New Directions for Organization Theory

New Directions for Organization Theory

Problems and Prospects

JEFFREY PFEFFER

New York   Oxford
OXFORD UNIVERSITY PRESS
1997

Oxford University Press

Oxford   New York
Athens   Auckland   Bangkok   Bogota   Bombay   Buenos Aires
Calcutta   Cape Town   Dar es Salaam   Delhi   Florence   Hong Kong
Istanbul   Karachi   Kuala Lumpur   Madras   Madrid   Melbourne
Mexico City   Nairobi   Paris   Singapore   Taipei   Tokyo   Toronto

and associated companies in
Berlin   Ibadan

Copyright © 1997 by Oxford University Press

Published by Oxford University Press, Inc.
198 Madison Avenue, New York, New York 10016

Library of Congress Cataloging-in-Publication Data
Pfeffer, Jeffrey.
    New directions for organization theory : problems and prospects / by Jeffrey Pfeffer.
      p.   cm.
    Includes bibliographical references and index.
    ISBN 0-19-511434-5
    1. Organizational sociology.   2. Organizational behavior.
  3. Social control.   I. Title.
  HM131.P4168   1997
  302.3'5—dc20   96-33593

9 8 7 6 5 4 3 2 1
Printed in the United States of America
on acid-free paper

Preface

I would probably have never written this book or the *Handbook of Social Psychology* chapter that was its progenitor had the decision been a rational one. Since the last time I had attempted such an effort in the early 1980s, the field of organizational behavior had continued along the path of increasing growth, differentiation, and paradigm proliferation that made undertaking any sort of overview or review of the field an "almost impossible" effort—a phrase used repeatedly by colleagues who were kind enough to provide advice and comments on the attempt. But within days of receiving the invitation to do the chapter for the fourth edition of the *Handbook*, I learned I had almost a complete blockage of the coronary arteries feeding the left side of the heart (which meant a "coronary event"—I love the language of physicians—would be instantly fatal) and, consequently, I needed open heart surgery. "What should I do about this invitation?" I asked my wife and best friend, Kathleen. "Say yes," she replied. "That will give you something to look forward to and a feeling that you will have a future." It seemed like a good idea at the time, so I did say yes, and following all of the principles of escalating commitment that we know so well, wound up writing first a long chapter and then this book.

The task proved to be a formidable one, and I am quite resolved not to do it again. Making sense of such a diverse field and deciding what to cover and what to leave out is invariably both difficult and an undertaking that can never fully please anyone except the author, and not even that person on a regular basis. When I sent out the book manuscript for comments, and when I sent out a working-paper version of the chapter (completed before the book, although who knows if it will have appeared in print before the book does), I invariably got what Bob Sutton came to call the "me, me, me" response. "This is a Rorschach test," said Sutton, and he was, as usual, right. The modal comment I received was something along the lines of "why didn't you include more [or anything] about my favorite topic, which is also among the most important in the field?" And, "how could you have overlooked citing some of my most important and very best papers?" which the authors of these messages were often kind enough to enclose so I wouldn't have to expend too much effort tracking them down. At first I took all of this as a compliment—surely people must think this writing will be influential and important to be willing to spend effort lobbying for the inclusion of their favorite material. After a while, however, I realized it reflected an egocentric view of the field that is an almost inevitable outcome of the absence of agreed-upon paradigms and frameworks. Years ago Jerry Salancik and I had shown that when there was uncertainty to resolve, social similarity came to play an important role in decision processes. Given the prevalent uncertainty and absence of agreement about the content and direction of organization studies, social similarity would again be expected to play a role in people's views of the field, and no one is more similar than ourselves.

So, let me begin with an apology. If I have failed to include your favorite work or to cite you sufficiently, it is not because I am necessarily ignorant of that part of the field or of your work, although I might be. It is because to keep this effort to manageable proportions, decisions did have to be made about what to leave in and what to leave out. These decisions were premised on my goal to provide an overview of the field for new entrants such as graduate students and scholars from adjacent disciplines. That implied focusing on what constitutes the most basic and fundamental questions about how to understand organizations and directing attention to what are some (not all) of the topic areas that have drawn increasing research attention and controversy. I make no claims for the ultimate wisdom of these choices—I did the best I could. I invite readers who don't like the choices I made to supplement this material with their own.

I very much appreciate the helpful comments on drafts of this material provided by Pam Haunschild, Joanne Martin, Charles O'Reilly, Bob Sutton, Michael Tushman, and Karl Weick. I have listened to their comments even if I have not, in every instance, followed their advice. I also appreciate the comments of Marjorie Williams of Harvard Business School Press, who was kind enough to read the manuscript even though the press did not wind up publishing it. The editors of the *Handbook of Social Psychology*, particularly Dan Gilbert, were very helpful in their guidance. And, of course, thanks to Herb Addison, my editor at Oxford University Press, for his guidance and confidence in the project. It has been a joy to work with Herb and the press, and I hope they feel the same way.

My life is made easier by my incredibly wonderful assistant, Katrina Jaggears, who did whatever I asked to help with the manuscript. My existence is made joyous and wiser by my beloved, my bride, my wonderfulness, the Amazing Kathleen. And, in a sense more real than I sometimes like to think about, my completing this book (and everything else since the fall of 1993) was made possible by Drs. James Avery and Joel Klompus, each of whom has both exceptional technical skill and a dedicated, total quality approach to medicine. All things considered, I am lucky indeed.

CONTENTS

New Directions for Organization Theory

1

The Development and Scope
of Organization Studies

We live in an organizational world. Virtually all of us are born in an organization—a hospital—with our very existence ratified by a state agency that issues a certificate documenting our birth. Under the current U.S. income tax regulations, if we are going to be claimed as a dependent on someone's tax return, within the first year of our life we will be issued a social security number by an agency of the federal government. When we die, a death certificate will be issued by another public bureaucracy and our passing may be announced by a newspaper organization. An organization will see to the disposition of our bodies, and other organizations will concern themselves with the disposition of our assets. And during the time in between, more than 90 percent of individuals living in the United States will earn their livelihoods working for an organization (as contrasted with being self-employed), having been prepared for employment by being schooled in educational organizations. "Organizations are all around us. Because of their ubiquity, however, they fade into the background, and we need to be reminded of their impact" (Scott, 1992, p. 3).

Not much more than a century ago, organizations were much less present in the social landscape. Public bureaucracies and business firms were both fewer and smaller in size. Boulding noted:

> [L]abor unions were practically non-existent. There were practically no employers' associations or trade associations. There were no farm organizations of any importance . . . National government absorbed . . . an almost infinitesimal part of the total national product . . . Outside of the Masons there were practically no fraternal organizations . . . Organizations outside the government were largely confined to the churches, a few local philanthropic societies, and the political parties . . . In place of the sparse fauna of 1852 we now have what seems like a vast jungle . . . Not only are there many more organizations . . . but the organizations are larger, better organized, more closely knit . . . Yet this

3

revolution has received little study . . . It has crept upon us silently. (1968, pp. 3–4)

And in times past, fewer people worked for others: "We look back after wage labour has won a respected position by two centuries of struggle. We forget the time when complete dependence on wages had for centuries been rejected by all who regarded themselves as free men" (Hill, 1964, p. 63).

One of the indicators of the importance of organizations is that with increasing frequency "organizations are singled out as the source of many of the ills besetting contemporary society" (Scott, 1992, p. 4). For good or ill, many of society's assets are managed by and controlled by organizations such as mutual funds, banks, and pension funds. Their decisions affect who will get credit, what investments and technologies will receive backing, and, as a consequence, which sectors of the economy will be developed, and how and where people live. "Organized" religion has spread, as have organized community and self-help groups, to do things that used to be done informally by neighbors in a community. Through their actions, these organizations define poverty and social problems as well as help determine their remediation. The fact that so much of our material and social welfare and life is inextricably bound up with organizations means that it is important to understand how they function and how they can be analyzed. As Stern and Barley have argued, it is important to study "how organizations affect the social systems in which they are embedded" (1996, p. 146).

The field of organization studies, developed to understand these ubiquitous social entities, comprises an interdisciplinary focus on (a) the effect of social organizations on the behavior and attitudes of individuals within them, (b) the effects of individual characteristics and actions on organizations, with a particular emphasis on the efficacy and, indeed, the possibility of potent individual influence (e.g., through leadership) in organizational systems, (c) the performance, success, and survival of organizations, (d) the mutual effects of environments, including resource and task, political, and cultural environments on organizations and vice versa, and (e) concerns with both the epistemology and methodology that undergird research on each of these topics. As such, the study of organizations is broad in both its theoretical scope and empirical focus. For instance, social psychological theories and findings relevant to the above issues would appear as a subfield, and possibly a small one at that, in the domain of organization studies.

Given the breadth and scope of the field, which today reaches out to the humanities (Zald, 1993), one might well ask to what extent considering organization studies as a separate subject of inquiry makes sense, especially since the discipline's boundaries are so permeable. This question has traditionally been answered by the claim that the interdisciplinary nature of organization studies makes cross-level analysis and the advance of theory more likely through processes of cross-fertilization. However, there are clear trade-offs involved. Even as organization studies becomes broad enough in scope to include virtually all relevant methods and theoretical perspectives, this very breadth makes integration of knowledge or even cognizance of the entire domain of organization studies substantially more difficult.

Because of the scope and diffuseness of the subject matter, which has increased substantially over time, any treatment of organization studies must necessarily be somewhat arbitrary in its coverage and its organization. In previous incarnations of this book (Pfeffer, 1982; 1985), I chose to organize the material by focusing on different levels of analysis (individuals, coalitions, and subunits on one hand and the total organization on the other) and on different perspectives on action. This latter categorization differentiated among perspectives that emphasized rational choice and decision making, situational constraint and social influence, and a third perspective focusing on the emergent, almost random nature of organizational behavior. Although treatments by level of analysis are still common, particularly in texts on organizations (e.g., Northcraft and Neale, 1994; Wagner and Hollenbeck, 1992), and although differences in perspectives on action remain important, for the researcher or student trying to access the field what may be even more important are the fundamental concepts and models used and useful for understanding organizations and the controversies that characterize the development of the field. Consequently, what I have chosen to do in this book is first to give the reader some sense of the evolution and particularly the more recent history of the field and its scope and content and then to consider the relevant literature organized by the major issues and concepts that make sense of organizations and are relevant to those who live in and manage them.

To understand or analyze organizations, it is important to consider the locus of causality and whether that is lodged in individuals, situations, or some combination. The locus of causality directs where we place our research emphasis and how we go about understanding and affecting behavior. This topic constitutes the focus of chapter 2. It is the case that scholars, managers, and casual observers approach the analysis of organizations with a set of implicit or explicit models of behavior. These models both structure what we observe and learn and also affect the choice of how to intervene to change organizations and their members. Chapter 3 explores five various models and assumptions about behavior that distinguish some prominent, competing theories and approaches to organizational analysis, including the economic model, the social model, the retrospectively rational model, the moral model, and a cognitive, interpretive model of organizational behavior.

As developed in chapters 2 and 3, one important distinction among theories of organizations is the extent to which dimensions of the social structure are used to help understand behavior by analyzing the context and constraints within which behavior occurs. Chapter 4 presents an overview of the literature on demographic composition and its effects on organizations, one prominent example of the use of structural analysis to understand organizations and groups within them. Chapter 5 then considers mechanisms of social control. Control has been a major theme in organizational studies since it began more than 100 years ago and continues to be prominent in numerous literatures relevant to organizations, including culture and socialization, rewards and incentives, and leadership. Control has a hierarchical emphasis to it, but many of the decisions in organizations occur through processes of interpersonal influence that rely on power and negotiation rather than on formal systems and authority. Chapter 6 explores how power and social influence are developed and exercised and how negotiation, one important way in which interpersonal influence is employed, occurs. Since the beginning of organizational studies, one of its goals has been to understand variations and determinants of organizational performance. Chapter 7 considers some prominent approaches to analyzing organizational performance and how they have evolved. Subjects such as control and organizational performance speak to the managerialist orientation that has been and still is prominent in organization studies. This functionalist orientation has stimulated a reaction in critical theory, which seeks to remind us that "organizations can trample personal freedom and individual fulfillment" (Stern and Barley, 1996, p. 148). Chapter 8 provides a brief overview of what constitutes some elements of a critical perspective on organizations and organization studies. In the concluding chapter 9, some substantive topics, largely overlooked in recent writing, are considered, and I take up the question of the evolution of organization studies and whether or not we are increasing our understanding of these important social entities. Together these topics and their exploration permit us to begin to understand what we know and what we don't, to identify some important directions for future research, and to glimpse the extent to which research and writing has been unevenly distributed and some of the factors associated with the field's attention.

A number of conclusions or themes emerge from this overview of the field. First, the location of much of organization studies in business schools, and U.S. business schools at that, coupled with the profusion of theories and absence of paradigmatic consensus has led to a substantial overemphasis of economic models and logic. The field is unduly entranced by economistic thinking. This is unfortunate because social and social psychological modes of organizational analysis are potentially both more valid and useful. Second, the location of organization studies has also led to a focus on particular subjects (e.g., performance, survival, leadership, culture) and an emphasis on a more micro (individual or individual organization) level of analysis. The relationship between organizations and society and various social problems and issues is given only occasional attention (e.g., Stern and Barley, 1996). Critical perspectives are seldom seen in empirical analyses and are more frequently found in European writings. But as organization studies evolves in Europe and tends to be located increasingly in prominent schools of administration, one wonders about the future of the European critical tradition.

Third, the absence of paradigmatic consensus and the consequent value placed on uniqueness (Mone and McKinley, 1993), cleverness, and being interesting have not always led to research focusing on powerful but apparently obvious effects on organizational behavior. And, coupled with the occasional insecurity that comes from paradigmatic profusion and the vulnerability that creates, organization studies has often eschewed an engineering orientation, implied by being an applied social science, that was present at its founding (e.g., Thompson, 1956). Thus, the field is at once captivated by topics that have the appearance of being applied without always taking seriously issues of design, intervention, and change.

Organizations Defined

How are organizations distinguished from other social collectivities such as small groups, families, mobs, and so forth? Scott noted that "most analysts have conceived of organizations as social structures created by individuals to support the collaborative pursuit of specified goals" (1992, p. 10). Parsons (1956) distinguished organizations from other social collectivities by noting that organizations had some purpose or goal. Donaldson maintained that "organizations are created and sustained . . . in order to attain certain objectives" (1995, p. 135). The goal-oriented or instrumental view of organizations implies that organizations are collections of individual efforts that are coordinated to achieve things that could not be achieved through individual action alone (Pfeffer and Salancik, 1978, p. 23).

However, defining organizations in terms of goal pursuit is somewhat problematic, and there is a large literature that treats the concept of an organizational goal and whether or not the construct is meaningful (e.g., Simon, 1964). One problem is that many organizations have within them members or employees who either do not know the organization's goal or, if they do know it, do not necessarily support it. For instance, although the goal of most publicly held corporations in the United States is something like profit maximization or the maximization of shareholder value, many employees are more concerned with job security and their relative influence than they are about profits. In one contract manufacturer, employees, not knowing the elements of corporate accounting, thought that the more overtime they worked (and the higher their own incomes), the better. The goal of maximizing overtime, however, was not an organizationally sanctioned or even recognized goal. Moreover, the goal of maximizing shareholder value does not generate much commitment or excitement among most organizational participants.

A second issue is that there is evidence that even when a goal is clearly identified, if and when it is attained organizations often develop new goals—as if the goal of an organization, once created, was simply its own continued survival and perpetuation. In a notable example of this process, Sills (1957) studied what happened to the National Foundation for Infantile Paralysis (the March of Dimes) when a vaccine for polio—the reason for its existence—was discovered. As we know, the March of Dimes did not disband upon achieving this success but instead took on the task of understanding and assisting in the treatment of other diseases such as genetic birth defects that crippled children.

Or consider the case of the Interstate Commerce Commission (ICC), established by legislation in 1887 to "break up huge concentrations of wealth in the hands of the country's railroad magnates" (Sanger, 1996, p. 9). Although railroads came to face substantial competition from trucking and the power of the railroad magnates declined substantially, the organization's purpose evolved and it endured. Over the years its powers expanded substantially so that it "gained authority over trucks, buses, and virtually anything else that moved across state lines. . . . consumer complaints about moving companies . . . had to go through the I.C.C." (Sanger, 1996, p. 9). Although the deregulation movement of the late 1970s spelled its apparent demise, the ICC survived for some *fifteen years* after virtually all of its functions were removed. Stripped of its power to set transportation rates or to control entry to the industry except in very rare instances, the agency continued to collect reams of data on transportation rates and employ a considerable staff:

> the commission survived numerous assassination attempts. Richard Nixon tried to merge the I.C.C. out of existence in 1970. . . . Ronald Reagan tried to eliminate its budget. . . . Sheer inertia, bureaucratic guile and lobbying by companies that thought twice about what life would be like in a completely competitive marketplace resulted in reprieve after reprieve. (Sanger, 1996, p. 9)

Pfeffer and Salancik noted that "organizations are . . . a process of organizing support sufficient to continue existence" (1978, p. 24). Organizational survival receives focus as a goal because survival must be continually accomplished and is never automatic. As March and Simon (1958) noted, organizations provide inducements for social actors to participate in them and in return obtain contributions that become inducements for others. From this perspective, an organization is viable and survives only as long as the inducements–contributions balance is positive, such that the available inducements are sufficient to produce the voluntary contributions of participation and effort necessary to maintain the organization. Consequently, organizational survival is more problematic than the survival of some other social groups because resources and energy must be expended in order to keep the organization going. Individuals must be recruited and offered sufficient inducements to remain in the organization, resources to support the organization must be extracted from the environment, and even the very legitimacy of the organization and its activities must occasionally be maintained against opposition.

For the most part, organizations have at least one goal—the survival if not the growth of the organization. Individuals not interested in helping the organization perpetuate itself typically leave. Individuals' well-being and status are often at least somewhat related to the well-being and status of the organization in which they are a member or an employee, producing some commonality of interest in perpetuating the organization. This can be seen by noting how often individuals identify themselves by what they do and their employment and other affiliations. Membership in high-status organizations confers status on the member, and employment in an organization that is larger or earns more money typically brings larger financial rewards.

Another distinction between organizations and other social entities is that organizations are, in many (although not all) instances, formally recognized by some governmental entity. The family may have legal definition, but mobs and informal small groups do not. In the case of public agencies or public bureaucracies, the organization may be created by statute or charter and is funded to carry out certain tasks and responsibilities. But, even private corporations are granted charters by the state and as part of that process must submit articles of incorporation that state their purpose, even if only in general terms. And unincorporated businesses may file fictitious business name statements and other forms with the state to document and legalize their existence. In this sense, organizations have a connection to the state, which confers legitimacy that distinguishes them from less formal collectivities such as families, mobs, or informal groups.

Organizations can also be distinguished by the nature of their boundaries. Inclusion in an organization is something granted by that organization, frequently with some sort of formal designation such as a membership card or employee identification. One is born into a family, and expulsion from the family is unlikely if not impossible. The boundaries of small groups and mobs are clearly evanescent. It is seldom the case in less formalized groups that the task of boundary maintenance and demarcation becomes a significant and identified role, but this is common in organizations—hence the frequent description of organizations as being "formal." Although organizational boundaries are clearly permeable—after all, an open-systems view of organizations sees them as taking in various types of inputs and, after some transformation process, exchanging what is produced for resources to continue the cycle (Katz and Kahn, 1978)—permeability is to some degree under the control of the organization. Formal boundary-spanning units such as purchasing and human resources attempt to ensure that inputs meet specifications, while other boundary-spanning units such as marketing and public relations seek to develop external support and demand for what the organization does.

So, we can say that organizations are more likely than other social groups to have a goal of survival and self-perpetuation, have more clearly defined, demarcated, and defended boundaries, and often (although not invariably) have some formal relationship with the state that recognizes their existence as distinct social entities—obligated to pay taxes as an entity, capable of suing and being sued, and so forth.

The Evolution of Research and Writing on Organizations

Several trends are apparent in organization studies as the field has evolved since the mid-1980s. First, the field is increasingly, although certainly not exclusively, lodged in business schools. It has virtually disappeared in psychology and political science departments, particularly in the United States, and, although it seems to be enjoying some slight resurgence in sociology departments, still represents a comparatively small part of that field also. The study of management and organizations is currently growing, albeit from an extremely small base, in schools of engineering, particularly in departments of industrial engineering and engineering management. This concentration of organization studies in a professional school environment is a phenomenon with important consequences for both what is studied and how it is studied. And, the evolution of organization studies in various disciplines is informative about the development of the field and its orientations, for this history still affects many aspects of the content of organization studies.

The study of management and organizations had some substantial part of its origins in engineering, both mechanical and industrial. Shenhav documented the move to standardize mechanical parts and processes and to professionalize the discipline of engineering in the late 1800s. He noted that "beginning in the late 1880s, parallel to the attempts to standardize and systematize mechanical matters, the movement was extended more explicitly to organizational and administrative issues" (1995, p. 560).

> The extension of technical principles to social and commercial endeavors was based on the assumption that human and nonhuman entities are interchangeable and can equally be subjected to engineering manipulation. . . . Including organizational design within the jurisdiction of engineers was justified by their claim that the analysis of organizations "is to the enterprise what the engine diagram is to the designer" (*Engineering Magazine*, April 1908: 83–91). . . . The rise of this group marks the origin of management as a distinct phenomenon. (p. 561)

The rise of Frederick W. Taylor and scientific management in the early 1900s marked the culmination of the efforts to apply engineering principles to the design and management of work and ushered in the golden age of engineering. Between 1880 and 1920, the number of engineers in the United States grew from 7,000 to 135,000 (Jacoby, 1985).

> It is impossible to overestimate the importance of the scientific management movement in the shaping of the modern corporation and indeed all institutions . . . which carry on labor processes. . . . Taylor dealt with the fundamentals of the organization of the labor process and of control over it. . . . The successors to Taylor are to be found in engineering and work design, and in top management. . . . Work itself is organized according to Taylorian principles, while personnel departments and academics have busied themselves with selection, training . . . and adjustment of "manpower" to suit the work processes so organized. Taylorism dominates the world of production; the practitioners of "human relations" and "industrial psychology" are the maintenance crew for the human machinery. (Braverman, 1974, pp. 86–87)

Principles of scientific management involved the separation of the planning and design of work from its actual execution and the scientific study of work processes (using time and motion studies, for instance) to figure out the most efficient way of doing jobs. Concerns of the early engineering orientation to organizations and management remain in contemporary writing. The scientific study of work processes to enhance efficiency can be seen in the contemporary writing about reengineering and in the work-process continuous improvement programs in many assembly plants. The separation of work design and planning from its execution is evident in attempts to reintegrate planning and doing in self-managing teams and in the implementation issues raised by moves toward decentralization of control. Taylor (1903) maintained that his piece-rate system for rewarding work could end labor unrest and that the science-based system was impartial and above class prejudice (Shenhav, 1995, p. 567). Developing management processes that maintain labor peace and are fair remain important issues to the present day. And, the organization of writing and thinking about management and organizations "around engineering ideals rather than around religious, phil-anthropic, paternalistic, or social Darwinist ones" (p. 564) also continues to the present.

Although Taylorism and engineering remain influential in the literature, this orientation is now more likely to be found in business schools. Management concerns have diminished in schools of engineering. Industrial engineering de-partments have substantially diminished in importance over time compared to disciplines such as electrical, chemical, and civil engineering, which are based on physical, not social, sciences. To the extent industrial engineering has survived, much of its attention has shifted to production and operations management, which it views from a modeling or mathematical perspective emphasizing tech-niques such as queuing theory and linear programming. With only a few excep-tions, the study of organizations and management diminished substantially in in-dustrial engineering departments, which were themselves in some decline.

Since the 1980s, there has been some reversal in this trend, for two reasons. First, business education, particularly in private schools, is often offered only to graduate students. This permitted industrial engineering to offer engineering management to undergraduates, an attractive option in the educational market place. Second, concerns with the management of high-technology companies and the frequent transition of engineers from technical to managerial responsibilities as their careers progressed have led to a market-based demand for more emphasis on management topics in engineering schools. Nevertheless, concern with man-agement issues remains comparatively small in engineering colleges today, partic-ularly when one contrasts the present with the situation around the turn of the century, when engineering was taking a leading role in developing the study of management and organizations.

The study of organizations began in psychology with industrial and organiza-tional psychology, subspecialties within psychology departments. The *Journal of Applied Psychology*, first published in 1917, contained articles on subjects in ap-plied psychology—testing and measuring individual capabilities, interests, and at-titudes through various assessment instruments (the study of individual differ-ences), the effects of work environments on attitudes and, to a lesser extent, behavior such as turnover and performance, and the design (both physical and social) of jobs and work environments. Table 1-1 presents the titles of selected articles from the first several volumes of the *Journal of Applied Psychology* to illustrate both the enormous continuity in subject matter between then and now and the substantive focus of the early research in applied psychology.

Braverman argued that both industrial psychology and industrial sociology arose as handmaidens to the engineering orientation of Taylorism and can be best understood in that context:

> Shortly after Taylor, industrial psychology and industrial physiology came into existence to perfect methods of selection, training, and motivation of workers, and these were soon broadened into an attempted industrial sociology, the study of the workplace as a social system. The cardinal feature of these various schools

> . . . is that . . . they do not by and large concern themselves with the organization of work, but rather with the conditions under which the worker may best be brought to cooperate in the scheme of work organized by the industrial engineer. (1974, p. 140)

Industrial and organizational psychology first lost status and then position within the discipline, quite possibly because of its applied orientation and its role in supporting management and engineering. Today industrial psychology exists in relatively few psychology departments and virtually none of the most prestigious. The Society for Industrial and Organizational Psychology (SIOP) has split off from the American Psychological Association and now holds separate meetings. And social psychology's increasing emphasis on individual cognition on the one hand and personality on the other, with a deemphasis on groups and social influence (e.g., Markus and Zajonc, 1985) has left a growing gulf between more mainstream psychological research and organizational issues and problems.

In sociology, the study of organizations was at one time a central focus of the discipline. Many of the central figures in sociological theory—Weber (1947), Marx (1967), and Durkheim (1949)—contributed to the understanding of bureaucracy, the employment relationship, and the division of labor and basis of solidarity. A series of case studies of the Tennessee Valley Authority (Selznick, 1949), a gypsum mine (Gouldner, 1954), and a state employment agency and federal law-enforcement organization (P. M. Blau, 1955) began the process of developing empirically based general principles to describe organizational functioning. Although organizational sociology remains viable, particularly in comparison to industrial/organizational psychology, from 1990 to 1994 only 15 percent of the articles in the *American Sociological Review*, the discipline's leading journal, could be considered to concern organizations. Thus, organization studies' place within sociology is a small one, particularly compared to the study of stratification.

A similar erosion of interest in organizations is visible in political science. Many of the most prominent early figures in organization science came from

Table 1-1   Titles of Selected Articles from the 1917, 1918, and 1919 Volumes of the *Journal of Applied Psychology*

The Human Element in Business

An Absolute Intelligence Scale

Mental Tests for Prospective Telegraphers

What Can the Psychology of Interests, Motives, and Character Contribute to Vocational Guidance?

Human Engineering

Vocational Tests for Retail Saleswomen

Work on the Committee on Classification of Personnel in the Army

Training Course of the American Steel and Wire Company

Air Service Tests of Aptitude for Flying

The Learning Curve in Typewriting

The Relation of the General Intelligence of School Children to the Occupation of Their Fathers political science—people such as Herbert Simon (1947) and James March (March and Simon, 1958; Cyert and March, 1963). Many of the earliest studies of organizations were studies of public bureaucracies (e.g., P. M. Blau, 1955; Blau and Scott, 1962; Selznick, 1949), so there were many connections between public administration, at one point an important subfield of political science, and organizational behavior. However, as documented by Green and Shapiro (1994), the discipline of political science has evolved to a point at which it has lost its institutional roots (March and Olsen, 1989) and instead has come to be dominated by formal models of rational choice. By 1992, this particular theoretical perspective, rational actor theory, was represented in some 40 percent of the articles published in the *American Political Science Review*, the disciplinary association's major journal. This formal modeling, often based on economic assumptions and methodological apparatus, has left political science increasingly distant from the less mathematical methods that characterize theory and research in organization studies and also somewhat distant from the concerns of administration and practice. Public administration, as a major subfield of political science, has withered as the study of institutions has become less important in the discipline, replaced by an emphasis on voting, coalitions, and legislative behavior.

The study of organizations fit uneasily in basic disciplines such as sociology and psychology where it appeared to be too applied and became marginalized in engineering schools, which were more concerned with disciplines based on the physical sciences. But the study of management, administration, and leadership has always found a home in business schools because of continuing interest in subjects such as motivation, human effects on productivity and performance, and organizational structure and strategy. Although organization studies programs have at times been under attack in various business schools (e.g., Carnegie Mellon, Yale, Rochester) because of the field's absence of mathematical, formal rigor, demands for relevance from business schools' constituencies have ensured it a place in business school curricula where it is a required course at both the undergraduate and graduate levels.

Business schools are much more prevalent in the United States than in Europe, and as a consequence the location of organization studies primarily in business schools has given it a distinctly American flavor. Clegg has noted that "organization studies . . . have drawn on both a range of materials and theoretical approaches which have been too restricted" (1990, p. 1). His descriptions of the French bread industry, Benetton, and industrial organization in the Far East including Taiwan, Korea, and Japan consistently challenge ideas of efficiency, whether these are derived from the transaction cost theory of Williamson (1975) or structural contingency theory ideas (Donaldson, 1985). Clegg noted that "the major thrust of efficiency arguments has been towards predicting a convergence in the range of organizational forms to be found in modernity" (p. 151). The proliferation of forms actually observed—witness the difference between the bread industries of the United States and France—belies simple efficiency accounts. But, these differences are apparent only to the extent one's empirical and theoretical scope transcends the confines of single countries, particularly the United States.

The crucial factor is not that a manager or an organization is Japanese rather than American. . . . It is what being Japanese makes available in terms of normal ways of accounting for action, of calculating strategy, of constituting rationalities, of mapping cognitively, which is important. These matters . . . depend upon distinct and nationally variable institutional frameworks. . . . Action is never unbounded. It is framed within more or less tacit understandings, as well as formal stipulations, which enable different agencies to do not only different things but also the same things distinctly in diverse contexts. (pp. 150–151)

Thus, the history and location of organization studies are consequential because the environment of behavior, including scholarship, has important effects on that behavior. The increasing concentration of organization studies in business schools or schools of management has had a number of important effects on the development of the discipline. One such effect is the influence of adjacent disciplines. By being in a business school, organization studies has come to be located in close institutional proximity to economics. Economics has a well-developed scientific paradigm, considering it is a social science, with greater consensus concerning what are the important issues to be studied and what are appropriate styles of theory and methodological approaches (e.g., Pfeffer and Moore, 1980a,b; Lodahl and Gordon, 1972). Organization studies has no such paradigmatic consensus (Pfeffer, 1993). Economics also has prestige, in part because of its extensive use of mathematical formalism, and in part because many business schools (e.g., the University of California at Berkeley) emerged out of economics departments, making that the mother discipline. As a consequence, economic ideas have come to have significant influence on organization studies. The economic theories that have been imported most frequently into organization theory—agency theory, human capital theory, and transaction cost economics—almost invariably proceed from a theoretical position of methodological individualism, calculative rationality, and presumptions of self-interested behavior and effort aversion (shirking).

As an example of economic theory's growth in prominence in the study of organizations, consider the increase in the proportion of articles in two major journals that cite economics, either transaction cost economics or some version of agency theory. In 1975, just 2.5 percent of the articles in *Administrative Science Quarterly*, the major journal in the field, and 0 percent of the articles in the *Academy of Management Journal*, the publication of the major disciplinary association, had citations to economic literature. Within ten years (1985), 30 percent of the articles published in *ASQ* and 10 percent of the articles appearing in *AMJ* cited economics. By 1994, the percentages had increased to 45 percent and 28 percent, respectively, numbers strikingly similar to those tracing the growth of rational actor models in political science. It seems almost impossible to consider the evolution of organization theory, particularly in the future, without considering the influence of economics on the field's methods and substance.

The second effect of having organizations studies sited where professional education (of MBA students) and practical concerns loom larger is that such realities influence, even if only subtly, the topics chosen for study and the theoretical lens brought to bear on them. For instance, although there have been a number of critiques of the leadership literature (e.g., Lieberson and O'Connor,

1972; Pfeffer, 1977; Meindl, Ehrlich, and Dukerich, 1985), some of which particularly question whether leadership has an effect or whether we just like to believe in the controllability of the environment and hence have a "romance" with the concept of leadership, research and writing on leadership continues apace. The recent emphasis on charismatic leadership (House, 1977), the traits or personalities of effective leaders (House, Spangler, and Wyocke, 1991; Winter, 1987), and transformational leadership (Bass, 1985)—or leadership capable of accomplishing large-scale, systemic change in organizations—reflects the effect of an environment in which leadership training is big business. For example, the Center for Creative Leadership, which does leadership training as well as research and materials development on this subject, saw its revenues grow from about $6 million in 1985 to more than $30 million in 1994. Business leaders also want to believe they are having, or at least could have, profound effects on their organizations. Organizational culture—and whether such culture, seen as a social control system, can be managed to enhance organizational performance (O'Reilly, 1989)—is another topic in which the influence of practical concerns can be seen, as are the growing number of studies of the effects of pay practices and other human resource policies on organizational performance (e.g., Huselid, 1995; Pfeffer, 1994; MacDuffie, 1995), studies of organizational change, and research evaluating organizational interventions designed to enhance performance. Stern and Barley have argued that being lodged in business schools has "tugged organizational research toward issues of efficiency and effectiveness and away from larger, systemic issues" (1996, p. 154).

Using organizational culture as an example, Barley, Meyer, and Gash (1988) demonstrated how to empirically explore the influence of academics on practitioners and vice versa in a study that could serve as a useful model for explorations in other topic areas as well. Barley et al. contrasted two theories of knowledge transmission—"diffusion" and "political":

> Whereas diffusion theorists assume that academics frame problems for practitioners, political theorists contend that scholarly endeavors are ultimately defined by the interests of those who dominate society and by whose largess academics retain the privilege of pursuing research. . . . A more open view of the relation between academics and practitioners would begin by positing two worlds that exist as separate but interdependent social systems characterized by different traditions, languages, interests, and norms. Under such conditions, the direction and degree of influence might vary from issue to issue. (1988, pp. 24–25)

By analyzing the language, concepts, and content of literature written for academics and practitioners over time, Barley et al. were able to ascertain patterns of influence. They showed that academics and practitioners were initially interested in different aspects of culture and approached its study quite differently. However, the data suggest that "the rubric of practitioners' discourse remained stable over time, while the pragmatics of academic discourse changed. . . . Those who wrote for academics gradually placed more emphasis on the economic value of controlling culture and on rational control and differentiation" (p. 52), concerns of the managerial audience. Although their study does not show that the influence of practitioners necessarily exists for all subjects, the study is instructive in both its method and its results and is consistent with the claim made here about the influence of practical concerns on academic discourse, which results, to some degree, from where the study of organizations is sited.

Abrahamson (1996) has argued for the use of bibliographic indices both over time and across countries to examine the rise and fall of management fashions — topics and perspectives that are in or out of favor. For instance, he traced the rapid rise of interest in quality circles beginning around 1980 and the subsequent fairly rapid decline in 1984. Abrahamson argued that "fashionable management techniques must appear both rational (efficient means to important ends) and progressive (new as well as improved relative to older management techniques)" (p. 255). He noted that "intraorganizational contradictions, as well as changes in their economic and political environments widen certain organizational performance gaps creating incipient preferences influencing management fashion demand" (p. 275). The studies of Abrahamson and Barley, Meyer, and Gash (1988) demonstrate the importance and the feasibility of being more self-reflective as a field and empirically examining the rise and fall of various ideas and topic areas.

Of course, trends tend to set in motion forces to create their opposite. The increasing emphasis on productivity, performance, and the interests of organizations has prompted the development of a critical studies subdiscipline that focuses on the perspective of those who work in organizations in contrast to those who own or control them (Steffy and Grimes, 1986). Thus, for example, Martin (1992a) wrote about subcultures in organizations and has questioned whether culture can, in fact, be managed. Other writers have been concerned with the place of the powerless in organizations and organization theory, with the explicit objective of undermining what otherwise would be considered normal or legitimate ways of organizing (e.g., Mumby, 1988). Such writing occasionally focuses on women and minorities, who often do not fare well in the competition for salary and positions, particularly compared to their human capital endowments, and who some argue have been neglected in the writing about organizations (e.g., Omi and Winant, 1986; Nkomo, 1992). Still others have argued for a gendered or gender-based theory of organizations (Mumby and Putnam, 1992; Ferguson, 1984). Much of this literature argues that "theorizing constitutes organizations in particular ways" (Mumby and Putnam, 1992, p. 465) and, therefore, that science is an inherently political and subjective activity and should be acknowledged as such. Although the idea of radical or Marxist organization studies may at first appear implausible, there are quite important critical studies of social control in the work place (e.g., Braverman, 1974; Edwards, 1979; Burawoy, 1979), of the neglect of the worker in studies of high-commitment work practices (Graham, 1995), and of the interests and role of social class in organizational and interorganizational functioning (e.g., Palmer, 1983).

Yet another phenomenon that may partly derive from where organization studies has come to be located is the continuing profusion of theories and diminished consensus on what are the important research questions and directions and on what are appropriate research methodologies. Some have bemoaned this absence of paradigmatic consensus and argued it has created problems for doctoral student training (Zammuto and Connolly, 1984), impeded the acquisition of resources and legitimacy (Pfeffer, 1993), and made it difficult to keep up with the development of the field (Mone and McKinley, 1993). Webster and Starbuck argued that "ineffective theories sustain themselves and tend to stabilize a science in a state of incompetence. . . . Theories about which scientists disagree foster divergent findings and incomparable studies that claim to be comparable" (1988, p. 95).

Others have argued that this proliferation of theories and methods is healthy (Zald, 1993; Van Maanen, 1995b). Burrell and Morgan (1979) identified four worldviews or paradigms found in organizational analysis: functionalist, interpretive, radical humanist, and radical structuralist. The functionalist paradigm treats "organization as an aspect of a wider societal system that serves the interests of its members" (Morgan, 1990, p. 15). The interpretive paradigm challenges the certainty of the functionalist view, "showing that order in the social world . . . rests on a precarious, socially-constructed web of symbolic relationships that are continuously negotiated . . . affirmed or changed" (pp. 18–19). Morgan maintained that the radical humanist paradigm "is concerned with understanding the way humans construct a world which they often experience as confining . . . and with finding ways in which humans can exercise control over their own constructions that allow them to express and develop their nature as human beings" (p. 21). The radical structuralist paradigm, with roots in Marxist theory, emphasizes the importance of self-generated change and logics of action. Although Morgan (1983) recognized the inherent incompatibility of these various theoretical paradigms, he nevertheless argued for the benefits of paradigm diversity:

> The interpretation of diversity as opportunity . . . celebrates the possibility of obtaining new insights and understanding. Established paradigms . . . are recognized as providing at best partial modes of understanding which may be supplemented or even replaced by those of new paradigms. . . . The challenge of diversity is seen as resting on the potential it offers for developing new modes of understanding the phenomenon of organization. (Morgan, 1990, pp. 13–14)

While some see paradigm proliferation and incommensurability as a problem and others as a valuable dimension of the field, there is virtually no disagreement about the *fact* of more paradigm proliferation. Coupled with the substantial growth in the numbers of people doing research or being identified with the field, the absence of theoretical or methodological consensus has had the predictable result of increasing the amount of differentiation present in the field of organization studies. Thus, for instance, the Academy of Management now has 57 percent more divisions and interest groups than it did in 1980 and 38 percent more than it had in 1985. More specialized journals have proliferated, and there is a more Balkanized field as a result. As Lawrence and Lorsch (1967) noted about organizations in general, increases in differentiation necessitate more effective integration across the differentiated units. This integration, for the most part, has not occurred in organization studies.

There is a literature on how scientific disciplines evolve and change (Kuhn, 1970), how scientific work gets done, and how contests for control of intellectual agendas within fields are played out (e.g., Green and Shapiro, 1994; Parker, 1993). The emphasis in much of this literature is on power and politics. Thus, for instance, Hassard noted, "For Kuhn, the everyday reality of science is more akin to the lifecycle of the political community than to the dictates of formal logic. . . . Kuhn speaks of discontinuous periods of normative and revolutionary activity" (1990, p. 220). These writings about the evolution of scientific fields, always interesting, are particularly relevant for understanding the evolution of organization studies because research is so often housed in interdisciplinary settings (schools of business, management, or administration) where there are fewer strong disciplinary anchors to direct activity. For this reason, context probably matters more, and the future is less easily predicted, than in fields with more paradigmatic consensus and stronger social norms.

The Changing Organizational Landscape

The world that organization theory seeks to analyze and describe has changed in some important ways. Four of the more significant changes are (a) the increasing externalization of the employment relation and the development of the "new employment contract," (b) a change in the size distribution of organizations, with a comparative growth in the proportion of smaller organizations, (c) the increasing influence of external capital markets on organizational governance and decision making, and (d) increasing salary inequality within organizations in the United States, compared both to the past and to other industrialized nations. These changes, to be documented below, pose some challenges for organization theory. Most directly, they beg for explanation. If people are working in different arrangements than in the past, if managerial discretion is now more constrained by financial markets, if pay is becoming more unequal, and if large organizational size now seems to be more of a burden and less of a benefit, then organization theory should have something to say about why these changes have occurred. Unfortunately, much of organization theory is silent about the structuring of the employment relation (Pfeffer and Baron, 1988) as well as about the size distribution of organizations, with population ecology (Hannan and Freeman, 1989) being a partial exception. Granovetter noted, "One might suppose that the frequently demonstrated importance of size would have stimulated an interest in its determinants, or at least its marginals; but such discussions are absent from the sociological literature" (1984, pp. 323–24). Although some work has documented the increasing influence of the capital markets and the erosion of managerialism (G. F. Davis and Thompson, 1994), there is, again, little explanation for why these changes have occurred, particularly in comparison with what has or has not gone on in other countries. Commenting on the study of wage inequality, Baron and Pfeffer noted that, although the study of inequality had a long history in sociology and economics, "remarkably little has been done to bring the firms back into the study of inequality, particularly in ways that are true to the social and relational nature of work organizations" (1994, p. 190).

Second, these and other changes in organizational form and functioning challenge organization theories that have been developed to explain a context that has shifted. For instance, what is the relevance of a literature on organizational culture in a world in which a high proportion of the work force works part-time or as independent contractors, with such limited attachment to firms that culture and cultural control is almost irrelevant? Or, what is the relevance of resource dependence theory (Pfeffer and Salancik, 1978), which proceeds from the assumption that managers take action to manage external uncertainty and dependence, even when such behaviors are not profit enhancing, in an environment in which shareholder return reigns supreme? What does a literature on careers, premised implicitly on the idea of advancement within an organization, have to say about situations in which small firms, without career ladders, and employment relationships, without much long-term connection to employers, are increasingly prevalent?

All four of the changes mentioned above are readily documented. Considering the organization of the employment relationship, Cappelli has written, "Internalized employment arrangements that buffered jobs from market pressures are giving way to arrangements that rely much more heavily on outside market forces to manage employees" (1995, p. 563). Pfeffer and Baron (1988) have referred to "externalized" employment to denote arrangements such as working off-site, working part-time or as temporary help, or being an outside contractor, all of which diminish the connection and attachment between the worker and the firm in which the work is done. If one includes both temporary and part-time work as well as outside contracting for business services in the category of contingent work, Belous (1989) estimated that in 1988 some 25 to 30 percent of U.S. employees were contingent or externalized employees. By 1985, part-time work constituted about one-quarter of all employment in California (Dillon, 1987). Applebaum (1987) has commented on the fact that "the majority of externalized workers no longer perform unskilled clerical tasks; many are professionals, such as nurses or accountants" (Davis-Blake and Uzzi, 1993, p. 195).

Moreover, the trend toward the externalization of employment seems to be quite strong. Cappelli, using unpublished Bureau of Labor Statistics data, reported that "direct employment in temporary help agencies has more than tripled since 1985" (1995, p. 580). Dillon's (1987) study of flexible employment in California reported that the number of temporary employees grew some 800 percent between 1972 and 1985, more than seven times the rate of growth in nonagricultural industries. The largest private employer in America is now Manpower, Inc., with 560,000 workers (Castro, 1993). Christensen reported that the number of part-time employees "doubled from 1968 to 1992, and much of that growth was due to increases in the number of involuntary part-time workers" (1995, p. 8). Between 1970 and 1990, the nonagricultural work force in the United States grew by 54 percent, but the number of individuals involuntarily employed part-time increased by more than 120 percent (Kilborn, 1991). Mishel and Bernstein reported that, as of 1989, 78 percent of employers used independent contractors to do work that could be done by employees, that 97 percent used temporary help, and that these figures had increased substantially in just three years (1995, p. 229). Between 1974 and 1984, the business services industry doubled employment, outstripping the growth even of industries providing services to consumers (Howe, 1986).

Externalization is not just a U.S. phenomenon. Atkinson (1984) documented the rise of externalized work in the United Kingdom. Bresnen and Fowler reported that a survey published in 1987 indicated that "77 per cent of the 584 firms surveyed used contractors for at least some activities, and, of these, 40 per cent showed an increase in use over the previous three years" (1994, p. 849). As in the United States, externalization has expanded:

> subcontracting has not only been used more in traditional ancillary services — such as cleaning, catering, transport, maintenance and security—. . . but has also begun to replace the use of conventional employment . . . in a much broader range of occupational groups such as design engineering, marketing, and publicity. (p. 849)

Job security is also a thing of the past. Wyatt Company (1993) reported that 72 percent of employers in their 1993 survey had layoffs in the previous three years, and Louis Harris and Associates (1991) reported that 50 percent of the surveyed firms had laid off substantial numbers of employees in the previous five years. The American Management Association reported that in each of the years from mid-1989 to mid-1994 an average 46.2 percent of the firms reported a workforce reduction. Moreover, "downsizing tends to be repetitive: on average, two-thirds of the firms that cut jobs in a given calendar year do so again the following year" (1994, p. 1). Cappelli (1995), reviewing the evidence on average job tenure, concluded that average tenure for men had declined. These changes have had predictable effects on morale and commitment. Using unpublished surveys performed over decades, Cappelli noted that there has been "a sharp decline in employee attitudes in the 1980s, especially regarding commitment to the employer" (1995, p. 586). A survey of middle managers (*Training*, 1992) found that only 2 percent of middle managers believed that dedication to one's employing organization was a key to success.

The trend toward externalizing employment has tended to differentially affect women and minorities. Pfeffer and Baron (1988, p. 270) noted that the growth rate of employment in business services during the 1974–1984 decade was almost twice as high for women as for men (136 percent versus 79 percent). Self-employment in business services tripled over the same period, with women accounting for most of that growth (Howe, 1986). Women are also disproportionately affected by the trend toward part-time employment. Because in the United States health insurance and pension benefits are tied to employment status, and because one's likelihood of being covered by union or non-union due process procedures and the salary one earns is affected by the size of one's employing organization (Stolzenberg, 1978), the changing conditions of employment have important social consequences.

The size distribution of organizations has also been shifting, with the trend being toward a higher proportion of smaller organizations (Granovetter, 1984), although the size of individual establishments (the units in which work is performed) has been fairly stable since the 1920s. Some of this shift may be explained by the changing composition of the economy, in which services now play a comparatively more important role. In 1982, the proportion of the U.S. work force employed in services equaled the proportion employed in manufacturing (Granovetter, 1984, p. 324), the first time this had happened. In general, service organizations are smaller than manufacturing organizations (p. 325), although the consolidation in financial services (banks and insurance companies) indicates that this is not invariably the case. But, even in manufacturing, smaller organizations are more numerous than in the past. This trend toward smaller size is consistent with the propensity to contract out tasks and to use more contract labor, reducing the size of the core organizations. The largest organizations—for example, the Fortune 500—have been shedding employees. Christensen reported that the largest companies, those in the Fortune 500, "reduced their work forces by 2.5 million employees between fiscal years 1983 and 1993" (1995, p. 2), a decrease of 18 percent. The fact that employment has continued to grow in the economy as a whole means, by definition, that there has been a shift to smaller organizations. Castro reported that "the number of people employed full time by *Fortune* 500 companies has shrunk from 19% of the work force two decades ago to less than 10% today" (1993, p. 43). Scherer (1980) has reviewed evidence indicating that economies of scale in production occur at relatively small establishment sizes, so that the economics of production do not dictate the need for large-size organizations.

Granovetter's (1984) comparative analysis of size distributions of organizations in Sweden, the United States, and Japan reported that there were comparatively more small organizations in Japan and that Sweden's size distribution of establishments was comparable to that in the United States. The Japanese manufacturing sector has typically operated with an emphasis on building networks of suppliers and using a great deal of outside contracting, which permitted the core firms to have fewer employees. To the extent this way of organizing production is increasingly the case in the U.S. economy, then a trend toward a similar and smaller size distribution of firms might be expected. Indeed, the emphasis on specialization, comparative advantage, core competencies, and similar strategies is consistent with both the changing nature of the employment relationship and the changing size distribution of organizations that one observes.

The size distribution of organizations is important because size is related to numerous other organizational characteristics such as having an internal labor market, formalization, complexity and differentiation in jobs, and having full-time employees (Kalleberg and Van Buren, 1996, p. 54). Size also affects organizational rewards, even net of other factors associated with size. Kalleberg and Van Buren (1996) reported that organizational size was positively related to the receipt of fringe benefits and to perceived promotion opportunities and was negatively related to job autonomy. They found that the frequently reported positive relationship between size and earnings was no longer statistically significant when other mediating factors related to size (such as unionization and the presence of an internal labor market) were controlled.

A third substantial change in the organizational context has been the growing power of the external capital markets and the corresponding diminished autonomy of managers, at least in publicly traded companies. Berle and Means (1932) first noted the issue of the separation of ownership from control and argued that with widely dispersed share ownership among many comparatively small investors, managers could operate effectively without oversight. The top executive largely controlled the selection of the board of directors, which ostensibly was to oversee this individual (Pfeffer, 1972c; Demb and Neubauer, 1992), and each individual shareholder was typically too small to make it cost effective to attempt to intervene in corporate governance. Although there were arguments over the empirical facts—the extent to which large firms were or were not owner-controlled (e.g., Zeitlin, 1974)—the presumption was that at least some substantial fraction of large, publicly traded firms provided their managers with substantial discretion to pursue interests such as growth (Baumol, 1959; Marris, 1967) or the enjoyment of various perquisites (Williamson, 1964).

In the 1980s, this managerial discretion began to erode substantially. The change occurred in part because of the development of an active market for corporate control (Manne, 1965). In this market, assets that are not being fully utilized or properly managed by current management are bid away by others who then manage these assets more efficiently. The market for corporate control has developed as riskier forms of financing—for example, through junk bonds—have become more institutionalized and as normative prohibitions on hostile raids or takeovers have diminished (Hirsch, 1986). Kaplan observed that of the 150 largest U.S. industrial corporations in 1980, by 1988 some 21.9 percent had been taken over or merged and another five had gone private in management buyouts, a situation he correctly characterized as "a very active U.S. takeover market" (1994, p. 515). Kaplan's study also demonstrated that this change in the context of corporate control was, to this point, primarily a U.S. phenomenon, with only 2.5 percent of comparably sized Japanese companies being merged during the same period.

Loss of managerial autonomy results not only from the risk of having the assets currently controlled by management bid away in a hostile takeover or tender offer if they are not being effectively employed. It is also the case that dispersed share ownership itself is a thing of the past, with large pension funds such as CALPERS (the state of California's pension fund), TIAA-CREF (a pension fund for college and university faculty), and other large retirement plans as well as banks and mutual funds now controlling a significant majority of the shares in many large corporations. These large shareholders have discovered that simply selling their shares if they are dissatisfied with management is difficult. Given the large concentration of institutional ownership, market liquidity for large blocs is possibly limited. There are also the transaction costs (brokerage fees) associated with securities sales. Consequently, these institutions have become considerably more active in pressing management for desired changes that would presumably serve shareholder interests. And, particularly for the public pension funds, run by "outsiders" to the corporate world, there are few normative constraints or social ties to reduce the ardor with which such corporate reforms are pursued. Although such shareholder rebellions are still comparatively rare events, they are increasing in frequency and by this very fact have taken on a more taken-for-granted and institutionalized aspect.

The increased potency of capital market control of the corporation has been reflected in the changing backgrounds of senior corporate executives—to deal with financial markets, it is helpful to have a background in finance. Fligstein (1991, p. 322) argued that analyzing the backgrounds of chief executives helps one understand both actual power and the perception of functional importance. Fligstein (1987; 1990) has documented the shift in the backgrounds of chief executive officers during the twentieth century from generalist entrepreneurs at the beginning of the period, to those with manufacturing backgrounds, to those with a sales background. In the current period, most CEOs have a background in finance.

There have been other important changes in the world of organizations that also have escaped much analysis in the literature. For instance, there is evidence that rewards within organizations are increasingly dispersed, and this dispersion is much greater in the United States than in other industrialized countries. Abegglen and Stalk (1985, p. 192) showed that the ratio of the salary paid to company presidents in Japan to the salary paid to newly hired employees has decreased from a pretax ratio of 110 times in 1927 to 23.6 in 1963, 19 in 1973, and 14.5 by 1980. On an after-tax basis, by 1980 the ratio of president to new employee compensation in Japan was just 7.5 times. And, this difference in executive compensation cannot be explained by differences in pay levels, for the average level of pay in Japan in the 1980s was comparable to that in the United States and in Western Europe. In contrast, Crystal reported that in the United States, "where [the] typical CEO earned total compensation (excluding perquisites and fringe benefits) that was around 35 times the pay of an average manufacturing worker in 1974, a typical CEO today earns pay that is around 120 times that of an average manufacturing worker and about 150 times that of the average worker in both manufacturing and service industries" (1991, p. 27). He further noted that these large gaps were not to be found in Japan, Germany, France, and the United Kingdom. Even in the United Kingdom, whose business community and economy is most closely aligned with the United States, the differential between CEO and average worker pay was under 35 times. Although the topic of wage dispersion has occupied a great deal of public attention in the United States, and although it is clear that wage dispersion is produced, at least in part, by forces operating within organizational labor markets (Baron and Pfeffer, 1994), this subject has not drawn much theoretical or empirical attention in the organizations literature.

The changing environment for corporate control, changing size distributions of firms, changing wage dispersion within organizations, and the profound changes in the governance of the employment relation have not to this point played a large role in affecting the research agenda of organization studies. In some ways, this is because the discipline is frequently almost as unconcerned about context and history as other related disciplines, such as economics, that have been deservedly criticized for such theoretical and empirical lacunae. As already noted, organization theory is not only largely housed in U.S. journals, it is also largely focused on U.S. organizations and ideas. In a comparative study of the development of organization theory, Guillen argued:

> the adoption of models or paradigms of organizational management does not necessarily follow from their scientific credibility and is not solely determined by economic and technological factors. . . . Managers in different countries adopted . . . paradigms in selective ways during the twentieth century, depending on the problems they were facing and such institutional factors as their mentalities and training, the activities of professional groups, the role of the state, and the attitude of the workers. (1994, pp. 1–2)

It is also the case that the field has tended to eschew engagement with concerns of public policy. The changing nature of the employment relationship and its differential effects on women and minorities, the changing structure of wages in firms, and the increasing influence of shareholder capitalism over what might be called a stakeholder model all have profound social implications. For the most part, however, the field has been content to leave public policy debates to economists and, to a lesser extent, sociologists, even though much of the phenomena of interest occur *in* organizations.

This neglect is unfortunate because a comparative—both over time and across place—research approach has much to recommend it for testing theories and models more rigorously and helping to discover the extent to which analytical perspectives are bound by either period, location, or both. Neglect of policy tends to keep the field of organization studies on the sidelines in debates about issues in which it potentially has much to contribute. In thinking about the various perspectives on organizations to be discussed below, the changing features of organizations—both those highlighted here and others—should be kept firmly in mind. One way of evaluating organizational models and theories is to ask to what extent they provide a productive way of understanding and predicting the evolving nature of organizations.

2

Understanding the Causes of Behavior

Perhaps the most fundamental question addressed by organization studies is how we are to understand what causes behavior. The question is important for those seeking to affect organizations and is equally important for those doing research on them, for, depending on how it is answered, attention focuses on some factors or variables and away from others. For much of its history, organization studies was dominated by a situationalist perspective, in which the causes of behavior were sought in the environment of the individual. Thus, for instance, in learning and operant-conditioning perspectives (Luthans and Kreitner, 1975; Nord, 1969), behavior is seen to be a function of its consequences, and analytic attention is therefore directed at understanding the cues that trigger behavior, the consequences that follow the behavior, schedules of reinforcement, and the relative efficacy of rewards or punishment (O'Reilly and Weitz, 1980) in altering behavior. The large literature on job design (Hackman and Oldham, 1980) asked what dimensions of jobs—things such as autonomy, variety, and the feedback received—affected employee motivation and job satisfaction. Studies of job attitudes such as satisfaction with pay, with the job overall, and with co-workers typically looked to the environment—the level of pay received, job characteristics, the availability of alternatives, what co-workers thought and said (Salancik and Pfeffer, 1978a)—as the critical explanatory factors.

There were a number of reasons for the situational emphasis, but certainly two are a legal environment that made focusing on individual differences more difficult and a political context in which social problems and their solutions tended to be located in the environment and—for good or ill depending on one's perspective—the role of individual choice and responsibility were deemphasized. As to the first point, a landmark legal case, *Griggs v. Duke Power*, established the principle that if the application of selection criteria such as written tests had an adverse impact on groups protected by the various civil rights statutes, such as women or minorities, so that they scored less well on that screening device, then the test or selection standard had to be validated in order to be employed. Validation, of course, not only involves determining whether test scores predict subsequent performance but can entail selecting more broadly from the applicant pool (to avoid restriction-of-range problems) and then following those selected to see if their scores on the test predicted their performance. Moreover, since expectations for performance are often self-fulfilling (e.g., Archibald, 1974), a true validation study must gather test scores when an individual enters the organization and then keep them secret until they can be compared to performance measures that are uncontaminated by knowledge of the individual's scores. This process is quite costly and could be undertaken only by comparatively large organizations, and then only for those jobs that had enough incumbents to make the effort worthwhile (e.g., Howard and Bray, 1988). The practical effect of the *Griggs* decision and its vigorous enforcement by the Equal Employment Opportunity Commission was to make employment testing less important in selection and socially suspect.

Without reviewing in detail the political and social history of the Great Society of President Lyndon Johnson or other social reforms, it seems clear that the 1960s and 1970s were periods in which social interventions to affect the environment of behavior were seen as important. Early childhood education and development was emphasized in the Head Start program, the establishment of Legal Aid promised to give poorer Americans access to the court system for redress of problems, and the federal role in education was greatly expanded in an effort to provide better and fairer educational opportunities in the belief that this would aid social mobility. By contrast, the current political climate emphasizes individual choice and responsibility. Subsequent Supreme Court decisions have weakened the requirements for demonstrating the adverse impact of tests or other screening devices. Legal services for the poor are under attack, and current budgeting and legislation seek the devolution of responsibility for education away from the federal government. This different social context with its focus on the individual has surely helped shape what organizations scholars study as well as the perspective they bring to that endeavor.

It is not just the historical context that affects how causes for behavior are perceived. There is also accumulating evidence that the attribution of causes of behavior is significantly affected by cultural norms and values. In a set of experiments, Morris and Peng tested the idea that:

> dispositionalism in social attribution . . . reflects an implicit theory about social behavior that is more widespread in individualist cultures than in collectivist cultures. . . . An implicit theory about a domain is acquired from culturally bound experience with events in the domain and with public representations of the domain (e.g., folktales, sacred texts, laws, and works of art). . . . In highly individualist cultures, such as the United States, persons are primarily identified as individual units . . . and they are socialized to behave according to personal preferences. In highly collectivist cultures, such as China, persons are primarily identified as group members . . . and they are socialized to behave according to group norms, role constraints, and situational scripts. (1994, p. 952)

In an experiment in which subjects watched cartoon displays of physical and social events and reported their causal perceptions, Morris and Peng (1994) predicted and found that American and Chinese would differ significantly in how they attributed behavior in the social situation, with the Americans emphasizing internal forces and the Chinese emphasizing external pressures. A second study found that attributions for mass murders reported in the newspaper differed systematically between Americans and Chinese. "American reporters attributed more to personal dispositions and Chinese reporters attributed more to situational factors" (Morris and Peng, 1994, p. 961). This research is important because it suggests that attributions of causality and psychological phenomena such as the fundamental attribution error (L. D. Ross, 1977) are *not* invariant across cultures. Consequently, the growing interest in dispositional explanations for organizational behavior is almost certainly a Western if not strictly an American phenomenon, and we need to be much more sensitive to the culturally embedded character of our explanations of causality and, for that matter, the culturally and socially embedded character of our models of behavior.

The 1980s and 1990s have witnessed a renewed interest in research seeking the causes of individual behavior and attitudes not in a person's particular organizational or social environment but rather in the individual's own personality or dispositions. One of the strongest statements of this view was made by Schneider, who argued, "the attributes of people, not the nature of the external environment, or organizational technology, or organizational structure, are the fundamental determinants of organizational behavior" (1987, p. 437). He argued this was true because organizations would tend to recruit, select, and retain people on the basis of individual attributes, and consequently, those attributes would come to constitute the basis of the organization. The attraction-selection-attrition (ASA) cycle would operate to produce homogeneity over time; thus, "the situation is not independent of the people in the setting; the situation *is* the people. . . . Structure, process, and culture are the *outcome* of the people in an organization, not the cause of the behavior of the organization" (Schneider, Goldstein, and Smith, 1995, p. 751). Of course, some formulations stress the interaction between persons and situations (e.g., Chatman, 1991; O'Reilly, Chatman, and Caldwell, 1991), but the resurgence of interest in individual differences as an important way of understanding organizational behavior has been both vigorous and controversial.

The Search for Individual Dispositions

The search for individual differences, operationalized as cross-situational consistency in behavior or attitudes, was largely dormant by the 1970s. For instance, the study of leadership traits produced limited success in uncovering consistent dimensions of personality or finding robust effects of individual attributes on outcomes of organizational interest. Vroom summarized that research: "There appear to be a few traits which tend to distinguish leaders from non-leaders. . . . The differences tend to be small in magnitude with large amounts of overlap between the distributions of scores of leaders and followers. . . . There is considerable variance across situations" (1976, p. 1529). Vroom also noted that there were important problems in inferences of causality in much of the research—leadership roles may create differences in traits rather than the traits being responsible for accession to positions of leadership.

This neglect of individual differences has now changed substantially. A search of *Psychological Abstracts* revealed that the average annual number of articles dealing with personality traits increased some 41 percent from the period 1974–1986 to the period 1987–1992. Examining the *American Business Index*, which only began in 1985, and considering only articles that concern both organizational behavior and personality, I found that there were 9% more articles per year in the period 1989–1992 than there were in the period 1985–1988.

Weiss and Adler (1984) wrote an influential piece that has stimulated much of this renewed interest. They argued that the failure to find dispositional effects of any empirical consequence in organizations was possibly more a matter of poor theory and methods than the fact that dispositions didn't matter. They noted that it was often the case that personality scales were grafted, almost as an afterthought, onto studies being done for other reasons. Therefore, the particular construct being measured was not always logically related to the rest of the study design. Funder and Colvin (1991) argued that counting specific behaviors was too restrictive a way to assess consistency across situations. They maintained that coding behavior in terms of its social effect or psychological meaning was more valid, because that would relocate "the essence of behavior from its superficial appearance to the meaning it has for the person or the effect it has upon the social environment" (p. 774). Judge argued that "not all personality constructs are equally efficacious in predicting attitudes and behavior" (1992, p. 32), and that the research on dispositions had not necessarily focused on the most important dimensions. Chatman (1989) maintained that personality or individual differences constituted an overall gestalt and that investigating single facets or dimensions at a time would inevitably fail to capture the substance of individual differences. Thus, neither personal dispositions, nor situations, nor the meaning of cross-situational consistency had been adequately assessed; it was premature to conclude that dispositions didn't matter.

The availability of panel data, particularly data measuring job attitudes, prompted renewed interest in and study of cross-situational consistency. A year after the Weiss and Adler paper appeared, Staw and Ross (1985) published a paper that, despite its acknowledged theoretical and methodological flaws, spawned a resurgence of interest in individual differences in organizational behavior and provided a substantive direction for that interest—namely, a concern with positive and negative affect. The Staw and Ross study used a single-item measure of job satisfaction from the National Longitudinal Survey of Mature Male Workers (who were between forty-four and sixty-five years old) and examined the stability of that measure over time, comparing responses in 1966, 1969, and 1971. They found that although the measure of job satisfaction was comparatively more stable (the longitudinal correlations were higher) for men who remained in the same company or in the same occupation compared to those who changed either or both—providing some evidence for the importance of the situation—it was still the case that even in the case of the most change, the stability in job satisfaction was statistically significant. They concluded that "satisfaction in 1966 was the strongest and most significant predictor of 1971 job attitudes. Neither changes in pay nor changes in job status accounted for nearly as much variance as prior job attitude" (p. 475). Staw and Ross took this result to indicate that job satisfaction was a stable individual characteristic, such that some people tended to be happier than others regardless of their circumstances. Staw and Ross went on to argue that one possible reason that various organizational interventions (such as job redesign) were not always as effective as their advocates hoped was that "many situational interventions may be prone to failure because they must contend with attitudinal consistency or a tendency for individuals to revert back to their basic dispositions" (p. 478).

In a critique of the relative variance claims made by Staw and Ross for dispositions compared to situations, Johns noted that there was a test-retest correlation of .84 for both job status and pay (the two situational factors considered in the study) over the five-year period examined. Consequently, "the situational changes against which Staw and Ross pitted prior job satisfaction were highly constrained" (1991, p. 90).

The most obvious problems with this initial study—use of a single-item dependent variable, definition of the personal trait of satisfaction from its stability over time, which is tautological, and failure to control for a number of alternative explanations for the results, such as the content of the jobs being performed—were overcome to varying degrees in subsequent studies. The basic paradigm—searching for longitudinal correlations in attitudes—remained essentially unchanged. Thus, for instance, Staw, Bell, and Clausen (1986) used data on personality collected at Berkeley on individuals when they were young to examine job satisfaction decades later. They found that personality did predict job satisfaction and that this result held even when the socioeconomic status of the individuals was statistically controlled. Gerhart (1987) replicated the Staw and Ross study using a sample of younger workers (who would presumably be more likely to experience more change in job conditions). He attempted to control for differences in job characteristics by assigning job characteristic scores to occupations on the basis of their descriptions in the *Dictionary of Occupational Titles* and by using those items from the Job Characteristics Inventory (Sims, Szilagyi, and Keller, 1976) that measured job complexity. He found that although there were important effects of job characteristics on job attitudes, the statistical significance of the cross-time stability in job satisfaction remained.

One issue in all of these studies is what stability in job satisfaction scores actually says about the existence of dispositions. Gutek and Winter (1992) argued that this apparent stability was not necessarily an indicator of some stable underlying trait but rather possibly an artifact of response-shift bias (Howard and Dailey, 1979). Response-shift bias raises the possibility that there is a change in the frame of reference used by the respondent in answering questions about job satisfaction so that the stability in job attitudes is illusory. Gutek and Winter wrote:

> evaluation of the job is confounded with a change in frame of reference that accompanies a job change. . . . Respondents may be using a different frame of

reference each time job satisfaction is measured during a longitudinal study, especially if they have changed jobs between the two measurements. . . . The job change "intervention" expands their conception of the possible range of job satisfaction and thereby affects their Post job change ratings of job satisfaction. (1992, pp. 62–63)

Gutek and Winter noted that there were three kinds of job-satisfaction ratings: (1) a rating of job satisfaction at an earlier time, possibly when the individual was in a different situation, which they referred to as "Pre"; (2) a rating of job satisfaction at the present time, called "Post"; and (3) a retrospective rating of job satisfaction for the conditions of the initial period, called "Then." Terborg, Howard, and Maxwell (1980) have presented evidence that the comparisons of Then/Post measurements were more similar to objective ratings of change in behavior than were the Pre/Post ratings. Furthermore, Terborg, Howard, and Maxwell showed that "the retrospective technique was robust to problems of saliency, priming, and order effects, and Then ratings were not biased by memory distortion or social desirability" (Gutek and Winter, 1992, p. 64).

In three separate studies, Gutek and Winter found "no consistency of job attitudes across job situations when we designed studies that took into account the possible occurrence of a response shift bias among job changers." The ratings of different jobs were essentially independent, but these ratings "should have been correlated if people are predisposed to be satisfied or dissatisfied" (1992, p. 75). They concluded that the "fact" of cross-time consistency in job satisfaction was artifactual and not robust.

Another issue highlighted by the Staw and Ross study and Gerhart's replication and extension is the meaning and measurement of situational versus dispositional effects. In a sample, responses over time may be highly correlated even if those responses differ significantly across the two periods, as long as the relative scores of the subjects remain stable (Newton and Keenan, 1991). Thus, for example, an intervention that raises everyone's job satisfaction significantly may still leave the relative ranking among individuals unchanged, implying stability when, in fact, there is change. In a study of British engineers whose course satisfaction was measured while still in school in 1980 and whose job satisfaction was measured in 1982 and 1984, Newton and Keenan (1991) reported a statistically significant correlation between job satisfaction measured two years apart ($r = 0.24$), a significant correlation between course satisfaction and job satisfaction four years later ($r = 0.15$), but no relationship between course satisfaction and job satisfaction two years after graduation ($r = 0.03$). However, there were also significant changes in the level of job satisfaction (and alienation) over time, with the results indicating that, on the whole, respondents were less satisfied with their jobs than they were with their university courses. This study demonstrated that, by using an over-time correlation measure, one would infer some degree of stability (note that the amount of variance explained at a later time by scores at the previous time is quite small), but looking at the differences in means, one would infer statistically significant change. Some scholars have explicitly defined a dispositional perspective in terms of the stability of rank-ordering of individuals across situations, even if and when "these consistent individual differences . . . [are] superimposed on overall *level* differences that reflect that some work environments are generally more satisfying than others" (Watson and Slack, 1993, p. 182).

Any theory emphasizing the importance of dispositions must necessarily answer the question of where such dispositions originate. One possible answer is genetics, and a series of studies of twins has sought to demonstrate the heritability of both job attitudes and vocational interests. These studies have capitalized on the availability of data gathered on twins, some of whom were separated at birth and raised apart—something that is important in order to be able to empirically distinguish between genetic heredity and environment. Arvey, Bouchard, Segal, and Abraham (1989) estimated that about 30 percent of the observed variation in general job satisfaction could be attributed to inherited or genetic factors. Lykken, Bouchard, McGue, and Tellegen (1993), studying vocational and recreational interests in pairs of twins, found that about 50 percent of the variation in interests was associated with genetic variation. They also found a higher degree of correlation in the monozygotic twins than for the dyzygotic twins, the latter having less genetic material in common. Note that the amount of heritability implied by these studies is substantial—in some cases exceeding 50 percent.

There have been a number of methodological critiques of the twin studies. Cropanzano and James (1990) noted that if the twins were raised in similar environments—a plausible assumption—comparing environmental with inherited influences would not be valid. But perhaps the biggest issue is that, "absent information regarding *how* the process works, one wonders *what* is inherited" (Judge, 1992, p. 44, emphasis in original). There have been numerous studies demonstrating the likelihood that intelligence is inherited, at least in part, and has a genetic component (Bouchard and McGue, 1981; Seligman, 1992; Hernstein and Murray, 1994). Intelligence, moreover, has been shown to affect numerous life outcomes such as career success (O'Reilly and Chatman, 1994). The question posed by the twin studies is whether the observed relationship between job satisfaction and vocational interest scores across sets of twins is the consequence of the heritability of job affect and career interests or of the heritability of intelligence and the effect of intelligence on career interests and job satisfaction (see also Judge, 1992). This distinction, however, is not necessarily critical to those who argue that the heritability of traits and their stability and existence are important, not the particular mechanisms or even the particular traits that are inherited. Thus, for instance, Lykken et al. noted, "the experiences people seek, and the effect of those experiences on their developing interests, are influenced by traits of physique, aptitude, and temperament . . . that are themselves substantially genetically influenced" (1993, p. 658).

One critical problem faced by research on the dispositional bases of organizational behavior has been to identify not only the source of dispositions but also a consistent, replicable set of meaningful dispositions. As noted previously, the work on the stability of satisfaction over time led naturally to an interest in the possibility that one important individual trait was a propensity to be happy or unhappy. This corresponded nicely with work in social psychology on positive and negative affect and has resulted in a number of empirical studies. Watson, Clark, and Tellegen (1988) reported on the development of scales for positive and negative affect and evidence that these are, in fact, two orthogonal dimensions. Costa and McCrae (1988) reported six-year test-retest correlations of 0.82 for positive affect and 0.83 for negative affect, providing evidence of the stability of this disposition over time.

Levin and Stokes (1989) argued and provided evidence that negative affectivity was related to measures of job satisfaction. Their experimental study manipulated task characteristics by giving some subjects the job of rating graduate student applications and others the task of copying transcripts. They selected subjects that were either in the highest or lowest quartile of the scale of negative affectivity. Their empirical results indicated that although task condition explained some 53 percent of the variation in job satisfaction while negative affectivity accounted for only 4 percent, even in the two very different task conditions the effect of negative affectivity was statistically significant. Watson and Slack (1993) studied eighty-two employees at Southern Methodist University, measuring them initially on scales assessing positive affect and negative affect. Subsequently, subjects were retested on these personality measures and also completed job satisfaction and job change measures. Although there was significant attrition in the group, through both voluntary turnover and firing, the initial measures of affect were unrelated to whether or not the subjects remained employed at SMU. Measures of temperament showed good test-retest consistency, with correlations ranging from 0.63 to 0.74. Also, initial measures of positive and negative affect were correlated with job satisfaction almost two years later, and, in fact, the correlations between affect at the time of the initial measurement and subsequent satisfaction were of about the same magnitude as contemporaneous correlations between the dispositions and job satisfaction when measured at time 2. Moreover, even when (perceptual) measures of job characteristics were partialed out in the analysis, the effect of positive and negative affect remained.

Of course, positive and negative affect are not the only critical dimensions of personality. Another advance made in the study of dispositions has been convergence on the importance of five core dimensions of personality—the so-called Big Five (e.g., Barrick and Mount, 1991; Digman, 1990; L. R. Goldberg, 1990). The Big Five factors are: extraversion, agreeableness, conscientiousness, emotional stability, and openness to experience (Barrick and Mount, 1993, p. 111). This is an important advance because one of the criticisms of dispositional research has been that it was atheoretical and tautological. For instance, Judge and Hulin commented on the proliferation of "empirical studies linking traits to outcomes, with often only tangential relations to a well-developed theoretical framework" (1993, p. 389). The search for personality dimensions has at times involved finding some regularity in behavior and then naming that regularity a personality dimension; at other times it has involved factor analyses of questionnaire responses, which data has been used to empirically uncover dispositions. These factor-analytic solutions were not always stable across subject populations, and the search for dispositions was criticized for attempting to capitalize on empirical regularities.

O'Reilly and Chatman (1994) have noted that although there has been a renewed interest in the effects of individual characteristics on organizational behavior, one characteristic absent in this literature is intelligence, or general cognitive ability (GCA). This is despite the evidence that intelligence is in part inherited and is stable over time and, most important, the evidence that "general cognitive ability predicts job performance in all jobs" (Hunter, 1986, p. 340). A number of studies using large samples (e.g., Ree and Earles, 1991; Austin and Hanisch, 1990; Campbell, 1990) have shown cognitive ability to predict job performance and occupational choice even better than measures of specific aptitudes. O'Reilly and Chatman (1994) obtained measures of the intelligence (using Graduate Management Admission Test scores) and motivation (using the Adjective Check List as part of a personality assessment) of a set of MBA students while they were in their first year of business school. After these students graduated (either three and a half or four and a half years later), O'Reilly and Chatman measured current salary, number of job offers received on graduation, number of promotions, the increment in salary compared to the salary received on graduation, and the ratio of the number of offers received to the number of interviews students had while looking for a job when they graduated. The study controlled for previous work experience, sex, age, citizenship, and college major. O'Reilly and Chatman found virtually no main effects for either intelligence or motivation but uncovered a statistically significant interaction that predicted current salary, number of offers, and number of promotions.

House, Howard, and Walker (1991), employing the AT&T data (Howard and Bray, 1988), found that verbal ability was correlated .83 with verbal ability measured some twenty years after the initial measurement. Quantitative ability was not as stable, with the correlation over twenty years being just .40. Nevertheless, both dimensions of intelligence were much more stable than any of the other dispositions measured by House and his colleagues and, moreover, had statistically significant effects on managerial attainment, measured in terms of the level of responsibility achieved. For those interested in the effect of individual differences on what happens to people and how they perform in organizations, it would seem that intelligence or mental ability would be an excellent research focus. Furthermore, including measures of intelligence in studies of the effects of other dispositions would permit research to eliminate this factor as an alternative explanation for the results.

Another advance in the literature on traits has been the recognition of the need to both theoretically and empirically distinguish between moods, or states that can be induced experimentally by manipulations such as giving subjects cookies or that vary naturally, from more stable and enduring traits such as positive or negative affect. George (1989; 1991) has shown that although there is some relationship between mood and positive and negative affect, the constructs are empirically distinct. Mood at work has been related to absence and prosocial behaviors and to organizational outcomes such as sales. The evidence in these studies does seem to suggest that mood has a stronger effect on the various dependent variables than does disposition. In some sense that is not surprising, as mood is a characteristic of the moment and might therefore be expected to be more proximately relevant to current behavior than a more generalized affective orientation.

Problems with the Dispositional Perspective

Although there has been a plethora of articles and substantially increased interest in exploring the effect of individual traits on behavior in organizations, this literature is not without its problems. First, there remains ambiguity about the definition of some of the traits, including even the Big Five. Barrick and Mount acknowledged that "some researchers have reservations about the five-factor model, particularly the imprecise specification of these dimensions" (1991, p. 3). These reservations flow logically from the fact that "while there is general agreement among researchers concerning the number of factors, there is some disagreement about their precise meaning" (p. 3). For instance, the first trait is extraversion/ introversion, associated with the characteristics of being sociable, talkative, and assertive (p. 111). However, Hogan (1986) has interpreted this dimension as consisting of two components, ambition and sociability. Extraversion, ambition, sociability, and talkativeness are not necessarily conceptually identical. Similar imprecision exists for virtually all of the traits. For instance, conscientiousness has also been called conformity or dependability and has been referred to as the will to achieve because of its association with various educational achievement measures: "As the disparity in labels suggests, there is some disagreement regarding the essence of this dimension" (Barrick and Mount, 1991, p. 4).

Similar problems affect the interpretation of positive and negative affect, which have been most often measured and theorized as if they were statistically independent dimensions. But the independence between the constructs seems to depend on measurement and methodological issues (Chamberlain, 1988; Diener, 1990). Diener concluded that "there is not replicable evidence across samples and methods that positive and negative affect are . . . unrelated" (1990, p. 14).

Second, although some studies have measured the stability of dispositions across time, those dealing with positive and negative affect, for example, such concern about ensuring that stable traits are identified and validated is not necessarily the norm. For example, several authors have employed the inaugural addresses of U.S. presidents to measure presidential personality (e.g., House, Spangler, and Wyocke, 1991; Spangler and House, 1991; Winter, 1987). Winter coded inaugural addresses for achievement, affiliation, and power-motive imagery. However, he chose to code a single speech—the first inaugural address. Although a number of the presidents were reelected and therefore gave second inaugural speeches, and since many had been in public life for years and so had given speeches that could also have been analyzed, there was no attempt in *any* of the studies of the effects of presidential personality to establish that presidential personality, as a reasonably stable underlying construct, had been measured by using the same method to assess consistency over time.

Indeed, Winter's own data permit one to explore an alternative interpretation for his results—namely, that the imagery in the speeches reflects not the personality of the president but rather the political ideology of the president's party. Winter (1987) reported the scores for the U.S. presidents he studied. Considering only those from the twentieth century, Democratic presidents scored, on average, 62.8 on the standardized power-imagery measure while Republican presidents scored

49.5. Democrats scored 60.1 on affiliation while Republicans scored 51. Thus, across political parties there are differences that provide a plausible explanation for the differences in imagery observed, without relying on the construct of personality.

Nor is there increased attention to measuring the stability of dispositions in more recent research, conducted long after this problem was discussed (Davis-Blake and Pfeffer, 1989). For example, in a study of the effect of the individual characteristic of cooperativeness and of being in a more cooperative culture on cooperative behavior, Chatman and Barsade (1995) measured individual cooperativeness at a single point in time, using a scale that had not been shown to be stable over time.

Third, there is evidence that dispositions or elements of personality appear to change in response to learning, experience, and exposure to different situations. House, Howard, and Walker (1991) found that the level of managerial responsibility AT&T employees had attained at one point in time had a statistically significant effect on the will to manage at a later time. Kohn and Schooler (1978; 1982) reported that individual traits such as self-direction and tolerance for uncertainty changed depending on the particular jobs that people held over time.

Fourth, the definition of dispositions is frequently imprecise with respect to the stability implied in the definition or to the distinction between dispositions and other psychological constructs. Thus, House, Shane, and Herold wrote, "Dispositions generally are viewed as tendencies to respond to situations . . . in a particular, predetermined manner. Furthermore such tendencies may vary in their temporal stability, their activation state, and their usefulness in explaining behavior under different conditions" (1996, p. 205). That article also noted that while personality characteristics were the most stable dispositions, "needs, motivates, preferences, and attitudes . . . need not be viewed as stable" (p. 205). This muddies the distinction between individual dispositions and other psychological states, including mood, which are readily induced (e.g., Isen and Levin, 1972; Brief, Butcher, and Roberson, 1995).

Fifth, many of the effects of dispositions, particularly on outcomes of organizational interest, are incredibly weak if not nonexistent. O'Reilly and Roberts, using a sample of 578 officers and enlisted men in a high-technology navy unit, found "no significant relationship between intrinsic traits and job satisfaction" (1975, p. 148), once factors such as rank and tenure with the navy were controlled. Barrick and Mount (1991) performed a meta-analysis of the effect of the Big Five personality traits on job performance, reviewing 117 studies conducted between 1952 and 1988 that covered some 24,000 individuals. They reported that the magnitudes of the estimated true correlations between these personality dimensions and job proficiency, training proficiency, and various career outcome measures such as salary, turnover, and tenure were less than 0.10. Tett, Jackson, and Rothstein's (1991) meta-analysis of the personality-job performance relationship in ninety-seven field studies found that the average corrected correlation between personality and job performance was 0.19. Hough et al. (1990), examining the validity of six personality traits in a sample of over 9,000 individuals in the U.S. military, found predictive validities for a variety of job-related criteria in the 0.20s. The average correlation between the traits and both technical proficiency and general soldiering proficiency was 0.04. The outcomes best predicted by the traits were physical fitness and military bearing. These reviews indicate that dispositions invariably account for 4 percent or less of the variation in outcomes such as job performance.

Examination of some specific studies illustrates the point that even when statistically significant correlations with personality dimensions are found, the effect sizes are often minute. Bluen, Barling, and Burns's (1990) study of the relationship between personality and the number of policies sold by life insurance brokers found a correlation 0.09 with impatience-irritability and 0.18 with achievement strivings. The same study showed that experience (organizational tenure) correlated 0.39 with the number of policies sold, demonstrating that work experience was a better predictor of current sales than personality. George's (1989; 1991) studies of the effects of positive and negative affectivity found that absenteeism from work correlated −0.10 with positive affectivity and 0.08 with negative affectivity. She also reported that positive affectivity was correlated 0.10 with a measure of altruism, 0.02 with indicators of customer service, and 0.00 with sales performance. Her studies found that state or mood had a stronger effect than dispositions on the outcomes assessed, but she reported that the strongest effects on absence were job tenure, age, being paid on commission, and full- or part-time employment status, all situational factors.

Sixth, many of the studies of dispositions make virtually no effort to control for plausible situational factors that might also explain the results. An important consequence of failure to control for situational causes is that the unique effects of situations and dispositions become impossible to untangle, and there is the potential for misattributing situational effects to dispositional causes.

Both self-selection and organizational selection result in the nonrandom assignment of individuals to organizational conditions (Schneider, 1987). In this sense, much research on individual attitudes and behaviors in organizational settings consists of quasi-experiments. In these quasi-experiments, modeling only dispositional determinants of behavior can lead to biased estimates of effects. Achen's (1986) book on the problems involved in making causal inferences from data generated by quasi-experiments discussed this point at length. He demonstrated that "an accurate assessment of a quasi-experiment depends on explicit modeling of both the behavioral outcome of the experiment *and* the assignment to treatment groups" (p. 37). Achen showed that, unless the assignment process is modeled, the results of quasi-experiments are frequently worthless. In organizations research, modeling the assignment process requires estimating the effects of organizational characteristics (such as the selection and reward system) that both cause individuals to be in particular organizations and that also cause many of the dependent variables being studied. Cropanzano and James (1990) have made a similar point in their critique of the study of twins.

It should be noted that not every study of individual dispositions suffers from all of these problems. For instance, Judge and Hulin made a carefully drawn distinction between "affective disposition, defined as the tendency to respond generally to the environment in an affect-based manner, and subjective well-being, the level of overall happiness and satisfaction an individual has with his or her life" (1993, p. 388) and were quite precise in their measurement models. O'Reilly and Chatman (1994) also have taken care to measure the traits carefully, ensure their validity, and control for at least some situational factors. But the problems are pervasive enough in the literature so that readers should keep them in mind in evaluating this research.

Person by Situation Interaction and Fit

Rather than emphasizing dispositions or situational influences on behavior, some formulations have argued that it is the interaction between the two that most successfully accounts for behavior in organizations. As Pervin and Lewis (1978) have summarized, interactional psychology encompasses some five meanings of interaction between a person and a situation: descriptive interaction (describing interpersonal relationships and behavior in terms of the individuals involved and the situation or context), statistical interaction, additive interaction (two or more variables having additive effects), interdependent interaction (in which individual traits and situational variables compose a complex system and changes in one variable may have different effects on other variables), and reciprocal action-transaction interaction (a variable is influenced by its own effects on other variables). George (1992) has noted that tests of the interactional perspective in the organizations literature are quite rare. To the extent there have been explorations of this perspective, they have generally taken one of two forms: (1) examining conditions under which particular dispositions have more or less effect on some criterion and (2) developing measures of and examining the consequences of person–situation or person–job fit.

Barrick and Mount (1993), following up on the long-standing argument that personality would have more effect in situations that were relatively weak or had fewer demands (Bem and Allen, 1974; Bem and Funder, 1978; Mischel, 1977), hypothesized that job autonomy would moderate the relationship between personality and managerial performance. Studying 154 participants in a U.S. Army training program, they found that job autonomy, as rated by the respondents and their supervisors, did moderate the relationship between conscientiousness and extraversion and supervisors' ratings of performance. Earlier, Lee, Ashford, and Bobko (1990) had found that job autonomy moderated the relationship between Type A personality and job performance and job satisfaction, reporting that individuals scoring high on the Type A scale had the highest job performance and satisfaction under conditions of greater autonomy.

Some of the first studies of job characteristics examined whether those characteristics of the job environment affected individuals with different traits differently. Hackman and Lawler (1971) found that growth need strength moderated the relationship between job characteristics and motivation and satisfaction, such that individuals with high growth need strength were more affected by the motivating potential of jobs than those with low growth need strength. O'Reilly, distinguishing individuals by whether their orientation to work was primarily expressive (desiring achievement and self-actualization) or instrumental (desiring job security and high financial rewards), found support for the idea that "respondents with high expressive orientations toward work" were "more satisfied in challenging jobs while low expressive types" were "comparatively less satisfied in challenging work" (1977, p. 41). Steers and Spencer (1977) reported that the need for achievement moderated the relationship between job autonomy and supervisory ratings of performance, and Mowday and Spencer (1981) reported statistically significant moderating effects of the need for achievement on the relationship between autonomy and absenteeism but no moderating effect when turnover was the dependent variable. However, the results for the need for achievement as a moderator of the relationship between job conditions and outcomes are not consistent. For instance, Evans, Kiggundu, and House (1979) found that need for achievement did not moderate the relationship between job autonomy and performance in a study of 343 managers and supervisors in an automobile assembly plant.

Judge (1993) pursued the idea that the relationship between job satisfaction and turnover—a relationship that has been consistently observed but is often quite weak—might be moderated by an individual's affective disposition. He followed up on an insight by Weitz that suggested "some individuals generally gripe more than others" (1952, p. 203). For individuals who were generally happy, job dissatisfaction was hypothesized to be more likely to produce turnover than for individuals who were generally dissatisfied. Using data collected from 234 nurses working in a Midwestern clinic, Judge found that "employees with a positive disposition who were dissatisfied with their jobs were much more likely to quit" (1993, p. 399). Note that virtually all forms of statistical interaction are represented in the studies just described. In some, personality moderates the effects of the environment on various outcomes; in others, environmental characteristics, such as the strength of the situation or the amount of autonomy, moderate the relationship between personality and various outcomes; and in yet other studies, personality moderates the relationship between an attitude, job satisfaction, and some behavior, such as turnover, that might be expected to logically follow from it.

The second form of interaction that has been studied is the idea that the degree of person–situation fit can be assessed and is an important predictor of outcomes such as success and turnover. Chatman (1989; 1991) has suggested that the ability to predict and understand behavior in organizations would be improved by assessing person–organization fit through the use of a Q-sort methodology. The methodology operationalizes Bem and Funder's (1978) suggestion of the importance of matching templates—descriptions of the context that are comparable to the ways in which individuals are characterized.

Chatman, Caldwell, and O'Reilly (1995) have noted that different situations place different demands on people, so that what is important is the fit between individual predispositions and the requirements of the job or situation. Their study compared the personality profiles of MBA graduates to the personality profiles developed by asking sixty raters to assess "those personal characteristics that are important in determining success during the first five years of a person's career as a manager" (Chatman et al., 1995, p. 11). They found that the degree of

correspondence between an individual's personality profile and the template produced by the raters was significantly related to salary several years after graduation
as well as to the increment in that salary over the starting salary received, controlling for other factors such as gender, age, ethnicity, and intelligence as measured
by scores on a standardized admissions test. O'Reilly, Chatman, and Caldwell
(1991) found that the greater the degree of correspondence between an individual's values and the organization's culture, the higher the level of performance, the
longer the individual stayed in the organization, and the greater the expressed
commitment to the firm. Chatman (1991) reported that the congruence between
organizational culture and personal values was a better predictor of tenure and
performance in the job than either of the factors alone.

Chatman and Barsade (1995) found that cooperative individuals behaved
more cooperatively when they worked in an experimentally induced cooperative
culture. Interestingly, their study demonstrated that cooperative individuals
tended to vary their behavior more depending on whether or not they were in an
individualistic or cooperative culture, while more individualistic individuals
tended to be less responsive to cultural norms. This result suggests that an individualistic culture, if it is created by recruiting individualistic people, is more robust,
at least in the United States. That is because the cooperative people will change
their behavior more to conform to the individualistic culture, which then will
become even more individualistic in its orientation. But since individualists conform less to social pressure, the reciprocal form of transformation—moving from
an individualistic to a collectivist set of norms—is much less likely.

The idea that person–organization fit is important seems intuitively sensible,
and certainly the results of these studies indicate that fit does predict important
organizational outcomes such as turnover in carefully conducted studies in which
fit is measured around the time of organizational entry and outcomes are measured at a later date. However, it is important to recognize that much of this
research does not assess stable traits or dispositions but rather more transient and
malleable individual attitudes and values. For instance, both Chatman (1991) and
O'Reilly et al. (1991) assessed person–organization fit by examining the relationship between new employees' preferences for various types of organizational cultures and more senior employees' descriptions of the actual organizational culture. But such preferences for cultural characteristics are quite likely to change
as a consequence of experience and as a result of organizational socialization
efforts. Chatman (1991) reported that attendance at firm social events and time
spent with a mentor significantly increased person–organization fit during the
first year on the job, so that the degree of person–organization fit at the time of
organizational entry accounted for less than 40 percent of the variation in fit a
year later. Thus, one can agree that person–organization fit is important, but note
that this degree of fit is in part a consequence of organizational efforts to change
individuals through socialization and inculturation processes and may or may not
reflect the interaction between stable individual traits and organizational situations. For this reason, research using individual dispositions as assessed in a formal
personality assessment process to predict managerial success by using the correlation with a rater-generated profile of managerial characteristics is an important

step in validating the usefulness of the personal disposition–situation fit argument (Chatman, Caldwell, and O'Reilly, 1995).

The Costs and Benefits of the Person–Situation Debate

There are a number of authors (e.g., George, 1992; House et al., 1996) who argue that organization studies should accept the interactionist perspective—situations, individual traits, and their interactions are all important—and stop debating the point. George, for instance, argued that "rather than mimicking the debate that raged in psychology over these same issues, it will probably be much more fruitful to try to understand the effects of person factors, situational factors, their various types of interactions, and the processes governing these interactions on organizational phenomena" (1992, p. 192). House et al. referred to the person–situation controversy as a "pseudo issue" and suggested that "it is more meaningful to ask how dispositional variables and organizational variables interact in evoking behavior" (1996, p. 220). Pervin (1985) and Carson (1989) also expressed exasperation with the continuing disputes about *whether* individual traits mattered or *which* were more important in general. The argument seems to be that the debate diverts time and attention away from advancing knowledge about organizational behavior.

The continuing controversy does, however, potentially have some positive benefit. First, the very fact of controversy, debate, and the passions aroused thereby provide attention, energy, and emphasis on this particular subset of the field. Thus, somewhat ironically, critiques of the dispositionalist perspective in organization studies (e.g., Davis-Blake and Pfeffer, 1989), and the responses they generated (e.g., House et al., 1996), have probably stimulated more and better work on this topic than might otherwise have occurred (see also Kenrick and Funder, 1988). As Mone and McKinley (1993) have argued, organization studies, in part because of its pre-paradigmatic nature, values uniqueness and things that are interesting possibly more than many scientific fields do. To the extent this is the case, the very controversy of the debate provides a measure of how interesting and novel the subject is and thus encourages more research activity.

Second, there is little doubt that critiques of the dispositionalist view have stimulated the substantive development of the study of individual traits. Without the critiques concerning the conceptual ambiguity of traits, methodological issues including failure to control for relevant situational influences and to use appropriate methods, and the very meaning of dispositions, one might question whether the field would have seen the advances in method and conceptual development witnessed particularly over the past several years.

The point about the relevance and usefulness of controversy is a general one for the field of organization studies, for this particular controversy is not the only one that has engaged the field. The fundamental issue is whether knowledge will be better developed by accommodating a number of points of view or whether the very absence of accommodation, particularly initially, stimulates deeper and more insightful thinking and analysis, to the ultimate benefit of the development of both theory and data.

Some Lessons Learned

This brief review of the person–situation debate in organization theory highlights a number of issues that bedevil the field and appear throughout the literature considered in this book. First, almost without exception, no consideration is given to the possibility that the answer to the question of where is the most productive place to search for the causality of behavior in organizations varies both over time and particularly over place. This is not to say that to have a valid theory of individual dispositions one should be able to locate a set of core dispositions that are invariant regardless of culture or context. Quite the contrary. The argument is that, instead of asserting generality under conditions where it is unlikely to hold, the study of organizations would be well served to explore whether the underlying dispositional dimensions vary and in what way across cultures and, similarly, to assess the extent to which dispositions or situations vary in their explanatory power over time and place. This entails much more than the few efforts at exploring some versions of interaction that are presently available in the literature.

Second, this literature is almost totally decoupled from the profound changes that were described in chapter 1 concerning the organizational landscape. This is not inevitable. Although one might be hard pressed to find a dispositional argument that could account for the rise in the prominence and power of capital market discipline over managerial behavior, one might think that exploring the causes of increasing wage inequality, or the effects on individuals' self-concepts or other dispositions of changing work arrangements, would occupy a larger portion of the field's research attention.

Third, consistent with much of the literature we will see in this book, the person–situation debate almost never engages concerns of important public or social policy, even though it is obviously highly relevant to some of those concerns. Whether behavior is caused by relatively stable, individual dispositions or by situations clearly has profound implications for efforts to enhance organizational performance. The locus of causality for behavior is important in considering the extent to which individual selection and testing—for employment, for placement in various ability tracks in school, for promotion, and for access to training and development opportunities in organizations—is beneficial or harmful and how it might be done more effectively. Although the issue of the social consequences of how the causes for behavior are defined has been occasionally raised (Davis-Blake and Pfeffer, 1989), there has not been very much discussion of the policy implications of this concern in almost any forum in the organizations literature. As such, the contributions of other social sciences come to dominate even if and when organization studies has important things to say about an issue. This diminishes both the importance and the impact of organization studies, an unfortunate outcome for many reasons.

3

Five Models of Behavior

Answering the question of how we are to understand behavior in organizations requires not only locating the causality for that behavior—in persons, situations, or their interaction—but also developing basic assumptions or premises about behavior that guide theory building and direct empirical testing. Simon noted, "Nothing is more fundamental in setting our research agenda and informing our research methods than our view of the nature of the human beings whose behavior we are studying" (1985, p. 303). In some ways, these assumptions or characterizations of behavior are related to the issues already discussed—do they emphasize the effects of social context or, alternatively, individual attributes and choices?—but they also involve yet additional controversies about the nature of behavior. Moreover, as Frank perceptively noted, our assumptions and models of human behavior have consequences, as they have a tendency to become self-fulfilling (see also, McGregor, 1960):

> Views about human nature have important practical consequences . . . They dictate corporate strategies for preventing workers from shirking, for bargaining with unions, and for setting prices. . . . [O]ur beliefs about human nature help shape human nature itself. . . . Our ideas about the limits of human potential mold what we aspire to become. (Frank, 1988, p. 237)

Zajonc (1980, pp. 202–203) made much the same point in discussing research on social perception and social cognition: "Social perception and social cognition create a social reality by affecting both the perceiver and the objects perceived. . . . Thus, I have argued, social perception requires equal attention on both sides: on the side of the observer or perceiver, and on the side of the objects perceived."

Although many models of behavior are possible, here I identify and describe five of the most important models of action and choice that are prominent in organization studies. In each instance, we want to examine the underlying assumptions, the research directions these models have produced, and their implications for understanding organizations. The five models are (1) the economic model; (2) the social model; (3) the retrospectively rational model; (4) the moral model; and (5) a cognitive, interpretive model.

There is, of course, a first question as to what extent these models should be evaluated by the veracity of their assumptions or by the empirical confirmation of their predictions. Friedman (1953) articulated a position that has often been repeated: models (and he was referring to economic models) should not be evaluated on the validity of their assumptions but rather on the validity of the predictions generated by such models. A variant of this position is the natural-selection or competition argument. This argument maintains that even though, in a particular instance, a firm or individual may not engage in rational or profit-maximizing behavior, over time, competitive selection pressures will ensure that these decisions, individuals, or firms diminish in relative frequency (Becker, 1962). In this sense, there is no need to show how various adaptive, efficient practices arise, because "it is implicitly assumed that inefficient ones will have failed the test of the marketplace" (Granovetter, 1985, p. 30).

Although this epistemological position is still generally the rule in economic analysis, it has been subjected to numerous criticisms for the logical fallacies it contains (Samuelson, 1963; Simon, 1963). Blaug (1980) has offered a critique of natural selection, adaptive reasoning. Boland (1979) has noted that the basic purpose of a theory is to explain, and to rely solely on whether or not the predictions are valid is foolish. "When predictions prove to be valid, we do not know why, and hence are unable to foretell under what conditions they will continue to hold or fail, or may need to be adapted" (Etzioni, 1988, p. 17).

One argument is that unrealistic models or theories may offer an advantage in simplicity or parsimony over their more realistic but complex competitors. Simon discussed the trade-off between theoretical simplicity and the assumptions that were required by the theory:

> Occam's Razor has a double edge. . . . Occam understood his rule as recommending theories that make no more assumptions than necessary to account for the phenomena. . . . A theory of profit or utility maximization can be stated more briefly than a satisficing theory. . . . But the former makes much stronger assumptions than the latter about the human cognitive system. . . . The two edges of the razor cut in opposite directions. (1979, p. 495)

The arguments over the bases for evaluating models of behavior help to distinguish between the economic model and the others reviewed below, most of which have been created to more accurately and completely capture empirical reality, even at some cost in simplicity or elegance.

Resolving this issue about realism versus parsimony involves trade-offs, and different fields and different theorists make those trade-offs differently. A parsimonious and, in economics, mathematically elegant theory simplifies or neglects institutional details that vary by time, place, and circumstance, but it may do so at the expense of a more complete model that can capture all of the institutional complexity. Ronald Coase, writing about the old institutional economics, made his choice on the side of theoretical elegance: "Without a theory they had nothing to pass on except a mass of descriptive material waiting for a theory, or a fire" (1983, p. 230). As Scott has noted, "the battle between the particular and the general, between the temporal and the timeless, is one that . . . theorists continue to confront" (1995, p. 5).

Economic Models of Organizational Behavior

Economic models are growing in prominence in the social sciences generally (Dosi, 1995), particularly in political science (Green and Shapiro, 1994), sociology (Coleman, 1990), and organization studies (e.g., Milgrom and Roberts, 1992; Eisenhardt, 1989). At one time, there was an institutional economics that was similar in many respects to institutional analysis in sociology (Scott, 1995), but that form of analysis was supplanted by neoclassical analysis and a new institutionalism that shares much of its theoretical assumptions and methods of reasoning with the neoclassical approach. In the organizations literature, one can find citations to economic models in such fundamental topics as organizational design and structure, rewards and incentives, control, decision making, career attainment, organizational performance and survival, the structure and evolution of the employment relation, gender and race discrimination, interorganizational relations, and numerous others. In fact, one is hard pressed to think of many substantive areas in which economic models are not cited, even if only as providing an alternative hypothesis.

Although there are a number of variants of economic models of behavior, they all share a number of features. First and foremost, behavior is presumed to be rational—intentionally chosen on the basis of the best information available at the time to maximize the individual's utility (or preferences). Although "all of the social sciences have a stake in rationality analysis . . . what distinguishes economists is that they push the approach further and more persistently" (Williamson, 1995, p. 22). Economics obviously admits the idea of bounded or limited rationality (e.g., Simon, 1978), but economic models "still tend to define 'bounded rationality' as an imperfect approximation of the 'unbounded' one" (Dosi, 1995, p. 5). Embedded in this conception of rationality is the idea that preferences are exogenous (Jacoby, 1990), and few variants consider the possibility that preferences are shaped by social institutions and should therefore be the subject of analysis rather than taken for granted or assumed.

An important extension of the rationality principle is the idea that social arrangements are designed to achieve efficiency and, over time, inefficient ones will disappear. Natural selection, if not conscious managerial decision making, ensures that organizational as well as individual action achieves rationality. The time frame involved may be quite long, however. In discussing whether or not power processes could supplant efficiency in affecting organizations, Williamson and Ouchi wrote, "power considerations will usually give way to efficiency—at least in profit-making enterprises, if observations are taken at sufficiently long intervals, say a *decade*" (1981, pp. 363–364; emphasis added). Williamson (1995) has contrasted the idea of efficiency with that of power and has vigorously maintained that power cannot account for organizational outcomes. Organizational design, practices governing the employment relation, and patterns of interorganizational relations that survive over time are all efficient, according to Williamson, and do not reflect the operation of political interests and relative potency of those interests. This assertion means that literature assessing the effects of power and interests on these organizational arrangements provides a partial test of the economic model of organizations.

Second, virtually all economic models proceed from a theoretical apparatus invoking methodological individualism. That means simply that institutions or organizations are seen as aggregations of individual preferences and actions or at times as a nexus of contracts and agreements (Jensen and Meckling, 1976). Organizations are viewed as having no substantive reality apart from this function of aggregating preferences or agreements. Williamson argued that organizations are simply another type of "contractual instrument, a continuation of market relations, *by other means*" (1991, p. 162; emphasis in original).

Third, economic models emphasize comprehensiveness and often proceed from an assumption of equilibrium. Coase has argued that one reason economic analysis has been successful in moving into related social sciences is that the analysis of systems equilibria focuses on systemic interdependencies and is a mode of analysis "more likely to uncover the basic interrelationships within a social system" (1978, p. 209). The focus on equilibrium conditions and the assumptions of market competition tend to assure a more deterministic outcome from the analysis. In emphasizing equilibrium conditions, modern economics demonstrates less concern with "path-dependence," or the idea that what has happened in the past is important for understanding the present and predicting the future. Both history and process are less important in this form of theorizing, which Jacoby has called "timeless and placeless" (1990, p. 32), with no emphasis on how the economy acquired its features and how these vary.

Although many social science theories share an assumption that individuals pursue self-interest, a number of the economic theories that have penetrated organization studies, such as transaction cost economics and agency theory, take the idea of self-interest one step farther and emphasize opportunism, or self-interest pursued with guile and deceit (Ghoshal and Moran, 1996). As Ghoshal and Moran noted, there is an important distinction between opportunism and self-interested behavior:

> Opportunism is a stronger form of the self-interest assumption of motivation. . . . The two are distinguished primarily by whether or not individuals can reliably be expected to obey rules or keep promises. Self-interested behavior, in the received view, is presumed to be constrained by obedience and faithfulness to promises. Opportunism is not. (1996, p. 17)

Opportunism includes "the making of false or empty, that is, self-disbelieved threats and promises in the expectation that individual advantage will thereby be realized" (Williamson, 1975, p. 26). In a similar vein, agency theory implies that "agents have opportunities to misrepresent information and divert resources to their personal use" and that "cooperative effort is plagued by opportunities for malfeasant behaviour" (Nilakant and Rao, 1994, p. 650). In this sense, many economic theories differ from other social sciences in their assumptions about the extent to which human behavior is strictly instrumental and unconstrained by morals or values, except when behavior may be discovered and have consequent adverse effects on reputational resources.

The presumption of opportunism, an "extreme caricature" (Milgrom and Roberts, 1992, p. 42) of human behavior, is critical to at least some variants of the economic model. For instance, Williamson noted that "but for opportunism, most forms of complex contracting and hierarchy vanish" (1993, p. 97). Ghoshal and Moran, summarizing transaction cost theory, noted that "opportunism—the seeking of self-interest with guile—is the ultimate cause for the failure of markets and for the existence of organizations" (1996, p. 17).

Because people are presumed to act in a self-interested fashion to maximize their utilities, and because individuals are presumed to have a disutility for expending effort, economic models invariably view employees as effort-averse, unlikely to do what the organization wants and needs without some form of incentive, sanction, or combination of both. Baron has noted:

> The image of the worker in these models is somewhat akin to Newton's first law of motion: employees remain in a state of rest unless compelled to change that state by a stronger force impressed upon them—namely, an optimal labor contract. Various incentive features . . . are claimed to provide forms of insurance that overcome workers' reluctance to work. (1988, p. 494)

Moreover, because individuals are concerned about their own preferences, and these preferences may not be identical to those of owners and managers or across levels in an organizational hierarchy, as already noted, agency problems are presumed to be pervasive. "Agency theory holds that many social relationships can be usefully understood as involving two parties: a principal and an agent. The agent performs certain actions on behalf of the principal, who necessarily must delegate some authority to the agent" (Donaldson, 1990, p. 369). Agency problems arise when the desires or objectives of principals and agents diverge—a condition thought to be virtually ubiquitous—and when it is expensive or difficult for the principal to actually monitor or verify the agent's behavior (Eisenhardt, 1989). Agency theory deals with the topic of contracts—how to devise efficient systems for aligning the interests of the agent with those of the principal, particularly given the fact that the difference in the tolerance for risk (agents are presumed to be more risk averse than principals, in part because they frequently have less capability for diversifying their risk) may make a strictly performance-based incentive scheme for the agents costly because they would need to be compensated for bearing that risk.

There is some evidence that formal training in economics is significantly related to the use of economic reasoning and behavior (Larrick, Morgan, and Nisbett, 1990). Economic reasoning includes the sunk-cost rule (only future benefits and costs should be considered in a decision), the net benefit rule (that action with the greatest net benefit should be chosen), and the opportunity cost rule (the real cost of engaging in some action is the loss of benefits available from pursuing the next best course of action) (Larrick, Nisbett, and Morgan, 1993). Larrick et al. reported that "people who use these rules are more likely to have more successful life outcomes . . . college seniors . . . had higher grade point averages . . . and faculty . . . had higher salaries" (1993, p. 345). Frank, Gilovich, and Regan (1993) summarized studies indicating that individuals with economics training tended to defect more frequently in prisoner's dilemma experiments and tended to give less to charity. However, Arkes and Blumer (1985) reported no effect of previous courses in economics on not considering sunk costs in decision making, and Fischhoff (1982) has also concluded that many attempts to train people to avoid decision biases were unsuccessful. The two sets of results together suggest that behaving on the basis of classical economic assumptions may provide individual benefit, although whether or not it provides general social or even organizational benefit is open to question and depends on the amount of voluntary cooperation required for system effectiveness.

Because of the emphasis on methodological individualism and the efficiency of market-mediated transactions, the question naturally occurs as to how and why institutions, such as organizations, arise at all. One approach to answering this question is provided by transaction cost economics (Williamson, 1975). As reviewed by Williamson, the basic elements of the model are (1) the transaction is the basic unit of analysis; (2) transactions vary with respect to their frequency, uncertainty, and asset specificity, which affects how easy it is to redeploy the assets to other uses; (3) there are a set of generic modes of governance, including markets, hierarchies, and intermediate forms; and (4) the basic prediction is that "transactions, which differ in their attributes, are aligned with governance structures, which differ in their costs and competence" (1995, p. 27) in a way so as to minimize transaction costs.

These governance problems arise because of bounded rationality and uncertainty, which make the future impossible to foresee perfectly and make contracting for all possible future states of the world unfeasible. One might wonder why the parties involved don't simply handle contingencies as they arise. The answer, of course, is that each individual is presumed to be a utility-maximizing person interested in attaining his or her own interests and so cannot be trusted. This particular economic model of behavior has within it assumptions of the same sort of untrustworthy behavior typical of the genre—in this case, opportunism. "By opportunism, I mean self-interest seeking with guile. This includes, but is scarcely limited to, more blatant forms such as lying, stealing, and cheating. Opportunism more often involves subtle forms of deceit" (Williamson, 1985, p. 47).

Transaction cost models also provide an account for the presence of hierarchy in organizations, where the degree of hierarchy is defined as the extent of centralization of power and control (Williamson, 1985). Under the usual adaptive logic, hierarchy exists because of its efficiency: "the least hierarchical modes, in both contracting and decision-making respects . . . have the worst efficiency properties" (Williamson, 1985, p. 231).

If the reader is having trouble accepting the behavioral premises or assumptions of these models, it is not surprising. Not only are these models at variance with much of social psychological theory—for instance, theories emphasizing intrinsic motivation (Lepper and Greene, 1975; Deci, 1975)—they also contradict much current management practice that deemphasizes hierarchy, individual monetary incentives, and control. Furthermore, the economic model of behavior presents an extremely unflattering portrait of human behavior. "Typically, such organizational economic actors seek personal wealth, status, leisure, or the like. . . . Accordingly, their behavior as potentially shirking or opportunistic agents can be curbed by vigilant monitoring, together with incentive schemes based around money, promotion, negative sanctions, and the like" (Donaldson, 1990, pp. 371–372). To the extent such theories of behavior, when implemented in actual organizational policies and practices, produce the very behavior expected (i.e., become self-fulfilling prophecies), to the extent such theories of behavior are growing in importance in the social sciences, and to the extent such theories are at variance with basic ideas in sociology, social psychology, and organization theory, it seems clear that this is a substantial and important arena in which these social sciences need to challenge these models of behavior.

Problems with the Economic Model of Organizational Behavior

Strong critiques of the economic model of behavior have been offered by economists, political scientists, and sociologists, albeit with surprisingly little effect on the prominence of these models in the social science literature generally or the organizations literature specifically. Green and Shapiro (1994), after commenting on the substantial growth of rational choice models in political science, noted that such dominance could not be explained by the validity or power of this approach. "The stature of rational choice scholarship does not rest on a readily identifiable set of empirical successes" (p. 5). They noted that the rational choice models made predictions that were either trivially obvious or frequently empirically incorrect. In questioning their usefulness as a foundation for understanding politics, Green and Shapiro commented, "the case has yet to be made that these models have advanced our understanding of how politics works in the real world" (1994, p. 6).

Hirsch, Michaels, and Friedman (1987) contrasted the "clean" models of rational choice theories with the "dirty hands" of social sciences, such as social psychology and sociology, that actually empirically investigate the world. They argued that being too removed from the empirical world risks being unable to account for the variety actually observed and "incompetent to address the cultural side of life in society" (p. 325). Leontief (1985), himself a Nobel-prize winning economist, criticized the absence of original data in economic research and noted that of the articles appearing in the *American Economic Review* throughout the 1970s, half contained no data at all, and of the four or five articles that did contain original observations, two studied pigeons and mice. Mueller noted that "in one of the major collections on organizational economics, the ratio of empirical papers to nonempirical papers is 1:14 (Barney and Ouchi, 1986)" (1995, p. 1226).

When data are employed, because of the belief in the theory, almost any massaging of the data to get it to conform to the theory is acceptable. The data used are frequently previously collected for other purposes, and assumptions and variables are added on an ad hoc basis (Etzioni, 1988, p. 18) to improve the fit between theory and data. This makes it hazardous to evaluate the validity of the models' predictions: "When we defend the maximization paradigm by pointing to the similarities between its predictions and observed behavior, we often overlook the fact that the empirical 'success' of many economic models is principally derived from accommodating adjustments in complementary hypotheses" (Cross, 1983, p. 3).

The assumptions of adaptive efficiency characteristic of these models almost invariably lead to tautological reasoning. Practices are presumed to be efficient because of their very existence—if they were inefficient they would disappear—and thus the logic of economic science as it is practiced is, given a particular empirical observation, to derive a proof that demonstrates the efficiency properties of what has been observed.

As one example, consider the analysis of seniority-based wage systems in organizations (Lazear, 1979; 1981). In most organizations and for many jobs, there is a positive relationship between experience and earnings. But, it is not likely in all organizations and jobs for which this relationship holds that an individual's productivity goes up linearly with experience. So, the question is, Why not pay workers each period on the basis of their productivity for that period, thereby inducing effort to attain those contingent rewards? What Lazear demonstrates is that a payment scheme that rewards employees less than their marginal product when they are young and more when they are old can motivate effort because there is now an incentive for the more senior workers not to shirk—if they are discovered and fired, they lose the deferred compensation inherent in being paid more than they are producing. And, younger workers are motivated to work hard and stay with the firm so they can enjoy the benefits of higher earnings when they have more experience. Since this story begins with an empirical fact and then makes economic sense of that fact, it does not do a very satisfactory job of accounting for the recent trends away from this sort of payment system—although I have no doubt that such a change could be readily accounted for by an efficiency-based account if economic theorists were called to do so. This tendency toward tautology has been noted by Sen (1977), Arrow (1982), and Latis (1976), among others.

Another problem is that the methodological individualism characteristic of these models either ignores organizations and institutions almost completely or treats them as a residual category required by some form of market failure or contracting problem. Clegg noted that "economic approaches to organizations . . . operate with a particular set of a priori values: these are that organizations are an aberration from a more natural form of economic activity. This more natural form is that of exchange on the market" (1990, p. 61). Simon, who also won the Nobel prize in economics, has critiqued even the new institutional economics for its relative neglect of organizations:

> A fundamental feature of the new institutional economics is that it retains the centrality of markets and exchanges. All phenomena are to be explained by translating them into (and deriving them from) market transactions based upon negotiated contracts, for example in which employers become "principals" and employees become "agents." . . . The new institutional economics is wholly compatible with and conservative of neoclassical theory. . . . In general, the new institutional economics has not drawn heavily from the empirical work in organizations and decision-making for its auxiliary assumptions. . . . Until . . . the existing literature on organizations and decision making [is] taken into account, the new institutional economics and related approaches are *acts of faith, or perhaps of piety*. (1991, pp. 26–27; emphasis added)

Cooperation, necessary in the interdependent activities that characterize organizations, is ubiquitous. Economic approaches to understanding organizations must, then, develop an approach that reconciles the assumption of self-interested, utility-maximizing behavior with the observed organizational world. Critiquing the approach of organizational economics to understanding this fundamental issue of cooperation, Mueller (1995) argued that the individual utility-maximization assumption shared with other versions of economics prevented accounting for instances in which cooperation was sustained even when this behavior conflicted with self-interest. He concluded:

> OE [organizational economics] has put forward a largely static model with little empirical grounding of how a governance structure can secure cooperative outcomes. . . . The fact that economics makes cynical assumptions about the motivation of human beings has been emphasized previously. . . . Economics-based attempts to explain behavior in organizations lack what has become a basic understanding in organization theory, namely the ability to analyze members' motivations and behavior as varying depending upon situational contingencies. (p. 1230)

Economics has a particularly difficult time dealing with interorganizational cooperation. That is because ties of sentiment and friendship and the peer obligations thereby activated are presumed to exist among persons within an organization but not among larger social entities intent on maximizing shareholder wealth and efficiency. Granovetter sought to extend Coase's (1937) original question as to why firms exist: "parallel to Coase's 1937 question is another of at least equal significance, which asks about firms what Coase asked about individual economic actors: why do they coalesce into identifiable social structures?" (1995, p. 94). In their study of the keiretsu, the interfirm networks in Japan, Lincoln, Gerlach, and Ahmadjian concluded:

> We see the big-six *keiretsu* groups as . . . *networks*, and we interpret their economic role as one of collective action maximizing the joint welfare . . . of the membership by restraining both the bearing of risks and the appropriation of returns by individual firms and substituting what appears to be a group-administered allocation plan. The actions of groups . . . are . . . not necessarily

rational for its strongest members. Indeed, why the best-performing corporations . . . maintain their membership is, at least to economists viewing firms as rational utility maximizers, perhaps the greatest puzzle posed by the *keiretsu* phenomenon. . . . There is a collective logic to the *keiretsu* phenomenon that, in our view, is not reducible to rational optimizing on the part of individual firms. (1996, p. 86)

In addition to cooperation, another important feature of organizations is uncertainty (Thompson, 1967). Analyzing how agency theory and transaction cost economics deal with this issue, Nilikant and Rao noted:

> The applicability of principal-agent models is limited to two settings: (a) where performance standards are precise and knowledge of the effort-outcome relationship is complete, and (b) where performance standards are precise but knowledge of effort-outcome relationships is incomplete. . . . Second, even in the settings where they are applicable, principal-agent approaches . . . are unrealistic to the extent that they presume that performance in organizations results exclusively from individual-contributor jobs, exaggerate the degree to which individuals are work averse, and emphasize the quantity of effort at the expense of the quality and type of effort. (1994, p. 652)

A third prominent and important feature of organizations is authority. Economic models, particularly transaction cost approaches, maintain that authority is an efficient way of coping with information problems and opportunism and, in fact, is one of the sources of efficiency in organizations as contrasted with markets that lack authority relations. As an explanation of authority relations, however, the approach is sorely deficient:

> First, even if we accept the strategy of explaining governance structures in efficiency terms, the literature has not examined the possibility that authority opens up new avenues for opportunism. Hence, on the transaction cost school's own criterion for good organizational design, we still lack a full explication of the efficiency advantages generated by authority relations. Second, I have argued that the underlying functionalist explanatory strategy is weak. A number of causal mechanisms might conceivably be used to ground this approach but each candidate mechanism is open to significant objections. (Dow, 1987, p. 33)

But perhaps the most compelling critique of the economic model, at least as it has been applied to understanding organizations, is its difficulty in making unique predictions about empirical results. Consider first an issue that is well within the scope of the new institutional economics of Williamson and others and is a prominent feature of the new organizational landscape—should an economic exchange be incorporated inside the organization's boundaries or left to market-mediated transactions? Given the significant change over time in the extent to which the employment relation has been internalized and the change in the size distribution of organizations that has occurred, in part, because of the more extensive use of contracting arrangements rather than vertical integration, one might think that economic analysis would provide a compelling answer as to why labor was first internalized in the employment relation as market-mediated transactions were supplanted and now is being increasingly externalized once more.

But it doesn't. Davis-Blake and Uzzi, studying the use of temporary help and independent contractors, concluded that "the use of externalized workers is determined by multiple factors and is affected by the costs and feasibility of externalization, by the structure of the organization, and by the interests of external groups" (1993, pp. 216–217). After reviewing the arguments of Williamson (1975) and others for the development of internal labor market arrangements that substituted for spot labor markets, Pfeffer and Baron (1988, p. 263) concluded:

> the internalization of employment and the development of long-term employment relations is alleged to convey diverse benefits on organizations. . . . There is a problem with the above tale, however: it neglects some costs of internalization and long-term employment. . . . Even more importantly, it neglects the fact that perhaps the most visible and prominent trends in the structuring of work arrangements . . . involve "taking the workers back out" of their organizations. (1988, p. 263)

One problem is that one of the crucial variables the theory employs to predict whether transactions are better left to the market or incorporated inside the organization, asset specificity, is arguably as much a consequence of the decisions about how to organize as it is their cause. A firm that has decided to internalize its employment will be much more likely to engage in training and to organize jobs on the presumption of worker continuity; a firm that has decided to rely on temporary help and contract labor will invest less in training and will find ways to organize production so that long-term attachments by workers are unnecessary. A quick consideration of the various ways in which work is organized in the automobile industry provides an example of this. Moreover, the theory does not anticipate the empirical reality of many firms that organize transactions both through markets and hierarchies. For instance, most food franchisers have both company-owned stores (hierarchy) and franchised operations (market-mediated relations). Except as a transitional state (which is not the case), the economic models of organizations would predict either one or the other arrangement (but not both) in a particular case depending on asset specificity and other contracting issues.

Moreover, there is evidence that both institutionalization and power theories of organizations occasionally are more successful than some presumption of rationality or efficiency in explaining both organizational structure and employment practices. Pfeffer and Cohen (1984) found that, controlling for other factors including size and technology, the use of internal labor market practices was positively related to the presence of a personnel department and negatively related to the extent of unionization. Unions and personnel professionals are both potent political groups in organizations. Baron, Dobbin, and Jennings (1986) argued that modern human resource management practices, implemented under government pressure during World War II, were maintained after the war in part through the activities of personnel professionals and with the support of personnel associations. Internal labor market arrangements and modern personnel practices obviously provide a more important and central role for the personnel function in organizations, and it is therefore not surprising that these innovations in personnel administration would be favored by personnel administrators. What is significant is the evidence that their presence and power affected the adoption of these practices.

J. R. Sutton et al. (1994), using longitudinal data on 300 American employers over the period 1955–1985, explored what factors were associated with the adoption of disciplinary hearing and grievance procedures for nonunion salaried and hourly employees. Controlling for numerous other factors plausibly related to technical or efficiency reasons for adopting these practices, they observed strong positive effects on adoption of having a personnel office and having a labor attorney on retainer and strong negative effects of having a union contract (pp. 963–964). With respect to personnel professionals and labor lawyers, they noted that "these professionals actively interpret legal doctrine—typically overstating the legal threat to employers—and disseminate recipes for compliance as a means for enhancing their prestige, autonomy, and authority within organizations" (pp. 949–950).

In a study of hiring selectivity that measured the use of educational requirements, the use of tests, and whether or not the establishment screened on traits that presumably assessed worker reliability and attachment to the labor force, Cohen and Pfeffer (1986) found that technical or rational requirements, such as the amount of technological change and the importance of training, accounted for less of the variation than did the presence of a personnel department and the extent of unionization. Unions care about organizational selectivity because of their concern that such procedures are used to weed out individuals who might be sympathetic to unions. Considering the results from the studies of the determinants of internal labor market practices, the adoption and persistence of bureaucratic personnel practices, the adoption of due-process grievance mechanisms, and the evidence on hiring standards, the evidence strongly suggests that political factors do account for how the employment relationship is governed.

Some studies suggest that rational considerations also have limits in their ability to account for organizational structures, particularly in public sector organizations. J. W. Meyer and Rowan (1977) argued that organizational structure was often decoupled from any actual effect on organizational operations. Rather, organizations adopted structural forms that signaled compliance with social demands, including demands for accountability and for the appearance, if not the reality, of rationality. Thus, organizational design and organizational behavior could bear little connection to each other. Organizational structure was best understood as a response to social pressures for legitimacy and conformity to normative requirements. In a study of school organizations in California, J. W. Meyer, Scott, and Deal (1981) found support for these ideas. Similar forces affect private sector organizations as well. In a study of the adoption of the multidivisional organizational form in large firms, Fligstein (1985) found a statistically significant effect on adoption, once that form had become institutionalized, of being in an industry in which other, similar firms had already adopted the M-form. This result provides evidence of the effect of imitation on the adoption of a particular structure, net of factors related to efficiency.

The dominance of the economic model of behavior comes from a number of factors other than the validity of its assumptions or its empirical support. Its mathematical elegance provides status and makes it less accessible to the untrained, which lends it prestige. How can something carry prestige if anyone can do it? Conversely, some technique or line of reasoning accessible and understood only by the few carries the value imparted by scarcity (Cialdini, 1988). The paradigmatic consensus born out of a way of thinking about problems provides the field with greater potential for unity of thought and action, always a major advantage in political contests (Pfeffer, 1992).

Furthermore, economists have taken a number of strategic behaviors to enforce and maintain theoretical hegemony (R. Parker, 1993). S. Cole has argued that "one of the primary mechanisms through which consensus is maintained is the practice of vesting authority in elites" (1983, p. 137). R. Parker (1993) has documented the dominance by graduates of elite schools in the discipline of economics. And those who do not conform to the orthodoxy of the discipline are excluded from its most prestigious positions, regardless of the importance of their ideas or their general scholarly reputation. The case of Robert Reich, secretary of labor in the Clinton administration, offers a good case in point:

> Although the general approach of Mr. Reich is increasingly shared by others, his specific work has nevertheless been criticized by trained economists, mostly on the grounds that he is a lawyer, not a Ph.D. in economics. . . . That criticism has been one reason that Mr. Reich . . . has failed to get a tenured professorship at the Kennedy School, where he has been a lecturer . . . for more than a decade. . . . The criticism of Mr. Reich's credentials . . . has intensified with his appointment last week as chief of the economics transition team. (Uchitelle, 1992, p. 17)

But perhaps the most important reason for the persistent dominance of the economic model as a way of understanding organizations is its implicit ideology. The economic model presents a benign view of social organization. By stressing markets and the operation of voluntary exchange, power, coercion, and exploitation are left out of view. Employment relationships are voluntary—if someone doesn't care for his or her employer, the person simply finds another one. One's persistence in a particular exchange, including the exchange of work for wages, is taken as prima facie evidence of the person's revealed preferences. The implication is that the particular exchange is preferred to other available alternatives, or else the person would pursue one of those options. Thus, the economic model permits and, in fact, encourages one to avoid dealing with or even thinking about the potential conflict of interest between individuals and organizations and about issues such as power and social control. The idea of voluntary exchange implies that social control is accomplished readily and without coercion—and surely this is a much more benign portrayal than in the ethnographic studies of actual workplace relations (e.g., Burawoy, 1979; Graham, 1995; Kunda, 1992).

Granovetter has also noted that the attractiveness of economic logic lies in its way of dealing with the problem of social order, coordination, and control:

> It has long been recognized that the idealized markets of perfect competition have survived intellectual attack in part because self-regulating economic struc-

tures are politically attractive to many. . . . Competition determines the terms of trade in a way that individual traders cannot manipulate. If traders encounter complex or difficult relationships, characterized by mistrust or malfeasance, they can simply move on to the legion of other traders willing to do business on market terms; social relations and their details thus become frictional matters. (1985, p. 484)

In this regard, economics shares with many other social sciences, including some versions of organization theory, a perspective that sees "all that is *real* as *necessary*, all that exists as inevitable, and thus the present mode of production as eternal" (Braverman, 1974, p. 16). At the end, however, regardless of its ideological comfort and the active exclusion of dissenters, there is little evidence that the economic model's dominance in the literature derives from the ability to make nontrivial predictions about organizational issues.

The Social Model of Behavior

Economic models exclude social context or social relations almost entirely, except tangentially and indirectly. For instance, one could potentially incorporate the welfare of others or one's relationship with others into the typical economic utility function, but the analyses seldom do so. Lazear (1995) did discuss peer pressure in attempting to develop an economic rationale for team-based compensation. But the inclusion of these more social considerations is still within the context of individual utility maximization and choice: "Norms can be thought of more rigorously as the equilibrium level of effort that results when an organization punishes deviance" (pp. 49–50).

What might be termed a social model of behavior, in contrast, emphasizes the embedded nature of behavior (Granovetter, 1985). P. M. Blau has noted, "The fundamental fact of social life is precisely that it is social—that human beings do not live in isolation but associate with other human beings. . . . The study of social structure . . . centers attention on the distribution of people among different positions and their social associations" (1977, p. 1). Social models emphasize that "one's behavior is rarely explicable without reference to previous and persisting effects of interaction with others and the overall pattern of such interactions in groups" (Granovetter, 1986, p. 31). Organizational behavior is "embedded in concrete, ongoing systems of social relations" (Granovetter, 1985, p. 487). Pfeffer and Salancik, outlining the resource dependence perspective on interorganizational behavior, argued that "to understand the behavior of an organization, you must understand the context of that behavior. . . . Organizations are inescapably bound up with the conditions of their environment" (1978, p. 1). Social models of behavior emphasize the context of behavior more generally and networks and social actors' positions in them and their social relations more specifically as causal explanations.

Several studies have demonstrated that individuals' perceptions of their work environment, including task characteristics, are affected by what others say. White and Mitchell (1979), O'Reilly and Caldwell (1979), and Weiss and Shaw (1979) demonstrated experimentally that social cues from co-workers affected subjects' judgments about task characteristics. Interaction with others, then, helps to frame what we notice about our environment and how that environment is evaluated (Salancik and Pfeffer, 1978a).

Not only affective responses but also cognitive structures are affected by social influence. Walker (1985), for instance, studied judgments about means–ends connections associated with success for software products as a measure of cognition in a software firm. He found that network position was a stronger and more stable predictor of differences in cognition than either the particular function the individual held or the type of product the person worked on. Ibarra and Andrews (1993) explored the effects of individual attributes, formal position, and network connections in explaining variation in individuals' perceptions of work conditions in an advertising firm. The basic argument was that people would share perceptions with others to whom they were proximate, in communication network terms. Their results suggested that network factors shaped job-related perceptions, even when individual attributes and formal position effects were accounted for.

Krackhardt and Porter (1986) examined organizational turnover as a process that was socially mediated. Their study gathered data on friendship and interaction patterns in fast-food restaurants. They reported that turnover was clustered both in time and social space. When members of a friendship group began to leave, other members soon followed. As a consequence, turnover tended to snowball, with the propensity for turnover among individuals being related to patterns of social interaction.

Granovetter's (1974) study of job-finding behavior discovered that individuals who located their jobs through personal contacts tended to earn higher salaries and to stay in their jobs longer (i.e., they were more satisfied with them) than those who found their positions through more impersonal mechanisms such as newspaper advertisements. The study also found that personal contacts were particularly important in locating managerial jobs, as contrasted with technical or professional jobs. This is undoubtedly the case because of the more uncertain nature of managerial work and the consequent difficulty of making evaluations of managerial candidates (Kanter, 1977). Under conditions of uncertainty, personal social relations become more necessary, because they are more effective than impersonal mechanisms in resolving that uncertainty (Salancik and Pfeffer, 1978b). Granovetter's work, and subsequent research that has related promotion or salary in organizations to network positions (e.g., Burt, 1992), has defined another form of capital to correspond to the economists' notions of individual human capital—namely, social capital, which is a function of one's position in the social structure and can be assessed only with reference to that structure.

The social model of behavior also has implications for understanding the behavior of organizations as units, because what an organization does is significantly affected by who it is connected to and what they do. Galaskiewicz and Wasserman noted that ties between boundary-spanning personnel, including directors, "act as a conduit to disseminate ideas and innovations throughout an organizational field" (1989, p. 456). In a similar vein, Haunschild wrote that director ties "render events that are otherwise distant more proximate . . . creating an immediate concrete example that may encourage imitation" (1993, p. 568).

Studying the adoption of the poison pill antitakeover defense, G. F. Davis (1991) found that firms that had board of director interlocks to other firms that had adopted poison pills were themselves more likely to do so, controlling for other factors. "Being tied to one other adopter increased the rate by about 61 percent, ties to two other adopters nearly doubled the rate, and firms with six ties to other adopters subsequently adopted at about 2.5 times the rate of comparable firms with no ties" (p. 605). Mizruchi (1992) observed that interfirm linkages affected the likelihood that firms would make campaign contributions to particular political candidates.

Strategy is also affected by interfirm ties. Greve (1995), studying the abandonment of corporate strategy—in this instance, a particular radio format—observed a social contagion effect from both market contacts and other units within the same corporation. In a subsequent study concerning the adoption of a particular radio format, Greve (1996) observed a social contagion effect on the adoption of a specific market strategy, with the contagion effect being particularly pronounced for other stations with the same corporate ownership. Haveman (1993) studied the entry of California savings and loans into six new markets over the 1977–1987 period: direct investment in real estate, mortgage-backed securities, nonresidential mortgages, consumer loans other than mortgages, commercial loans, and other services (e.g., insurance). For direct investment in real estate, nonresidential mortgages, and mortgage-backed securities, Haveman found evidence of imitation—firms were more likely to enter a market in a given period the greater the number of large firms and the greater the number of profitable firms that had previously done so. Although this study did not measure interfirm linkages as precisely as Davis or Greve, it provides additional evidence consistent with the idea that firms are influenced by the behavior of others in their environment.

There is evidence that interfirm relationships help to account for organizational structures and do so net of technical factors. Palmer, Jennings, and Zhou (1993) reported that interlocks with multidivisional firms influenced the adoption of the multidivisional structure. L. R. Burns and Wholey (1993) studied the adoption and abandonment of the matrix organizational form using a sample of more than 1,300 hospitals over the seventeen-year period 1961–1978. Matrix management is a particularly interesting structural innovation to examine, because it "constitutes a shift from vertical-functional authority toward a hybrid, function-by-product organization. . . . Matrix structures are team-oriented arrangements that promote coordinated, multidisciplinary activity across functional areas, broad participation in decisions, and the sharing of knowledge" (p. 107). As such, they are almost diametrically different from the emphasis on hierarchy in transaction cost economics. The empirical results showed no effect of organizational scale on matrix adoption, but there were some positive effects of task diversity, a technical factor predicted to be associated with the need for a matrix structure. Their results show much stronger and more consistent effects of social influence on both adoption and abandonment of matrix structures:

> the prestige of a hospital influences not only its decision to adopt . . . but also the decisions of neighboring hospitals. . . . Other significant effects suggest that professional media . . . and regional and local hospital networks . . . are influential. Our results thus suggest that organizational networks influence the diffusion of administrative innovations in much the same way that they influence the spread of technological innovations. (p. 130)

Mizruchi and Stearns (1994) found that having a banker on a firm's board increased the level of borrowing. Galaskiewicz and Burt (1991) reported that corporate officers responsible for philanthropy that were similarly positioned in the interorganizational network evaluated potential contribution recipients similarly. Galaskiewicz and Wasserman (1989), studying patterns of corporate giving in the Minneapolis-St. Paul area, found numerous examples of the importance of network connections. Nonprofits received more money from corporations that previously gave money to other nonprofits whose directors sat on the focal nonprofit's board. And, firms gave more money to nonprofits that were previously funded by companies whose CEOs or philanthropy officers were personally known by the firm.

Haunschild (1993), examining the acquisition activity of 327 firms, found that firms imitated the acquisition activities of firms to which they were tied through directorships. In a subsequent study, Haunschild (1994) found that the size of the acquisition premia paid by firms in takeovers was related to the premia paid by their interlock partners as well as to the size of premia paid by other acquirers using the same investment bank. The evidence from the studies of charitable giving and corporate takeover activity is consistent with the idea that network influences are particularly important when there is more uncertainty, for social communication is useful in resolving that uncertainty (Festinger, 1954).

The Effect of Social Ties on Organizational Performance

Network linkages not only affect behavior through a process of modeling and social contagion but also directly influence the flow of resources and legitimacy to organizations. Baum and Oliver (1991), examining childcare service organizations in the Toronto area, found that organizations with institutional linkages were substantially more likely to survive as competition increased. Palmer et al. (1995) reported that firms run by managers and directors who were more central in the structure of interfirm ties were less susceptible to predatory takeover.

D'Aveni (1990) examined the effect of an organization's management being in elite networks on filing for bankruptcy, controlling for economic and financial factors. He argued that the social prestige and connections of senior management were important, because "their prestige influences creditors to support the existing top management's right to continue in control of the firm without supervision by the bankruptcy courts" (p. 121). He tested the idea that:

> managerial prestige contributes to the legitimacy of firms by influencing social exchanges on three levels of analysis: interpersonal relationships, interorganiza-

tional transactions and societal-level . . . interactions. On the individual level, prestige helps to maintain an illusion of competence and control by influencing interpersonal reactions to the individual. . . . Prestige is taken as an indication the manager is competent, credible, and trustworthy. . . . Prestigious managers contribute to the belief that the debtor firm will be trustworthy in its relationship with others and will conform to elite values and norms. (pp. 121–122)

D'Aveni measured five status characteristics: "membership in the political elite, membership in the military elite, membership in elite educational circles, membership in webs of board directorates, and previous acceptance into the ranks of high ranking corporate officers" (p. 128). His results confirmed the effect of managerial membership in elites on bankruptcy. For instance, "lack of top managers with cooptive links to potential creditors . . . appears to have had a significant detrimental effect on organizational survival," and "managerial membership in . . . the inner circle of the economic elite . . . [is] significantly associated with bankruptcy" (p. 131).

Because network linkages are consequential for obtaining resources, resource dependence theory predicts that interorganizational linkages such as mergers (Pfeffer, 1972b; Burt, 1980; Finkelstein, 1996), joint ventures (Pfeffer and Nowak, 1976), and board of director interlocks (Pfeffer, 1972c; Burt, Christman, and Kilburn, 1980) will develop to manage transactions interdependencies (Pfeffer and Salancik, 1978). The studies of interlocking directorates (e.g., M. P. Allen, 1974; Dooley, 1969; Pfeffer, 1972c; Pfeffer, 1973) have generally found that board composition is "influenced primarily by the market position of the firm and the company's needs to reduce uncertainty and secure resources from actors in its environment" (Galaskiewicz et al., 1985, p. 404). Burt, Christman, and Kilburn reported that "each of the directorate ties considered (establishments connected through corporate boards by ownership, direct interlocking, and indirect financial interlocking) tends to occur where there is market constraint and tends to be absent in the absence of constraint" (1980, p. 837). However, not all studies have found support for this hypothesis. Galaskiewicz et al. (1985), in a study of 116 corporations in a single metropolitan area, found no effect of the market position of firms.

Similarly, studies of merger behavior (Burt, 1980; Pfeffer, 1972b) have found that patterns of mergers were predicted by patterns of resource interdependencies, measured by transactions among economic sectors. Finkelstein (1996) again found evidence for a resource dependence effect but also found that the strength of this effect varied by time period. There is also some evidence that firms that develop linkages to manage constraints emanating from the environment enjoy superior economic performance (Pfeffer, 1972a; Burt, 1983). But the evidence here is mixed, in part because there is not much difference in the use of interorganizational linkages to manage constraints. Burt noted, "successfully coopting market constraints appears to be an attribute of all industries rather than a variable distinguishing industries in terms of their ability to obtain profits in excess of the profits to be expected from their relative levels of structural autonomy" (1980, p. 922).

Davis and Thompson (1994) have argued that efficiency-oriented approaches to understanding corporate governance and behavior, such as agency theory and transaction cost economics, are limited in their explanatory ability because of their neglect of social influence and the fact that organizations are embedded in networks of social relationships. They accounted for the rise of shareholder activism during the early 1990s using a social movement framework that emphasized the social contagion of demands for reform in corporate governance. It appears that understanding intraorganizational as well as interorganizational behavior benefits from explicit attention to social influences activated through network structures.

Network ideas may have even more importance and predictive power outside of the United States with its emphasis on individual action and rewards. For example, networks are particularly important in understanding Japanese organizations and their interactions (Gerlach, 1992). A study of the six major *keiretsu* by Lincoln, Gerlach, and Ahmadjian (1996) found that these interorganizational networks performed important resource and risk reallocation functions. In particular, they noted: "The *keiretsu* . . . equalize the fortunes of their members, smoothing inequality in financial returns across participating firms at any given time, and perhaps over time as well, for any given company. These adjustments amount to "taxing" prosperous members to guarantee the survival and hasten the recovery of financially troubled affiliates" (p. 68).

Network Concepts

There are a number of important concepts and ideas in network analyses of organizations. One concept has to do with the fact that, among social actors, "weak ties" often offer advantages over stronger ties. One of the ironies uncovered by Granovetter (1973; 1974) was the relative importance and effectiveness of comparatively weak ties among individuals in the job-finding process. Although one might think that strong ties, such as friendship or kinship, would be more useful in activities such as job finding, this was not the case. Although strong ties create a closer bond between individuals, people to whom one is more strongly tied are more likely to be in the same social network and thus provide redundant contacts and information. Weak ties link individuals to different and more diverse sets of contacts and consequently provide less-redundant information and social relations compared to strong ties.

Network models of organizations have been developed most completely by Burt (1992), who has also developed a computer program, Structure, to implement his method of social network analysis. Burt's basic ideas of structure concern structural equivalence, constraint, and structural holes. If a social unit has the same relations with others as another unit (which could be an individual or a firm), the two social entities are considered to be structurally equivalent. Because they have the same pattern of social relations, the entities are competitors, even if they are not aware of each other. Burt has noted, "competition is a matter of relations, not player attributes" (p. 3). Reanalyzing data on the diffusion of the antibiotic tetracycline (Coleman, Katz, and Menzel, 1966), Burt (1987) found that structural equivalence was a more powerful predictor of diffusion than was social contagion. In social contagion models of diffusion, the argument is that information or an innovation diffuses through direct social contact or ties (e.g., you talk to a colleague who tells you about the new product, and then you are more likely to adopt it). This mode of analysis, emphasizing direct social contact, has a long history in sociology. For instance, Lazersfeld, Berelson, and Gaudet (1944) demonstrated that individuals who voted for a particular political party tended to have friends affiliated with that party. Burt found that individuals in structurally equivalent positions—competitors—were more likely to adopt some innovation once it had been adopted by their competitors even in the absence of direct contact. Thus, competition, as defined by the network measure of structural equivalence, was a better predictor of diffusion than social contagion.

Constraint is also defined in terms of one's network of relations. A given organization, for instance, is constrained to the extent that it transacts with other organizations and has few alternatives to those organizations, while the organizations themselves have diffuse or unconcentrated transactions. Conversely, one has power in exchange relations to the extent that one has options and transacts with others who themselves are highly constrained. Burt (1980; 1983) has shown that measures of network constraint can predict profitability and interorganizational relationships, such as board of director interlocks, designed to co-opt or otherwise mitigate such constraints.

Finally, a structural hole represents separation between nonredundant contacts and is similar, in some respects, to the idea of weak ties. When contacts, members of one's own network, are not themselves linked, Burt (1992) argued that there could be profit in serving as an intermediary—not directly linking the parties but mediating transactions among them. Burt has theoretically derived and empirically tested the idea that "players with a network optimized for structural holes, in addition to being exposed to more rewarding opportunities, are also more likely to secure favorable terms in the opportunities they choose to pursue" (p. 30). This is because the social actor in the middle can play the parties off against each other and can also profit from arranging transactions that otherwise might not occur. Indeed, Burt has defined this role of being an intermediary as an important component of entrepreneurship.

Recently, Podolny (1993) has developed a fourth important concept for understanding social networks, that of status. Status is defined as "the perceived quality of that producer's products in relation to the perceived quality of that producer's competitors' products" (p. 830). Status is determined not only by the objective quality of the good or service but, particularly when that quality is difficult to directly assess, by the ties a given organization maintains with buyers, other producers, and third parties. For a producer of a given level of quality, status translates into higher revenues and lower production costs (p. 837). Given the advantages of attaining higher status and the advantages that accrue to those organizations with high status, two important questions emerge. First, what keeps other organizations from acquiring status and therefore disturbing the stability of the status order? And second, why doesn't one or a subset of the highest-status producers come to totally dominate the market?

The answers to both questions come from the fact that status is produced, in part, through network linkages, and this fact provides both opportunity and constraint. Although lower-status organizations may seek to form linkages with higher-status producers in order to enhance their status, there is little or no incentive for the higher-status organizations to want those linkages formed. Indeed, to the extent that higher-status organizations do form linkages with lower-status entities, their own status is potentially at risk. This idea also helps to answer the question about the limits of market dominance:

> Since the relationship between actual and perceived quality is mediated by the producer's ties to others in the market, the producer invariably changes how it is perceived if it broadens relations with others in the market. . . . To the extent that a higher-status producer attempts to expand into the position of a lower-status competitor, it changes its reputation and thus alters the cost-and-revenue profile that provided it with the initial advantage. As a result, just as status processes help reproduce inequality by constraining those at the bottom of the status hierarchy, so status processes also place limits on the higher-status producer's expansion into the lower end of the market. (Podolny, 1993, pp. 844–845)

Podolny (1993) showed that the percentage spread in debt underwritings (the gross spread divided by the dollar amount of the bond offering) was negatively related to the status of the underwriting firm, indicating that, as predicted, higher-status investment banks enjoyed a cost advantage that resulted from their status and permitted them to underbid their lower-status competitors. Podolny (1994), studying which banks formed relationships with others, found that there was an effect of market uncertainty on this process. When uncertainty was greater, organizations tended to engage in transactions with those with whom they had dealt in the past, and they tended to engage in transactions with those of similar status. These results suggest that the status hierarchy will be particularly stable under conditions of greater uncertainty, because it is under precisely those circumstances that transactions, and presumably other relationships, will be most restricted by history and status similarity.

Other Social Models of Organizational Behavior

In some sense, network models of organizations arose out of the resource dependence perspective (Pfeffer and Salancik, 1978), which was filled with network imagery and concepts but did not employ formalized network measures or methods in the empirical research. Both approaches depart from the "rationalist, individualistic perspective" that "has denied both the reality of organizations as institutions . . . as well as the embedded and at times quasi-political character of organizational action and choice" (Pfeffer, 1987, p. 25). The resource dependence perspective, however, focuses attention not just on the social effects on behavior but also on the fact that organizations have a reality apart from "serving as settings and apart from the various people who were in them at any point in time" (p. 26). As such, the theory is a reaction to the view, increasingly common in both economics and political science, that "formally organized social institutions" are "arenas within which . . . behavior, driven by more fundamental factors, occurs" (J. G. March and Olsen, 1984, p. 734). Resource dependence departs from economics because of its emphasis on uncertainty reduction and power apart from considerations of efficiency. It departs from a Marxist or intraclass perspective on organizations, discussed in chapter 8, because of its emphasis on "actions serving the interests of and being organized by organizations rather than families, individuals, or a social class" (Pfeffer, 1987, p. 27). And it departs from at least some variants or implications of a network perspective in its emphasis on organizations as social units with an existence distinct from the members.

The basic arguments and premises of the resource dependence perspective are readily summarized:

> (1) the fundamental units for understanding intercorporate relations and society are organizations; ours is a society of organizations (Presthus, 1978); (2) these organizations are not autonomous, but rather are constrained by a network of interdependencies with other organizations; (3) interdependence, when coupled with uncertainty about what the actions will be of those with which the organization is interdependent, leads to a situation in which survival and continued success are uncertain; and, therefore, (4) organizations take actions to manage external interdependencies, although such actions are inevitably never completely successful and produce new patterns of dependence and interdependence. Furthermore, (5) these patterns of dependence produce interorganizational as well as intraorganizational power, where such power has some effect on organizational behavior. Organizations tend to comply with the demands of those interests in their environment which have relatively more power. (Pfeffer, 1987, pp. 26–27)

Institutional theory is another important variant of a social model of behavior. Scott argued that institutional theory broadened the conception of the environment considered in some other organization theories: "To the earlier emphasis on the importance of the technical environment—resources and technical know-how—institutional theory has called attention to the importance of the social and cultural environment, in particular, to social knowledge and cultural rule systems" (Scott, 1995, p. xiv). One variant of institutional theory has emphasized cognitive, mimetic processes in which organizations, particularly when confronted with uncertainty, resolve that uncertainty by imitating what appears to be prevalent practice (DiMaggio and Powell, 1983). Scott wrote: "We seek to behave in conventional ways . . . that will not cause us to stand out or be noticed as different. . . . We attempt to imitate others whom we regard as superior or more successful. One principal indicator of the strength of such mimetic processes is prevalence: the number of similar individuals or organizations exhibiting a given form or practice" (p. 45). Another variant of institutional theory emphasizes conformity deriving from the taken-for-granted or assumed character of social life. Zucker noted that "institutionalization is rooted in conformity—not conformity engendered by sanctions . . . nor conformity resulting from a 'black-box' internalization process, but conformity rooted in the taken-for-granted aspects of everyday life. . . . Institutionalization operates to produce common understandings about what is appropriate and, fundamentally, meaningful behavior" (1983, p. 5).

Although some (e.g., DiMaggio, 1988) have argued that institutional theory deemphasizes the role of interests as contrasted with resource dependence or network perspectives, Scott argued that "institutional theory reminds us that interests are institutionally defined and shaped" (1987, p. 508). What institutional theory has emphasized is the role of the state and external authority in imposing organizational arrangements and the fact that organizational structures and processes may serve to legitimate organizations rather than to advance technical efficiency.

In comparison to economic models, social models of behavior deemphasize individual characteristics but rather emphasize the relationship and connection among social actors. One achieves promotions, for instance, not so much as a consequence of one's individual human capital (Becker, 1964) but because of one's location in the social structure. Turnover is related to the turnover of one's social contacts (Krackhardt and Porter, 1986), job attitudes are affected by the attitudes of others in one's social environment (e.g., Thomas and Griffin, 1983) and particularly by those in one's communication network (Ibarra and Andrews, 1993), and one's ability to find a job depends importantly on social relations (Granovetter, 1986). Status and associated perceptions of quality depend on the status of those organizations (or individuals) to which one is tied (Podolny, 1993). Organizational survival and economic success depend on the pattern of connections to other organizations (Pfeffer and Salancik, 1978).

Although we know that organizations are, fundamentally, relational entities, and that the environment of organizations is composed of other organizations and filled with transactions and other interchanges among them, many theories and analyses take the individual or the organization alone as the unit of analysis and fail to incorporate ideas or measures of social structure into either theory or empirical research (Pfeffer, 1991, p. 800). The social model of behavior avoids this pitfall even as it challenges more individualistic conceptualizations of organizational and interorganizational behavior.

Some Problems with the Social Model

Although the social model of behavior and associated network ideas have enjoyed a great deal of empirical support, particularly in the domain of interorganizational relations, predictions of network relations and their effects have not been consistently observed, and there is some disagreement over how to measure network ties. The problem arises because ties among organizations are frequently multiplex and potentially accomplished through a number of mechanisms including joint ventures, other forms of alliances, as well as board of director interlocks. The public availability of data on board composition has resulted in a large amount of empirical research focusing on this particular mechanism for linking organizations. One complexity is that interlock ties can be "sent" (a manager or CEO of the focal organization sits on another organization's board), "received" (another organization is represented on the focal organization's board), or "neutral" (the two focal organizations are linked because representatives from each serve on another organization's board and meet in that context). As Palmer et al. (1995) have noted, there is much debate about the relative importance of sent and received interlocks compared to neutral interlocks, which are often called weak when compared to more direct interlocking. Some studies find effects of neutral interlocks (Palmer et al., 1995) and not of stronger ties, but there are few a priori predictions about which type of tie should be important in a given study. Reviewing much of this literature, Fligstein and Brantley concluded that "we should abandon our concentration on . . . directors as a source of network data, in general, and financial linkages across boards of directors, in particular, unless their possible relevance can be specified theoretically" (1992, p. 304).

Further complicating the issue, many studies that ostensibly use network language don't employ network methods for analyzing the actual structure of the network but use very reduced measures instead. For instance, Palmer et al. (1995) measured connections in terms of the number of sent industrial and commercial bank interlocks, the number of received industrial and commercial bank interlocks, and the number of neutral industrial and commercial bank interlocks. They measured industrial and banking interlocks separately because of the important role of banks in some theories of how organizations are linked (e.g., Soref and Zeitlin, 1987). Numbers do not indicate the importance of the particular organizations linked by a tie, and these studies typically don't measure centrality, closeness or proximity, and similar indicators of network structure.

Using formal network models requires a great deal of data on relations among individuals or organizations, data which often are not available. Thus, for instance, studies of interorganizational relations from a resource dependence or structural autonomy perspective use data not on the specific transaction interdependencies of given organizations but rather the patterns of transactions among economic sectors. This is because specific organizational transactions data are not available. As Finkelstein (1996) noted, however, this presents a problem of aggregation bias in the data. Gathering data on ties among individuals to model career mobility (Burt, 1992) requires a lot of information, so such studies are typically confined to just one or a very few organizations. But this type of design necessarily limits the researcher's ability to explore conditions under which network effects are stronger or weaker or to compare measurement models directly in different settings. In this sense, network models of organizations are richly detailed depictions of social relations, but the empirical specificity constrains the empirical research process.

Finally, it should be acknowledged that the social model of organizational behavior is a useful and productive way of understanding how information, structures, decisions, and other policies and practices diffuse across social actors. This model, however, does not have as much to say about how the various practices or structures arise in the first place. In that sense, the social model is potentially a useful complement to other perspectives on the source of behavior in organizations.

The Retrospectively Rational Model of Behavior

While economic models tend to emphasize prospective, intentional rationality, an alternative perspective emphasizes the retrospectively rational nature of behavior

(Aronson, 1972). The retrospectively rational model suggests that individuals and organizations will take actions to make sense of or to appear to be consistent with previous choices. There are two important variants of the retrospectively rational model—one that emphasizes a "cooler" cognitive process of self-perception and one that implicates "warmer" social psychological processes such as commitment and self-justification.

The basic premises of the self-perception model are well enough known in psychology to bear only brief recitation. First, behavior may be initially mindless, habitual, or automatic (Langer, 1983) or, alternatively, produced by other salient influences; behavior is not always prospectively chosen to be consistent with preferences—indeed, one of the intended consequences of engaging in some activity is *discovering* what one's true preferences are (J. G. March, 1978). Second, individuals, particularly when questioned or called to account for their behavior, prefer to appear sensible, logical, and consistent, if for no other reason than as part of a strategy of self-presentation (Alexander and Knight, 1971); in this sense, individuals act as if they were lay social scientists inferring the causality of their own behavior (Kelley, 1971). Third, when questioned about their attitudes or behaviors, individuals will look to their own past statements and actions and to the external environment for explanations as to the sources of those attitudes or behavior; this process has been referred to as self-perception (Bem, 1972) or retrospective rationality (Staw, 1980). Because there are social norms valuing consistency, individuals will often attempt to behave in a fashion consistent with the attitudes and beliefs they have inferred they hold by retrospectively examining their own past behavior, thereby creating a situation in which the past comes to affect the future through its influence on self-perceptions and attitudes.

Weick's (1964) study of the effect of cognitive dissonance on performance is a good example of studies of this type. In the study, individuals agreed to do a difficult cognitive task after they learned they would get a smaller reward for participating in the study than they had expected. "Those that were deprived most severely rated the subsequent task more interesting and were three times more productive at performing it than were people who felt less deprived" (Weick, 1993, p. 11). Faced with the prospect of a greatly diminished reward for something they were committed to do, individuals made sense out of their commitment by evaluating the intrinsic interest and worth of the task more highly. And, "by working hard and solving more problems, they created a situation that confirmed the sensibleness of agreeing to participate in the first place" (p. 11). Thus, a process of commitment caused individuals to cognitively revalue a task, and having engaged in that revaluation, they proceeded to act differently, working harder than those that had not gone through the same degree of cognitive revaluation created by the diminished external reward.

Thus, one particularly important formulation of this perspective notes that if there are no salient extrinsic reasons for engaging in some activity—such as large external rewards or the threat of important sanctions—individuals will come to believe that they are doing the activity because they truly like it. This is the insufficient justification paradigm that is discussed thoroughly in the literature on behavioral commitment (Kiesler, 1971; Salancik, 1977) and cognitive dissonance

(Festinger, 1957). By contrast, if individuals are provided with salient extrinsic reasons or constraints for doing something, particularly when such rewards or sanctions are not customary (Staw, Calder, Hess, and Sandelands, 1980), they will see the activity as less interesting and attractive. Consequently, the provision of extrinsic rewards and controls, including surveillance, can undermine intrinsic interest in, enjoyment of, and motivation to do task activities (e.g., Deci, 1975; Lepper and Greene, 1975; Enzle and Anderson, 1993).

The commitment or self-justification variant of retrospective rationality postulates a more active process than mere self-perception. Individuals—to maintain their self-identity, to appear to others and themselves to be acting consistently, to make their past decisions appear sensible or turn out well, to avoid the political costs of being discovered as having made a mistake—will persist with a course of action and, at times, even escalate their commitment to it. The prediction is the greater the commitment, produced through an investment of resources, the more perseverance there will be.

The implications of both variants of the retrospectively rational model of behavior are almost completely at odds with those of economic models and with other theories emphasizing the importance of extrinsic rewards. The self-perception version suggests that incentives may be counterproductive and that pay-for-performance schemes may actually reduce performance (Kohn, 1993). It is, therefore, not surprising that particularly the early work by Deci (1975) is known by economists. Economists and others have tended to dismiss much of this research because it (1) frequently used children as subjects, (2) was experimental and therefore appeared to some as artificial, (3) couldn't really be generalized to organizational settings because it dealt with different activities, "(learning vs. working), the people involved are different (children vs. adults), and the purpose is different (developing vs. earning a living)" (Montemayor, 1995, pp. 943–944), and most important, (4) on occasion introduced incentives or surveillance into situations—for example, free play or recreation—in which they would not normally be expected, as contrasted with organizational situations in which incentives and control would be a more natural part of the environment. Although these are valid concerns, they are not a significant challenge to this model of behavior, because a number of studies have tested the rationalizing model of behavior with adults in field situations and found results consistent with the theory.

Staw (1974) studied ROTC cadets and capitalized on the introduction of the draft lottery during the Vietnam War to test the effects of insufficient justification. Some men joined ROTC under a two-year program that was less committing, and others joined and were committed to serve as officers upon completion of the program. Once having joined ROTC, when the draft lottery was held, some individuals learned because of the number assigned to their birthday that they would have been likely to be drafted, others learned that the odds of their being drafted were very low, and still others learned they had intermediate odds. Those with low odds of being drafted in a program that permitted them to withdraw did so. Those with high odds of being drafted remained in the less-committing ROTC program and had reason to be pleased with their decision to be in the more committing program. But those men who were committed to ROTC but discovered they had a high draft number (low probability of being drafted) faced a problem. They joined ROTC to avoid the draft and serve under better circumstances as commissioned officers, but now they learned that they might not have had to serve; they no longer had an extrinsic reason for being in ROTC. But because of their contractual commitment, they could not withdraw. As might be expected under insufficient justification predictions, this group earned higher grades in their ROTC courses and expressed the most favorable attitudes toward the program compared to the cadets with extrinsic reasons for being in ROTC. They made sense of their commitment in the presence of insufficient external justification by finding, within the program, benefits and elements to enjoy and appreciate.

O'Reilly and Caldwell (1980), in a study of 108 MBA graduates, examined the effects of the bases of job choice on job satisfaction and commitment. They found a "positive relationship between intrinsic decision factors [intrinsic interest in the job itself, personal feelings about the job, etc.] and satisfaction and commitment" (p. 561). They also found evidence that "decisions made under external constraints, that is, decisions based on a concern for family and financial considerations, are inversely related to job satisfaction and commitment" (p. 563). O'Reilly and Caldwell (1981) studied the effects on MBA graduates of the number of offers they received and whether or not they took the highest offer. They predicted that graduates who had several job offers and who accepted a job that did not pay the best among the offers should have fewer extrinsic reasons for their choice than those who either took the best offer or had only one offer and, consequently, should be more committed to the job. They found that, consistent with this prediction, individuals who took their initial offer with fewer external reasons for doing so in fact were more satisfied with the job and stayed in it longer.

In a third field test of these ideas, Caldwell, O'Reilly, and Morris (1983) studied both satisfaction with and intrinsic interest in an evening MBA program on the part of 132 students, some of whom received more generous employer-provided subsidies for attending the program than others. They found that sufficiency of justification effects depended both on orientation toward the activity and beliefs about the subsidy. Specifically, "providing an educational subsidy is associated with lowered task interest for employees who are expressively oriented. . . . Failure to provide an extrinsic reward is related . . . to increased interest for those who do not [believe] the subsidy is a normal employee benefit" (p. 506).

One implication of this retrospective rationalization argument is that once individuals are committed to some organization or activity, additional incentives probably will not increase their motivation or positive affect and can, in fact, undermine their positive attitudes and actions. Pfeffer and Lawler (1980), studying college and university faculty, found a positive relationship between overly sufficient justification (salary was higher than would be predicted based on experience, productivity, and other characteristics) and job satisfaction for faculty who had been in their organizations for a shorter period of time. For faculty with longer organizational tenure, who were more committed to the organization as a consequence (Sheldon, 1971), there was no relationship between compensation and satisfaction or intentions to look for another job.

It is important to recognize that it is the self-perception and rationalization of behavior, not something inherent in intrinsic or extrinsic rewards, that account for these results. To demonstrate this, Porac and Salancik (1981) conducted an experiment in which the addition of one extrinsic reward, extra credit for taking part in the experiment, undermined the effect of another extrinsic reward, money. They argued that the addition of a new, salient reward undermined the value of another reward, because it provided yet another explanation for the person's behavior. Moreover, because attribution of causality and self-justification are the critical processes, the undermining effect of extrinsic rewards or surveillance can be diminished by providing alternative explanations for the external control. Thus, for instance, Enzle and Anderson (1993) found that the effect of surveillance to undermine intrinsic task interest was eliminated when the surveillance was explained either as necessary to make sure the equipment was working properly or to satisfy curiosity. But the undermining effect was evident when either no explanation was provided or an explanation emphasizing control was given.

These findings are important because there are situations in which it is necessary to use extrinsic rewards or surveillance in order to obtain the desired behavior, but at the same time there is a desire not to eliminate intrinsic interest in the task. As Cialdini et al. noted, "External rewards and sanctions do work (Eisenberger, 1992); and when nothing else does, it becomes necessary to generate . . . desirable behavior. Yet, the immediate gains . . . can be undercut and reversed by the presence of these same external constraints when independent, long-term interest in the activity is considered" (1994, p. 1). Their study of children's writing demonstrated that by attributing an action undertaken under the influence of a controlling reward to a stable trait of the actor, the undermining effect of the external control was neutralized.

The attribution and self-perception of behavior mean that Frank's (1988) observations on the importance of the models of behavior for creating that behavior are very much on target. Strickland (1958) found that subjects placed in a situation where they monitored one subordinate (a confederate of the experimenter) more closely than the other came to believe the more closely monitored individual needed more surveillance and could not be trusted as much, even though there were no objective differences in the performance of the two. Strickland wrote of the supervisor's dilemma, in which "the supervisor . . . may become victimized by his own previous supervisory behavior" (p. 201). Not only does close supervision not provide the supervisor an opportunity to learn about unsupervised work efforts, but the action of supervising can cause the individual to make sense of that behavior by coming to believe that this activity was necessary to get the work done. Lingle, Brock, and Cialdini found that individuals "who become involved in covert surveillance may feel a need to justify their actions by generating evidence that the surveillance effort is worthwhile" (1977, p. 423). Their study demonstrated that surveillance can stimulate entrapment activities that increase the frequency of the undesired behavior, therefore reaffirming the need for the surveillance activity.

Furthermore, those closely supervised can develop a self-perception that they are not trustworthy or intrinsically motivated and may then continue to act on those self-perceptions. Constraints provide an external explanation for engaging or not engaging in a behavior, thereby potentially negating intrinsic motivations that might otherwise control the behavior. Wilson and Lassiter (1982) conducted an experiment in which subjects had an opportunity to cheat on a trivia quiz but where the incentive to do so was minimal. They found that subjects exposed to a more severe threat against cheating actually cheated more frequently than subjects exposed to a milder threat or than control subjects exposed to no threat at all. They concluded that "broad applications of threats . . . can be counterproductive, because they may increase interest in the undesirable behaviors among the large number of people who had little desire to perform them in the first place" (p. 818). In this way, the mental models of behavior that form the basis for actions can come to be true even if they were initially incorrect—they set up a cycle of behavior that confirms the assumptions of the models.

The commitment or self-justification version of the rationalizing model is also at odds with economic conceptions of rational decision making. Economics suggests that sunk costs should not matter in decision situations. Once resources have been expended, they are "sunk" and cannot be regained, no matter what one does. Therefore, rational choice models suggest that decisions should be based solely on incremental analysis—whether the expenditure of additional resources will provide benefits greater than the costs of those resources. In contrast, the rationalizing model suggests that individuals may want to justify their previous commitment, evidenced by the expenditure of resources, by persisting in the behavior. Also, not demonstrating continued commitment to a previously chosen course of action to some extent acknowledges that one has made a decision error, and this can be politically risky as well as threatening to one's self-esteem. Better to persist and hope that things will turn out all right or that one will be rewarded for the positive attribute of perseverance.

Arkes and Blumer provided a number of demonstrations, both experimental and field, of the sunk cost effect—"a greater tendency to continue an endeavor once an investment in money, effort, or time has been made" (1985, p. 124). In a field demonstration of this effect, individuals who came to a ticket window to purchase season tickets to the Ohio University Theater's 1982–1983 season were randomly assigned to one of three conditions: (1) paid the normal price ($15); (2) were sold the ticket at a $2 discount; or (3) were sold the ticket at a $7 discount. "The seller explained to the latter two groups that the discount was being given as part of a promotion by the theater department" (p. 127). Because the discounts were randomly assigned, "the groups should not have differed on the costs and benefits they could have anticipated by attending each play" (p. 128). Since the different price tickets were color coded, it was possible to precisely determine how many persons in each condition attended each performance. The results indicated that the "no discount group used significantly more tickets (4.11) than both the $2 discount group (3.32) and the $7 discount group (3.29)" during the first half of the season, although there were no differences among the groups in the second half of the season (p. 128).

Staw and Hoang (1995) demonstrated the effect of commitment and sunk costs in a field study of the National Basketball Association. They showed that draft order—how early a player was drafted—was a statistically significant predictor of the amount of playing time even over a five-year period, controlling for performance in the preceding year, position, and injuries. They also found that draft order affected a player's career length and the likelihood of being traded, again with performance and other factors statistically controlled. Players taken earlier in the draft were less likely to be cut from a team or traded. Staw and Hoang discovered that being traded was negatively associated with subsequently being retained by the new team and with playing time, even with performance held constant. They interpreted this latter result to mean that "the further teams were from the original drafting of players, the less committed they were to them" (p. 491), and this reduced commitment had predictable effects on player use and retention.

Another arena in which commitment effects have been demonstrated is the performance appraisal process. Bazerman, Beekun, and Schoorman (1982), in an experimental simulation of a managerial situation that involved making a promotion decision, found that "subjects who were responsible for the promotion decision gave higher pay increases and bonuses, evaluated the manager's potential more favorably, and projected higher sales and earnings than did the subjects who were not responsible for the promotion decision" (Schoorman, 1988, p. 58). Schoorman (1988) replicated this result in field research conducted in a large public sector organization. He found that when the individuals filling out performance appraisal ratings had input into and agreed with the promotion or hiring decision for the person being rated, the performance appraisal score was more positive than when the rater did not have input into the decision. Schoorman reported that "the escalation effects accounted for 6% of the variance in performance appraisal ratings" (p. 60), which was more than the variance accounted for by the measures of clerical ability that were used to actually select employees for the jobs. Having once made or agreed with a hiring or promotion decision, the way to make sense of or rationalize that choice was apparently to evaluate the performance of the selected individual more positively.

The "Rationality" of the Rationalizing Model

Not all of the studies of sunk cost necessarily demonstrate behavior that is irrational using decision theory logic (Northcraft and Wolf, 1984), as many of the experimental situations involved scenarios in which it would be rational to increase or continue investment. For instance, in the counter game reported by Brockner and Rubin (1985), players paid one cent for each click of a 600-point counter, received an initial stake of $5, and therefore had a 5/6 chance of winning a prize of varying size, ranging from $2 to $20. "In most conditions, the expected value of the game is positive, and the appropriate strategy is to enter and never quit. However, the average amount invested in these games is quite low" (Heath, 1995, p. 41). And, the marginal returns to subsequent investments, given one has not yet won a prize, actually increase over time. The available evidence seems to suggest that people escalate commitment when they do not set a budget and when incremental costs and benefits are difficult to track (p. 47). Heath summarized the existing literature:

> There is currently no evidence that people will make errors of escalating commitment when marginal investments are explicit. . . . The literature provides no clear demonstration of such errors because previous demonstrations of "escalating commitment" with explicit investments did not provide relevant information about marginal costs and benefits. . . . When researchers omit information about benefits . . . their studies may not control subjects' expectations about the benefits of a marginal investment. Subjects may assume that benefits increase as sunk costs increase. . . . Other studies . . . do not control for expectations about costs. (1995, p. 52)

Heath (1995), in a series of experiments, tested the idea that people set mental budgets for investments and resist exceeding those budgets as they track their expenditures against the budgets. He warned about the problem of de-escalation of commitment even in the presence of high marginal returns because of adherence to the mental budget model:

> when benefits come from completing a project, investments toward the end of a project produce increasingly high marginal returns. In situations where there is learning, previous investments may decrease marginal costs and increase marginal benefits by moving people down a learning curve. Mental budgeting predicts that in such situations people are more likely to make errors of de-escalating commitment (p. 53).

The rationalizing model of behavior may, in fact, be quite rational, using a noneconomic, commonsense definition of the term. Commitment to decisions may make political sense and demonstrate persistence in the face of adversity, a characteristic that is often valued. After all, if you hire an individual and then aren't committed to this decision when the person makes a mistake, it may be more difficult to attract other, talented individuals to work with you. In a study demonstrating the different weights more- versus less-experienced managers give to persistence, Staw and Ross (1980) presented subjects with a decision-making case in which a hypothetical manager had behaved in either a consistent or inconsistent fashion, allocated either many or few resources, and had achieved either success or failure. Subjects in each condition had to evaluate the administrator and recommend the size of a raise. Staw and Ross found that all three conditions were positively associated with the evaluations given: being successful, behaving consistently, and using as few resources as possible were positively related to both the evaluations and the size of the raise recommended. The study used different subject populations—evening MBA students who had full-time jobs, psychology undergraduate students, and undergraduate business students. Staw and Ross found that who did the evaluating affected the weight given to the three factors. They noted that the evening MBA students gave performance the smallest weight in evaluating the manager and showed the greatest difference in the evaluations of consistent versus inconsistent administrators. The results suggest that business experience, for whatever reason, tends to lead to a greater value being placed on consistency and persistence: individuals who persist can come to be evaluated more positively than those who don't maintain their commitments, making perseverance rational for those individuals.

Commitment can also be sensible in that the very commitment can have positive effects on results. Consider, for instance, the Staw and Hoang (1995) study of the effects of draft order on playing time and being retained in the NBA. Why might it make sense to play someone more than might be warranted by that individual's performance in the previous year? Because there is evidence that playing time itself positively affects future performance: "We regressed performance for years 2 through 5 on prior year's performance, prior year's time on the court, draft number. . . . The results of these four analyses supported a straightforward investment hypothesis. . . . An increase in performance was associated with the investment of prior playing time" (p. 489).

Moreover, Staw and Hoang wrote about "the vagaries of forecasting talent" (p. 477) and also did an analysis that demonstrated that "draft number" was "a significant predictor of subsequent performance during players' second and third years in the NBA" (p. 488). Consequently, "draft order does appear to contain some useful information." Given these facts, some persistence in following one's initial predictions concerning talent might appear to be justified.

In the world outside of the experimental laboratory, the rationalizing model may be more rational than sometimes thought. That is because performance is not necessarily fully determined by preset factors and is affected by expectations and by the resources that individuals receive as a consequence of commitment, such as an opportunity to gain more experience. Moreover, performance is often ambiguous in terms of its assessment, which means that acts of commitment can change the evaluation of results. In this real world, the effects of both self-perception and commitment on subsequent behavior and performance help to create the very results that the rationalizing model seek to explain. These feedback cycles—resulting from both self-perception and commitment—to subsequent attitudes, behavior, and dimensions of performance would seem to warrant more attention not only to evaluate the ability of the rationalizing model to account for behavior but also to establish its implications for actually managing behavior.

The Moral Model of Behavior

Recently, there has been growing interest in models of behavior that move away from the neoclassical economic paradigm but in some instances retain a focus on individual or organizational rational choice. These models differ from the economic model of behavior in their core assumptions. Etzioni (1988, p. 4) has articulated the core assumptions of one behavior model that includes morals. First, a moral model postulates that individuals pursue not only pleasure (as they do in the utilitarian approach) but also morality. Consequently, "individuals are, simultaneously, under the influence of two major sets of factors—their pleasure and their moral duty" (p. 63). Second, this perspective emphasizes the fact that individuals choose means, not just goals, and these means are chosen on the basis of their values and emotions. Because moral and utilitarian considerations are qualitatively different, they cannot be traded off against each other (p. 71). An individual obtains "a sense of affirmation . . . when a person abides by his or her moral commitments" (p. 36). Third, the neoclassical presumption of the primacy of the individual is modified to account for the fact that social collectivities, including organizations but also including neighborhood and ethnic communities, are important decision-making units.

Frank (1990) has counterposed what he has called the self-interest model with a commitment model of behavior. Frank (1988; 1990) first reviewed the various "rational" reasons to forgo short-term self-interest, such as building a reputation for being trustworthy, as well as evolutionary or selection mechanisms that might produce more cooperative behavior. For example, the fact that people who cheat in transactions and are discovered will probably not have too many more opportunities to cheat again means that those who remain in the arena of exchange are probably not going to behave completely opportunistically. Frank distinguished these more sophisticated versions of self-interest from his view of commitment, which he described thus: "The motive is not to avoid the possibility of being caught, but to maintain and strengthen the predisposition to behave honestly. . . . *It is this change in my emotional makeup . . . that other people may apprehend*" (1988, p. 95, emphasis in original).

There is extensive empirical evidence consistent with the moral model of behavior, particularly as it is contrasted with a model of attitudes and behaviors resulting from the operation of simple self-interest. However, most of the relevant research does not deal with organizational contexts or problems, which leaves an important research agenda—applying the ideas of the moral model of behavior to organizations.

There have been studies showing that political behavior is not completely explainable by the idea of self-interest. Voting is a public-spirited act—it requires some effort, but the odds that a given individual's vote will be consequential for determining the election outcome is almost infinitesimally small. Hirschleifer (1985) reviewed studies showing that there was a correlation between the expected closeness of the election and voting—people were more likely to vote when the election was thought to be close, as self-interest would predict—but the relationship was comparatively small. Barry (1978) presented data indicating that closeness of the election accounted for about 9 percent of the variation in voter turnout, while a citizen duty score, a measure of moral obligation, accounted for between 30 percent and 40 percent.

Sears and Funk (1990) reviewed numerous studies of the role of self-interest in accounting for the political opinions of Americans on issues including race, taxes, crime, and war. They concluded that only about one-quarter of the self-interest terms in regression equations met even minimal standards of statistical significance and that the average bivariate correlation between a measure of self-interest and the corresponding political attitude was about 0.07, indicating that even when statistically significant, self-interest contributed in only a small way to explaining political attitudes. By contrast, symbolic predispositions, which include the possibility that "people may be socialized to respond to public issues in a principled and public-regarding manner" (Sears and Funk, 1990, p. 169), had considerably greater explanatory power. Similar results emerged from studies not of political attitudes but of actual voting. Sears et al., reviewing a number of these voting studies, concluded that "symbolic attributes (liberalism, conservatism, party identification, and racial prejudice) had strong effects, while self-interest had almost none" (1980, p. 679).

There is evidence that individuals behave altruistically and according to moral precepts and, by so doing, ignore simple self-interest. As one example, experiments show that many people mail back presumably lost wallets to strangers without taking anything (Hornstein, Fisch, and Holmes, 1968). Hornstein, Masor, and Sole (1971) found that some 64 percent of subjects who had an opportunity to return a lost contribution to a fictitious institute doing research in medicine did return the money. Latane and Darley (1970), in a study conducted in New York City, found that when strangers were approached by the researchers (in disguise) requesting aid, a high proportion furnished help.

The economic model of behavior has emphasized the free-riding problem—the tendency of individuals to take advantage of the efforts of others and shirk in situations in which the benefits are collective and cannot be distributed in proportion to individual contribution or performance. Discussions of the free-riding problem dominate consideration of group-based incentive schemes in organizations such as profit or gain sharing and lead many economists to believe that collective ownership of assets, as in a cooperative form of organization, is inherently inefficient. Thus, for instance, Williamson wrote that "cooperatives are unable to retain superior managers, who are induced to leave by offers of better pay in capitalist firms" (1985, p. 266).

There is only one problem with all of this concern for the free-riding problem—empirical evidence indicates that it is often not much of a problem at all: "A large number of experiments, under different conditions, most of them highly unfavorable to civility, show that people do not take free rides, but pay voluntarily as much as 40 percent to 60 percent of what economists figured is due to the public till if the person was not to free ride at all. The main reason: the subjects consider it the 'right' or 'fair' thing to do" (Etzioni, 1988, p. 59).

Another review of the literature on free riding came to the same conclusion:

> The logic of the problem of collective action is both compelling and illuminating. The problem with this logic, however, is that the empirical evidence for its ability to predict actual behavior is either scant or nonexistent. . . . Under the conditions described by the theory as leading to free riding, people often cooperate instead. . . . In over 13 experiments we have found that subjects persist in investing substantial proportions of their resources in public goods despite conditions specifically designed to maximize the impact of free riding and thus minimize investment. The prevalence of such economically "illogical" behavior was replicated over and over again. (Marwell, 1982, pp. 208, 210)

Etzioni (1988) has reviewed a set of studies that indicate that for moral issues, activities or behavior that have been deemed to be sacred, the calculative approach does not do very well in explaining behavior and, instead, nonmarkets exist. He concluded, "in any given society and period, certain items are not considered legitimate material for exchange. . . . As a result, market models are expected to depict the relations poorly at best; socio-economic conceptions that include moral as well as economic factors are necessary" (p. 81).

Institutional theory in some of its variants has a normative component: "emphasis . . . is placed on normative rules that introduce a prescriptive, evaluative, and obligatory dimension to social life" (Scott, 1995, p. 37). Selznick defined institutionalization as "to infuse with value" (1957, p. 17). Holm has noted that "the study of institutions is the study of norm-governed behavior" (1995, p. 398). J. G. March and Olsen, arguing for the importance of institutions for understanding politics, noted the importance of social obligations in understanding behavior: "To describe behavior as driven by rules is to see action as a matching of a situation to the demands of a position. Rules define relationships among roles in terms of what an incumbent of one role *owes* to incumbents of other roles" (1989, p. 23, emphasis added).

An interesting illustration of the effect of the normative order on the adoption of specific organizational practices is provided by Tolbert and Zucker's (1983) study of the diffusion of municipal civil service reform in the United States during the period 1885–1935. Early in the period, which cities adopted reforms could be predicted on the basis of characteristics that might be reasonably argued to account for the need and desire for reform: larger cities, cities with a larger proportion of immigrants, and those with a higher proportion of white-collar to blue-collar workers were more likely to adopt reform. Although city characteristics were strongly predictive of adoption of civil service reforms during the early period from 1885 to 1904, the effects of these characteristics became weaker over time so that by 1935, city characteristics no longer had predictive power. Tolbert and Zucker interpreted this result as demonstrating normative influence: "As an increasing number of organizations adopt a program or policy, it becomes progressively institutionalized, or widely understood to be a necessary component of rationalized organizational structure. The legitimacy of the procedures themselves serves as the impetus for the later adopters" (p. 35).

The normative order is importantly influenced by the actions of the state, which has important coercive and regulatory powers. Baron, Dobbin, and Jennings (1986), examining the diffusion and implementation of modern personnel practices, observed an important discontinuity at the time of World War II. At that point, the state intervened in organizational administration—for instance, forbidding strikes, demanding personnel records so that an inventory of manpower could be maintained and managed, and limiting wage increases. Baron et al. noted that "these interventions . . . fueled the development of bureaucratic controls by creating models of employment and incentives to formalize and expand personnel functions" (p. 369). Bridges and Villemez (1994), analyzing a matched sample of employees and employers from Chicago in the early 1980s, found that both government influence in the industrial sector and how close organizations were to the public sector had important effects on the development and spread of due-process procedures and bureaucratic control.

The conclusion from this brief review of relevant empirical evidence seems inescapable: social and individual values matter in understanding behavior and are often more powerful predictors than simple conceptions of self-interest. In determining the normative order, both prevalence and the actions of legitimate authorities, such as governments, are important. Consequently, understanding the emergence of norms and moral conceptions in organizations, and examining their effects on behavior, are important research tasks.

The Interpretive, Cognitive Model of Behavior

Cognition is explicitly present in most of the models already considered. The economic model often presumes rational choice, a cognitive process. Indeed, one of the prominent critiques of the rational decision-making foundations of economic theory has proceeded by showing how human judgment and decision processes frequently violate the principles of rational choice (Tversky and Kahneman, 1974). The moral model of behavior proceeds from its own version of rationality, which includes moral values in the decision calculus. The retrospectively rational model of behavior is concerned with the connection between cognition and action but posits that on many occasions cognitions follow actions to rationalize or justify them rather than guiding action prospectively. What distinguishes what I have termed an interpretive, cognitive model of behavior from the others is its focus on the sensemaking and perception processes and the extent to which researchers using this approach on occasion separate cognition from objective reality. In that sense, many versions of the cognitive model argue for a relativism that makes them attractive to critical theorists and other postmodern conceptions of organization science that bemoan the machinelike quality of much social science and organizational research.

The cognitive model is not readily summarized because it has numerous variants that emphasize somewhat different aspects of cognitive process. Some cognitive models, as we will soon see, emphasize the social aspects of cognition and become almost indistinguishable from the social model of behavior with its emphasis on social context. On occasion, writers in the cognitive tradition emphasize retrospective sensemaking based on commitment processes and in this sense become identical to the rationalizing model of behavior. Throughout, however, the interest in cognition is premised on the idea that behaviors and outcomes are better understood if we focus on the "cognitive processes that influence those behaviors and outcomes" (Gioia and Sims, 1986, p. 3).

Weick is probably the most consistent and forceful proponent of the cognitive view:

> An organization is a body of thought thought by thinking thinkers. . . . In reply to the question "what is an organization," we consider organizations to be snapshots of ongoing processes, these snapshots being selected and controlled by human consciousness and attentiveness. This consciousness and attentiveness, in turn, can be seen as snapshots of ongoing cognitive processes . . . where the mind acquires knowledge about its surroundings. . . . In these epistemological

processes, both knowledge and the environment are constructed by participants interactively. (1979, p. 42)

The relativism inherent in this conception of organizations can be readily seen in Weick's elaboration of these ideas. Thus, "an organization can be viewed as a body of jargon available for attachment to experience" (1979, p. 42). Or, "Organizations exist largely in the mind" (Weick and Bougon, 1986, p. 102). What do managers do? "Managerial work can be viewed as managing myths, images, symbols, and labels. The much touted 'bottom line' of the organization is a symbol, if not a myth" (Weick, 1979, p. 42). Managers traffic in images, and as such, "the appropriate role for the manager may be evangelist rather than accountant" (p. 42).

Note that this approach differs in some important respects from other treatments of the symbolic role of management (Pfeffer, 1981b) and the use of political language and symbols (e.g., Edelman, 1964). For instance, Edelman noted, "Political analysis must, then, proceed on two levels simultaneously. It must examine how political actions get some groups the tangible things they want . . . and at the same time it must explore what these same actions mean to the mass public and how it is placated or aroused by them" (p. 12). Edelman's comment that "it is not uncommon to give the rhetoric to one side and the decision to the other" (p. 39) and Pfeffer's argument that substantive outcomes and "the attitudes, beliefs, norms, and values which are generated around them" (1981c, p. 180) may be loosely coupled both speak to the existence of a substantive reality apart from cognition that is implicitly denied if one takes Weick's position literally.

Individuals' beliefs about the causal relationships in an organizational setting can be represented in a cause map: "participants edit their own organizational experience into patterns of personal knowledge. A representation of that knowledge is called a *cognitive map*. A cognitive map consists of the concepts and the relations a participant uses to understand organizational situations" (Weick and Bougon, 1986, p. 106).

Bougon, Weick, and Binkhorst (1977) measured the cause maps of members of the Utrecht Jazz Orchestra. In these maps, a -1 indicated an inverse relation, a 0 indicated no relation, and a $+1$ indicated a positive relationship between the entries in the rows and columns. It is possible to obtain the entries (which represent behaviors, contextual factors, and outcomes such as the difficulty of the piece, the amount of rehearsal time, and the quality of the performance) from the organizational members themselves or to provide the members with a list based on preliminary interviewing. But in either case, to assess the similarity of cause maps one must present the same set of stimulus materials to each organizational member. Summing across all the orchestra members provides an average map of the causal structure as seen by the organizational members and a "consensual view of what the orchestra is" (Weick and Bougon, 1986, p. 112). Bougon (1983) has developed one possible method for measuring cause maps in organizational contexts. Although the cause map idea and method is interesting, it has not come to play a prominent role in subsequent empirical research, possibly because collecting these data is an arduous task.

One might ask, Where do cognitive representations of organizations come from? At one point, Weick and Bougon suggested that "when people build cognitive maps, they start with outcomes, small experiments, and consequences. . . . These perceived regularities form the raw materials for cognitive maps" (1986, p. 105). This conception is consistent with that seen in attribution theory, viewing individuals as lay social scientists. The implication that a great deal of cognitive effort goes on in organizations is inconsistent with the view that much behavior is mindless (Langer, 1983) or is controlled by rules and standard operating procedures (Cyert and March, 1963). All this cognitive activity is also inconsistent with Mintzberg's (1973) depiction of managerial work as involving little time spent reflecting or thinking as compared to acting or interacting with others.

Subsequently, Weick argued that behavioral commitment is the critical process underlying cognition in organizations: "behavioral commitment is a stimulus to build . . . coherent world views out of whatever resources are at hand. . . . Justification can become an important source of social structure, culture, and norms. . . . Organizations begin to materialize when rationales for commitment become articulated. . . . Justifications can easily be transformed into organizational goals because these goals themselves are so general" (1993, pp. 12–13). This view of cognition as being based on behavioral commitment obviously makes the cognitive model of organizations very similar to the retrospectively rational model already discussed.

Although research on the cognitive model of organizations will sometimes use the phrase "social cognition" and will frequently invoke the term "organization," much of the work is actually quite silent on the obvious social and contextual influences on the processes of attribution, sensemaking, and constructing of causal maps that go on. In this sense, the cognitive model of organizations is consistent and in fact may derive from the trend in social psychology to downplay, empirically if not in the language used, the social, relational reality of organizational life. Although there are exceptions to this tendency, they are relatively few. As R. A. Baron has noted, "social psychology has undergone nothing short of what some have described as a *cognitive revolution*. During this transformation, the primary emphasis of the field shifted from social *behavior* (interpersonal relations and group processes) to social *thought*—how we think about others and interpret their characteristics, words, and deeds" (1993, p. 64, emphasis in original). Mimicking this trend in organization studies may not have been the wisest choice. Inattention to the social aspect of organizational life and the corresponding emphasis on individual cognition coupled with the difficulties of actually mapping cognitive structures has left the cognitive model in the position of being more of a metaphor for writing about organizations than a major stimulus to empirical research.

Conclusion

Unfortunately, the relative prevalence of the various models of behavior in the organizations literature and in managerial discourse about organizations is only loosely related to the degree of empirical support they enjoy or the reasonableness of their assumptions. Apparently, models of behavior often take on a religious quality, adopted or rejected on the basis of belief or aesthetics rather than on the basis of scientific evidence. So, even though organizations are inherently social and relational entities, there is great interest in the economic model of behavior in spite of the fact that many of its variants proceed from a position of methodological individualism that denies the very reality of the institutions and organizations being explained. Even though self-perception and commitment processes have been repeatedly demonstrated in both field and experimental situations, and these perspectives have important implications for the effects of surveillance, incentives, and other forms of external control, the insights of these models are seldom incorporated in either the research on or design of organizational incentive systems. Even though moral considerations loom large and often dominate self-interest in studies of political behavior, a moral model of organizational behavior has yet to be developed or explored to any great extent.

Perhaps the greatest difficulty is that the models often seem to simply ignore each other. Empirical explorations that attempt to compare and contrast at least some of the various competing models of behavior—the economic model, the social model, the retrospectively rational model, and the moral model—are substantially less common than warranted. Because these theoretical perspectives affect the practice of management, the formulation of public policy, and the conduct of research, attention to their assumptions, evidentiary base, and implications would seem to be critical for anyone doing research on organizations.

4

The Effects of Organizational
Composition

As discussed thus far in this book, underlying all organization theory and research is the basic question, How are we to understand organizations? One variant of a social model of behavior that has drawn sufficient research attention to merit more extended consideration is an approach to organizational analysis emphasizing the effects of social composition.

Although many organization theories have psychological or social psychological foundations (Mowday and Sutton, 1993), which emphasize attitudes, dispositions, and cognitive processes, one important portion of the field employs a structural perspective. "This focus on structure tends to direct attention . . . toward the enduring properties of the relations among actors that both constrain and enable action to occur" (Pfeffer, 1991, p. 789). Structural analysis explains "patterns of social relations in terms of properties of social structure, not in terms of the assumptions made, whether or not these are derivable from psychological principles" (P. M. Blau, 1977, p. 246). Although structural accounts may rely on psychological principles or assumptions, these are not always directly tested or even examined in the analyses. The structural perspective relies on the social model of behavior for its core assumptions and so emphasizes the effect of context on behavior. One advantage of analyzing organizations in terms of the effects of their composition is that such analyses rely on more readily observable variables (Pfeffer, 1983; Hambrick and Mason, 1984). Weick has noted the advantages of analyzing organizations in terms of observable behaviors and other properties:

> There are several places in the organizational literature where investigators seem to resist defining their concepts in terms of observable actions by individuals in the mistaken belief that, in doing so, they will have to explain the actions psychologically. If . . . properties can be defined in terms of observable individual behaviors, there is a better chance the empirical research . . . can be made more cumulative. (1969, pp. 31–32)

One subtle but important implication of the social model, with its emphasis on the effects of social influences, is that not every social entity is going to be equally available to exert influence. Thus, there is the argument that patterns of social relations are explained not solely on the basis of motives but "on the basis of external *opportunities* for social relations created by population composition and the structure of positions in the social environment" (Huber, 1990, p. 2, emphasis added). What this means is simply that who you interact with and are therefore influenced by and, in turn, influence, is a function of the existing social structure. If you never have contact with Democrats because of the particular composition of your social environment, your political attitudes will be affected accordingly. If an individual's social environment is made up almost exclusively of males, the opportunity for interaction with women is limited simply by the composition of the social group, regardless of the individual's interest in inter-acting with women. This latter example is particularly relevant, as we will see below, in understanding women's networks and careers in numerically male-dominated environments. As an empirical illustration of this compositional effect, P. M. Blau and Schwartz (1984) explored patterns of intermarriage among racial, occupational, ethnic background, and birth-region dimensions in a sample of metropolitan areas. They acknowledged that individuals would prefer to associate with similar others. However, exercising this preference is constrained by the available interaction partners. Blau and Schwartz demonstrated that the relative size of various demographic groups affected the observed rate of intermarriage.

Many explorations of structural effects have examined the impact of varying group composition in terms of salient demographic differences such as age, orga-nizational tenure, gender, or work background (Pfeffer, 1983; Stewman, 1988). These studies usually proceed from the empirically justifiable presumption that similarity is an important basis of interpersonal attraction and contact (Berscheid and Walster, 1969) as well as the assumption that background and contact matter for understanding behavior. In the organizations literature, structural effects have been explored most completely in the literature on organizational demography, a related literature on the effects of the composition of top management teams, and a literature that has explored the effect of gender composition on work-related outcomes such as wage and position attainment. A part of the literature on gender composition examines how this affects social networks, and through such network connections, mobility prospects.

Organizational Demography

Kanter's (1977) argument that proportions have an important effect on the experi-ences of those in the minority was an explicit recognition of compositional effects. She wrote, "If one sees nine X's and one O, the O will stand out" (p. 210). Kanter argued that women in token status suffered from being more visible and thus under more intense scrutiny and came to be stereotyped, seen as representative of the group (women) rather than as distinct individuals. Differences between those in token status and the majority were exaggerated because the presence of persons who were different made the similarities among those in the majority more salient. Kanter argued that the pressures that confronted someone in token status made success difficult, particularly in organizational contexts such as management positions in which trust and interpersonal communication were important. Her research identified three sources of stress:

> Because their "differentness" is highly visible, tokens feel that they are always under scrutiny. . . . Because they are symbolic representatives of their "type," tokens experience added pressure to perform well, since this may determine future opportunities for other individuals in their social category. . . . One response to performance pressure is to overachieve; another is to avoid calling attention to oneself or one's accomplishments. . . .
>
> The second source of stress, *boundary heightening*, results from majority group members' tendencies to exaggerate their own commonalities as well as their differences from tokens. . . .
>
> The third source of stress, *role entrapment*, involves typecasting by dominants. (P. B. Jackson, Thoits, and Taylor, 1995, p. 545)

Spangler, Gordon, and Pipkin (1978), empirically examining Kanter's ideas, found that women in law schools in which they constituted less than 20 percent of the student body spoke up less in class, earned lower grades, and tended to go into more "female" law specialities compared to women in a law school in which they constituted about a third of the class. Jackson, Thoits, and Taylor, studying 167 elite black leaders in the United States, found that "numerical rarity by race and by gender significantly increased symptoms of depression and anxiety" (1995, p. 543).

Pfeffer (1983) proposed that age and tenure distributions, as well as gender and race composition, were consequential for understanding organizations. In particular, he argued that organizations that had more discontinuous tenure distributions were more likely to experience intercohort conflict and consequently greater turnover. Organizations consisting almost solely of long-tenured people lacked demographically adjacent individuals to link newcomers into the organization. In a series of studies of organizations including university departments, top management groups, and nurses in hospitals, heterogeneity in organizational tenure was observed to be positively related to turnover (McCain, O'Reilly, and Pfeffer, 1983; W. G. Wagner, Pfeffer, and O'Reilly, 1984; Pfeffer and O'Reilly, 1987). Furthermore, those individuals who were most demographically distant or dissimilar were more likely to leave.

Demographic diversity can occur along several dimensions—age, tenure in the organization, gender, education and training, and so forth. This fact raises two questions. First, are certain of these bases of heterogeneity more important in affecting organizational outcomes such as turnover than others? Second, what happens when organizational populations are quite heterogeneous along a number of dimensions simultaneously? Studying turnover among top management teams in fifty-one banks and using a number of measures of heterogeneity, Jackson et al. (1991) reported that only age-based diversity affected turnover rates. Alexander et al. (1995), in a study of nursing turnover in a set of 398 U.S. community hospitals, found that both heterogeneity in educational preparation and diversity in tenure were significantly and positively related to increased turnover. However, they found that heterogeneity in employment status (full- versus part-time) was related negatively to turnover. They also examined whether or not heterogeneity had a curvilinear relationship with tenure, under the argument that very high levels of diversity "will improve communication, interaction, and social integration, because the barriers to such interactions are broken down by the presence of small, similar size of groupings" (p. 1459). Their study did not find any evidence of this curvilinear effect, but the underlying idea, derived from P. M. Blau's (1977) discussion of heterogeneity and group size and the effects on in-group versus out-group communication, is worth exploring in other settings.

Alexander et al. also explored the effects of heterogeneity along multiple dimensions. They argued that if organizational "members manifest differences on multiple demographic characteristics, it becomes more difficult to create homogeneous groups that exhibit internal consistency on every demographic dimension" (1995, p. 1460). Consequently, they expected that multiform heterogeneity would result in reduced turnover compared to settings in which there was heterogeneity only on one dimension. Their empirical results were consistent with their prediction "that when heterogeneity is high on multiple dimensions, organizations are likely to experience lower turnover among their members" (p. 1472).

These studies hypothesized that demographic dissimilarity hindered interpersonal communication and, consequently, social integration and interaction; they also hypothesized that it was through these effects that turnover occurred. However, because of data limitations, the research tended to relate measures of demographic heterogeneity directly to outcomes such as turnover without exploring the mediating mechanisms. Some studies have more directly examined the consequences of demography for interpersonal evaluation, communication, and integration, finding support for the basic argument. Tsui and O'Reilly (1989) found that, after controlling for an individual's own demographic characteristics, the greater the difference between that person's age, education, race, and gender and that of his or her supervisor, the lower the supervisor's ratings of the subordinate's effectiveness and the greater the degree of role ambiguity experienced by the subordinate. This result suggests that demographic differences affect the performance evaluation process and have important consequences for rewards and recognition that are likely to be linked to turnover, motivation, and performance. Zenger and Lawrence (1989) examined age and tenure effects on actual communication in technical work groups, finding that more heterogeneous groups had less interpersonal communication.

O'Reilly, Caldwell, and Barnett (1989) studied twenty work units with seventy-nine respondents. They measured cohesiveness, satisfaction with co-workers, and the amount of socialization with other co-workers off the job. These three components formed a scale with satisfactory reliability that they called social integration. The study was important because it explored the consequences of individual-level processes (the extent to which a given individual was different from the rest of the group and a measure of how integrated that individual was) and of those operating on a more macro level (the extent of demographic heterogeneity in the group as a whole and the amount of group-level social integration). Their "results show group-level tenure homogeneity to be associated with lower turnover rates of individuals, with group-level social integration as a moderator. . . . Furthermore, this process is not merely the aggregate of an individual-level process, since individual-level social integration does not affect the turnover rates" (p. 33). The results of this study demonstrated substantive as well as statistical significance. Individuals in the group with the least social integration had an estimated turnover rate *nine* times as high as would be expected without this effect of demographic diversity. By contrast, individuals in the most integrated group had an estimated turnover rate 94 percent lower than it would have been without this effect of demographic cohesion.

A further study of processes that undergird the effects of composition and demography demonstrated that the greater the work-unit diversity, the lower the levels of psychological attachment, operationalized as commitment, attendance at work, and turnover intentions (Tsui, Egan, and O'Reilly, 1992). This study also found that the effects of heterogeneity were not constant across demographic groups, with whites and males evidencing larger negative effects from being in more demographically heterogeneous units than nonwhites and women. This finding raises the point that being different in a specific work setting is not the whole story; there are also institutional or societal expectations about organizational composition and individual status, power, and rewards that affect how individuals react. Wharton has argued that "researchers should . . . examine how organizational arrangements help to evoke . . . distinctions at both the individual and group levels" (1992, p. 57) and her recourse to social identity theory linked the study of what happens inside organizations to broader concerns of social categorization.

The importance of the social context for understanding the effects of demography is nicely illustrated by a study of Japanese top management teams (Wiersema and Bird, 1993). They found, first of all, that there was less diversity in top management teams in Japan than there was, on average, in the United States. This reflects Japanese organizations' policies of promotion from within, slow evaluation and promotion, and an emphasis on consensual decision making. But, even though there was less heterogeneity in Japanese top management teams, the effect of what heterogeneity there was on turnover was substantially *stronger* than that observed in studies of U.S. managers. Heterogeneity on the dimensions of age, team tenure, and the prestige of the university attended were all significantly correlated with team turnover. In Japan, there is less heterogeneity in senior management, but heterogeneity also has a larger effect than in the United States.

The distribution of length of service in an organization affects not only turnover and interpersonal processes such as conflict and social integration; it also effects innovative activity and organizational change. At the group level of analysis, R. Katz (1982) reported that research and development project groups with either fairly short (less than one and a half years) or fairly long (greater than five years) average tenure in the group were less productive than groups intermediate in average tenure. He argued that this was because in groups with fairly short tenures, individuals spent a lot of time organizing themselves and learning how to work together and access necessary information and expertise distributed across group members. In groups in which individuals had worked together on average quite a long time, the negative effect on performance came from restricted communication and hence less search and access to new information, particularly from outside the particular project group, than might be optimal.

Much of demography's effect on organizational change and adaptation comes through its impact on career processes in organizations. Stewman (1986) has shown that "the commonly held view that organizational pyramids necessitate declining career chances the higher one rises in the organization" is inaccurate (Stewman, 1988, p. 175; see also Stewman and Konda, 1983). Rather, career chances depend most importantly on the rate of organizational growth and to a lesser extent on the rate of voluntary quitting. Thus, individuals in organizations that cease growing face substantially more limited promotion prospects, and this effect on careers has implications for attracting and retaining talent.

As a nice illustration of this phenomenon, S. Morris (1973) examined the development and evolution of the U.S. railroad industry, one of the first industries to have organizations operating on a national scale and one in which many of the early management practices originated. However, some time after its creation the industry stagnated, both in terms of its competitive success and in terms of its management-systems innovation. Morris argued that much of the problem from the 1920s onward was a consequence of the industry's demography. The railroads grew quite rapidly around the turn of the century and then abruptly stopped growing. This left them with a fairly young management cadre, but without the business that created additional management positions, producing blocked promotional opportunities for new organizational entrants. With few prospects for mobility, new organizational entrants left, and recruiting of talent became more difficult. When one considers that this was a period in which the average level of education was rising, management practices were evolving as large companies increasingly populated the landscape, and technological change was also accelerating, the loss of expertise resulting from the inability to attract and retain young managerial talent was substantial. Thus, a particular demographic situation generated personnel problems that left the organizations not well suited to solving the performance problems, generating a cycle of decline that can be observed in other industries as well.

Demography may make adapting to changing environmental conditions more difficult. T. L. Reed (1978) studied the U.S. Foreign Service and its apparent inability "to change rapidly in response to the shift in the complexity of international relations in World War II and thereafter" (Stewman, 1988, p. 188). Reed argued that this problem arose from the organization's opportunity structure, which was based on seniority and typically had long waiting times before someone could advance to the more senior grades. Because of this recruitment and advancement process, there was "an extended time lag . . . to get new recruits into the middle and senior levels of the expanded areas of responsibility" (Stewman, 1988, p. 188) and thereby bring new expertise and points of view into the foreign policy development process.

Demography affects not only the rate of succession and adaptation but also elements of the choice of a successor. In particular, Pfeffer and Moore (1980a) found that academic departments that had more long-tenured individuals tended to choose new department heads more frequently from within the department. If for no other reason than availability, demography will affect succession—one is more likely to choose a successor from within an organization if there is an abundance of senior individuals with the requisite experience from which to choose.

Determinants of Demography

As Mitman has noted, most of the research literature on demography has explored the effects of demographic distributions on various outcomes, and "only a small number of studies have focused directly on the origins and determinants of demographic patterns" (1992, p. 5). Because organizational demography is determined "by the past history of the social composition of net flows into it" (Stinchcombe, McDill, and Walker, 1968, p. 221), understanding organizational demography requires understanding demographic composition at some initial point and the subsequent flows into and out of the organization. Because the processes of organizational entry, internal transitions such as promotion, and organizational exits are themselves affected by demographic composition (e.g., the studies cited above on turnover and the tendency for recruiting to reproduce friendship and social composition), the evolution of an organization's demography over time is a dynamic process with important feedback loops. External labor market conditions, government regulations such as antidiscrimination and affirmative action requirements and the vigor with which these are enforced, and economic factors such as the rate of industry growth or decline are among those forces that affect entry and exit processes and the consequent organizational demography. Although modeling the dynamics over time imposes substantial data requirements, to the extent demography is an important explanation for organizational processes and outcomes, understanding demographic dynamics is an important undertaking.

One notable example of what might be done in the study of the determinants of demography is a study of gender integration in the government of the State of California (Baron, Mittman, and Newman, 1991). Using a linear partial-adjustment model, the study examined the determinants both of the "target level" of segregation—"a minimum level of gender segregation that is possible, given the organizational configuration, toward which the agency is posed to adjust but which social forces might resist" (p. 1376)—and the speed of adjustment to that target level. The research employed quarterly staffing data over a six-year period for all state agencies that described the ethnic and gender composition of each job title within each agency—detailed data that permit quite fine-grained analysis. Baron et al. found that both initial segregation levels and the speed of adjustment were related to the same factors:

> Segregation . . . was markedly lower in large agencies and those with high proportions of female and nonwhite employees and was somewhat higher among agencies that lacked an affirmative action program, were unionized along craft

lines, were clerical intensive, derived their mandate from the state constitution [and consequently were presumably less subject to legislative influence], reported objective quantitative output measures (i.e., had well-defined core technologies), were not dependent on the General Fund for revenues, or experienced frequent chief executive turnover. (p. 1385)

The study also found that agencies with female heads adjusted faster, as did agencies that grew faster and faced more scrutiny. The effect of employment growth on demographic change is likely to be an effect observed in many different organizational contexts, as is the importance of political interests, in this study represented by unions and the amount of legislative oversight and pressure from the state personnel board. The methods and models employed in this study are broadly applicable to the study of demographic change in general and should have stimulated more follow-on studies than they did.

A second example of an analysis of changes in organizational demography over time is Haveman's (1995) study of the entry rate, the exit rate, the average tenure, and the dispersion in tenure for managers in savings and loans. She noted that "explanations of organizations' tenure distributions must be rooted in explanations of job mobility, because movement of employees into and out of the labor force and movement of employees between organizations drives individual tenure and thus drives changes in organizations' tenure distributions" (pp. 588–589). Haveman found that the rate of entry into organizations was positively affected by the industry merger rate, dissolution rate, and firm acquisition rate as well as by the industry birth and dissolution rate. Average tenure was positively affected by the industry dissolution rate and negatively by the firm acquisition rate. Tenure dispersion was positively related to both the industry birth rate and the industry merger rate. Haveman's study also indicated that larger and older organizations' demographies are affected differentially by industry dynamics.

Most of the existing research on the determinants of organizational composition has focused on the proportion of women or minorities as the dependent variable to be explained. Studying the gender composition of college and university faculties, Tolbert and Oberfield (1991) found that there was a smaller proportion of female faculty when there were more slack resources and that there was more female faculty the higher the proportion of female students. This latter finding is consistent with research by Borjas (1980; 1982; 1983), who explored the connection between the proportion of minorities and women in constituencies for agencies served by the federal government and the hiring and salary of women and minorities in those agencies. He argued that to maximize political support, agencies that served minorities and women would tend to match the demographics of their client population in their employees. He did find that the demographic composition of the groups served by agencies strongly affected both the proportion of women and minorities hired and their relative wages (compared to white men)—agencies serving women, for instance, employed a higher proportion of women and the women's earnings were more similar to men's. Tolbert and Oberfield's first result, on the effect of resource levels, echoes the results of other studies that have also found that women tend to work in organizations that have fewer resources (e.g., Szafran, 1984; Pfeffer and Davis-Blake, 1987). Although studying the determinants of gender and race composition of organizations is obviously important, it would be useful to have studies of other demographic factors such as age and tenure in the organization and, as in the Haveman (1995) and Baron et al. studies described above, to have these changes dynamically modeled.

Top Management Teams

At about the same time as Wagner et al. (1984) were studying how demographic diversity affected turnover in top management teams, Hambrick and Mason (1984) were proposing an "upper-echelons" theory of management that emphasized the organizational effects of the composition of the top management group. Their argument was that both strategic choices and organizational performance were related to the characteristics of the top management team because of the presumption "that top managers structure decision situations to fit their view of the world. . . . A central requirement for understanding organizational behavior is to identify those factors that direct or orient executive attention" (Finkelstein and Hambrick, 1990, p. 484). Hambrick and Mason argued:

> a manager, or even an entire team of managers, cannot scan every aspect of the organization and its environment. The manager's *field of vision*—those areas to which attention is directed—is restricted, posing a sharp limitation on eventual perceptions. Second, the manager's perceptions are further limited because one *selectively perceives* only some of the phenomena included in the field of vision. Finally, the bits of information selected for processing are *interpreted* through a filter woven by one's cognitive base and values. (1984, p. 195)

This meant that the individual's worldview was probably related to his or her functional background, education, and experience, all of which affected the information one attended to and how one processed that information. Consequently, research on the characteristics of top management teams has emphasized heterogeneity in functional backgrounds, the amount of time the team has spent working together, and other indicators of experience, diversity and similarity. The other important emphasis in this literature has been the focus on characteristics of the *team*, as contrasted with the research linking strategy and organizational performance to the characteristics of the chief executive (e.g., Carlson, 1972). The evidence suggests that team effects are important in understanding organizational change and performance. Tushman, Newman, and Romanelli noted that "the data are consistent across diverse industries and companies. . . . An executive team's ability to proactively initiate and implement frame-breaking change *and* to manage convergent change seem to be important factors which discriminate between organizational renewal and greatness versus complacency and eventual decline" (1986, p. 15).

For instance, Finkelstein and Hambrick (1990) examined 100 organizations in the computer, chemical, and natural gas industries. They found that long-tenured managerial teams tended to have more persistent strategies and that the strategies and performance more closely conformed to industry norms. They also found that the effects of top management team composition were strongest in those competitive environments that permitted managers the greatest decision-making discretion. This result is important in reminding us that any effects of top management teams will be stronger in environments that permit managerial discretion and in which performance variation is consequently greater. Bantel and Jackson (1989) observed a negative relationship between top management team tenure and organizational innovativeness. Wiersema and Bantel (1992), measuring corporate strategic change as the absolute change in the level of diversification, found that firms that had individuals in top management who were younger, had less average organizational tenure, and had higher levels of education, more training in the sciences, and longer tenure working together in the top management team tended to experience more strategic change. Their results suggest that cognitive perspectives are reflected in demographic measures of team composition.

O'Reilly, Snyder, and Boothe (1993) explored the effects of top management demography in a sample of twenty-four electronics firms, defining the top management team as those who reported directly to the CEO. They measured turnover, organizational change, performance, and top management team dynamics in terms of how positive these dynamics were using a seven-item scale. The study controlled for company age, firm size, and the size of the top management team. Consistent with other studies, they found that increased heterogeneity within the team was negatively associated with team dynamics and was positively related to turnover. They also found that "heterogeneity within the executive team is significantly linked to less structural change, whereas homogeneity is positively associated with change" (p. 167). They noted that "when an executive team operates in a turbulent context, there may be an important premium on their ability to function effectively as a group and to avoid conflicts and misunderstandings that can slow them down and deflect their attention" (p. 172). Thus, ironically, the heterogeneity that brings different information and perspectives can also have dysfunctional effects, particularly if it is not managed effectively.

The O'Reilly et al. (1993) study is one of the few that have explored the process through which top management team demography operates. In another study of this process, K. G. Smith et al. (1994) used data from fifty-three high-technology firms to test a direct model of the effect of top management team demography on organizational performance, a model in which demography affected performance through its influence on interpersonal processes, as well as a model in which process itself had direct effects. Figure 4-1 shows the three ways in which process and top management team demography might affect organizational performance. Controlling for past performance, firm size, industry demand, and competition, K. G. Smith et al. (1994) found that demography affected intervening processes such as informal communication, which in turn affected sales growth and return on investment. They also observed direct demographic effects of heterogeneous experience and heterogeneous education on these two measures of performance as well as direct effects of informal communication and social integration.

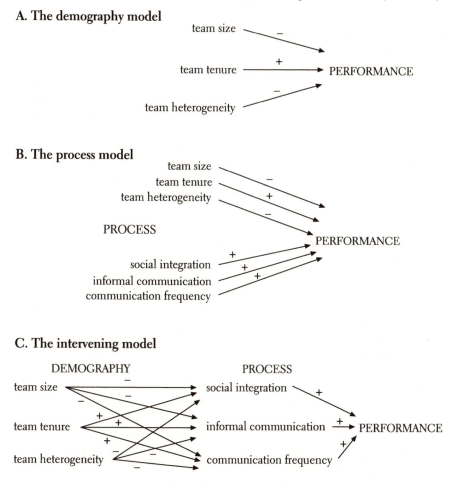

A. The demography model

B. The process model

C. The intervening model

Figure 4-1   Models of the Effects of Demography on Performance. *Source:* K. G. Smith et al., 1994

These latter two studies are noteworthy because they are exceptions to much of the upper-echelon literature that has been almost completely unconcerned with processes of interaction among individuals. Recall that the organizational demography literature focused on issues such as intercohort conflict, succession, career advancement, and so forth—all of which are also issues within the top management team. What most of the upper-echelon research has done, however, is to simply aggregate individual characteristics—for example, average length of tenure in the team or the organization, average education—but it has not explored the consequences of varying *distributions* of these characteristics for the processes of conflict and career advancement that one would also expect to be important in top management groups.

Virtually all of the top management team literature has focused on the *consequences* of upper-echelon composition. That, of course, leaves the question of how senior management composition emerges in the first place. Demographic similarity may play an important role in understanding this process. Westphal and Zajac (1995) examined 413 large corporations over the period 1986–1991. They found that when the chief executive was more powerful, new directors appointed to the board tended to be more similar to the existing CEO. When the board was more powerful, new directors were demographically more similar to the existing board members. They also found that the greater the demographic similarity between the chief executive and the board, the more highly compensated was the CEO, even when other factors affecting compensation were statistically controlled. Their study presents an upper-echelon case of the type of homosocial reproduction—the tendency to hire and promote similar others—that Kanter (1977) had described more generally.

Another study of the filling of senior-level college and university administrative vacancies also illustrates the importance of demography for the construction of senior management teams. The literature suggests that there is both a tendency to choose similar others and a propensity for jobs to become categorized by gender and race depending on their composition (Bielby and Baron, 1986). Konrad and Pfeffer (1991) found that a woman or a member of a minority was more likely to be placed in a vacant college administrative position (1) the higher the proportion of women (or minorities) in similar positions in the labor market as a whole; (2) the higher the proportion of women (or minorities) in senior administrative positions in the organization; and (3) if a woman (or minority) had been the previous occupant of the position. They found that each of these effects was significant, even with the others in the model, which meant that the gender or race of the position's previous occupant affected the gender or race of the new occupant even with labor market supply and the power of the demographic group in the senior administration statistically controlled. The study provided evidence that positions were typed by the characteristics of the previous occupant and also for the importance of the proportion of women in comparable positions in the labor market and in the administrative hierarchy in the specific organization for predicting the characteristics of those hired to fill vacant positions.

It is important to recognize that the top management teams literature, emphasizing the effects of senior team composition on organizational change, strategy, and performance, represents a reaction to perspectives on both organizational behavior and strategy that deemphasize the role of action and choice:

> organizations were disembodied, or perhaps, "beheaded," by many in the academic community. . . . Essentially mechanical models came to the fore. An organization's structure was seen as determined by such factors as environment, technology, and size. . . . In the ecologist's framework, the environment was the centerpiece. . . . Organizational variation was largely random, accidental, or rooted in history. . . . Even the field of strategy . . . lost sight of senior executives. . . . Strategy scholars become preoccupied with product life cycles, portfolio matrices, industry and competitor analysis, . . . experience curves, and generic strategies. (Finkelstein and Hambrick, 1996, pp. 4–5)

John Child's (1972) article on strategic choice argued that political considerations loomed large in understanding organizations and their structures. Child noted that "many available contributions to a theory of organizational structure do not incorporate the direct source of variation in formal structural arrangements, namely the strategic decisions of those who have the power of structural initiation" (p. 16).

The top management team literature provides evidence that backgrounds, which, of course, represent individual history and learning, are important in understanding organizational dynamics. More important, it focuses attention on the composition and interrelationships of the senior management team. This focus stands, for instance, in contrast to the literature on leadership, which, for the most part, examines the correlates and consequences of *individual* leader behavior—even though we know that, outside of the experimental laboratory, leaders seldom act alone in their roles. By demonstrating the importance of top management team dynamics and the effects of composition on those dynamics, this research has implications for constituting top management teams and for executive and leadership development, implications that remain to be more fully researched and explored.

Gender, Networks, and Careers

The effects of composition and structural relationships have been particularly prominent in studies attempting to understand problems confronting women and ethnic minorities in organizations. Many studies have reported that women fare better within organizations when they are in comparatively larger numbers. For instance, Izraeli (1983), studying the attitudes of union representatives in worker's committees in Israel, found that women in more gender-balanced committees deemed women to be as effective as men while women in male-dominated committees thought that women were less effective than men. Heery and Kelley (1988), studying local British unions, found that women in office were more likely than men to encourage women's participation. Alexander and Thoits (1985) and Spangler, Gordon, and Pipkin (1978) reported that female students' grades were lower in male-dominated departments. Tidball (1980) argued that one reason women graduates from all-women's colleges did so well subsequently was the presence of a greater proportion of women faculty members. Sackett, Dubois, and Noe (1991) reported that the performance ratings obtained by women were lower when their proportion was less than 20 percent and that this diminished performance assessment held even with job and firm variables statistically controlled.

Mellor (1995), in a study of fifty-six northeastern locals of a single union, examined the effects of the varying gender composition of local unions' offices on women's and men's ratings of their competence, their ability to participate in local activities, their desire to participate, and their perceived acceptance. His study distinguished between gender representation, defined as the ratio of women officers to women members, and gender composition, based on a count of women and men in local office (p. 709). He concluded:

gender composition in local office did have a positive influence on women's ratings but did not influence men's participation ratings. Women in locals with a higher composition of women in office reported higher competence and opportunity to participate in local activities. . . . Women in locals with a greater representation of women in office reported greater opportunity and desire to participate in local activities as compared with women in locals with lower representation. (pp. 714–716)

Ely (1995) argued that it was not just the proportion of women but where in the hierarchy of power they were located that mattered. Using both quantitative and qualitative data, she found that sex roles were more stereotyped and women rated themselves less positively in firms with relatively low proportions of senior women. But, Gutek, Cohen, and Konrad (1990), examining the sexual harassment of women at work, found that the higher the proportion of women up to a point, the more sexual behaviors and sexual harassment there was. The relationship was curvilinear, because in an organization that was composed solely or virtually entirely of women, there would be no sexual harassment. Their results reflected the greater amount of contact between men and women when there were more women in the work place.

An alternative perspective argues that women and minorities fare worse and face more discrimination when they are in larger proportions (Blalock, 1967). The logic is that "a larger minority is thought to represent a greater perceived threat to the economic and political security of the majority" (South et al., 1982, p. 587). If there are only one or a few women or minorities, these individuals themselves may face more pressure and less social support, but because they are few in number, they may be different but are not a threat. In larger numbers, they may be perceived as a threat or as competition, and this can engender more forceful hostility on the part of the majority. "Members of the majority group are assumed to respond to competitive threats posed by a large minority by actively denying minority group members access to . . . rewards" (p. 589). Writing about the effects of increasing proportions of women, Allmendinger and Hackman noted, "The Kanter position is that things will get better, mainly because of what the women are doing; the Blalock position is that things will get worse, mainly because of how the men are reacting" (1995, p. 427).

South and his colleagues administered a survey to employees in six offices of a government agency. They examined the effect of the gender composition of the work group on the frequency of contact with co-workers and the amount of encouragement for promotion from male and female co-workers as well as from a male supervisor. The results showed that there was less contact with male co-workers and more contact with female co-workers the higher the proportion of women in the work group, but there was no effect on the amount of contact with a male supervisor. There was no statistically significant effect of group gender composition on promotion encouragement from male co-workers, but the higher the proportion of women in the work group, the less encouragement there was from both the male supervisor and from female co-workers. South et al. (1982) argued that both contact and competition effects were important, and which was stronger depended not only on the particular proportions but also on the specific context. In another study of this issue, Toren (1990) found that the greater the proportion of women on the faculty of Israeli universities, the lower were their academic ranks relative to those of their male colleagues. And, Wharton and Baron (1987) reported that men in mixed-gender work settings had lower levels of job satisfaction.

Allmendinger and Hackman (1995) studied seventy-eight symphony orchestras in four countries that varied in the proportion of women members. This is a particularly appropriate setting, because "variation associated with both organizational tasks and member talent is relatively low across both orchestras and nations" (p. 428), eliminating alternative interpretations for the results of gender composition. The study collected questionnaire data from a sample of orchestra members on a number of dimensions including (1) the organizational features of the orchestra, such as integrity as an ensemble, player involvement, and recognition; (2) behavior of the music director; (3) orchestral processes, such as the quality of relationships and musical outcomes; (4) player motivation and satisfaction; and (5) specific satisfaction with features such as management, work relationships, and job security. They found that gender composition was significantly related to nineteen of twenty-two dependent variables, with there being less effect on the music director's behavior. "Almost all of the dependent measures decline significantly as the proportion of women in an orchestra increases from token to more substantial levels. However, 10 of the 19 significant effects exhibit a statistically significant reversal of the decline at some point on the gender composition spectrum" (p. 435). Moreover, ratings by observers of two features, integrity as an ensemble and orchestra structure, matched the members' survey descriptions and also evidenced a negative effect for increasing proportions of women (p. 443). The study also found that it was "*men* who respond most strongly to changes in organizational gender composition" (p. 443). The study is consistent with the view that "things really do get more difficult . . . as more women enter traditionally male organizations, at least until a state of gender balance is achieved" (p. 454). The importance of this line of work is to note that there are competitive effects from increasing the proportions of those in token status in a work context, and these need to be considered along with the effects of contact and social support.

Konrad, Winter, and Gutek have drawn a useful distinction between theories that consider proportions and numbers by themselves and those that bring in the status characteristics of those in greater or lesser proportion as being important in understanding organizational dynamics:

> "Generic" composition theories assume that the important factor affecting individuals in work groups is whether they are in the majority or in the minority and that the specific demographic characteristics of the majority and the minority do not add anything to the prediction of individual behavior and outcomes. . . . "Institutional" composition theories assume that members of different demographic groups will react differently to being in the minority or the majority, depending upon the social significance of particular demographic characteristics in society at large and in the particular organization. (1992, pp. 116–117)

Their data from eighty-nine work groups provided support for an "institutional" version of the effects of composition. The authors found that "women holding superior positions in predominantly male work groups experienced the most undesirable social outcomes of any group" (p. 116).

Although women themselves sometimes may do better in larger proportions, organizations and occupations in which they constitute a larger proportion frequently offer fewer rewards. For example, the proportion of women administrators in colleges and universities has been found to be negatively related to the salaries earned by both men and women administrators (Pfeffer and Davis-Blake, 1987). Baron and Newman (1990), studying the California Civil Service, reported that the proportion of women and minorities in a given job was negatively related to the prescribed salary for that job, even when education and experience requirements were controlled, and this effect helped explain changes in prescribed wage rates for positions in the state civil service over time. Shenhav and Haberfeld (1992) found that both men and women scientists in disciplines employing a higher proportion of women had lower earnings. England et al. (1988) have reviewed the extensive evidence demonstrating that, at the occupational level of analysis, wages are negatively related to the proportion of women in the occupation.

Pfeffer and Davis-Blake's study of academic administrators observed an important nonlinearity in the relationship between the proportion of women and wages. At very low and at very high percentages of women, when the addition of a few more women would not make a great deal of difference in how the organization and its work was seen, the negative effect of an increase in the proportion of women on salaries was less than around a tipping point, a value at which work apparently became reclassified as being "women's work" and consequently devalued.

The organization- or job-level effects of the proportion of women on wages probably occur because of the societal devaluation of women's work. It is important to note that these results contradict human capital theory, with its emphasis on individual abilities and experience, for they demonstrate a compositional effect on economic outcomes net of individual differences.

What may be of equal interest, however, are the more micro-level processes occurring within organizations that affect women's progress. These processes involve the availability of similar others with whom to form close relationships and the trade-off between network relations that provide social support through stronger ties and network relations that provide access to a wider range of information and contacts but entail weaker ties.

Because there are, in most organizations, fewer women (and minorities) in high-status positions in the hierarchy, in most contexts men and women differ in the opportunity to have informal interaction with same-gender others who are also instrumentally useful (Ibarra, 1992; 1993b). Because there are preferences for same-gender relationships, particularly for providing the social support that requires strong social ties, women have social networks and task-related, instrumental networks that overlap less than men's. Thus, the difference in men's and women's career attainment is not simply that men and women have different network structures—because there are no such differences (Brass, 1985; Ibarra, 1992)—but because men and women have different capabilities to convert positional resources into a network advantage (Ibarra, 1995). Harlan and Weiss (1982) reported that men and women managers did not differ in their reliance on informal networks. However, "women with minority status reported that access to influential groups required sustained effort, whereas men . . . reported that access was gained without effort" (Mellor, 1995, p. 707).

There is evidence that the position or prestige of an individual with whom a person is connected and how many contacts the person has with such individuals affect that person's mobility and occupational and wage attainment. "Access to people with specific resources . . . creates a correlation between theirs and yours" (Burt, 1992, p. 11). For instance, studies have demonstrated that the occupational prestige of a given person's job is affected by the occupational prestige of a personal contact leading to the job (Lin, 1982; Lin, Ensel, and Vaughn, 1981). Boxman, De Graaf, and Flap (1991) found that individuals with larger contact networks obtained positions that paid better than those with smaller networks.

The evidence also indicates that information networks that are larger and that have fewer indirect ties among those in the network (i.e., that have more structural holes [Burt, 1992]) are related to advancement (Burt, 1992; Podolny and Baron, 1995). In a study of the careers of senior managers in a high-technology firm, Burt found that "managers with networks rich in structural holes get promoted faster and at a younger age than do their peers" (1992, p. 115). Studying a high-technology company in California, Podolny and Baron (1995) found that mobility through the salary system in a one-year period was positively related to the number of new ties formed after the most recent shift in salary grade. This means that, in order to remain mobile, an individual must reconstruct his or her network on a continuing basis as that person's career advances, because each change in position means a change in the instrumentality of various actual and potential network ties.

But, if women are more likely to develop strong ties and if developing cross-gender ties are more difficult, then they are disadvantaged in their ability to develop new relationships compared to their male counterparts. Although some of this disadvantage may derive from gender-based differences in the importance of social (as contrasted with instrumental) ties, a lot of the difference is because of the difficulty of developing social support and task-related information networks that overlap and because of the scarcity of same-gender contacts as women advance in organizations.

Consistent with this line of reasoning, Ely (1994) found that women in firms with fewer women in senior positions were less likely to perceive senior women as role models, less likely to base identification on gender, more likely to perceive competition in their relations with women peers, and less likely, therefore, to find social support in their peer relationships. Ely's results support the view that the proportion of women in senior ranks in organizations is a critical variable, because it affects women's social identity and consequently the kinds of relationships they form and networks they build.

Similar issues confront minorities in organizations. Ibarra reported that "when human capital variables, such as tenure and graduate education, and positional resources, such as rank and potential for advancement, were held constant, minority and white middle managers in comparable jobs differed in the homophily and intimacy of their organizational network ties" (1995, p. 693), with minority ties being less homophilous and close. This evidence is consistent with structural constraints on network patterns, although the study also found strategic differences in network behavior that differentiated high-potential from other minority managers.

There is compelling evidence that network relations predict career success (e.g., Burt, 1992). This has led to discussions of the concept of social capital, to complement ideas such as human capital and cultural capital. Burt defined social capital as "at once the resources contacts hold and the structure of contacts in a network" (1992, p. 12). He distinguished social capital from human capital by noting that human capital is a property of an individual while social capital is "owned" jointly by the parties to a relationship. If the relationship is severed, one's social capital that originates in that relationship disappears. An individual's social capital depends on his or her structural position in the social system. Although there may be some ability to strategically affect one's social relations, this ability is clearly constrained by, among other things, the social composition of the environment in which one is operating. Also, building network ties and maintaining social relations takes time, and thus investment in networking must be balanced against alternative activities. The fact that studies of career attainment are able to explain variance from a knowledge of network relations provides support for the social model of behavior and for the importance of the social context in understanding organizations.

Conclusion

The available research evidence seems compelling that although demography is not destiny, there are important compositional effects on perseverance and conservatism in decision making, interpersonal conflict and turnover, and social integration and communication. Demographic similarity affects the choice of those placed in positions of authority. The literature clearly suggests that compositional effects in organizations and work groups are consequential and that these structural factors constitute a powerful environment within which other processes operate. Therefore, this literature means that (1) one of the ways in which the environment affects organizations is through demographic processes and (2) environmental determinism is limited in its explanatory power, simply because different organizational demographies often lead to different organizational behavior even in similar environments.

Compositional effects constrain the operation of network processes, as the literature on women and minorities in organizations nicely illustrates. One's social network is affected, although not completely determined, by the comparative availability of different types of individuals in the immediate environment. In this sense, the study of organizational demography complements the social model of behavior, with its emphasis on social influence, which often operates through interpersonal networks or structural equivalence. Composition helps to determine the content of those influences and the composition of the networks through which social influence travels.

In a fashion similar to other areas of organization studies, there has been a tendency to overlook the structural context within which individual behavior occurs. The leadership literature is a good example of this, in its neglect of the effect of managerial team composition on leader behavior. What the research on demography and social context has done is to bring these issues of structural constraint back into focus. A large number of substantively important empirical contributions suggest that one ignores the effects of social composition at some peril. Demography has a tendency to perpetuate itself—to use Kanter's (1977) apt phrase, to exhibit "homosocial reproduction." And demography has effects on organizations ranging from innovation and change to strategic decision making to the welfare of women and minorities in those organizations. As such, the study of organizational demography reminds us yet again of the social, relational nature of organizations and has provided both theoretical ideas and some empirical apparatus for taking these ideas seriously.

5

Mechanisms of Social Control

The various models for understanding organizations developed in chapters 3 and 4 and the discussion in chapter 2 concerning the locus for causality of behavior have as their goal being able to explain, predict, and ultimately influence organizational behavior. Although each perspective has its own specific implications for controlling behavior, control is at once the essential problem of management and organization and the implicit focus of much of organization studies. As Braverman noted, "control is . . . the central concept for all management systems" (1974, p. 68) and is a fundamental issue in organizations.

Organizations, after all, are composed of individuals who are working interdependently to produce some good or service. Even holding aside issues of incentives and motivation, the very fact of interdependence requires coordination to ensure that activity results in the efficient production of the organization's output. What would happen in an automobile plant if there were no social controls of any kind to determine when people would start work and what they would do? Almost certainly there would be chaos. Coordination and control are necessary, and how to achieve these ends efficiently and, in some formulations, humanely, are fundamental organizational issues. Kunda has written:

> Purposeful collective action, whatever its circumstances, requires the coordination of activities of a diverse and heterogeneous membership. There is, however, an inherent conflict between demands organizations place on the time and efforts of their members and the desires and needs of members when left to their own devices. Thus, the age-old management dilemma: how to cause members to behave in ways compatible with organizational goals. (1992, p. 11)

The various models of behavior have quite different implications for how to best achieve the requisite level of social control and coordination, and assumptions about human behavior inevitably undergird all organizational control systems. What is often not done, either by the theorists or by organizational managers, is to make these assumptions explicit. O'Reilly and Chatman provided a good definition of control in organizational settings: "control comes from the knowledge that someone who matters to us is paying close attention to what we are doing and will tell us if our behavior is appropriate or inappropriate" (1996, p. 161).

The control process begins with recruiting and selection, in which organizations try to find individuals who already possess necessary skills and attitudes that make them good prospects for being productive. Uncovering who is a good employment prospect and possesses the requisite qualities is inevitably an uncertain undertaking. One cannot always directly observe motivation, diligence, or intelligence. Consequently, in the recruiting process, organizations frequently rely on signals or proxies for the underlying quality being sought.

> According to Spence (1974), a signal is any observable indicator, of a quality or qualities, that meets two criteria: (1) the indicator must be at least partially manipulable by the actor and (2) the marginal cost or difficulty of obtaining the indicator must be nonzero and inversely correlated with the actor's level of quality. A college diploma is a signal of productivity because its attainment is at least partially within an individual's control and because it is more difficult for those who lack organizational skills (or other such attributes that help constitute productivity) to obtain a college degree. (Podolny, 1993, p. 831)

R. Collins (1979) has analyzed the use of educational credentials as a hiring criterion, in particular as signals of conformity to social values including diligence, motivation, and fitting in. His review of the evidence indicated that the rise in the level of education in the United States could not be traced to technical factors such as the changing skill mix of occupations or to the upgraded skill requirements within occupations. Rather, there is evidence that "education has been used as a means of cultural selection" (p. 32). R. Collins (1974; 1979) developed a theory of hiring criteria based on the organizational requirements for loyalty. He argued that "public trust" organizations–organizations emphasizing "a public image of service, ideals, safeguards and/or confidentiality" (1979, p. 33)– would require more loyalty than market organizations. He found that, net of size, technological change, and other factors, public trust organizations did have higher educational requirements than did market organizations, and that at virtually all employee levels, the organization's control type was the single most important predictor of educational requirements (p. 42). Edwards (1976) also noted that organizational selection procedures often seemed to reward conformity and the willingness to subordinate oneself to social controls.

The existing theory and evidence suggests that (1) selection is an important part of the control process; (2) conformity to social norms and dominant cultural values is an important criteria being sought, particularly by certain types of organizations; and (3) because such characteristics are difficult to observe directly, indirect indicators or signals, such as educational attainment and job stability, are often used by organizations seeking employees with those characteristics.

Once hired, individuals encounter varying degrees of socialization and training (Pascale, 1985) to help them understand what is expected and to come to want to do those activities. Individuals also receive wages, the possibility of promotion, and other benefits—incentives designed to induce them to remain in the organization and to work hard in its interests. Also, people work most often in hierarchies under supervision. How well they are led may also affect their attitudes and behavior.

Because control and coordination are such ubiquitous issues, virtually the entire organizations literature concerns this topic, at least indirectly. This chapter discusses four mechanisms of social control: (1) the use of rewards and incentives, including "negative" rewards and surveillance; (2) commitment and socialization processes; (3) organizational culture; and (4) leadership. Each of these processes is a fundamental mechanism of social control in organizational settings and is intended to direct and motivate behavior, and each has stimulated substantial research and theoretical interest and controversy.

There is an important difference in emphasis across these mechanisms of social control. Rewards and incentives work primarily on the environment of employees, and the literature on organizational rewards almost invariably proceeds from the presumptions of the economic model of behavior. As such, reviewing the literature on rewards and compensation will permit us to see in yet another research context to what extent the predictions of the economic model of behavior are, in fact, empirically supported and under what circumstances. The use of rewards and incentives as mechanisms of organizational control varies over time and place depending on the degree of acceptance and dominance of the economic perspective on organizational behavior. By contrast, commitment, culture, and some aspects of leadership try to engage and change fundamental decision premises, self-perceptions, beliefs, and values and frequently work on the emotions using social psychological principles, using the heart as well as the head. As such, these control strategies are premised largely on the retrospectively rational and, to a lesser extent, the social and moral models of behavior.

Interest in rewards and incentives—a rational basis of control—and normative control, based importantly on social psychological principles, has waxed and waned over time and, contrary to some accounts (Edwards, 1979), has not simply evolved from coercive to normative control (Barley and Kunda, 1992). Table 5-1 reproduces Barley and Kunda's depiction of the succession of different managerial

Table 5-1   Succession of Managerial Ideologies

Ideology	Era of Ascent	Tenor
Industrial betterment	1870–1900	Normative
Scientific management	1900–1923	Rational
Welfare capitalism/human relations	1923–1955	Normative
Systems rationalism	1955–1980	Rational
Organizational culture	1980–present	Normative

From Barley and Kunda, 1992, p. 364.

ideologies over time. These bases of control have fluctuated over time because of the fundamental tension between community and individual self-interest that forms the basis for the various control systems:

> each sensed that industrialization was problematic because it juxtaposed two contrasting paradigms for social order. These two forms of social organization were given different names by different scholars. Weber wrote of the "communal" and the "associative." Durkheim contrasted "mechanistic" with "organic" solidarity. . . . However, the essence of their vision was the same. In a Gemeinschaft, people share a common identity, are bound by common values and traditions, and partake of a way of life that contrasts sharply with the competition, individualism, and calculative self-interest associated with the Gesellschaft. The central dilemma identified . . . concerned the integrity of the social fabric. How could relations based on utilitarianism and rational calculation remain integrated and socially fulfilling? (p. 385)

Barley and Kunda found no evidence that changes in managerial ideology followed changes in the quality of labor relations in the United States. Although "heightened labor activity may . . . have fanned interest in human relations during the 1940s . . . rhetorics of organizational culture and commitment unambiguously arose in an era of declining labor militancy" (1992, p. 389). Rather, they found that "surges of normative and rational theorizing occurred, respectively, in conjunction with periods of contraction or expansion" (p. 391). They argued, "Rational and normative rhetorics both promise managers greater productivity and profitability but advocate radically different means for obtaining these ends. . . . Rational rhetorics should surge when profitability seems most linked to the management of capital. Conversely, normative rhetorics should surge when profitability seems to depend more on the management of labor" (p. 389).

Their study of the shifting language and preference for control of different types reminds us that particular control strategies are invariably historically and contextually located. That makes it important to understand how mechanisms of organizational control vary not only across time but also across different social contexts. Technologies of organizational control, and the models on which they are implicitly or explicitly premised, are neither timeless nor ubiquitous in their validity, a factor seldom acknowledged in the relevant literatures.

Rewards, Incentives, Sanctions, and Surveillance

There are a number of fundamental issues in the literature on rewards and incentives:

1. What determines the incentive structure organizations actually employ with different groups of people? For instance, why is there pay for performance on an individual basis in some organizations but pay for seniority in others? Within a given organization, why are some jobs paid more on the basis of individual performance than others?
2. What are the effects of various amounts, forms, and distributions

of incentives on individual and organizational behavior and performance?

3. To administer contingent rewards, there must be some degree of monitoring or surveillance of either behavior or results. What are the effects of this surveillance?

4. In addition to the use of incentives and rewards, there is also the
possibility of controlling behavior through punishment or sanctions.
What determines when these are used and what are their effects?

Throughout the discussion that follows, I focus on pay, which is the principal
(although not the only) reward in organizations. But A. Kohn (1993) argues that
the issue isn't what is given as a reward but rather the fact that something—
praise, a prize, or pay—is provided contingent on the focal person exhibiting
some desired behavior. Thus, the issues and principles discussed are general, but
the focus on pay has the advantage of more directly engaging a lot of the empirical literature and confronting the predictions of the economic model most directly. Although there has recently been much more empirical research on pay
practices in organizations, stimulated by the availability of data sets on managerial
compensation collected by various compensation consulting firms, definitive answers to any of the questions posed must await further research.

There are several facts one needs to keep in mind in thinking about these
issues. First, the bases of rewards are changing, particularly in the United States
but almost certainly elsewhere as well. One basic dimension of the change is the
growing emphasis on variable pay—pay that changes depending on the performance (or skill) of the individual, his or her work group, or organization and a
corresponding deemphasis on paying simply for time worked or for seniority. The
change can be seen most dramatically in the pay of senior managers such as chief
executive officers. Useem (1996), studying the compensation of the seven top
executives from forty-five large companies over the period 1982–1995, reported
that the proportion of managers' total compensation that was variable increased
from 37 percent to 61 percent. The proportion of variable pay for CEOs increased even more, from 41 percent in 1982 to 70 percent, in 1995. The biggest
change was an increase in the use of long-term incentive pay.

Nor is the increase in variable pay plans confined to senior management.
Ledford, Lawler, and Mohrman (1995) reported the results from surveys of the
pay practices of the Fortune 1000 (the 500 largest industrial and 500 largest service firms) conducted in 1987, 1990, and 1993. Between 1987 and 1993, the
proportion of firms using individual incentives for at least 20 percent of their work
force increased from 38 percent to 50 percent; the proportion using gain sharing
for at least some of the work force increased from 7 percent to 16 percent; and
the proportion of firms that had an employee stock ownership plan covering at
least 20 percent of the work force increased from 53 percent to 62 percent. The
proportion of firms using profit sharing for some of the work force actually declined slightly over the period, from 45 percent to 43 percent. Although the
growth in some of these innovations in incentives is modest, there is little doubt
that there is much more experimentation occurring with incentives throughout

organizations (Kanter, 1987), with the emphasis being to link pay to performance, thereby making pay more contingent or variable. Increased use of variable pay is also evident in other countries besides the United States. Wood, in a study of 135 manufacturing plants in the United Kingdom, reported that "some form of merit pay was claimed to be used in 50 per cent of plants, and profit-sharing in 25 per cent, and moreover, the adoption of both increased between 1986 and 1990, by 13 per cent in the case of merit pay and 8 per cent in the case of profit-sharing" (1996, p. 60).

This movement is quite consistent with operant conditioning principles (e.g., Skinner, 1953; Luthans and Kreitner, 1975), which emphasize the connection between actions and their consequences. These changes are congruent with the economic model of behavior, with its emphasis on incentives, particularly externally controlled and administered incentives, as being important. Indeed, one of the important challenges to the economic model has been the historically relatively small relationship between pay and performance, even for senior-level executives (Baker, Jensen, and Murphy, 1988). Jensen and Murphy noted, "actual compensation contracts look very different form those predicted by economic theory. The failure of theory to explain actual compensation arrangements suggests that the theory is wrong" (1987, p. 43).

Second, reward practices vary dramatically across organizations and even more dramatically across cultures. There are large, well-known, and effective firms (e.g., Mars Candy, Southwest Airlines) that use virtually no merit pay. There are others, such as Hewlett-Packard, that do use individual merit pay. There are countries, with Japan and Korea being notable cases, in which pay is based primarily on seniority, to a lesser extent on position, and virtually not at all on individual differences in merit or performance, although these practices may be changing. There are companies and countries in which pay is emphasized as the primary mechanism for controlling and directing behavior, and there are countries and companies in which pay is deemphasized, with control being achieved in other ways and rewards and recognition being more symbolic than economic. The distribution of rewards also varies dramatically across companies and cultures, with large dispersion in rewards characteristic of some but not others.

This substantial variation in pay practices is interesting and important for two reasons. First, if some pay practices were invariably more effective than others regardless of the context, one would expect to see more uniform adoption of these more effective practices as a response to competitive pressure. Second, because of the strong ideological component of pay—practices are frequently based more on beliefs about behavior than on hard evidence (A. Kohn, 1993)—this is a topic in which there is much more good theory than field-based empirical results that inform the theory. Thus, there is an important opportunity for research progress.

Determinants of Pay and Pay Systems in Organizations

What do we know about how pay is determined and why it varies across organizations? Unfortunately, not as much as we might like. Mitchell, Lewin, and Lawler concluded their review of the compensation literature by stating, "The use of alternative pay systems in the American labor market is a result of a complex set of economic, historical, and institutional forces. A folk wisdom has grown up around the different types of plans" (1990, p. 87). Much of what we do know about pay and incentive schemes is, however, at variance with predictions from the economic model of behavior.

We know that pay is less differentiated in union as contrasted with nonunion settings and that pay is more strongly related to seniority and is seldom related to individual performance differences in unionized work places (Freeman and Medoff, 1984). We know that even in nonunion private corporations that have performance appraisals and presumably some form of merit pay, pay is often significantly related to seniority and is not much related to performance if at all (Medoff and Abraham, 1980; 1981). There are substantial gender and race effects on pay (Jacobs, 1992; Johnson, 1978; Sigelman, Milward, and Shepard, 1982), evidence of discrimination in the wage determination process and that economic returns are affected by more than an individual's human capital.

Leonard (1990), in a study of about 20,000 executives, found that pay was related to the degree of organizational hierarchy—executives in flatter hierarchies earned less. Lambert, Larcker, and Weigelt (1993), studying more than 4,000 executives in 303 different companies, found that the relationship between pay and other factors such as performance, the number of people supervised, or chief executive power varied greatly across industries. This suggests that managerial labor markets are not completely efficient and that there are important industry (and undoubtedly company and national) differences in the wage determination process.

In a challenge to strictly economic, efficiency-based conceptions of the pay determination process, Lambert and his colleagues found effects of managerial power on pay. For instance, they reported a positive association between the level of executive compensation and the percentage of the external board members who had been appointed by the chief executive; they also reported statistically significant effects for virtually all of their other measures of managerial power such as the percentage of stock owned by the chief executive. Other evidence also suggests the importance of power in the salary determination process. A study by Pfeffer and Konrad (1991) of academic salaries found that power had a main effect on pay and positively affected the returns to research productivity and years of experience, with more powerful individuals enjoying greater returns. Several indicators of individual power were employed in that study: (1) receiving outside research funding, (2) having an outside job offer, (3) extensive contact and communication with individuals in other institutions, and (4) a scale composed of responses to questions asking about the level of involvement in departmental affairs and perceptions of opportunities to influence policies in the department and in the broader institution. Moore and Pfeffer (1980) found that more powerful departments on two campuses of the University of California were able to achieve greater acceleration in salaries for their faculty members even when measures of departmental quality and size were controlled.

A study of Australian establishments (Drago and Heywood, 1995) explored predictions from the so-called new economics of personnel literature (Hart and Holmstrom, 1987), which relates pay schemes to the ease of monitoring worker effort, as well as predictions from the managerial strategic choice literature (Kochan, Katz, and McKersie, 1986). The reported results for the use of various pay systems such as piece rate, group pay, and profit sharing were both complex and did not consistently support either theoretical perspective. For instance, the use of piece rates was *positively* related to the proportion of long-tenured employees. This result is exactly opposite to the predictions of the new economics of personnel literature, which argues that "firms will tend to avoid more immediate wage incentives, such as piece rates, where the expected job tenure of workers is long, since increasing wages over the employees' life-cycle provides a less costly alternative" (Drago and Heywood, 1995, p. 508). They also reported that the use of piece rates was *higher* the larger the proportion of managers, which contradicts the prediction that individual incentives provide an alternative to direct supervision. And they reported that the use of piece rates was less the *larger* the proportion of casual labor—but one would expect that it would be casual workers, with no long-term attachment to the organization or their fellow workers, who would most require individual incentives to induce effort. They did find, consistent with the strategic choice–managerial strategy predictions, that there was more use of profit sharing in organizations that had quality circles or other systems to encourage worker participation.

Wood's (1996) study of U.K. manufacturing plants found no statistically significant relationship between the use of high-commitment work practices and any particular payment system. His study did find that the proportion of pay comprised of profit sharing payments was associated with the use of high-commitment work practices, which means that "when profit-sharing is taken seriously, it is likely to be in conjunction with" high-commitment management (p. 64).

We know that pay is strongly related to performance in professional sports (e.g., Harder, 1992), but even here there is some evidence of racial discrimination (Kahn and Sherer, 1988; Scully, 1974). Of course, performance is quite measurable in professional sports, and, moreover, there is an efficient national labor market (for experienced players who can change teams) that makes the strong pay–performance connection expected.

From a study of college and university faculty (Konrad and Pfeffer, 1990), we know that research productivity, a measure of performance, had a larger effect on pay in private, higher quality institutions, in institutions governed by collective bargaining agreements, in institutions in which there was more collaboration on research and more social contact among faculty, in departments that had chairpersons with shorter, fixed-length terms and had norms emphasizing research, and in fields with more highly developed scientific paradigms. However, even in contexts in which productivity could be readily assessed and in which merit was ostensibly emphasized, the effect of productivity on salary was quite small. Being one standard deviation above the mean for research productivity produced only a 5.5 percent increment in salary. The results suggest that paying for productivity is more likely where productivity can be more unambiguously assessed (fields with more-developed paradigms), in contexts in which there is more contact (both social and research), which also provides more information about performance, and in places where the social norms and values emphasize productivity.

The interpretation that paying for productivity is more likely when there is less uncertainty and ambiguity about measuring performance and administering salaries makes sense of the apparently anomalous finding that returns to productivity were actually *higher* in institutions in which faculty were covered by collective bargaining agreements. Konrad and Pfeffer noted that "unions . . . open the salary determination process to scrutiny by the members and instill due-process procedures that increase the certainty . . . in the salary determination process. In the absence of collective bargaining, salaries may be determined by the arbitrary and occasionally secret decisions of administrators" (1990, p. 265). Although some unions have eschewed merit-based considerations in determining pay, the American Association of University Professors "advocated a more professional system in which teaching and research excellence would be rewarded" (p. 265). The results from the study overall support the importance of perceptions of fairness in process as being a necessary condition for pay to reflect productivity.

We are inclined to think of faculty labor markets as being reasonably efficient. Faculty have few organization-specific skills and interorganizational mobility is frequent. Efficient labor markets are presumed to result in fairly equal returns to dimensions of human capital or performance regardless of where one is located. But Konrad and Pfeffer reported that context—the particular organization and its attributes—mattered a great deal in determining returns to productivity:

> Consider those individuals who were in settings that were above the median, simultaneously, on resource levels, paradigm development, research emphasis, research collaboration, and who worked in high quality institutions. . . . Individuals producing research at a rate that is one standard deviation above the mean in their fields lost more in salaries if they were in the wrong organizational context than they would have lost had they simply worked less hard and produced less research, falling to the mean level. (1990, p. 277)

There is evidence from a study of college and university administrators (Pfeffer and Davis-Blake, 1990) that there is less pay dispersion in public colleges (where salaries are more likely to be known), when there is more promotion from within, and in more socially homogeneous organizations. A study of wage dispersion in more than 1,800 academic departments (Pfeffer and Langton, 1988) found greater inequality in wages in private colleges, in larger departments, and in settings in which people tended to work on research alone. More social contact among department members and more participative departmental governance were both associated with less dispersed salaries. The evidence is consistent with the explanation that more social contact and publicness of information diminish salary inequality in organizations.

Given the prominence of the economic model of behavior, with its emphasis on incentives, the question naturally arises as to why there has not been more incentive-based compensation or why incentives are so small even when performance can be fairly unambiguously assessed (Frank, 1984). Lazear (1989) has argued that when teamwork and cooperation are important, individually based rewards can reduce the incentive to cooperate. Milgrom and Roberts (1988) have argued that merit systems that provide very different rewards can encourage unproductive political behaviors as individuals jockey for those rewards.

Studying this issue empirically, Pfeffer and Davis-Blake (1992) found that salary differentiation was related to turnover among academic administrators, with those lower in the salary distribution being particularly affected by pay dispersion. Pfeffer and Langton (1993), studying college and university faculty, found that the greater the pay dispersion, the lower the job satisfaction, and that paying for performance and greater pay dispersion were associated with diminished levels of research productivity and with a smaller likelihood of working collaboratively on research. They noted that such adverse effects of wage dispersion were particularly pronounced for individuals with shorter tenure (who were less committed), in public colleges (where pay is more likely to be known), and in departments that had less highly developed scientific paradigms (there was less consensus on standards of evaluation and performance). Cowherd and Levine (1992), using a sample of 102 business units, compared the pay and inputs of lower-level employees to those of top management to compute a measure of pay equity. They found that the greater the degree of pay equity across classes of employees, the higher was the level of product quality. Thus, one answer as to why there is not more use of differentiated incentives is that at least in some contexts they have negative consequences.

Many of the studies of pay determination process have focused on CEO pay. The basic message of these studies is that, at least historically, there has been either no or a very weak relationship between CEO pay and company performance, where performance is measured in almost any way (Crystal, 1991; Main, O'Reilly, and Wade, 1995; Miller, 1995). Instead, CEO pay seems to be related to organizational size, to the industry in which one works—with there being a premium for working in unregulated and more competitive and risky industries—and to the composition of the compensation committee of the board of directors. O'Reilly, Main, and Crystal (1988) found that there were important social influences in the pay determination process (see also Main, O'Reilly, and Wade, 1995). Specifically, CEOs in companies in which members of the compensation committee were themselves more highly compensated in their own roles as CEOs earned more, controlling for other factors—a result the authors interpreted as meaning that salaries were set in a process of social comparison. Compensation committee members who themselves were well paid would be more generous when setting the salaries of others because those salaries would not look high by comparison. O'Reilly and his colleagues also discovered that this result was particularly strong when the compensation committee directors had joined the board after the CEO had assumed his position—which probably meant that they owed their positions to the CEO and therefore were more under his influence. Main et al. (1995) further reported that demographic similarity between CEOs and members of the compensation committee, an important basis of interpersonal attraction (Berscheid and Walster, 1969), was positively related to CEO pay.

The literature on CEO pay has attempted to provide an explanation for the increasing difference in pay between CEOs and the rest of the organization—an explanation that is consistent with principles of economic efficiency—by developing a tournament model of executive compensation. The theoretical problem is nicely described by Lazear and Rosen (1981, p. 847): "On the day that a given individual is promoted from vice-president to president, his salary may triple. It is difficult to argue that his skills have tripled in that one-day period, presenting difficulties for standard theory" that relates wages to human capital or to productivity. The basic idea behind the tournament model is that vice presidents (or those one level below the CEO) compete for the top job. In order to induce maximum effort, the "prize"—the salary earned when one achieves that position—must be sufficient to compensate for the effort and the probability of achieving the prize. So, Rosen (1986) "has shown that top prizes of a disproportionate size are theoretically necessary to motivate tournament survivors so they will not rest on past achievements or winning as they enter the final contest. Elevating the top prize has the effect of lengthening the career ladder for high-ranking contestants" (O'Reilly et al., 1988, p. 260).

The predictions of the tournament model are straightforward—the lower the probability of winning the contest, or the greater the number of contestants, the greater the difference in salary should be to compensate for this reduced expected payoff. This model would suggest, for instance, that as organizations have flattened their hierarchies, salary differences across levels would be expected to increase to induce effort on the part of those who now have a lower expectation of being advanced because of the greater number of people competing for the fewer number of promotions. In one empirical test of this model, its predictions were found not to hold. O'Reilly et al. (1988, p. 266) reported that, controlling for other factors, the number of vice presidents was *negatively* related to CEO compensation (and to the difference between the salaries of CEOs and vice presidents). Moreover, also inconsistent with tournament ideas, the average vice-presidential salary was positively related to CEO salary. The fact that the tournament model is inconsistent with the evidence has, unfortunately, not diminished its popularity as an explanation for the rise in CEO compensation.

It is possible and indeed likely that because of the prevalence, particularly in the United States, of belief in the economic model and its associated assumptions, pay systems may be designed for legitimation—to signal to outsiders that the firm is well managed and doing the right thing by implementing incentives to tie senior executive pay to performance. Westphal and Zajac (1994) studied 570 of the largest corporations over a two-decade period, examining not only which firms adopted long-term incentive plans but which firms actually used them. They discovered that a substantial fraction of firms announcing the adoption of long-term incentive schemes in their proxy statements never actually used such plans to set compensation and that this separation between form and substance was particularly likely in organizations that had poor prior performance and powerful chief executives. This result suggests that pay and pay systems have important symbolic and legitimating aspects.

Evidence on the Effects of Incentives

The effects of incentives, particularly individual incentive schemes, are empirically ambiguous, in sharp contrast to the claims made in some of the economics literature about optimal incentive arrangements. The literature on the effects of pay is plagued with methodological problems, and most of the studies that use existing compensation data bases and that claim to examine the effects of incentives fail virtually completely in this effort. This is because of the failure to control for a number of highly plausible alternative interpretations of the results. Most important, it is critical to distinguish between *incentive* effects, which are presumed to result from increased motivation and diligence, and *information* effects. Incentive schemes do more than just motivate effort. They also tell people specifically what is valued and comparatively more important in the particular setting and how, therefore, to allocate attention and effort among competing objectives. In that sense, incentives are similar to goal setting (E. A. Locke and Latham, 1990), establishing explicit objectives and letting individuals know what is expected and important. The goal-setting literature is quite clear that setting specific and demanding goals, by itself, can have a powerful effect on performance (e.g., E. A. Locke and Bryan, 1966; E. A. Locke, Frederick, Lee, and Bobko, 1984; E. A. Locke and Latham, 1990). Moreover, the introduction of incentives is also frequently accompanied by the introduction of information—about workers' performance and productivity, for instance, or about workers' productivity compared to some standard or to that of other workers. This information is often new as productivity data or comparisons may have been nonexistent in the work place. Knowledge of results has also been found to have profound effects on behavior and to be one of the elements that determines the motivating potential of jobs (e.g., Hackman and Oldham, 1980). Few studies, particularly those relying on archival data, have recognized these critical theoretical distinctions, and virtually none have attempted to empirically examine them.

There is another important methodological issue that plagues many if not most of the studies of the effects of incentive systems. The choice of pay system parameters is not exogenous, and "differences in pay policies may reflect systematic forces. . . . Failure to model the causes of variation in pay policies . . . may bias . . . empirical results" (Ehrenberg, 1990, p. 90).

Why might incentives not work? Incentives can actually undermine intrinsic motivation, as already discussed, and can also undermine performance on tasks that require higher levels of judgment and creativity. Amabile (1985) found that having creative writers just think five minutes about receiving a reward caused them to write less creatively. Amabile, Hennessey, and Grossman (1986) found that on a series of tasks ranging from making collages to inventing stories and using subjects of various ages, the simple promise of reward diminished creativity. Summaries of the research literature on the effects of rewards (McGraw, 1978; A. Kohn, 1993) suggest that rewards are particularly detrimental to performance when the tasks are intrinsically interesting enough that rewards aren't necessary and when the task is complex enough that there are no simple steps to solve it.

In considering the effects of incentives, it is important to recognize that contingent pay or pay for performance can be based on individual performance, subunit or work-group performance, the performance of the entire organization, or some combination. Welbourne and Cable have noted that "very little is known about how employees covered by various group incentives interpret the programs" (1995, p. 712). They also noted the absence of literature on the effects of group incentives on job satisfaction. There have been studies of some forms of group incentives, such as gainsharing, stock ownership, and profit sharing on organizational-level outcomes (e.g., Kaufman, 1992; Weitzman and Kruse, 1990; Rosen, Klein, and Young, 1986; Jones and Kato, 1993). There has not been much study of the effects of group or organizational incentives on individual behavior and attitudes. The distinction among the unit of analysis rewarded should be kept in mind in thinking about incentives and behavior.

It is also the case that wage incentives are effective only to the extent that the measurement system that underlies them measures the right thing. Most incentive systems are premised on the idea of individual merit and confront the problem of interdependence. They all too often solve this problem by measuring the wrong thing, and not very well. Simon provided a compelling critique of the typical pay scheme and why it would probably not be effective:

> If the indices used to measure outcomes are inappropriate, either because they do not measure the right variables, or because they do not properly identify individual contributions, then reward systems can be grossly inefficient or even counterproductive. . . . In general, the greater the interdependence among various members of the organization, the more difficult it is to measure their separate contributions. . . . But of course, intense interdependence is precisely what makes it advantageous to organize people instead of depending wholly on market transactions. . . . Although economic rewards play an important part in securing adherence to organizational goals and management authority, they are limited in their effectiveness. Organizations would be far less effective systems than they actually are if such rewards were the only means, or even the principal means, of motivation available. (1991, pp. 33–34)

As implied by the foregoing discussion, the evidence on the effects of variations in pay policies in organizations on performance is mixed. Leonard (1990) found that firms with long-term incentive plans enjoyed greater increases in return on equity over the period 1981–1985, but he also reported that corporate success was not related to the *level* of executive pay or to the steepness of the pay differentials across ranks—a measure of the reward for achieving promotion. Abowd (1990), in a study of 16,000 managers, found that the sensitivity of managerial compensation to performance was related to measures of shareholder return but not to accounting measures of performance. This result is somewhat surprising, since executive pay tends to be set more frequently on the basis of the achievement of objectives measured by the accounting system. Asch (1990), examining an incentive program for navy recruiters, found a positive effect of financial incentives, but there were also some negative results. The best recruiters (based on historical data) produced less as they approached the prize eligibility date, and after winning a prize, recruiters enlisted fewer recruits. Studying managers in a single company, Kahn and Sherer (1990) reported that managers for whom bonuses were most sensitive to performance performed better the following year, even when past performance was statistically controlled. However, the same study found that differences in the sensitivity of merit pay to performance had no significant effects on subsequent performance—thus, bonuses had an effect on performance but merit pay did not.

A longitudinal study tracing the implementation of merit pay in a government bureaucracy reported no relationship between merit pay and performance (Pearce, Stevenson, and Perry, 1985). Marsden and Richardson (1994), studying the use of individual performance pay in the Inland Revenue department in the United Kingdom, reported that performance pay had little motivational effect and may have demotivated some employees.

In a study of 8,000 workers in the United States and Japan, Levine (1993) found that employees receiving high wages were less likely to quit, were more satisfied with their pay, and reported a higher level of effort on the job. These results support the idea that paying above-market wages may be rational because it results in lower turnover costs and more employee effort, but Levine's data do not speak to the issue of the effects of contingent pay practices.

The principal controversy in the pay literature concerns the use of individual incentives (as contrasted with group or organizational incentives), and particularly the effectiveness of contingent or merit pay. Deming and many other of the quality gurus have bemoaned the use of individual merit pay, arguing that it frequently rewards or punishes workers for things over which they have little control, since they don't often control the system of production within which they work (Gabor, 1990). They also maintained that merit pay practices often leave workers discouraged and dissatisfied and create internal organizational competition and conflict.

Other authors have noted that individual merit pay practices are inconsistent with many of the underlying precepts of high-commitment work practices. For instance, Beer et al. maintained that "by making pay contingent upon performance (as judged by management), management is signaling that it is they—not the individual—who are in control" (1984, p. 114). Consequently, "performance-related pay may lower the individual's feeling of competence and self-determination and run counter to an intrinsic reward policy" (Wood, 1996, p. 55). Because "out-put based incentive schemes, and particularly piecework, are . . . very much identified . . . with the past emphasis on a Taylorist control strategy and the ills associated with it" (p. 56), many argue that piecework and other individual incentive schemes conflict with the ideas of commitment, involvement, and intrinsic motivation.

Besser's study of pay practices at Toyota Motor Manufacturing in Kentucky found evidence of high productivity, quality, and discretionary effort in a work setting in which equal pay was the norm—"81 percent of TMM's employees receive roughly the same pay with distinctions based on job category, not individual performance" (1995, p. 388) Besser noted that most motivation theories (e.g., Lawler, 1981) focused on the individual and took what motivated the particular individual as given. By contrast, "Cole's (1979) contention and the argument of this paper is that large Japanese firms take a much more active role in shaping

employee motivation than organizations are usually given credit for. They do this
. . . by turning small work groups and company ideology into official reward
mechanisms with powerful consequences for individual motivation" (p. 387). Adler's (1992) study of New United Motor Manufacturing also documented an instance of extremely limited use of differential monetary rewards in a system that
was highly effective by any measure.

A good portion of the literature on the effects of incentives has focused on
the connection between CEO incentive schemes and organizational performance. This research is frequently plagued by two problems. One is that the
choice of incentives is not exogenous. For instance, a CEO who anticipates improved corporate performance and a rising stock price is much more likely to
want to be paid with stock options or incentive compensation. Thus, a study that
simply finds a contemporaneous correlation between incentive compensation and
performance may have the causality reversed—the incentives may be implemented because of the enhanced performance (Leonard, 1990). Second, the assumptions that CEOs, already exceedingly well compensated, will work harder
for some extra compensation and that a single individual, even a CEO, can profoundly affect the performance of large organizations are both suspect. There is
little evidence, for instance, that CEOs who have long-term incentives as part of
their compensation package in fact manage companies who do better in terms of
economic returns over time (Crystal, 1991; but, see Leonard, 1990).

There are more consistent results on the effects of incentives in studies of
sports. There is, for instance, evidence that larger prizes produce better scores in
golf tournaments (Ehrenberg and Bognanno, 1988; 1990), even controlling for
the quality of the players who choose to participate. A study of race car drivers
found that larger prizes produced greater speed but also more accidents (Becker
and Huselid, 1992). Of course, many sports, including golf and race car driving,
involve comparatively little interdependence among the contestants. This absence
of important task-related interdependence is the exception, rather than the rule,
in most work organizations. Consequently, results from studies of incentive effects
in sports need to be generalized to other settings with some caution.

Monitoring and Surveillance

In order to reward or sanction behavior or results, one must be able to assess
them. The development of electronic monitoring capability has undoubtedly
shifted the balance toward monitoring behavior as contrasted with monitoring
outcomes, but in either case surveillance has important consequences. By 1990,
more than 10 million workers were subjected to electronic performance monitoring. Moreover, this monitoring is moving from covering only fairly low-skilled
workers doing simple tasks (such as data input or telephone work) to work done
by professional, technical, and managerial employees (e.g., Garson, 1988). For
instance, physician treatment practices, such as the number of drugs prescribed
or tests ordered, are increasingly gathered in data bases, compared to norms, and
used to influence physician behavior.

There is evidence that electronic performance monitoring results in increased stress (Amick and Smith, 1992; Smith, et al., 1992; Irving, Higgins, and Safayeni, 1986), decreased job satisfaction (Irving, et al., 1986; Grant and Higgins, 1989), increased feelings of social isolation (Aiello, 1993), and an increased tendency to believe that the quantity of work is more important than its quality (Shell and Allgeier, 1992). The evidence from several studies is consistent with the social facilitation prediction that computer monitoring decreases performance on more complex tasks (Aiello and Svec, 1993) while it can increase performance on very simple tasks (Aiello and Chomiak, 1992).

One might wonder, in an era in which there is increasing emphasis on building employee commitment, on working in teams, and on devolving responsibility as organizations take out layers that make work more complex, how there can be a concomitant increase in electronic and other surveillance activities—a practice that research indicates often produces effects opposite those being sought by the high-commitment work practices so frequently discussed. One avenue to pursue in understanding this apparent contradiction is to note that, virtually without exception, the studies of surveillance (and other forms of external control) have asked about their effects on those *subject to* these practices. For the practices to persist, in spite of their often deleterious consequences, it would seem useful to understand their effects on those *administering* the practices. It is quite possible that the control, or at least the illusion of control, produced by implementing surveillance, and the higher level of involvement and responsibility that accrues to those who more closely supervise and monitor work, may explain why those who administer such practices persist in using them even if the results are not always positive.

A similar set of issues concerns the use of sanctions. There have now been a large number of studies of managerial succession showing how various conditions such as the power of the CEO and the firm's ownership moderate the relationship between performance and turnover (e.g., Ocasio, 1994; Salancik and Pfeffer, 1980). With few exceptions, these studies have not asked whether or not firing those associated with poor performance subsequently improves the performance of the organization. Gavin, Green, and Fairhurst distinguished two strategies of managerial control, particularly in situations of poor performance: "Managers may utilize a judicial approach which has its focus on using primarily punitive measures as a deterrent to future poor performance incidents. . . . Alternatively, a problem-solving approach may be used which can be characterized as more interactive, cooperative, and non-punitive in nature" (1995, p. 209).

Gavin et al. (1995), in a laboratory experiment, found partial support for the ideas that managers use consistent control strategies over time, that they are more likely to be punitive the worse the level of performance, and that subordinates perceive punitive control strategies as less just. O'Reilly and Weitz (1980) studied the behavior of managers in a large retail chain. They found a positive correlation between the use of sanctions, such as warnings and dismissals, and unit performance. They argued that how managers treated poor performers sent an important signal about the performance culture of the organization. The fact that firing is often a form of ritual scapegoating (Gamson and Scotch, 1964) is well known but sometimes overlooked in both theory and empirical research. As Zajac and Westphal (1995) reminded us, all organizational incentives (and sanctions) have a symbolic, public face to them and can be partly understood in that context.

Commitment and Socialization Processes

Commitment is based on the rationalizing model of behavior: if an individual can be induced to do something and this behavior cannot be attributed to some powerful external force such as a reward or sanction, the person will become more committed to the action and to its implications for other attitudes and behavior. Because this commitment results from a process of self-perception (Bem, 1972) and dissonance reduction (Festinger, 1957), it represents a change in individuals' perceptions of themselves and the world. Consequently, commitment processes create fundamental change in perceptions and attitudes, and in that sense commitment represents a form of internal control that does not need to rely nearly as much on continuing surveillance and reward. Commitment may, therefore, be a much more efficient as well as more effective means of coordinating and managing behavior. "Willingness of employees at all levels to assume responsibility for producing results—not simply 'following the rules'—is generally believed to be a major determinant of organizational success" (Simon, 1991, p. 37).

Salancik (1977) has argued that commitment arises under the conditions of choice or volition, publicness, and explicitness. Without choice, there is no implication of the behavior for the individual's beliefs or perceptions. All of the literature is consistent in emphasizing the importance of choice—or at least the appearance of it—in building commitment (e.g., Cialdini, 1988; Kiesler, 1971). Publicness makes it harder for the person to deny having done the action and in that sense binds the person and his or her choice more closely together. Explicitness means that behaviors are more committing to the extent they have a clear, logical relationship to subsequent behaviors and attitudes. So, the act of taking a lower-paying job from among many offers (O'Reilly and Caldwell, 1980; 1981) represents a choice that has explicit implications—one must really like the job and the organization if one is willing to forgo more money elsewhere to be there. And a job choice is almost inevitably a public decision—known by one's friends and family and obviously by one's co-workers and those whose offers have been declined.

One of the more customary times in which to activate the mechanism of commitment is when an individual joins an organization. If the organization makes the recruiting process difficult and demanding, individuals who are not seriously interested and committed will drop out during the process. But those that persevere will be much more committed and loyal—after all, if they didn't really want to join the organization and have the particular job, why would they have gone through so much? Graham (1995), in a participant observation study, described what it was like to be hired into Subaru-Isuzu. She was told that 30,000 people had applied to work at the company (p. 20). First, she had to take a battery called the General Aptitude Test (GAT), which consisted of "nine written and four dexterity tests" (p. 21). Then, having scored sufficiently well, she received a letter saying she was selected to "enter Phase I of a two phase pre-employment assessment activity" (pp. 21–22). The assessments, involving working in groups, were tiring and stressful. It took more than six months to get hired (p. 31):

> The reactions of the training class members to the selection process ran from "grueling" and "demanding" to "fun." . . . Everyone agreed, however, that they had never worked so hard to land a job. The general sentiment was that we had really accomplished something and were among a select few. . . . In order to maintain their status in the selection process, most applicants were forced to make some degree of sacrifice. (p. 31)

Similar selection processes have been described at New United Motors (Adler, 1992), even though in this instance, under the United Automobile Workers contract, the workers had recall rights and the evidence is that even union "troublemakers" were rehired if they applied. Adler noted that "each applicant for the manager, Group Leader, Team Leader and Team Member positions had to pass the same three-day assessment test" (p. 120). Initially, 78 percent of the 3,200 hourly applicants were rejected, although most who persisted were later hired. Why reject those who were later going to be hired? This process tends to create the feeling of being in a special, highly selected work force. It is also a process that requires perseverance, and this persistence in efforts to get a job will result in more commitment to that job. Nor are these commitment tactics used and useful only for hourly workers. At Data General (Kidder, 1981), two project leaders, West and Alsing, used a process called the "signing up" to ensure that those recruited onto a team of engineers to design a computer had consciously chosen to undertake a difficult and demanding task and would therefore be willing to sacrifice themselves and work hard for the project:

> "It's gonna be tough," says Alsing. "If we hired you, you'd be working with a bunch of cynics and egotists and it'd be hard to keep up with them."
> "That doesn't scare me," says the recruit.
> "There's a lot of fast people in this group," Alsing goes on. "It's gonna be a real hard job with a lot of long hours. And I mean long hours." (pp. 65–66)

There is, of course, a potential downside to commitment—namely, a resistance to change and an irrational perseverance in behavior. Staw (1976) and Brockner (Brockner and Rubin, 1985; Brockner, Rubin, and Lang, 1981) have both examined escalating commitment to failing courses of action and some of the conditions under which such perseverance occurs.

It is interesting that the study of commitment in the empirical organizations literature seems to be most often associated with some kind of organizational or individual pathology—some error in decision making. Thus, for instance, there are case studies of commitment to building sites for the World's Fair in Vancouver (Ross and Staw, 1986) even in the face of massive cost overruns, and persistence in building nuclear power plants and resistance to closing them down (Ross and Staw, 1993) even when confronted by budget overruns and technical problems.

There are numerous studies of the escalating commitment involved in recruitment to a religion, a cult, or a self-help group (e.g., Barker, 1984; Galanter, 1989; O'Reilly and Chatman, 1996). Many of these groups emphasize recruiting others, as a way of cementing the individual's own commitment to the organization through the activity of proselytizing. Admitting one has made a mistake by joining is always difficult: "Est trainees rarely will complain later; they more often will boast of their exceptional bargain in personal fulfillment. . . . The alternative to claiming this is to admit that they were conned and didn't even have the courage to walk out in the middle. Very few people will admit to that" (Baer and Stolz, 1978, p. 60).

It seems paradoxical that, even as the organizations literature emphasizes the pathologies of commitment such as escalation to failing courses of action and seduction by cults, building organizational commitment is seen by most practicing managers as something that is desirable, not dysfunctional:

> Much research literature focuses on ways of developing and enhancing commitment among employees (Mowday, Porter, and Steers, 1982), suggesting that organizations view commitment as a desirable attribute. Support for this perspective is shown by studies linking commitment with a variety of work behaviors including voluntary turnover (Mowday, et al., 1982), employee performance (Meyer, Paunonen, Gellatly, Goffin, and Jackson, 1989), organizational citizenship (O'Reilly and Chatman, 1986; Shore and Wayne, 1993), and absenteeism (Mowday, et al., 1982). (Shore, Barksdale, and Shore, 1995, p. 1593)

That is why there is so much interest in understanding the psychological dynamics of commitment and culture (O'Reilly and Chatman, 1996). Some may object and argue that commitment to decisions and organizational commitment are two different phenomena. They are different in their apparent desirability, but the research literature is clear that they are produced by similar psychological dynamics.

Pascale's (1985) discussion of socialization practices in organizations speaks both to how socialization is accomplished and to the deeply ambivalent attitudes toward socialization and commitment that seem to characterize Americans and particularly academics. Writing about this ambivalence, he noted, "Mention the term 'socialization' and a variety of unsavory images come to mind. . . . Americans, dedicated by constitution and conviction to the full expression of individuality, regard 'socialization' as alien and vaguely sinister. . . . The underlying dilemma of socialization is so sensitive to core American values that it is seldom debated" (pp. 27, 37).

Socialization is "the systematic means by which firms bring new members into their culture" (Pascale, 1985, p. 27). Pascale identified seven steps that constituted the socialization process. The first step is "careful selection of entry-level candidates" (p. 29), a process observed in the various Japanese automobile plants operating in the United States as well as in organizations such as Southwest Airlines. The second step entails "humility-inducing experiences in the first months on the job" (p. 30) that dislodge the individual's old habits, behaviors, and social identity. This part of the process proceeds on the premise that for there to be a fundamental change in values and behaviors—the goal of socialization—the individual must be confronted with evidence that his or her previous social identity won't bring comfort in the new organizational environment. Hard work, long hours, and the social isolation that derives from spending so much time at work all help to make the individual susceptible to social influences emanating from within the organization. The stress makes the individual open to these influences. The corporate hazing also has some of the same effects as other forms of hazing: it produces a perception that the organization must be worthwhile—otherwise, one's willingness to suffer so much would be inexplicable. As Aronson and Mills explained, "Persons who go through a great deal of trouble or pain to attain something tend to value it more highly than persons who attain the same thing with a minimum of effort" (1959, p. 177).

The third part of the socialization process involves thorough training through exposure in the field to the organization's operations and to individuals who exemplify its values. Many retail organizations, such as grocery and department stores, emphasize putting new employees in the store, regardless of their subsequent anticipated career path, to ensure that they fully understand the organization and what it is about. Career advancement is slow so that sufficient time is spent getting thoroughly socialized to the organization's values and behaviors.

The fourth step in the socialization experience entails paying close attention "to systems measuring operational results and rewarding individual performance. Systems are comprehensive, consistent, and triangulate particularly on those aspects of the business that are tied to competitive success and corporate values" (Pascale, 1985, p. 31). What is measured is what is attended to, and measurement therefore helps to create as well as to reinforce a set of values and norms.

The fifth step in the socialization process involves strict adherence to the organization's core values. As Pascale (1985, p. 32) noted, subjecting oneself to an intense socialization experience puts oneself at the mercy of the firm and leaves one quite vulnerable. In order to convince individuals that socialization will not work against their interests, the organization must build and maintain a bond of trust with its employees. That means making promises that ensure individuals' well-being, and it means keeping those promises. For instance, at New United Motor Manufacturing, the union and its members gave up the right to strike over work rules, company contributions to the Supplemental Unemployment Benefits scheme of General Motors, and the protection of numerous job classifications in return for higher wages and a promise of no layoffs. When this no-layoff policy was sorely tested in 1987 and 1988 because of inadequate sales of the company's cars, the organization found ways of meeting the commitment. The comptroller and general manager stated, "There's no question in my mind but that the commitment to no layoffs and the ability of managers to operate on a day-to-day basis in a way that supports this underlying philosophy are absolutely crucial to our success. Team members know that when they contribute ideas for more effective operations they are not jeopardizing anyone's job" (Adler, 1992, p. 123).

The sixth step in the socialization process is developing reinforcing folklore, stories, and legends that validate the organization's culture and its aims and that interpret history in ways consistent with its values. Finally, "consistent role models and consistent traits are associated with those recognized as on the fast track" (Pascale, 1985, p. 33). In other words, through whom it rewards and recognizes, the organization sends a consistent message about what behaviors and attitudes it values.

Van Maanen and Schein (1979) proposed six socialization tactics that could vary along a bipolar continuum. As reviewed by Ashforth and Saks (1996, p. 150), these socialization tactics were (1) collective versus individual (were newcomers grouped together or handled individually?); (2) formal versus informal (were newcomers separated from the rest of the organization or not?); (3) sequential versus random (was there a fixed sequence of steps required to assume a new job role?); (4) fixed versus variable (was there a specified timetable for the socialization process?); (5) serial versus disjunctive (was the new member socialized by an experienced member?); and (6) investiture versus divestiture (are the newcomer's identity and personal characteristics affirmed or stripped away?).

Ashforth and Saks found that, on the one hand, "the six tactics of institutionalized socialization were negatively related to role ambiguity, role conflict, stress symptoms, and intentions to quit and positively associated with job satisfaction, organizational commitment, and organizational identification" (1996, p. 169). This suggests that more extensive and formalized socialization has positive effects on those subjected to it. On the other hand, institutionalized socialization was negatively related "to both attempted and actual role innovation at four months and to actual role innovation at ten months" (p. 169). But the trade-off between innovation and change and reduced stress and enhanced job satisfaction may be more apparent than real. As Ashforth and Saks noted, the issue is what is learned, not how it is taught, that is important, and it is possible to inculcate norms that encourage innovation in an institutionalized socialization process.

The evidence suggests that commitment is intentionally built and managed. There is evidence that the psychological and social psychological processes that produce commitment are reasonably well understood. There is also literature that suggests deep ambivalence about commitment, be it to a decision or an organization. Being committed is, almost by definition, to some degree a loss of personal freedom and choice—to be committed to an organization is to stay with it even in the absence of rational reasons to do so. It is this aspect of commitment that some find troubling. But, it is important to recognize that individuals often choose commitment and to be committed. Institutionalized socialization produced less role stress and higher job satisfaction. Thus, commitment has obvious positive effects for organizations but also for the individuals who are committed as well.

Organizational Culture

Although closely related to the idea of control through commitment and socialization, the topic of organizational culture is somewhat distinct. Commitment is one important mechanism through which strong cultures may be built (O'Reilly and

Chatman, 1996), but the concept of culture incorporates more than simply commitment. Kunda defined culture as:

> a learned body of tradition that governs what one needs to know, think and feel in order to meet the standards of membership. . . . When applied to organizational settings, culture is generally viewed as the shared rules governing cognitive and affective aspects of membership in an organization, and the means whereby they are shaped and expressed. Of particular concern have been the shared meanings, assumptions, norms, and values that govern work-related behavior; the symbolic, textural, and narrative structures in which they are encoded; and—in the functionalist tradition—the structural causes and consequences of cultural forms and their relationship to various measures of organizational effectiveness. (1992, p. 8)

Pettigrew has defined culture in a similar fashion:

> in order for people to function within any given setting, they must have a continuing sense of what that reality is all about in order to be acted upon. Culture is the system of such publicly and collectively accepted meanings operating for a given group at a given time. This system of terms, forms, categories, and images interprets a people's own situation to themselves. . . . The offspring of the concept of culture . . . are symbol, language, ideology, belief, ritual, and myth. (1979, p. 574)

The definition of the concept of culture has occasionally been contested and lacks consensus. Some (Reichers and Schneider, 1990) have argued that culture is conceptually not distinguishable from the construct of organizational climate. Culture has been defined and measured at different levels of analysis, including the group, the entire organization, or even the industry (e.g., Chatman and Jehn, 1994). O'Reilly and Chatman have noted that some "define culture as what an organization *is* while still others argue that it is what an organization *has* (Schein, 1985; Smircich, 1983)" (1996, p. 159). O'Reilly and Chatman offered a definition that is grounded in the view of culture as a form of organizational control: "we define culture as a system of shared values (that define what is important) and norms that define appropriate attitudes and behaviors for organizational members (how to feel and behave)" (p. 160). Defined in this way, one can ask, empirically, to what extent there is agreement about values (consistency) and to what extent violations of organizational norms and rules are sanctioned severely (the intensity with which values and beliefs about appropriate behavior are held). This definition is, therefore, quite amenable to empirical, quantitative measurement and, moreover, links culture with other social psychological constructs such as norms and values.

Given the disagreements about the definition of culture, it is not surprising that there is also a variety of opinions about how to operationalize and measure the concept. One approach, the Organizational Culture Profile (O'Reilly, Chatman, and Caldwell, 1991), employs a Q-sort profile comparison process that asks respondents to put fifty-four value statements into a set of nine categories from "most characteristic of my firm's culture" to "most uncharacteristic of my firm's culture." The sorting process permits fewer cards at the extremes than in the middle. The procedure produces a measure with good test–retest reliability. With an average of thirty-five respondents from fifteen firms in various service industries, Chatman and Jehn (1994, p. 531) observed a high degree of consensus within firms, although the extent of consensus varied, as might be expected as some firms had stronger cultures than others. In several studies using the OCP, a consistent set of seven factors emerged: "(1) innovation, (2) stability, (3) an orientation toward people, (4) an orientation toward outcomes or results, (5) an emphasis on being easygoing, (6) attention to detail, and (7) a collaborative or team orientation" (p. 534). Chatman and Jehn demonstrated that even within the service sector, individual firms had unique cultures. They also found that "industry differences explain more variance than organization differences for six of the seven culture dimensions" (p. 537). It seems fair to state that progress has been made in operationalizing the concept of culture and developing measurement procedures that produce results consistent with theoretical expectations and that are replicable. As noted below, however, fragmentation in the culture research literature, compared to the literature on personality and organizational behavior, for instance, has resulted in less borrowing of measurement processes across studies and consequently less cumulation of results.

Since the mid-1980s there have been a plethora of both scholarly and practitioner-oriented books on the subject of culture. Barley, Meyer, and Gash (1988, p. 33), searching six bibliographic data bases, noted that the total number of papers published annually on organizational culture increased from less than twenty in 1979 to about fifty in 1984 and to close to 130 in 1985, an exponential rate of growth. Some of this activity has been stimulated by the idea that strong cultures are positively related to economic performance (e.g., Kotter and Heskett, 1992; Dennison, 1990), that managing culture is possible (e.g., S. Davis, 1984; O'Reilly, 1989), and that culture is an effective managerial method used in exemplary organizations such as Hewlett-Packard (e.g., Deal and Kennedy, 1982). Barley et al. also noted that "the upsurge of interest in organizational culture in large part reflected the back-to-back commercial success of three bestsellers that spoke of culture under various guises. . . . By attracting attention in both the academic and managerial communities, organizational culture attained the status of a dominant idea in a relatively short period of time" (1988, p. 32).

Not all empirical studies have found a relationship between strong cultures and performance (e.g., Siehl and Martin, 1990), and even those that have uncovered an effect have noted the relationship is often complex. Thus, for instance, Kotter and Heskett found that in order to enhance performance, culture needed to be matched to the firm's strategy, and even then, "strategically appropriate cultures will not promote excellent performance over long periods unless they contain norms and values that help firms adapt to a changing environment" (1992, p. 142).

Unfortunately, the vast amount of writing on the subject of organizational culture has been accompanied by a fragmentation that makes this topic domain an excellent exemplar of the costs of an absence of paradigmatic consensus. There is agreement on the fact that "research on organizational cultures is highly fragmented. Empirical research addresses a wide variety of content themes and research subjects. With regard to theory, researchers employ different ontological as well as epistemological assumptions, research programs, concepts, and methodologies" (Ebers, 1995, p. 129). Thus, for instance, Martin (1992a), in an overview of the literature, distinguished among three competing perspectives on organizational culture: (1) an integration perspective emphasizing consistency in the relationship among cultural manifestations, relatively great consensus among organization members, and the exclusion of interpretive ambiguity; (2) a differentiation perspective emphasizing inconsistency in the relationship among cultural elements, consensus only within subcultures, and a channeling of ambiguity outside subcultures; and (3) a fragmentation perspective that sees complexity in the relationship among cultural manifestations, a multiplicity of views rather than either subcultural or total organizational consensus, and a focus on ambiguity.

Ebers noted that although the interpretive stance of much field research might be useful for understanding cultural phenomena and the "theoretical heterogeneity of organizational cultural research contributes to richness of ideas and intellectual scrutiny" (1995, p. 131), the domain of culture research incurred some costs as well from this fragmentation. The nature of the research literature on organizational culture makes it "difficult to bring the various research findings into relation and to consolidate what has been learned" (p. 132).

Ebers (1995, p. 153) developed a typology of organizational cultures reproduced here in Table 5-2. There are a number of advantages of this typology. First, it considers the fact that "it might be fruitful not only to consider the intensity and dispersion of a particular set of cultural orientations . . . but also their domain of validity" (p. 157). Second, the typology highlights the various bases of individual compliance to cultural values, a distinction not often emphasized. And the typology highlights both the internal self-regulatory consequences of culture and also the possibility of culture serving external legitimation and adaptive uses. In short, the typology, based on the existing literature on culture, defines not only four ideal types but, more important, some critical dimensions along which conceptions of culture can be usefully described.

Even as the academic debate about culture has proceeded, the world of practice took ideas as they were deemed useful and implemented them. So, as some academics argued about whether or not culture could be managed, in some organizations, particularly many high-technology organizations, it was quite effectively managed. Kunda's (1992) ethnographic study of cultural control in a high-technology firm obviously uncovered instances of resistance and control failure — there is no system of management control, including the use of financial incentives, that works perfectly. But what was striking was the extent to which there was management consciousness about what they were doing and their overall effectiveness in accomplishing what they sought to do. Even as some debated about how to change cultures, or whether culture change can be directed, organizations ranging from Ford (Pascale, 1990) to Sears were doing it.

Culture as a social control mechanism is important because it offers several advantages over external control accomplished through rewards and sanctions. In order to manage behavior through external control, it is generally necessary to know in advance what behaviors or outcomes are important and are to be re-

Table 5-2   Typology of Organizational Cultures

	Cultural Ideal-Types			
Characteristic	Legitimate Culture	Efficient Culture	Traditional Culture	Utilitarian Culture
Origination of content	Environmental norms and values	Constituencies' demands on performance	Members' values, beliefs, and traditions	Members' (self-) interests
Basis of validity	Ideology	Adequate performance	Affiliation	Psychological and legal contracts
Focus	External support; legitimacy	Outcomes; expertise; planning; control	Trust tradition; long-term commitment	Achievement; just allocation of rewards and contributions
Basis of individual compliance	Identification; ideological pressures for conformity	Social and material sanctioning	Internalization	Calculations of consequences
Co-ordination of actions	Normative regulation	Shared teleology	Dramaturgical and communicative action	Interlocking interest and strategic action
Characteristic setting	Public institutional setting; performance difficult to assess	Structurally interdependent groups; monitored; performance readily assessable	Groups with stable membership, long history, and intensive interaction	Small, heterogeneous groups of regularly convening individuals with mutual interests and purposes

From Ebers (1995, p. 153).

warded. Because of task complexity and because of unanticipated circumstances, this foresight is not always possible. A second problem is that, as already noted, relying on external rewards or sanctions requires some supervisorial effort or surveillance, and this effort can be both costly and counterproductive. Indeed, in some situations, supervisorial control is simply impractical. Consider an airline that intends to compete on the basis of outstanding levels of service, such as Virgin Atlantic. How could one possibly monitor the numerous interactions between customers and airline personnel, many of which take place in dispersed locations during flights? As Kunda wrote, cultural control is "designed to minimize the use and deemphasize the significance of traditional bureaucratic control structures—hierarchical and functional differentiation, economically motivated performance—and to elicit instead behavior consistent with cultural prescriptions" (1992, p. 218).

A third issue is that external controls are more likely to evoke psychological reactance, particularly when such controls are first introduced into a situation. Reactance theory suggests that individuals do not like to lose freedoms, and the imposition of external constraint is a relatively obtrusive intervention that may elicit feelings of constraint. Ironically, psychological reactance (Brehm, 1966) can produce rebellious behavior that in turn makes further control even more necessary (e.g., Pfeffer, 1994). Cultural control largely overcomes this problem because controls come from the internalization of values and from peer enforcement. In systems of cultural control, "there is evidence of a decentralization and a deepening of control: performance of the member role and particularly of the extensively articulated beliefs and emotions it prescribes is 'supervised' by a broader group of control agents—practically anyone who is a member of the organization" (Kunda, 1992, p. 219).

O'Reilly and Chatman (1996) noted that there were four mechanisms through which organizations attempted to manage culture. Systems of participation in organizational decision making, a frequent feature of high-commitment work organizations (Walton, 1985), provide individuals with the feeling that they are making choices. This perception of choice increases commitment to the organization and to the decisions made. Consider, for instance, the application of Taylorist principles of standardized work at New United Motor. In many settings, employees rebel against the regimentation of minutely standardized work procedures. This resistance was largely overcome at NUMMI by involving the workers themselves in the process:

> The first thing you do is teach workers the techniques of work analysis. Next . . . you get the workers as a group to time each other with a stopwatch. . . . After everybody has been timed, workers analyze what they think is the best performance and break that process down into little pieces. . . . All this leads to a way of doing the job that everybody agrees with. . . . The point is to get workers to participate in defining the standards and encourage them to constantly make suggestions to improve them. (Adler, 1992, p. 141)

Second, managers in organizations send signals about what is important and valued through mechanisms such as what they spend time on, what they ask questions about, and what they talk about (Peters, 1978; Pfeffer, 1981b). Language, symbols, and rituals are important in developing and maintaining a culture. Pettigrew wrote about "man as a creator of symbols, languages, beliefs, visions, ideologies, and myths, in effect, man as a *creator and manager of meaning*" (1979, p. 572, emphasis in original). Graham's ethnographic study of Subaru-Isuzu noted the importance of "certain words and actions which conveyed a sense of equality" (1995, p. 107). The team metaphor was consistently repeated, and workers were called associates. Symbolic measures also helped to reinforce the culture of equality and teamwork:

> Everyone, from the company president on down, wore the same basic uniform, parked in the same general parking lots, ate in the same cafeteria, and was restricted to a half-hour lunch period. . . . Clerical and management Associates worked together in one large room without barriers. . . . SIA used rituals and ceremonies to create a shared experience of belonging. These included morning exercises and daily team meetings. (p. 110)

Even though the equality and egalitarianism was not always authentic, the steps taken to provide evidence of these values did affect how employees felt about and reacted to their work environment.

Third, cultures are created through shared social information—informational social influence (Deutsch and Gerard, 1955). Particularly when people first enter an organization, they are often uncertain about what to do and what the rules of the game are. If they are exposed to consistent social information—consistency in norms—about expectations for behavior, they are likely to conform to those expectations. Consistency is often difficult to maintain under immediate performance pressures but is critical to building a strong culture and implementing cultural control, as Adler's reporting of the observations of a NUMMI manager indicated: "At GM, it's easy to slip into the mentality of 'just do it—I've got a production schedule to meet.' The biggest challenge for managers coming into NUMMI is the absolute commitment to consistency to all our principles, not just to a production schedule set by Marketing. At NUMMI, we've got to walk like we talk" (p. 127). Many strong-culture organizations attempt to manage the informational environment by isolating, either physically or socially, through hard work and inclusive social activities, individuals from other social influences that would be distracting or diversionary, such as other organizations or outside interests.

Finally, organizations shape behavior through reward systems, although such systems frequently don't use monetary rewards. Biggart's (1989) study of direct sales organizations, such as Mary Kay and Tupperware, found that such organizations used frequent meetings, recognition of achievements, awards, and even visits from a charismatic founder to reinforce behavior consistent with cultural values. Underlying all of these forms of cultural control is always the implicit threat that those who don't fit in will be expelled from the organization, and this fear of social ostracism is also a strong factor promoting conformity to the organization's core values and decision premises.

Leadership

Control in organizations is also exercised through individual, interpersonal influence, in which those in roles of authority motivate and direct others to act as they would like. This interpersonal influence is often called leadership, a subject big enough for a book, or many books, on its own. What is important is to understand the issues that currently concern this subject of research. Perhaps the foremost issue is whether or not leadership matters and, if so, in what situations individual leadership action is likely to be most efficacious. Second, there is a question as to whether leadership skills and behaviors can be learned; if so, to what extent, and what are the most effective ways of shaping and changing behavior to enhance leadership effectiveness? Third, and closely related, there is the question of what effective leaders do, in terms of specific behaviors and actions. Here we briefly review each of these issues.

Leadership Effects

Obviously, there are important differences on a variety of outcome variables depending on leader behavior—for instance, the original studies on the effects of democratic versus autocratic leadership demonstrated differences in both performance and subordinate attitudes (Lippitt, 1940), and other experimental studies over the years have also revealed leadership effects (see House and Baetz, 1979, for a review). The issue in the literature is not whether differences in leader behavior *might* matter but whether, given the sorting and filtering that goes on before people rise to leadership positions and the constraints under which those leaders operate, the effects of leadership are of substantive importance in actual organizational situations (Pfeffer, 1977). The argument that there is not much effect of leader behavior maintains this is because leader behavior, within natural situations, does not vary much across leaders, for two reasons: (1) external constraints and (2) a selection and socialization process that homogenizes those who rise to leadership positions.

Not only do organizations select those for leadership positions in a process that often constitutes homosocial reproduction (Kanter, 1977), but a labor market also constrains variation in who assumes leadership roles. Thus, for instance, Pfeffer and Davis-Blake (1986), studying National Basketball Association teams, argued that one reason why there may be no observed effect for coaches on team performance is that the choice of new coaches is itself constrained by past team performance. In general, it is probably reasonable to argue that effective and successful leaders or managers would prefer to work in better organizations, so that poorly performing organizations may have trouble in attracting the talent necessary to make things different. Pfeffer and Davis-Blake (1986) observed there was no direct effect of succession on performance. But, when the competence of the new coaches was included in the analysis (with competence assessed by previous win-loss record or by previous professional basketball coaching experience), there was evidence of a succession effect.

The very real constraints on leader behavior (and indeed all behavior in organizations) make it problematic to find leader effects even if and when they occur. Johns took as an example the proposition that "considerate behavior on the part of leaders will be positively associated with subordinate performance" (1991, p. 80). He noted that for this research hypothesis to be supported, the following conditions must exist:

1. The leaders in the sample must exhibit interpersonal variation in consideration.
2. Subordinates must be capable of detecting variation in consideration.
3. Subordinates must report variations in consideration on the . . . questionnaire.
4. Variation in consideration must lead to variation in subordinate behavior. . . .
5. Variation in subordinate behavior must be translated into variation in subordinate performance. (p. 80)

Johns noted that organizations might do things that restrict variation in leader consideration and that subordinate performance could be affected by equipment or other conditions. He noted that "constraints may exist that restrict required variance and thus threaten the hypothesis in spite of an actual true-score relationship between consideration and performance in the population" (p. 81). These comments on the effects of constraints on evaluating hypotheses are applicable to literatures other than that on leadership, but the arguments are particularly important in this context because of the very real selection and behavior constraints often encountered. These constraints at once reduce the likelihood of finding leadership effects and also make such effects less likely to exist.

Another variant of the argument to use caution in assessing the effects of leaders is that one needs to be careful in inferring effects of leader behavior in natural situations, because it is quite likely that managerial style itself adjusts to differences in performance. An observed relationship between leadership and performance might well be because performance causes leader behavior rather than the reverse (Lowin and Craig, 1968).

The debate about whether or not leadership matters has occurred on two fronts—theoretical and empirical. The empirical issue was joined with a study by Lieberson and O'Connor (1972) that decomposed the variation in sales, profits, and profit margins (profits/sales) for a sample of 167 large corporations over a twenty-year period to effects associated with year, industry, company, and leadership (as represented by the chief executive). The study found, not surprisingly, that there were much larger industry and company effects than leadership effects. Salancik and Pfeffer (1977) replicated this methodology in an examination of the effect of mayors on city budgets, specifically spending on different categories. Again, there was only a small effect of leadership observed. The methodology employed in these studies depends importantly on how the variance is decomposed (the order in which factors are considered) and also requires one to estimate a time lag (including no lag, or contemporaneous effects) between leadership succession and a change in the variable being studied. Moreover, effects were described in relative terms. In absolute terms, a small percentage change in either sales, profits, or budgetary expenditures can amount to a lot of actual dollars, given the size of the units that were examined.

Weiner and Mahoney (1981), using a somewhat different methodology that included more direct measures of company, industry, and period effects (e.g., organizational size, industry sales, and capital structure), observed substantially larger effects for leadership in their study of 193 business firms over a nineteen-year period. However, neither of their measures of leadership strategy explained much variance. They argued that "means to identify causal variables of leadership at the corporate level are needed" (p. 469). Meyer's (1975) study of government finance offices from 1966 to 1972 discovered that there were more changes in organizational structure in offices that selected new leaders compared to finance departments in which there were no changes in leadership.

Two studies illustrate different methodologies that are more useful and valid in assessing leadership effects. Lieberman, Lau, and Williams (1990) used Cobb-

Douglas production function models of factor productivity to examine the growth in both labor and capital productivity in six automobile firms over an almost forty-year period. The study is important, because it relied only on publicly available data and employed a different methodology for estimating leadership effects. The authors found that "the hypothesis of no top management effects can be rejected . . . for all of the firms except Toyota" (p. 1209). Moreover, the estimated effects were large. For instance, the results indicated that "Ford's productivity level in the initial year of Petersen's [the CEO] regime was 21% above the average initial year productivity level of all Ford executives over the sample period" and that "his [Petersen's] annual rate of productivity growth was 3.1% above the average of all Ford executives" (p. 1209).

If employed on a larger sample, this methodology, which permits the identification of specific magnitudes of effects of specific leadership regimes, would permit one to explore which specific factors associated with a change in leadership regime were responsible for increased or diminished productivity and productivity growth as well as the conditions under which leadership effects were larger and smaller. For instance, one inference from this study is that a well-defined system (the Toyota manufacturing system) negates the effects of changes in executive regimes but that executive change can have large effects when the firm in question is struggling to catch up with an industry leader. It is unfortunate that this line of research and associated methodology has not been pursued.

A second promising empirical line of inquiry is represented in a study of the performance of major league baseball players (Kahn, 1993). Kahn argued that a good manager would be (1) better able to turn player inputs into victories and (2) better able to cause players to perform better. He measured the quality of major league managers by their predicted salary based on performance. Player ability was measured by past performance. He concluded that "managerial quality was found to have . . . a positive . . . effect on team winning percentage, controlling for team offensive and defensive inputs, as well as on player performance relative to player ability" (p. 543). Kahn's study did not permit the estimation of whether this managerial effect persisted over time or rather represented just an initial change in performance. The basic ideas and methodology could potentially be applied to other sports and in other contexts in which both aggregate and individual performance was measurable.

The theoretical question was, why the persistent fascination with leadership? Calder (1977) and Pfeffer (1977) both argued that leadership effects were attributed, particularly in uncertain situations, to achieve a feeling of mastery or control (Kelley, 1971; Langer, 1983). In this sense, the study of leadership represented the fundamental attribution error (Nisbett and Ross, 1980) at work. Meindl, Ehrlich, and Dukerich commented on the prominence of the study and discussion of leadership: "it appears that the concept of leadership is a permanently entrenched part of the socially constructed reality that we bring to bear in our analysis of organizations. And there is every sign that the obsessions with and celebrations of it will persist. . . . Such realities emphasize leadership, and the concept has thereby gained a brilliance that exceeds the limits of normal scientific inquiry" (1985, p. 78).

Meindl et al. (1985) introduced the idea of the romance of leadership, an elevated belief in the efficacy of leaders and leader behavior. They found an inverse relationship between the relative number of doctoral dissertations concerning leadership and economic conditions, indicating that there was more interest in leadership when economic conditions were worse. They also observed a positive relationship between the number of articles published in the *Wall Street Journal* concerning leadership and firm performance and, in a set of experimental studies, found that extreme performance outcomes were more likely to result in attributions of leadership effect. In an analysis of their data that explored the extent to which there is a desire to attribute performance to human agency, regardless of hierarchical position, Meindl et al. observed statistically significant positive correlations between attributions to leaders and to subordinates in the experimental studies. The idea of the romance of leadership is persuasive, but again, there has been insufficient pursuit of an initially promising idea. Two directions would seem to warrant exploration. First, it is highly unlikely that people are born with the idea that leaders matter. The romance of leadership is learned, and that stimulates the question of how and under what conditions some come to believe in leadership effects more than others. It is likely that the degree to which people have a romance of leadership varies across cultures, with possibly more relevance in more individualistic cultures. Second, it would be worthwhile to explore factors other than extreme performance or performance problems that produce an increased attribution of leadership effects.

Even if one accepts both the empirical and theoretical critique of the leadership literature (and certainly not everyone does), the focus on leadership is quite understandable and rational, given a pragmatic orientation. Even if a leader's effects are constrained, someone in a leadership position must still do something. After all, one cannot affect general economic conditions or the history of an organization. Decisions about whom to choose for key positions remain, while occupants of those positions have to take some action, regardless of how efficacious that action may or may not be. In that sense, the arguments about leadership effects are theoretically interesting but possibly managerially and practically irrelevant—people must be chosen for positions, trained to be as effective as they can be in them, and, once in the jobs, do something, whether the impact is large or small. It therefore remains important to develop research that can at least help in addressing these three issues.

Nevertheless, the comments of Meindl and his colleagues are useful in helping us understand how the leadership literature has evolved. For instance, the current emphasis on building organizational vision and visionary organizations (Collins and Porras, 1994) and the relative neglect of leader behaviors such as consideration and initiating structure, behaviors that used to be studied (Fleishman, 1973)—are comprehensible given the less hierarchical nature of many of today's organizations. This has made the exercise of hierarchical, role-based leadership less relevant and the task of building the ability to take coordinated collective action in the absence of direct hierarchical authority more important.

What Do Leaders Do?

On the question of what effective leaders do, the leadership literature has been particularly interested in distinguishing charismatic or transformational leaders from transactional leaders. Bass (1985) argued that transactional leaders exchange rewards for behavior provided by followers while transformational leaders develop relationships with followers that inspire and stimulate them to forgo their own self-interest for some higher collective good. Shamir, House, and Arthur (1993) argued that noncharismatic leaders affected followers' cognitions, such as their calculations about the desirability of engaging in some behavior, and possibly their ability to perform specific tasks. By contrast, charismatic leaders affected followers' emotions and self-esteem or self-concept. Shamir et al. operationalized charismatic leadership as an interaction and communication process between a leader and others that results in the internalization of the leader's goals and values, a strong moral or personal (as contrasted with a calculative) commitment to those values and goals, and a tendency on the part of the followers to submerge their own interests and identity for the sake of the collectivity. House (1977) has noted that one charismatic behavior is articulating ideological goals, which he maintained had a more potent effect on the motivation and self-confidence of followers than more utilitarian or pragmatic objectives. Shamir et al. (1993) noted that, in comparison to noncharismatic leaders, charismatic leaders would tend to use more references to values and moral justifications, make more references to the collective, use more references to history and to more distant objectives, make more positive statements about followers' self-worth, and communicate higher expectations for the followers.

House (1977) argued that charismatic leaders differed from other leaders not only in their behaviors but also in their own personal characteristics. In particular, he linked the study of dispositions to the study of leadership by arguing that leaders that have charismatic effects on subordinates differed from those that did not have such effects in terms of their dominance, self-confidence, need for influence or power, and strong belief in the righteousness of their ideas.

Charismatic leadership is not likely to be exhibited equally in all circumstances. Shamir et al. (1993) argued that charismatic leadership is more likely to emerge under conditions of greater uncertainty and ambiguity—when performance cannot be easily quantified or measured, when means to achieve objectives are uncertain, and when it is difficult to link extrinsic rewards to individual achievement. They also noted that charismatic leadership is more likely under exceptional organizational conditions such as rapid changes in the environment, performance pressures, reorganizations, mergers, or sudden growth. Note that the conditions for the emergence of charismatic leadership are similar to those that Meindl et al. (1985) argued were associated with the romance of leadership. But that link is logical. The conditions that lead observers to attribute leadership and to want to feel control are precisely those conditions that would make the appearance of charisma more probable.

Because of the issues of attribution already discussed, experimental studies of charisma offer the cleanest exploration of these ideas. Howell and Frost (1989) conducted a study in which 144 second-year business students worked on a complex and realistic in-basket exercise as the experimental task. Participants were exposed to one of three leader behavior treatments—consideration, structuring, or charismatic—delivered by confederates who were provided scripts and had been trained to exhibit all three of the leadership styles employed in the study. The study also manipulated social information about the task by using co-worker confederates. Under one condition, co-workers expressed interest and enthusiasm, while in the other they expressed disinterest and boredom and made disparaging remarks about the relevance and usefulness of the exercise. Howell and Frost (1989) found that individuals who worked for charismatic leaders performed significantly better on the exercise, as rated by experts, and generated a wider variety of courses of action, indicating more flexibility and creativity. Furthermore, those subjects working for charismatic leaders reported significantly higher satisfaction and less role ambiguity and a better relationship with the leader. There was also a main effect of the social information manipulation.

The Howell and Frost (1989) study also begins to answer the question of whether leadership can be learned. Although there have been arguments that charisma emerges from certain distinct personality types (e.g., House, 1977; House, Spangler, and Wyocke, 1991), the Howell and Frost study demonstrated that, when people were given a script and training, various types of leader behavior can be exhibited, at least for a short period of time. The scientific exploration of whether leader behavior can be changed by various forms of training remains largely underdeveloped, but the burgeoning market for leadership courses and leadership training suggests at least that a substantial number of individuals and organizations believe that such learning is possible.

The literature on charismatic and transformational leadership also has something to say, indirectly, about some of the other mechanisms of social control. This literature suggests that the use of rewards and incentives, which is associated with transactional leadership, is likely to be less effective and possibly ineffective in ambiguous or stressful situations. And the literature on charisma is consistent with the implications of psychological commitment and organizational culture for developing control in organizations. Because the "rewards" offered by the charismatic leader are not tangible, abiding by the leader's requests creates a situation in which behavior has been altered for insufficient extrinsic reasons, which should lead to greater commitment to those behaviors. And, the organizational culture literature's emphasis on values is consistent with the similar emphasis in the transformational leadership literature.

There are a number of studies that have demonstrated the potency of informational social influence (e.g., R. W. Griffin, 1983; O'Reilly and Caldwell, 1979; see also Cialdini, 1988, for a review), such that we come to believe and to behave as others in our environment do and tell us to. Clearly, therefore, one of the critical roles of the leader is to interpret an ambiguous social reality, making sense of the situation in a way that can mobilize behavior and provide reassurance (e.g., Pfeffer, 1981b). This is accomplished through the use of language, and language is a powerful tool of leadership and social influence more generally. Pondy (1978), Weick (1979), and Peters (1978) have all emphasized the importance of language in the task of leadership. Eccles and Nohria noted, "To view management from a rhetorical perspective is to recognize that *the way people talk about the world has everything to do with the way the world is ultimately understood and acted in. . . .* The primary task of managerial language has always been to persuade individuals to put forth their best efforts in a collective enterprise with other men and women" (1992, p. 29). Consequently, "the basic task of management . . . is to mobilize action by using language creatively to appeal to the self- and collective identities of individuals" (p. 37).

The symbolic, rhetorical role of leadership would seem to rely on linguistic skills, having a good vocabulary, and possessing the ability to select images and language that reach and touch others. There is some case evidence that this is true. Eccles and Nohria (1992) compared the language of Jack Welch, CEO of General Electric and an individual who led it through an important transformation, with that of Roger Smith, the CEO of General Motors, who is generally acknowledged not to have helped the organization become better at competing in the automobile industry. They describe Welch's language as conveying "an imaginative vision of the future, a realistic portrayal of the present, and a selective depiction of the past which can serve as a contrast to the future" (p. 32). By contrast, Smith "externalized GM's problems" and never provided enough detail to his vision of building a twenty-first-century corporation to inspire action. Rhetoric that is effective in mobilizing action also maintains a balance between clarity and ambiguity:

> effective rhetoric aims to be clear but never *too* clear. It aims to be robust across as many different situations as possible, and to be flexible enough to incorporate the different meanings, emphases, and interpretations that different people will inevitably give to it. . . . The concept of robustness also implies that the rhetorical strategy should be dynamic, adjusting over time to evolving contingencies. (p. 35)

To the extent rhetorical skill is critical for leaders, leadership training might profitably involve training in drama and literature. It would be interesting to assess the extent of such training in conventional leadership education as well as to evaluate the effectiveness of this type of skill building compared to more cognitive and rationality-based leadership development. The literature on management as symbolic action presumes that there is enough uncertainty or ambiguity in situations such that language can direct and divert attention, creating meaning out of ambiguity. This symbolic role of management has been emphasized in writings about organizational culture (e.g., O'Reilly and Chatman, 1996) and is another link between these mechanisms of social control.

Can Leadership Be Developed, Taught, or Learned?

Management training, broadly defined, is big business indeed. Each year some 70,000 plus students graduate from MBA programs just in the United States, and business schools are developing and expanding all over the world. Books on leadership typically sell well, and leadership training for practicing managers is a boom industry in its own right. There have been literally decades of study about leader behaviors and their effects, and even the elements of charisma have been studied. Consequently, one might expect to see a large literature on whether or not leadership training makes a difference and which approaches are the most effective. However, such a literature is virtually nonexistent. As Gaziel noted, "it is . . . difficult to find reports on empirical investigations concerning the degree to which academic studies of management develop the skills and qualifications in their students required for successful performance of managerial roles" (1994, p. 341), and a similar scarcity of reliable research exists for other forms of management and leadership training as well. There are studies that rely on the self-reports of those who have experienced leadership training. Such reports should, of course, be viewed with a great deal of caution. Having invested time and energy in a course of study, one is likely to rationalize that investment by saying that it was helpful and useful. Moreover, many of these courses are at a minimum more pleasant than work and often allow students to bond with the other members of the class, and each of these effects would also be expected to produce high levels of participant-reported satisfaction with the programs.

Kirkpatrick (1979) has developed a useful overview of how to evaluate the effectiveness of leadership or, for that matter, any other kind of training. He argued that four criteria should be employed: (1) attitudes and perceptions of those who participated in the program; (2) learning, which refers to mastery of principles, concepts, facts, and techniques; (3) behavior, or whether participants actually do things differently as a consequence of having been exposed to the training; and (4) results, which refers to whether or not morale and turnover improves, whether economic performance is better, and so forth. Of course, doing a completely valid study of these four dimensions would be difficult, as the problems of inference are severe even with a control group design. Nevertheless, it does seem that given the substantial investment of effort, it would be useful to know whether the effort is worthwhile and, perhaps even more important, what forms of training and education are comparatively more efficacious under what circumstances.

In a study of the use of an assessment center process for developmental purposes, Engelbrecht and Fischer (1995) did find that the experience did have an effect even three months after participants had gone through it. Compared to a control group, those managers who went through the developmental assessment center process differed "in action orientation, task structuring, development, empathy, managing information, and probing. No significant difference was found in either synthesis or judgment. The results . . . indicate an improvement in managerial performance regarding the six . . . dimensions" (p. 397). Using behaviorally anchored rating scales, the study indicated that "the developmental assessment center process can . . . be considered to be accountable for 14.3% of the total variance in overall managerial performance . . . 3 months after center attendance" (p. 398). This study provides evidence that interventions can affect managerial behavior. It would be wonderful to have many more studies of this type, with samples large enough to indicate under what conditions these interventions have the greatest effect.

Conclusion

The subject of social control provokes ambivalence: on the one hand, it is a necessary and important part of organizations, but on the other hand, individuals want to believe that they are autonomous decision makers, exercising free will. Thus, there seems to be a preference for social control practices such as the use of financial rewards that have more of the character of a voluntary exchange and that don't rely on deeper social psychological processes such as commitment and emotion. Such control practices also fit more easily with the economic model of behavior, which is more ideologically attractive. It seems to be the case that U.S. organizations rely more on financial rewards than organizations in other cultures. This is also reflected in the disproportionate research attention on compensation. One wonders if this emphasis is because of individualistic, rational decision-oriented social values. The evidence does seem persuasive that control premised in culture, language, and socialization and commitment processes is quite effective, while the evidence on the efficacy of financial rewards is substantially more equivocal.

The ambivalence about the effects (if not the effectiveness) of social control is in part responsible for the development of a critical perspective on organizations and their control practices, a subject considered in chapter 8. And this ambivalence also has tended to result in the various social control perspectives talking past each other, thereby missing opportunities for studies contrasting and comparing the approaches. This remains an important research agenda.

6

Developing and Exercising Power
and Influence

Social control is often, although not invariably, embedded in a hierarchical process. Certainly leadership, the use of rewards and sanctions, and the development of an organizational culture all convey the implication of some central authority that is setting up the reward system, appointing the leaders, and establishing the corporate culture. For those living and working in organizations but not necessarily in the most senior positions, social control takes on another connotation—how to develop informal influence and power to achieve what one wants and needs for task accomplishment as well as for individual benefit.

The exercise of informal influence is important not only because of individual agendas, however. Changes in organizations have made lateral, nonhierarchical influence comparatively more important. Organizations have flattened their hierarchies, taking out levels of management as well as leagues of middle managers. There is simply less hierarchy left. The increasing emphasis on high-commitment or high-involvement work practices and the concomitant emphasis on self-managing teams (e.g., Katzenbach and Smith, 1993) means that the exercise of formal, hierarchical control is less consistent with organizational values and ways of organizing.

This deemphasis on formal authority has been hastened by the increasingly rapid pace of technological, social, and market change, with the corresponding requirement for organizations to reduce the time it takes to make decisions, design products or services, and bring them to market. The emphasis on speed means that few organizations can afford having decisions and information move up and down formal hierarchies of authority. As a result of these trends, there is increasing managerial and research interest in less formal ways of getting things done; these less formal methods rely more on power and influence, leverage individuals' positions in social networks, and entail ongoing negotiations among organizational participants. Consequently, the subjects of power and influence and the biases and problems that beset negotiations have drawn increasing scholarly attention.

Power and Influence

Power has had a bad name in social science research and is most often conspicuous by its absence from the literature. It is not just Williamson (e.g., Williamson and Ouchi, 1981) who has critiqued the concept and argued that it was neither necessary nor useful for understanding organizations. Courses about power and influence in schools of administration started only in the late 1970s and still exist in comparatively few institutions. A perusal of management texts at that time and even later reveals that power was often omitted entirely from consideration. When it was discussed, the emphasis was on a relatively simple conception of interpersonal power—French and Raven's (1968) bases of power (expert, reward, sanction, and so forth). Perrow noted that "the literature on power in organizations is generally . . . preoccupied with interpersonal or intergroup phenomena . . . or else it takes as the major dimension of power the relative and absolute power of levels in the hierarchy" (1970a, p. 60). Kipnis, Schmidt, and Wilkinson wrote that "organizational psychologists have not been particularly interested in studying the ways in which people at work influence their colleagues and superiors to obtain personal benefits or to satisfy organizational goals" (1980, p. 440). Although power may have always been important and certainly is becoming more so as hierarchical bases of authority erode under the environmental changes described above, power as an idea does not fit very well with either our conception of organizations and individuals as being rational utility and efficiency maximizers or with our social values that emphasize cooperation and deemphasize inequality in the access to social resources.

We are profoundly ambivalent about power (Pfeffer, 1992) and that ambivalence has led to recurrent questioning of the concept and its definition. Illustrating the pervasiveness of the ambivalence, Kanter noted, "Power is America's last dirty word. It is easier to talk about money—and much easier to talk about sex—than it is to talk about power" (1979, p. 65). John Gardner wrote, "In this country . . . power has such a bad name that many good people persuade themselves they want nothing to do with it" (1990, p. 55). Gandz and Murray, from a survey of 428 managers, provided empirical evidence of the ambivalence: although the managers overwhelmingly agreed with the statements "the existence of workplace politics is common to most organizations" and "successful executives must be good politicians," they also thought that "organizations free of politics are happier than those where there are a lot of politics" and "politics in organizations are detrimental to efficiency" (1980, p. 244).

After first considering the definition of power and issues of its measurement, we address three fundamental questions concerning power in organizations: (1) under what circumstances are power and influence more important in organizational decision making, and under what circumstances are political skills less critical for getting things done? (2) what are the important sources of power? and

(3) what are the strategies and tactics through which interpersonal influence is developed and exercised and power gets employed?

The Definition and Critique of the Concept of Power

Wrong defined power as the "intentional and effective control by particular agents" (1968, p. 676), a definition closely related to that offered by Russell: "the production of intended effects by some men on other men" (1938, p. 25). There are three key elements in the definition: the influence of some over others, the fact that power is not relegated to relations between superiors and subordinates but includes interactions among equals as well, and the idea that this influence is conscious and intended. Because of the concept of intent, Wrong saw power as narrower in its definition than the broader idea of social control: "When social controls have been internalized, the concept of power is clearly inapplicable. . . . We must distinguish the diffuse controls exercised by the group over social-ized individuals from direct, intentional efforts by a specific person or group to control another" (1968, p. 676).

Power is also sometimes distinguished from authority. Authority is authorized or legitimated power. The vesting of control in authorities not only makes the exercise of power appear less arbitrary and visible, it also reduces the costs of exercising power (Pfeffer, 1981b, p. 4). The exercise of authority is expected— that is why the authority is vested in certain roles and individuals in the first place. The exercise of power may not always be so welcomed.

In order to demonstrate influence or control, most definitions of power include the idea of overcoming resistance. Dahl (1957, pp. 202–203) defined power as a relation among actors in which one can get another to do something that the other would not otherwise have done. Emerson wrote, "The power of an actor A over actor B is the amount of resistance on the part of B which can be potentially overcome by A" (1962, p. 32).

There are also important distinctions made between power as a capacity and power as actually employed. Wrong noted, "power is usually defined as a *capacity* to control others. . . . The evidence that a person or group possesses the capacity to control others may be the frequency with which successful acts of control have been carried out in the past" (1968, p. 77). March also maintained that "there seems to be general consensus that . . . potential power is different from actually exerted power" (1966, p. 57). He wrote about what he termed activation models, which assume that "power is a potential and that the exercise of power involves some mechanism of activation" (p. 57).

The measurement of the concept of power, then, requires providing evidence of intentional effects on outcomes of importance and the ability to overcome resistance. As March has noted, this may be more difficult to do than first imagined. He contrasted power with models relying on chance:

> Suppose we imagine that each power encounter occurs between just two people chosen at random from the total population. . . . Further, assume that at each encounter we will decide who prevails by flipping a coin. If the total number of

encounters per person is relatively small and the total number of persons relatively large, such a process will yield a few people who are successful in their encounters virtually all of the time, others who are successful most of the time, and so on. . . . All of the chance models generate power distributions. They are spurious distributions in the sense that power, as we usually mean it, had nothing to do with what happened. But we can still apply our measures of power to the systems involved. (1966, pp. 51–52)

March noted that to distinguish power from chance, one needed to assess (1) whether power was stable over time, (2) whether power was stable over subject matter, (3) whether power was correlated with other personal attributes, and (4) whether power was susceptible to experimental manipulation. He argued that there was evidence for the presence of all of these conditions, and since that time in particular an extensive experimental literature on power (e.g., Cook et al., 1983) has emerged.

Nevertheless, March was concerned about the overuse of the concept of power in analyzing social decision situations. Because power was so ubiquitous and obvious in conversations about everyday life, there is a tendency "to assume that it is real and meaningful. . . . However . . . we run the risk of treating the social validation of power as more compelling than it is simply because the social conditioning to a simple force model is so pervasive" (1966, pp. 68–69). He also was concerned that because of the obviousness of power, it would come to be used as a residual category for explanation—a name for the unobserved variance in research studies. As Dahl noted, "a Thing to which people attach many labels with subtly or grossly different meanings in many different cultures and times is probably not a Thing at all but many Things" (1957, p. 201). Unless considered and studied quite carefully, the force activation model of power is quite difficult to disprove:

> It is clear from a consideration both of the formal properties of activation models and of the problems observers have had with such models that they suffer from their excessive a posteriori explanatory power. If we observe that power exists and is stable and if we observe that sometimes weak people seem to triumph over strong people, we are tempted to rely on an activation hypothesis to explain the discrepancy. (March, 1966, p. 61)

In studies of power, it is essential to measure power separate from its use and results and to define and measure power before the analysis of the social choice rather than after. Again, however, since these initial concerns, a number of studies have been reasonably successful in overcoming these empirical and theoretical difficulties. Nonetheless, it is wise to keep them in mind in evaluating the literature on power.

There is an alternative perspective that maintains that the very ability of respondents to so quickly identify power and to discuss it provides evidence of the validity of the concept. Perrow has argued forcefully for this position:

> Power is a preoccupation of the managers in the firms, as evidenced by the interview data. . . . Given the nature of the concept and the "reality," I am not disturbed that the term "power" has different meanings. . . . A single, consistent

meaning of power, or decomposition of the concept into various types, might be preferable, but I doubt it. The annual production of new typologies and distinctions . . . has been intellectually stimulating, but operationally a nightmare. . . . To tie respondents to only one meaning would violate their own perceptions of the complexity, as well as the reality, of power. (1970a, pp. 83–84)

Concepts are defined in fact by their operationalization, and consequently it is useful to consider how power has been measured. One approach has been to rely on reputation, with the presumption being that informants as individuals are both willing and able to provide information on the power of social units. Perrow's (1970a) study of power in twelve organizations asked respondents to rank each of the four groups (sales, production, research and development, and staff services, including accounting and finance) in terms of how much power they had. This procedure defines power as zero-sum through the measurement process. Perrow noted that such a simple question "does not reflect the complexity of the concept. . . . Yet . . . the internal consistency of subgroup perspectives suggests that the bald term 'power' does have some consistent meaning" (p. 63). A study of the power of subunits in breweries in Canada (Hinings et al., 1974) also relied on interviews and questionnaires to assess power. Studies of resource allocations in universities (Pfeffer and Salancik, 1974; Pfeffer and Moore, 1980b) assessed power, in part, by asking each department head to rate all the departments as to how much power they thought the departments possessed. In these latter cases, since ratings rather than rankings were used, power was not defined so as to be zero-sum.

The evidence is compelling that individuals understand the question and, moreover, that reputational indicators of power produce information that is highly correlated across respondents:

In the University of Illinois study, department heads were asked to rate, on a seven-point scale, the power of all of the departments being studied. Only one department head even asked for a definition of what was meant by the concept of power. . . . No department that was judged, overall, to be in the top third of the departments in terms of power was rated by a single individual as being lower than the top third. Similarly, no department that, overall, was rated in the bottom third in terms of power was rated by a single person as being higher than the bottom third. (Pfeffer, 1992, p. 55)

In part to overcome problems with reactivity and to be able to study power historically, which is obviously not possible if one relies solely on the reports of informants, other indicators of power have been developed. The studies of power in universities, for instance, assessed what were key committees in the university and then examined departmental representation on these committees as a measure of departmental power. The evidence indicated that this representational measure was significantly correlated with the measure of departmental power based on respondent reports, with a correlation of .61 at Illinois and .57 at the University of California (Pfeffer, 1981c, p. 59).

In corporations, power of various subunits can be similarly assessed by examining the functional backgrounds of senior-level executives such as the CEO or inside directors. For instance, the timing of the rise of attorneys to power at Pacific Gas and Electric can be ascertained by their representation in officer- and manager-level positions, where they increased from four in 1960 to eighteen by 1980 (Pfeffer, 1992, p. 58). Another measure of the power of attorneys in corporations is provided in a cross-cultural study by Miyazawa of U.S. based subsidiaries of Japanese firms. He measured the power and prominence of the legal department by its degree of professionalization, defined as "the employment of U.S. licensed lawyers as in-house lawyers and . . . the placing of a U.S. in-house lawyer at the head of the legal department" (1986, p. 100). In the typical Japanese corporation, the legal department is part of a general affairs department and tends to have lay people working on legal-related matters, so that using licensed attorneys represented a shift in the power of the department.

There are also suggestions in the literature that a reliable way to assess power is by examining its consequences (Pfeffer, 1992)—for instance, the salaries paid to people at comparable levels in different divisions, growth in budget, and so forth. As long as the assessment of power using one set of indicators, including effects of power on resource allocations, is used solely to predict other, distinct outcomes, there is no problem with this procedure. If power has been measured in a valid and reliable way, the various indicators should correlate with each other and should operate as theoretically expected in studies of power (e.g., the measures of power should be predicted by theoretically developed determinants of power and should explain outcomes that are presumably affected by power).

Finkelstein provided one of the most comprehensive evaluations of the measurement of power in corporations, albeit he was focusing on the power of individuals in the top management team. Many of his measures, however, could be generalized to other levels of analysis such as organizational subunits. He developed four separate indices of power. The first measured structural power, which "is related to the distribution of formal positions within an organization" (1992, p. 512). His indicators of structural power were the percentage of individuals in a top management team with higher titles than the given individual (for the CEO this number is 0), the total cash compensation received, and the number of official titles a manager held. The second power index measured ownership power. The indicators were (1) the percentage of a firm's shares owned by an executive, (2) the percentage of the firm's shares owned by the executive's family, and (3) whether or not the manager was the founder of the firm or was related to the founder and whether or not the manager was related to other senior managers. The third dimension of power assessed expert power. The measures were the number of different functional areas a manager had worked in, the number of different positions a manager had held in the firm, and whether or not the manager's functional background matched the requirements of the environment for particular expertise. The final overall indicator of power was called prestige power and "is related to a manager's ability to absorb uncertainty from the institutional environment" (p. 515). The four indicators of this dimension of power were (1) the total number of corporate boards a manager sat on; (2) the number of nonprofit boards a manager sat on; (3) the financial standing of the corporate boards of which an executive was a member; and (4) whether or not the manager had an elite education.

Finkelstein tested his measures of power on a sample of 1,763 top managers from 102 firms in three industries over a five-year period. A factor analysis of all of the indicators reproduced the four scales. Cronbach's alphas for each of the scales were reasonably high, ranging from .67 for prestige power to .83 for structural power. A second study that asked for the perceived power of individuals revealed that perceived power was most strongly correlated with structural power and prestige power and was not statistically significantly correlated with expert power and was only weakly correlated with ownership power. Finally, Finkelstein reported that the consideration of the power of senior managers permitted better predictions of diversification strategies than models that did not include the power indicators.

Conditions Affecting the Use of Power

Because of the inherent appeal of force activation conceptions of power, it is important to understand the conditions under which power is more likely to be employed. Salancik and Pfeffer (1974) argued that power and influence would be employed under conditions of resource scarcity and for critical resources or important decisions. If resources weren't scarce, there was little or no allocation problem and no need to mobilize power. Similarly, if the decision did not concern critical issues, there was little need to expend power resources on its determination. Their study of allocations of a number of different resources at the University of Illinois found evidence consistent with these predictions, although resource criticality and scarcity were too highly correlated for the items they studied to assess separate effects. For instance, the most critical and scarce resource, graduate fellowships, was correlated .44 with departmental representation on important committees, while the least critical and scarce resource, summer faculty fellowships, was correlated only .01 with that measure of power (p. 468).

A subsequent study of resource allocations to departments on two University of California campuses that varied in the scarcity of resources confronted again found support for the idea that power was used more under conditions of scarcity (Pfeffer and Moore, 1980b). Studying 295 management units in forty-six divisions of a large organization to explore the determinants of interunit influence attempts, Gresov and Stephens also found that resource constraints increased the likelihood of a unit's attempting to exercise influence. They noted that "proactive attempts to influence other units may lead to an alteration of work and information flows . . . that will change the extent and nature of demands on unit members and existing structures" (1993, p. 256), so that influence activity within a set of related units is one possible response to resource constraints and organizational design problems. They reported that interunit influence attempts were also more likely the lower the commitment to the status quo, the lower the managerial tenure, and the greater the managerial dissatisfaction with unit performance.

A somewhat different view of the relationship between slack and power behavior comes from V. E. Schein (1979). She distinguished between power-acquisition strategies and tactics related to the process of getting the work done and power processes "designed to promote the self-oriented objectives of the individuals. Objectives such as promotion or increased status are related far more to individual self-aggrandizement than they are to work-related objectives" (p. 290). She argued:

> it is proposed that the ratio of personal to work-related power acquisition behaviors is in favor of personal power . . . in high-slack systems, whereas the reverse is true in low-slack systems. . . . Vigorous competition in the environment will prevent managers from tailoring their activities to achieve their own personal end and will require more work-related behaviors. . . . The absence of such competitive conditions permits managers to pursue their own goals without obvious disruption of the system. (p. 290)

Schein's article did not provide any evidence for the claim that efficiency considerations would drive out at least some forms of power behavior—the most self-serving—and this remains an important empirical question. There is the problem with this argument that the very definition of how much slack or how much environmental pressure there is, the question of what is the most appropriate response, and the issue of which individuals or units are best suited to coping with the problem are all settled at least in part through a political process.

Surveys of managers by Gandz and Murray (1980) and Madison et al. (1980) asking what levels, functions, and decisions in organizations seemed to most involve the use of power revealed that power was used more in major decisions, such as reorganizations or personnel changes, and was used more at senior organizational levels, which also presumably deal with more important decisions. Their results also indicated that power was used more in areas in which there was more uncertainty and in which performance was harder to assess (e.g., staff rather than line production operations).

This idea that power would be used more under conditions of uncertainty or ambiguity has been examined in a number of studies focusing on science and academia. The basic idea came from a typology of decision situations developed by Thompson and Tuden (1959). They categorized decision situations according to whether or not there was agreement about goals or preferences and whether or not there was agreement about technology—the connections between actions and their consequences. A summary of their typology noted:

> computational decision making procedures involved in rational choice are used in decision making only when there is agreement both on the goals and on the connections between actions and outcomes. When there is no agreement on goals, compromise is required to reach a decision. When there is no agreement on technology, judgment is necessary to determine the best course in achieving consensually shared goals. And when there is neither agreement on goals nor on technology, an unstructured, highly politicized form of decision making is likely to occur. (Pfeffer, 1981, p. 71)

The operationalization of the operation of power in these studies has typically been to examine the extent to which resources are allocated to individuals who share an important social affiliation under varying conditions of uncertainty—for instance, to what extent do National Science Foundation grant allocations match the composition of the review panel, controlling for other factors, under varying degrees of uncertainty? The presumption in this research is that allocations based on social similarity or on shared social connections reflect the operation of influence and politics. In a series of studies that equated the degree of uncertainty with the extent to which a scientific field was paradigmatically developed (Lodahl and Gordon, 1972), it was shown that the greater the degree of uncertainty (or the lower the level of paradigm development characterizing a field), the greater the effect of politics on National Science Foundation grant allocations (Pfeffer, Salancik, and Leblebici, 1976), the choice of editorial board members (Yoels, 1974), and the publishing of articles (Pfeffer, Leong, and Strehl, 1977).

Pfeffer (1992) has also argued that power is used more when there are differences in point of view or disagreements that must be resolved. And social influence and politics will be used more when interdependence among subunits is higher, requiring more coordination of behavior and increasing the interdependence of that behavior.

Sources of Power

Research has identified numerous sources of power for both individuals and organizational subunits. Some sources of power are personal characteristics. R. W. Allen et al. (1979) interviewed eighty-seven managers, including thirty chief executives, in southern California electronics firms to assess their beliefs about the personal characteristics associated with being powerful and being effective in the use of organizational politics. The characteristics mentioned most frequently were: articulate, sensitive, socially adept, competent, and popular. The study raises two issues. First, in relating personal characteristics to power, one needs to be careful that the characteristics associated with power (for example, self-confidence or being popular) are not a *consequence* of power rather than its source. It is reasonable to argue that one will be more socially adept and popular to the extent one has power—these characteristics may be both products and sources of power. The characteristics may also not be independent of each other—articulate and sensitive people may be more popular as a result. Second, there is the question of the extent to which these characteristics are relatively fixed or are malleable. Some, such as sensitivity and articulateness, can presumably be affected by training in clinical skills and public speaking, respectively.

Other sources of power are structural, deriving from one's position in the division of labor or one's location in the network of communication. As Perrow noted, "the preoccupation with interpersonal power has led us to neglect one of the most obvious aspects of this subject: in complex organizations, tasks are divided up between a few major departments or subunits, and all of these subunits are not likely to be equally powerful" (1970a, p. 59). One structural source of power is the ability to cope with the uncertainty an organization faces (Hickson et al., 1971; Hinings et al., 1974). Since the form and amount of uncertainty can vary, depending on the particular decision and situation, so too do the characteristics associated with having power.

For instance, a study of 304 professionals in a research and development laboratory (Tushman and Romanelli, 1983) found that the type of person who had the most influence depended on the type of project—in applied research units, individuals who spanned boundaries were the most influential, while in technical service projects, with less uncertainty, those most central in the internal communication structure had more power. Boeker (1989), examining the power of subunits in semiconductor firms, discovered that founding conditions and the background of the entrepreneur that started the company affected relative power and the perceived importance of different functional units. Miyazawa's study of the status and professionalization of legal departments in thirty-six of the largest Japanese subsidiaries operating in the United States found that this varied by "the industrial specialization of the subsidiary" (1986, p. 152). Although the trading subsidiaries were the largest, they were among the least professionalized. By contrast, subsidiaries in the field of transportation equipment had comparatively larger legal staffs with higher-status personnel, because there were more legal risks, particularly pertaining to product liability and antitrust.

Another important source of power is the ability to provide resources for the organization. Studies of universities (Salancik and Pfeffer, 1974; Pfeffer and Moore, 1980b) found that those departments that brought in the most grants and contracts, with their associated overhead, had the most power. J. D. Hackman (1985) has referred to the ability to obtain critical resources needed by the institution as environmental power and found this to be related to university departments' power.

The ability to cope with uncertainty or to bring in resources is not enough—it is also important that the individual or work unit be central in the workflow and communication structure to develop and exercise influence. Pettigrew's (1972; 1973) case study of a computer purchase decision illustrated how a manager who sat astride the flow of communication was able to substantially influence the final decision through his ability to filter and selectively present information. Ibarra, investigating the effects of individual attributes, formal position, and network centrality on the exercise of influence, reported that centrality was more important for administrative innovation roles and was equal to formal position in its effects on exercising influence in technical innovation roles. She concluded that "an organization's informal structure may be more critical than its formal structure when the exercise of power requires extensive boundary spanning" (1993a, p. 471). Brass and Burkhardt (1993) also found that an individual's network centrality was significantly related to others' perceptions of that individual's power.

Power accrues to those who can more accurately assess the social landscape. Krackhardt (1990) studied a small entrepreneurial firm and compared perceptions of the friendship and advice network to the actual networks, as empirically assessed. Those with more accurate perceptions of the existing advice network were rated as being more powerful by others in the organization, although accurate perceptions of the friendship network were unrelated to perceived power.

Because power is used to obtain resources (Pfeffer and Salancik, 1974; Pfeffer and Moore, 1980b), power becomes self-perpetuating through the effective use of the resources so acquired. Boeker (1989) found that the power distribution established at the time of a firm's founding tended to persist in his sample of semiconductor firms. Studying subunits in health care clinics, Lachman (1989) observed that previous power position was the best predictor of subsequent power. One way in which power is self-perpetuating is through the impact of the effective use of power on an individual's reputation, which then becomes a source of power: "Most observers would agree that present reputations for power are at least in part a function of the results of past encounters. . . . Most observers would probably also agree that power reputation, in turn, affects the results of encounters" (J. G. March, 1966, p. 57).

Power also derives from formal position or authority. Brass and Burkhardt (1993) reported that level in the organizational hierarchy was significantly related to others' perceptions of a focal individual's power. Sometimes that formal position can be used to protect the powerholder from the consequences of poor performance. Boeker (1992) studied sixty-seven organizations over a twenty-two-year period and asked what happened to chief executives when organizational performance was poor. He found that powerful chief executives were able to survive performance downturns by displacing the blame onto their subordinates, who tended to be replaced when performance suffered. By contrast, less powerful chief executives, who had less power because they owned less of the company's stock and there were more outsiders on the board of directors, were not able to displace poor performance and fire their subordinates; rather, they were replaced themselves.

Power is built by doing favors for others. Studies of the power of chief executives and its effects consistently find that the higher the proportion of outside directors the CEO has appointed, the more favorably that individual is treated. The argument is that being appointed to the board by someone activates a norm of reciprocity, and one is tied to the individual who did the appointing. Wade, O'Reilly, and Chandratat (1990) noted that there was a higher incidence of the provision of golden parachutes—contracts that pay off executives if they lose their jobs because of a change in control of the corporation, through a takeover, for instance—for CEOs who had been able to appoint more outsiders to their boards.

Strategies and Tactics for Using Power

Studies of how power is actually employed are scarcer than studies of the determinants of power or the conditions under which it is used in organizations, for the simple reason that the empirical obstacles to conducting such analyses are greater. Pfeffer (1992) has proposed a number of tactics for exercising power: (1) those having to do with timing, including delay, waiting, and moving first; (2) interpersonal influence strategies such as social proof, liking, commitment, contrast, reciprocity, and scarcity (Cialdini, 1988); (3) strategic presentation of information and analysis and selective use of data to buttress one's case; (4) reorganization to consolidate power or to break up the ability of one's opponents to coalesce; (5) use of evocative, emotion-producing language to mobilize support or quiet opposition; and (6) use of task forces and committees to co-opt opposition. Most of these techniques were illustrated with examples, but a few have some systematic empirical study behind them.

An insightful article by Schwartz (1974) analyzed waiting and delay as both indicators of power and as ways of exercising power. Schwartz provided anecdotal examples to illustrate the general theoretical point:

> Waiting is patterned by the distribution of power in a social system. This assertion hinges on the assumption that power is directly associated with an individual's scarcity as a social resource and, thereby, with his value as a member of a social unit. . . . The person who desires a valued service generally cannot gain immediate access to its dispenser, but must instead wait until others are accommodated. . . . To be able to make a person wait is, above all, to possess the capacity to modify his conduct in a manner congruent with one's own interests. To be delayed is . . . to be dependent upon the disposition of the one whom one is waiting for. The latter . . . by virtue of this dependency . . . finds himself further confirmed in his position of power. (pp. 843–844)

Schwartz noted that waiting is a form of investment and, like other forms of investment and commitment, increases the value of the object being sought. If one did not think the person waited for was important or valuable, then one would have engaged in a senseless activity. Conversely, the more one waits, the more important and valuable must be that which is waited for, to make sense of one's own behavior:

> if we regard waiting for a scarce service as an investment or sacrifice in return for a gain, we may measure part of the value of the gain by assessing the degree of sacrifice occasioned on its behalf. . . . The subjective value of the gain is therefore given not only by the objective value of the service but also by the amount of time invested in its attainment. . . . The other's service becomes valuable (and he becomes powerful) precisely because he is waited for. (1974, p. 857)

These initial insights on the relationship between time, waiting, and power have not been extensively pursued in subsequent empirical study. This seems a shame, because, as Schwartz noted, "queuing for resources is . . . a fundamental practice of social organization" (1974, p. 842). Much could be learned about power distributions by examining patterns of waiting time, and the use of delay or waiting to create or ratify power remains to be empirically explored, particularly as to the boundaries beyond which this strategy may backfire.

In an attempt to systematically understand influence tactics, Kipnis, Schmidt, and Wilkinson (1980) developed a fifty-eight-item questionnaire focused on various targets of influence (peers, superiors, and subordinates) that was factor analyzed to extract eight dimensions of influence: assertiveness, ingratiation, rationality, sanctions, exchange, upward appeals, blocking, and coalitions. They found that the use of these influence tactics varied systematically with the context in which they were attempted. The higher the status of the target person, the greater the reliance on rationality tactics (e.g., writing a memo, using logic, or making a plan). Assertiveness was used more with lower-status targets, and exchange was used most frequently with co-workers. The reasons for exercising influence also affected the choice of tactics: personal assistance prompted the use of ingratiation, while efforts to improve a target individual's performance tended to rely on assertiveness and rationality. Kipnis et al. found that "respondents showed the least variation in choice of tactics when attempting to influence their subordinates. No matter what the reason for influencing subordinates, the use of assertiveness . . . accounted for the most variance for each reason" (1980, p. 450). The study found no effect of gender on the choice of influence tactics. Brass and Burkhardt (1993), studying how others perceive an individual's power, found that some behavioral tactics, such as the use of assertiveness, ingratiation, exchange, and forming coalitions with others, were significantly related to perceptions of power, and this effect was independent of structural position.

Kipnis and Schmidt (1988) explored how the influence tactics used by subordinates on their superiors affected their salaries, evaluations, and tension or stress. Based on responses to six scales, four types of influence styles were identified: (1) shotgun, typified by individuals who tended to use all of the influence strategies almost indiscriminately, and were particularly high on the use of assertiveness; (2) ingratiator, typified by individuals who scored high on friendliness and had average scores on the other scales; (3) bystander, typified by individuals who scored low on their use of all of the influence strategies, and (4) tactician, typified by individuals who scored high on the reason (or rationality) strategy and had average scores on the other scales. They found that men and women who used a shotgun style received lower performance ratings. For men, the style that worked best was the tactician. In a study of CEO salaries, Kipnis and Schmidt (1988) found that those that employed the tactician strategy earned more than those using other approaches. The shotgun style was associated with the most stress and tension. This study complements the earlier study of Kipnis and his colleagues that investigated the correlates of the use of different influence approaches by showing that different influence styles have different levels of effectiveness. One issue with all of the Kipnis studies is that they rely on self-reports of influence behavior, which may not be completely accurate. However, there is no reason to believe that the errors are systematically related to the effects being studied.

Gargiulo (1993) studied the use of co-optation to overcome political constraint in a cooperative agribusiness in South America. He found that, consistent with resource dependence (Pfeffer and Salancik, 1978) predictions, leaders tended to build ties of interpersonal obligation with people who directly affected their performance in the organization. When, however, such direct ties could not be built, because of interpersonal friction or fundamental differences about policy, effective leaders used a two-step process in which they built co-optive relations with others who could affect the behavior of the person on whom they depended. Pfeffer and Salancik (1977), in their study of resource allocations at the University of Illinois, discovered that department heads that (1) knew their department's comparative position along a set of possible criteria for resource allocation and (2) advocated those criteria in decision making were able to obtain more resources for their departments, even controlling for the power of the department.

Power is accomplished through talk. In an interesting analysis of some testimony from the Watergate hearings, Molotch and Boden investigated "the ways people invoke routine conversational procedures to accomplish power" (1985, p. 273). They noted that there were three faces of power:

The first face of power is the capacity to prevail in explicit contests. . . . A second face of power (somewhat less visible) is the ability to set agendas, to determine the issues over which there will be any explicit contest at all. . . . Our third face of power is the most basic of all: it is the ability to determine the very grounds of the interactions through which agendas are set and outcomes determined; it is the struggle over the linguistic premises upon which the legitimacy of accounts will be judged. (p. 273)

Their focus was on Senator Gurney's attempts to discredit the very damaging testimony of John Dean. Gurney was a Republican and a partisan defender of President Nixon; John Dean had been the president's legal counsel and provided evidence concerning Nixon's role in the Watergate cover-up. Gurney's strategy was to demand the literal truth, free of any interpretive context—to demand just the facts. When Dean could not provide this "literal truth" and sought to explain the circumstances of a particular conversation, Gurney used this as a way to discredit Dean's account. As Molotch and Boden noted, *"if all accounts are potentially vulnerable to the challenge that they are not really objective, then any conversationalist is open—at all times—to the charge of interactive incompetence"* (p. 274, emphasis in original). They concluded by noting that "demands for 'just the facts,' the simple answers, the forced-choice response, preclude the 'whole story' that contains another's truth" (p. 285). Gurney was able to translate his potential power advantage, derived from being a U.S. senator, the questioner in the proceedings, and Dean's admission of personal culpability in the events, into an interactional advantage through the use of a conversational ploy of asking only for the literal truth. In addition to providing a specific example of a conversational strategy used for exercising power, the Molotch and Boden study illustrates the potential for this line of analysis to illuminate other situations in which talk is part and parcel of how power is accomplished.

Emotion is, along with language, another important way in which influence is exercised in organizational settings. As Rafaeli and Sutton wrote, "The view that organization members routinely use expressed positive emotions as tools of social influence is ubiquitous in organizational behavior" (1991, p. 749). Expressed negative emotion can also be a potent influencer. Sutton's (1991) study of bill collectors found that negative emotions could be part of an influence strategy of negative reinforcement—when the debtor paid (or at least promised to pay), the anger and disapproval expressed by the bill collector stopped. Thus, the debtor was reinforced (a noxious external stimulus was removed) for agreeing to pay. "Bill collectors believe that expressed emotions such as anger, irritation, and mild disapproval serve as tools of social influence when such conveyed feelings induce anxiety in debtors, and debtors construe that escape from such anxiety will be the consequence of complying with the collectors' demands" (Rafaeli and Sutton, 1991, p. 750).

In an ethnographic study of bill collectors and Israeli police interrogators, Rafaeli and Sutton explored the use of emotional contrast strategies as tools of social influence. The principle is that "stimuli that are presented before, during, or after a given stimulus shape its meaning" (1991, p. 750), so that what is nice or noxious behavior is very much affected by the context in which that behavior occurs. Thus, for instance, Kipnis and Vanderveer (1971) found that subjects in the role of supervisor were more likely to give larger pay raises and higher performance evaluations to subordinates attempting influence through ingratiation when a hostile co-worker was present as contrasted to situations in which that hostile co-worker was not present. The Rafaeli and Sutton data suggested that five emotional contrast strategies were employed: "(1) sequential good cop, bad cop, (2) simultaneous good cop, bad cop, (3) one person playing both roles, (4) good cop in contrast to hypothetical bad cop, and (5) good cop in contrast to expectations of bad cop" (1991, p. 758). They argued that the presence (or threatened presence) of both styles of behavior made the good cop behavior appear nicer and the bad cop behavior appear nastier than if either were presented alone. They concluded that there were three mechanisms through which the perceived amplification of expressed emotion, accomplished by using emotional contrast strategies, worked:

> First, target persons may experience accentuated anxiety in response to bad cops and accentuated relief in response to good cops when there is a contrast. . . . They may acquiesce with requests for compliance in order to escape from the anxiety or fear. . . . Second, the contrast may accentuate the targets' perceptions that good cops are kind and helpful. As a result, the targets may feel pressure to reciprocate the kindness by complying with the good cops' wishes. Third, accentuated feeling of relief in response to good cops . . . may lead target people to develop trust in the good cops. (pp. 764–766)

Our understanding of power and influence processes has advanced substantially through research using multiple methods. What that work has not done yet is to explore the scope conditions for the various influence strategies and sources of power. We know less than we might about how strategies of social influence fail, about when theoretically predicted determinants of power don't predict actual power, and about when power is used in situations either more or less than predicted by the context. Consequently, some important research remains to be done.

Negotiation in Organizations

One of the important ways in which interpersonal influence is accomplished is through negotiation. Research on negotiation is an active area and therefore warrants attention distinct from other interpersonal influence issues. One reason research on negotiation has grown is that negotiation is ubiquitous in and between organizations (Lax and Sebenius, 1986). Individuals negotiate salaries and other terms and conditions of employment, they negotiate for budgets and other resources for their work groups, they may negotiate with suppliers or customers or with various regulatory or governmental bodies, and as members of a task force or team they may negotiate over preferred courses of action and decisions. Interpersonal influence is often exercised through a process of negotiation. Since the mid-1980s there has been an explosive growth in research on negotiations and a possibly even greater increase in courses and seminars dealing with the subject.

Up until the 1990s, virtually all of the literature on negotiation ignored context almost completely, focusing either on the structure of payoffs and relative power or on individual differences in negotiation behavior. More recently, much of the research has focused on cognitive biases because of the premise that "to negotiate most effectively negotiators need to make more rational decisions" (Neale and Bazerman, 1991, p. 1). This research builds on the extensive work on biases in decision making (e.g., Tversky and Kahneman, 1974) under the premise that "negotiation represents a special case of decision making" (Neale and Northcraft, 1990, p. 56). This cognitive emphasis contrasts with the game theoretic approach to analyzing strategic interaction in economics, an approach that implies that "the structure of the negotiation determines its outcomes. The behavior and cognitions of players during negotiations simply represent the unfolding . . . of the structure. . . . Similarly, game theory allows no explicit role for the social processes that behavioral scientists often argue characterize negotiation (Neale and Bazerman, 1991, p. 9).

The decision- or cognitive-bias approach also contrasts with an earlier focus on the effect of individual differences and personality on negotiation processes and outcomes. Neale and Bazerman, reviewing the extensive literature on the effect of individual differences such as gender, cognitive complexity, locus of control, self-esteem, and risk preferences on negotiations, concluded that "individual differences offer little insight into predicting negotiator behavior and negotiation outcomes" (1991, p. 4). These authors also eschewed emphasizing the effects of situations, not because situational factors such as power differences or a negotiator's particular audience or constituency are unimportant, but rather because these situational factors cannot typically be altered by negotiators.

A number of cognitive biases have been reliably uncovered, many of which are consistent with the more general literature on decision biases (Tversky and Kahneman, 1974). "A variety of heuristics have been identified which systematically distort the negotiation process and potentially bias negotiation outcomes. Four of these cognitive heuristics are framing, anchoring-and-adjustment, availability, and overconfidence" (Neale and Northcraft, 1990, p. 57). There is a tendency for negotiators to rely too much on available information (Neale, 1984). "Colorful, dynamic, concrete, and otherwise vivid or distinctive stimuli disproportionately attract attention and . . . influence decision makers' deliberations" (Neale and Northcraft, 1990, p. 59). As an example in a negotiating context, opportunity costs, the cost of an alternative forgone, are much less vivid than out-of-pocket costs and are therefore not given enough weight in negotiations (Northcraft and Neale, 1986).

The idea of framing comes from prospect theory (Kahneman and Tversky, 1979), which suggests that "decision makers are risk-averse when choosing between certain gains and the risk of larger or no gains, but are risk-seeking when choosing between certain losses and the risk of larger or no losses" (Neale and Northcraft, 1990, p. 57). The same outcome can be framed as a gain or a loss depending on the individual's initial negotiating position and expectations. Studies (e.g., Neale and Bazerman, 1985) have shown that positively framed negotiations result in more completed agreements, but negatively framed negotiations result in completed agreements of greater value (Neale and Northcraft, 1990, p. 58).

Anchoring-and-adjustment reflects the process by which an arbitrarily chosen reference point influences judgments and behavior. This phenomenon accounts for the importance of the initial offer in bargaining, which then anchors subsequent adjustments. Northcraft and Neale (1987) have shown how a house's listing price anchors the estimates of its market value, even for experienced real estate agents. Because of the importance of the initial bargaining position in anchoring future concessions (which move from this initial position), "tough-to-soft" (Chertkoff and Conley, 1967) and "door-in-the-face" (Coker, Neale, and Northcraft, 1987) negotiating strategies are quite successful. Negotiation research has also demonstrated that negotiators are frequently overconfident in their ability to obtain favorable outcomes (Bazerman and Neale, 1982). In a situation of final offer arbitration, negotiators believed their offer had a 67.8 percent probability of being accepted (Bazerman and Neale, 1982). This overconfidence decreased negotiators' willingness to make concessions (Neale and Bazerman, 1985). Research has shown that negotiators frequently overlook the opportunity to negotiate for mutual gains because of the assumption that the situation is zero-sum (Bazerman, Magliozzi, and Neale, 1985) and are trapped by previously adopted positions in a process of commitment (Northcraft and Neale, 1986). There is evidence that concessions by opponents are devalued (Stillenger et al., 1990) and that there is frequently little effort made by negotiators to try to understand their opponent's cognitive perspective or interests (Bazerman and Carroll, 1987), thereby missing out on some information that would be useful to formulating a more effective negotiating approach.

Although cognitive bias may be important, it is not everything in understanding negotiation or, for that matter, other behavior in organizations. Tetlock has identified much of this research as relying on one of two metaphors: (1) "the social perceiver as intuitive psychologist who strives for 'cognitive mastery of the causal structure of the environment' (Kelley, 1967, p. 193)" and (2) "the intuitive economist whose primary goal in life is the maximization of subjective expected utility" (1992, p. 334). He wrote, "the psychologist and economist research programs have largely ignored the social settings in which people make most decisions. Subjects in laboratory studies of cognitive processes rarely feel accountable to others for the positions they take. They function in a social vacuum . . . in which they do not need to worry about the interpersonal consequences of their conduct" (Tetlock, 1992, p. 335).

Recent research has brought social context into the study of negotiations (e.g., Kramer and Messick, 1995). Much as Tetlock (1985a) demonstrated that decision biases were affected by the presumed presence of a social context that made an individual accountable, this research on negotiation has demonstrated that the experimental induction of a particular social identity, accomplished on occasion by subtle changes in task structure (Larrick and Blount, 1995), have important consequences for activating cooperative or competitive behavior. Some studies on the effects of social context involve constituent accountability, where negotiators are acting on behalf of a larger constituency. "These studies find that when negotiators are accountable to constituents who are monitoring their performance, they are more likely to engage in noncooperative behavior during negotiation" (Kramer, Pommerenke, and Newton, 1993, p. 639). Under conditions of accountability, there is less likelihood of reaching agreement, concessions are reduced, and there is more use of competitive bargaining tactics. Tetlock has noted, "accountability to constituents . . . induces concern for appearing strong by refusing to make concessions. People respond by employing competitive bargaining tactics that, while obstacles to resolving conflicts of interest, are quite effective in protecting their images in the eyes of constituents" (1985a, p. 311).

Kramer, Pommerenke, and Newton (1993) examined the effect of making social identity and accountability salient in a two-person negotiation context. Social identity was manipulated by having the subjects, MBA students, list all the ways in which they were similar to other MBAs (high social identification) or to list all the ways in which they were unique or different (low social identification). Kramer et al. argued and found that in high social-identity conditions, negotiating outcomes would be more equal (there would be smaller differences in the scores earned by the two parties to the negotiation), because "decision making will reflect greater concern with the outcomes obtained by the other person" (p. 638). Accountability also increased the equality of negotiating outcomes, because "when individuals feel interpersonally accountable to another party, they are more likely to use an equality rule when dividing resources" (p. 640).

As Barley has noted, "In daily life, persons are almost always members of groups whose values and beliefs shape their behavior and cognition. People typically dispute and bargain as members of families, communities, cliques, and organizations, not as isolated actors whose judgment is unfettered by social relationships" (1991, p. 169). Consequently, this line of research is substantively important for understanding negotiation. It brings elements of the social model of behavior to the task of understanding this important social process.

In addition to bringing in social context effects, research has explored the effects of motivational and affective processes on negotiations. Carnevale and Isen (1986), for example, found that inducing a positive mood facilitated integrative bargaining. Kramer, Newton, and Pommerenke (1993) reported that individuals who were higher in self-esteem were more confident and optimistic prior to negotiating and more confident about their doing well in the negotiation process. Inducing a positive mood also increased negotiator optimism and confidence. They noted that "if negotiators maintain unrealistically optimistic beliefs about their abilities and outcomes, they may avoid accepting agreements that they perceive as falling short of their aspirations" (p. 125). Consequently, self-enhancing bias may be another factor that affects the negotiating process in important ways.

The rise of social cognition as a dominant theoretical perspective in the negotiations realm duplicates its prominence in much of social psychology. But particularly in the domain of interpersonal influence, the emphasis on cognitive biases and departures from rational decision making seems too limited. First, in spite of Neale and Bazerman's (1991) concern with the link between description and prescription, it is not clear that knowing about cognitive biases, or even training in them and how to overcome them, invariably alters subsequent behavior (but see Lehman, Lempert, and Nisbett, 1988).

In light of the numerous courses and training programs in negotiation, there is a paucity of research on what determines negotiator effectiveness and whether or not negotiation training has an effect. Neale and Northcraft (1986) contrasted the negotiation outcomes produced by professional corporate real estate negotiators with those produced by undergraduate and graduate business students. They found that there was no difference between amateurs and experienced negotiators in their susceptibility to the framing bias but that "experts were significantly more integrative (i.e., were able to achieve agreements of greater joint benefit) than were amateurs" (Neale and Northcraft, 1990, p. 69). Northcraft and Neale (1987) examined the anchoring-and-adjustment bias using both experienced real estate agents and students that asked subjects to estimate the value of a house. The anchor was the presumed listing price. The study found that experts did not overcome this decision bias better than amateurs and that, in fact, amateurs were more aware of the fact that the listing price was influencing their judgments. Neale and Northcraft concluded, "Experience . . . can lead to superior negotiator performance. However, the truly adaptive superior performance or expertise comes from having an appropriate strategic conceptualization of the negotiation process. . . . If cognitive bias in negotiation is preconscious, amelioration of bias will depend upon the identification of non-cognitive aids to decision making" (1990, pp. 71–72).

In an experimental study of the effects of assigned goals and training on negotiator performance, Northcraft, Neale, and Earley (1994) found evidence that training improved performance and that there was a significant training by goal setting interaction. In the study, the training manipulation consisted of a presentation on bargaining and negotiation in which the lecturer "defined negotiation, defined and described advantages of distributive and integrative negotiating strategies, and developed a model of transforming potentially distributive negotiations into integrative agreements" (p. 263). The data reported in their Table 2 (p. 265) reveals that subjects exposed to training increased their performance substantially, compared to control subjects who had only the benefit of experience in a prior negotiation. Thus, there is some evidence that training can have an effect, although how long and under what conditions remains to be examined. The effect of experience on negotiation outcomes is more equivocal, which calls into question how much learning occurs. There would seem to be real value in seeing what can overcome the cognitive biases that beset negotiators and if overcoming these biases affects negotiation outcomes.

A second problem with the almost exclusive emphasis on decision making and social cognition is that the neglect of situational factors because they are not presumably under the negotiator's control seems an unsatisfactory reason for avoiding their study. It is far from clear that some relevant situational factors, including changing the situation to make certain social identities and affiliations more or less salient, are not capable of being affected. And, the study of processes of interpersonal influence would benefit from a comprehensive exploration of what actually affects interpersonal influence before moving to judgment about what is and what is not capable of being altered.

Conclusion

The topics of power and negotiation again illustrate many of the issues that characterize and influence the development of organization studies. The topic of power is more likely to be comfortably located in a sociology or political science department than in a business school, with its emphasis on the economic model of behavior and on rational decision making. Thus, one might speculate that one consequence of the changing locus of organization studies has been less emphasis on power and influence than there might otherwise be, given the importance of the subject for understanding organizations.

Moreover, the study of power was particularly vigorous in the early 1970s—a time at which both the strategic contingencies (Hickson et al., 1971) and resource dependence (Pfeffer and Salancik, 1978) perspectives developed. The 1970s was a particularly political period, comprising both the end of the Vietnam War and the associated political protests and the resignation of Richard Nixon as a consequence of the Watergate scandal. The 1980s and 1990s have been much more politically quiescent; this fact, coupled with a sometimes difficult job market, may also have made power and influence less likely to be subjects of as much research attention.

Power as a topic also suffers from the problem of being politically incorrect. As noted in the discussion of views of control, we prefer a voluntaristic, choice-based conception of action. Considerations of domination and force, of getting one's way against opposition—which is, after all, a part of most definitions of power—perhaps are better left out of sight or discussion. The field's increasing embeddedness in an economic, rational conception of behavior is nicely coupled with its renewed emphasis on the individual as contrasted with the situation. Both rationality and a focus on the individual in isolation more easily permit neglect of issues of interpersonal influence.

To the extent the field borrows from psychology, then the cognitive emphasis in psychology becomes evident in the literature on negotiations. Moreover, there is a practicality to conducting research on negotiations that further pushes the literature in this direction. Subject pools are virtually nonexistent in business schools, which means that, if one wants subjects for experiments, one needs to capitalize on the availability of students in classes, for instance, on negotiation. Although it is possible to study cognitive biases in class settings, explorations of the effects of social context are much more difficult to conduct. So, context and influence of adjacent fields come to affect not only what is studied but how.

7

Organizational Performance

One important goal of organization studies is not only to be able to explain and predict outcomes within organizations but also to be able to understand why some organizations fare better than others. There is, of course, substantial managerial interest in understanding performance, but there are theoretical reasons as well for attempting to explain why some organizations do better than others. Performance differences, once generally apprehended, will almost certainly lead to attempts to mimic the more effective organizations. In that sense, performance differences create pressures for imitation. Second, to the extent that competitive markets function, both labor and capital will be drawn to more successful organizations, so that over time a continuing process of natural selection favors higher performing organizations. Thus, understanding what factors affect performance can help us predict what the distribution of organizational characteristics will look like in the future—those characteristics associated with success will be more frequently represented in the population because of processes of mimetic adaptation and natural selection.

The study of organizational performance is a vast topic and includes contributions from economics as well as organization theory. We focus here on three of the more prominent organizational approaches for understanding performance—structural contingency theory and the literature on organizational design, the population ecology of organizations, with its focus on competition and natural selection as a way of understanding organizational births and deaths, and the recent work on the effects of management practices, particularly with respect to how the firm manages its human resources, on organizational performance typically measured in terms of productivity, quality, or stock market performance. Another important perspective on performance, emphasizing the organization's network position and its connection to external sources of support, was considered as part of the discussion of the social model of behavior in chapter 3 and is therefore not repeated here. The evidence is clear, however, that an organization's network position and the resulting structural constraint has important effects on profitability (e.g., Burt, 1983).

A cautionary word is in order. Although all of economic theory and much of organization theory treats survival and performance as highly correlated—organizations that don't perform effectively don't survive—Meyer and Zucker (1989) provided evidence that there were frequently loose connections between performance, as measured by profits, efficiency, or productivity, and organizational survival. J. Blau (1984), studying more than 150 architectural firms, reported that those characteristics that permitted the firms to survive the early 1970s recession also made them less likely to grow in either sales or profits subsequently. Meyer and Zucker argued that organizations that persisted even in the face of poor performance—so-called permanently failing organizations—survived because they "yield benefits that motivate investment in and maintenance of them, but these benefits often accrue to those who are in one way or another dependent on organizations rather than to those who legally own or control them" (1989, p. 45). Although many of the examples of organizations whose survival is very loosely coupled to performance are in the public sector—for example, public transit systems—by no means is this phenomenon confined to the public sector. Factors that affect performance are not necessarily the same ones that govern survival, as Carroll and Huo reported from a study of newspapers: "At a general level our analysis suggests that institutional environmental variables, especially political turmoil, more strongly affect the founding and death rates of organizations . . . whereas task environmental variables more strongly affect the performance of ongoing organizations" (1986, p. 867).

There is a method for using measures of performance to help validate theory and to provide insight on performance differences that was once more commonly used than it is currently, although its validity and ability to generate potential insights remain. The method proceeds from the idea that a regression that pools the experience of many organizations (possibly over time as well) provides a parametrization of the optimal relationship between a set of independent variables and a dependent variable of theoretical interest. One can then use the coefficients from the regression to estimate, for each unit under study, a predicted value for the dependent variable. One would expect that the greater the difference in the observed actual value from the predicted value, the worse performance would be.

This approach was first demonstrated in an industrial scheduling context by Bowman (1963) and was subsequently used, for instance, in studies of board composition. In a study of hospital boards of directors:

> regression equations were constructed for each dimension of board size and composition, in this instance, the proportion of persons from agricultural organizations and from financial organizations on the board of directors. For each hospital . . . the absolute value of the difference between the predicted (from the regression equation) value for a dimension of board composition and the actual value is computed and used as an independent variable. In this case, the amount of volunteer support the hospital received is explained. (Pfeffer, 1973, p. 360)

This approach is, of course, applicable to contexts other than the effects of board composition (Pfeffer, 1972c; 1973) where it has been demonstrated to have a statistically significant association with various measures of performance. The method provides a way of operationalizing the idea of fit, using the actual empirical results from a sample of organizations under the assumption that, in the aggregate, observed relationships provide a reasonable estimate of the optimal (or at least better) connection between independent and dependent variables. This method could be used, for instance, in testing the consonance hypothesis from structural contingency theory (to be described below), although it has typically not been. It is a relatively straightforward way of incorporating performance into studies of other things, and it provides another way of testing the theory. If some set of variables are presumably related to a given independent variable of theoretical interest, then it is reasonable to explore whether or not deviations from the predicted relationships have consequences. To the extent they do, one can have somewhat more confidence in the underlying theoretical reasoning.

Structural Contingency Theory

In the mid- to late 1960s and early 1970s, the organizations literature was literally filled with articles from a structural contingency perspective that maintained: "1. There is no one best way to organize. 2. Any way of organizing is not equally effective" (Galbraith, 1973, p. 2). The first statement means that under different conditions such as variations in strategy (Chandler, 1962), size, technological unpredictability, or environmental uncertainty, differences in structural arrangements will be observed (e.g., Lawrence and Lorsch, 1967). The second statement, also known as the consonance hypothesis, means "that those organizations that have structures that more closely match" or fit "the requirements of the context" will be "more effective than those that do not" (Pfeffer, 1982, p. 148). Another implication of structural contingency theory is that "organizations adapt their structure by moving out of misfit . . . in order to restore effectiveness and performance. . . . Much structural change is seen as being positive and productive" (Donaldson, 1995, p. 33).

At one point, contingency theory seemed to be both widely accepted and noncontroversial (Schoonhoven, 1981, p. 349). With some notable exceptions (e.g., Donaldson, 1985), structural contingency theory has since virtually faded from the research and managerial literature scene. What happened to structural contingency theory reflects in part characteristics of the field of organization studies already discussed: (1) an attraction to the new and unique, which makes following through on any cumulative program of research difficult and unlikely—by the time of Schoonhoven's (1981) critique the major ideas were more than fourteen years old and consequently the field's attention was already beginning to shift; (2) an interest in ideas that are readily translated into action; and (3) a fascination with economic logic, which is almost invariably noncontingent. As such, the rise and fall of this brand of organizational analysis provides an example of what has happened elsewhere in the field as well as a possible forecast for the future for other, similar topics.

It is important at the outset to note that not all theories of organizational structure are contingent. For instance, in economics Williamson (1975) promulgated what has come to be known as the M-form hypothesis, which maintained that the multidivisional (M-form) structure was more efficient than either a holding company or a functional structure (U-form). Although one might argue that there was some implicit condition of large size implied—one could scarcely have an efficient multidivisional structure or perhaps even one at all in very small organizations—the prediction of the advantages of the M-form were largely non-contingent: "The organization and operation of the large enterprise along the lines of the M-form favors goal pursuit and least-cost behavior more nearly associated with the neoclassical profit maximization hypothesis than does the U-form [functional] organizational alternative" (p. 150).

The multidivisional form was presumably so effective because it at once separated the strategic and capital allocation function of management, performed at headquarters, from concerns with operational efficiency, located in the divisions. At the same time, the M-form internalized transactions that would otherwise be subject to the problems of recontracting under conditions of information asymmetry and small numbers bargaining and permitted more efficient capital allocation because of the better information possessed inside organizational boundaries. Williamson was particularly concerned with problems of commitment to unprofitable lines of investment in organizations, a problem, he maintained, that would be overcome by separating the capital allocation process from operational management: "existing activities embody sunk costs of both organizational and tangible types while new projects require initial investments of both kinds. The sunk costs in programs and facilities of ongoing projects thus insulate existing projects from displacement by alternatives which, were the current program not already in place, might otherwise be preferred" (1975, p. 121).

The fact that transfer pricing in multidivisional structures was a highly political and contested process filled with its own forms of inefficiency (Eccles, 1985) seemed to go unnoticed. Armour and Teece (1978), in a study of firms in the petroleum industry, did find that adoption of the multidivisional form provided economic gains until the point at which the form had been so widely diffused that there was no longer any competitive advantage to be achieved by its adoption. And Teece (1981), in a study comparing two firms in each of fifteen industries, one of which had adopted the M-form and one of which had not, also found a profit advantage for the M-form firms.

There were two problems with the M-form hypothesis as a theory of organizational structure. First, it did not capture the multidimensionality and complexity of organizational structures. A multidivisional firm still faced a range of choices about specifically what staff functions, such as human resources, research and development, and so forth, to place in the divisions and which to centralize (S. A. Allen, 1978). Furthermore, divisionalization by itself did not capture much of the range of design variables, including how much discretion to permit the divisions (the degree of centralization) and how to decide what products to put in one division rather than another (how to coordinate and apportion interdependence). As Starbuck noted, "organizations are complex entities with myriad measurable characteristics" (1981, p. 181). His review of the so-called Aston studies of organization structure (e.g., Pugh et al., 1968; 1969) noted that these studies took more than 1,000 measurements in each organization. Reducing this organizational complexity to a single construct such as divisionalization grossly oversimplifies the measurement and meaning of organizational structure.

Second, the theory did not fit the facts as they were being uncovered by empirical studies of organizational structures—namely, that structure seemed to vary quite systematically with an organization's strategy, size, technology, and conditions of the organization's environment (e.g., Pugh et al., 1969; Child, 1973; Child and Mansfield, 1972). Common sense suggested that the appropriate organizational arrangements must surely depend on what is being organized and the environment in which that organization has to operate; consequently, the ideas of structural contingency theory assumed prominence.

Figure 7-1 presents an overview of the major variants of structural contingency theory. The facets of organizational structure that have been examined include the size of the administrative component, formalization, centralization, the degree of both vertical and horizontal differentiation, and the degree of task specialization and complexity. The factors associated with variations in organizational structure have included strategy, technology, particularly the technology of production, organizational size, and dimensions of the organization's environment, including the degree of competition and the amount of uncertainty or change in the environment.

There has been more support for the proposition that structure varies predict-

Factors that affect structure	Structural elements affected

Strategy
  product differentiation
  price
	Form (Multidivisional, functional, matrix)

Size	Size of the administrative component

Technology
  production process
  information technology
  amount of variability
	Degree of bureaucratization
	  formalization (use of rules)
	  functional specialization
	  centralization
	  standardization
	  formalization

Environment
  uncertainty/unpredictability
  degree of competition
  amount of change
  resource munificence
	Differentiation
	  number of levels
	  number of departments/divisions

Figure 7-1 An Overview of Structural Contingency Theory

ably across organizational contexts than there has been for the consonance hypothesis, which maintains that a match between context and the structure best suited to that context is associated with enhanced organizational performance. Considering first some of the evidence on the effect of context on structure, there is evidence that organizational size has been among the most important predictors of structural variation. Blau (1970) argued that size produced structural differentiation but at a diminishing rate as size increased. Meyer (1972b), in a longitudinal study of state and municipal finance departments, found that size did cause structural differentiation. Other general findings from the literature on the effects of size are: larger organizations tend to be more formalized (Meyer, 1972a; Hall, Haas, and Johnson, 1967), more specialized (Child, 1973; Pugh et al., 1969), and less centralized (Meyer, 1972, Blau, 1973). Child (1975) and Khandwalla (1973) found that larger size was associated with increasing levels of the degree of bureaucratization.

Scott (1992) has reviewed the literature on the effects of technology on structure, where technology has most frequently been conceptualized in terms of its routineness, variability, or unpredictability. The basic argument is that nonroutine, variable, or unpredictable technologies require more flexible organizational arrangements such as decentralization and less formalization (Perrow, 1970b; Hage and Aiken, 1969). The literature on the environment has also emphasized uncertainty or variability (e.g., Duncan, 1972). Burns and Stalker (1961), in what is probably one of the first studies in the structural contingency tradition, found that a more mechanistic or bureaucratic structure was appropriate for more stable and certain environments while a more flexible, organic structure was both observed more frequently and was more successful in more dynamic and uncertain environments. There is also some evidence that competition or the degree of stress emanating from the environment is associated with more centralization of control (Pfeffer and Leblebici, 1973; Khandwalla, 1973).

There have also been a number of demonstrations of the relationship between strategy and structure. Rumelt (1974) found that more diversified firms were more likely to employ a divisionalized structure. Undiversified firms were more likely to retain a functional structure. Moreover, the evidence is that firms diversified first and then changed their structure, not the other way around, as would be expected if structure caused strategy (e.g., Rumelt, 1974; Channon, 1973) rather than the reverse.

Schoonhoven (1981) has detailed the extensive theoretical and empirical problems that beset the test of the consonance hypothesis. This hypothesis has received support in some studies (e.g., Woodward, 1965) but not in others (Mohr, 1971; Pennings, 1975). Schoonhoven noted that (1) "contingency theory is not a theory at all . . . it is more an orienting strategy or metatheory" (p. 350); (2) there is a lack of clarity by contingency theorists that they are, in fact, predicting interactions; (3) "theoretical statements fail to provide any clues about the specific form of the interaction intended" (p. 351); (4) relationships are assumed to be linear, even though there are many reasons to suspect nonlinearities; and (5) there is an assumption that effects are symmetrical, even though, again, there is reason to suspect asymmetry in the interactions.

Although Schoonhoven's study—which used patient outcome data as measures of effectiveness, hospital unit structure as the independent variables, as well as sophisticated analytical methods—did find support for some version of structural contingency theory, in many respects her carefully done study and thoughtful theoretical critique marked virtually the end of empirical research on organizational structure. To some extent this is surprising, given the proliferation of studies that had occurred and given the frequent reorganizations that continued to occur in the world of management and begged for guidance. The question is, What happened to structural contingency theory? Donaldson has argued that the newer organization theories are, in various ways, antimanagerial, and he attributes the demise of structural contingency to some antimanagement bias: "The view taken of managers and management is more negative in these newer theories than is the . . . positive model of managers implicit in most structural contingency theory" (1995, p. 24). The argument that the neglect of structural contingency theory was from some antimanagerial bias is implausible on its face, given the numerous topics that are receiving research attention ranging from culture to leadership in which the interests of organizations and their managers are clearly prominent if not preeminent. A more likely reason is that, as it came to be operationalized and elaborated, structural contingency theory was neither readily comprehensible nor useful.

As a usable theory of organizational performance, structural contingency theory had several problems. First, empirical support for the consonance hypothesis has been inconsistent. But that could conceivably be remedied by more careful studies and measures. A greater problem was that most of the concepts used in the theory were too abstract and were not decision variables (Argyris, 1972). For instance, formalization, centralization, and specialization are constructs that are most often measured as scales (e.g., Pugh et al., 1969) and seldom directly changed. Organizations change reporting relationships, the measures used to monitor performance, and the amount of budgetary discretion permitted to individuals at different levels in different departments, but they don't change "centralization" or "formalization." In his review of the Aston studies, "one of the most important clusters of organizational research during the last 20 years" (Starbuck, 1981, p. 167), Starbuck argued that one problem with this research was the difficulty of making sense of highly aggregated agglomerations of variables and constructs: "Several other macro variables appear to be confusing hodgepodges. . . . The correlations make little sense to me because the macro variables themselves lack meaning and validity" (p. 174).

This problem affects virtually all of the existing studies of structure. Argyris (1995) has argued that for knowledge to be actionable:

1. The generalizations should inform the users not only what is likely to happen under the specified conditions but how to create the conditions and actions in the first place. . . . (p. 5)
2. Propositions that are intended to be used . . . if used correctly should lead to the predicted consequences, and not to others that are counter to those predicted. . . . (p. 8)

3. The generalizations should be usable over time and under different conditions while, at the same time, usable in the individual case. (p. 9)

Structural contingency theory was too complicated to be easily comprehended or summarized, which is necessary if it is to be used by people who do not have the luxury of returning to the texts for guidance. The theory was too disconnected from decision variables actually controlled in organizations, employed concepts that were too abstract, and did not deal in robust, parsimonious ideas. That is probably why clear theoretical statements (Thompson, 1967; Galbraith, 1973) were used in designing organizations to some extent even as the theoretical research spawned by those ideas was not. There are important cautionary lessons in this tale for much of organization theory.

Organizational Ecology

Organizational ecology studies populations of organizations, with the individual organization as the unit of observation. Because inertia—defined not as "no change" but as the inability for organizations to change as rapidly as the environment—is seen as a prominent feature of organizations (Hannan and Freeman, 1984), changes in organizational populations arise largely through the processes of organizational birth and death as contrasted with the adaptation of individual organizations. "Organizational ecology investigates the role of selection processes" (Singh and Lumsden, 1990, p. 162).

Although the ability to reproduce (birth) and to survive (the converse of organizational mortality) may not be finely variegated measures of organizational performance or the performance of various types or forms of organizations, these are clearly consequential outcomes. Organizational ecology does, therefore, have something important to say about organizational performance. There is, however, one important caveat to keep in mind in thinking about the connection between ecology and an understanding of organizational performance: organizational mortality is not always a bad thing. Some organizational mortality reflects bankruptcy and the disappearance of the entity. Some organizational mortality is the result of poor performance and a depressed stock price or financial condition that compels a merger or buy-out. But some organizational mortality is the consequence of being successful and represents selling out as a way of cashing out. Because studies of organizational mortality never discriminate as to either the voluntary nature of the disappearance or the economic returns to those involved in the organization that disappears, inferences about performance and its determinants from life tables of organizational populations should be done with some care and caution.

In addition to studies of births and deaths, ecological thinking has been applied to study organizational performance measured more directly, a very welcome addition to this literature for the very reason that the meaning of organizational mortality is often quite ambiguous. In a study of banks in Illinois from 1987 through 1993 (Barnett, Greve, and Park, 1994), performance was assessed as return on average assets. This was a period in which the regulatory rules were evolving, both nationally and also in Illinois, which was modifying its limitations on branch banking to permit more branching. Barnett et al. examined the relative performance of multiunit and single-branch banks. They found a paradox: unit banks suffered from competition, but the survivors were more successful competitors from learning how to survive under intense competitive pressure. By contrast, "branch systems . . . circumvent and avoid competition by attaining positional advantage—but then forego [sic] the evolutionary benefits competition brings" (p. 25). The authors argued that "rather than strategy and structure driving competitiveness, it is competition that drives evolution, which is then shaped by the strategies and structures of organizations. Ironically, the more they mollify selection pressures, the more that strategies and structure allow organizations to survive regardless of their ability to learn from the market" (p. 24).

Ecology empirically defines organizations that are independent, competitive, or mutualistic with each other in terms of the effects of population density on births and deaths: "By ecological conception, shared fates among organizations indicate interdependence. When organizations negatively affect one another, they are competitive. When they enhance each other's viability, organizations are mutualistic" (Barnett and Carroll, 1987, p. 400). Thus, an ecological view of technological interdependence examines the effects of density of organizations with a given technology on the failure rates of organizational populations—if the presence of more organizations with a given technology increases failure rates, then there is evidence of competition; if they decrease failure rates, there is evidence of mutualism (Barnett, 1990). The nature of the interdependence among organizations is, therefore, defined by its consequences.

Hannan and Freeman (1984) argued that inertia itself was produced by environmental selection pressures and was not simply the consequence of managerial incompetence. They noted that "in modern societies organizational forms that have high levels of reliability and accountability are favored by selection processes. Reliability and accountability of organizational forms require that the organizational structure be highly reproducible" (Singh and Lumsden, 1990, p. 168), which favors structures that don't change.

The basic ecological argument is that organizational forms that are comparatively more suited to the environment or niche within which they are operating will fare better—that is, they will tend to exhibit a higher founding rate and a lower mortality rate. It is important to note that the operative phrase is "comparatively" more fit, for unlike economics, ecology makes no claims about optimality or even progress. If a better form is not present in the population, for whatever reason, it cannot triumph in the selection process, which means that there is no guarantee that the organizational forms that seem to be winning are optimal. Moreover, because survival depends on the fit or match between the characteristics of organizations and their environments, which constantly change, what is a better or worse organizational form obviously changes also. Thus, in the population ecology of organizations, there is never a best way to organize—only a way that has outperformed rivals in the past, given the conditions of the environment that prevailed at that time. Finally, it is important to note that while organizational ecology deals with selection pressures, those selection regimes may have political elements. There is no assurance that selection is only on the basis of efficiency or economic performance (Hannan and Freeman, 1989).

The empirical results of the numerous organizational ecology studies are readily summarized. First, there is a liability in newness (Stinchcombe, 1965), in that new organizations tend to fail at a higher rate than older ones. Singh and Lumsden summarized the arguments about why new organizations have higher failure rates:

> Young organizations and the individuals in them have to learn new roles. . . .
> A significant amount of time and effort has to be expended to coordinate these new roles for the individual actors and in their mutual socialization. . . . In dealing with external clients, customers, and other relevant actors, new organizations are forced to compete with existing organizations that have well-established client groups who are familiar with the organization. (1990, p. 168)

This is an interesting and nontrivial prediction, when one considers the fact that older organizations are likely to have greater inertia and be more difficult to change. A prediction founded just on considerations of adaptability, then, would predict a higher failure rate for older organizations, particularly in more rapidly changing environments that would require more change.

This age dependence of organizational mortality holds even when size is controlled—it is not the case that age dependence occurs simply because new organizations also tend to be smaller and smaller organizations disappear more frequently, although there is a liability of smallness (Aldrich and Auster, 1986). Smaller organizations have more difficulty raising capital, face diseconomies of scale in dealing with government regulations, and face problems in attracting labor in competition with larger organizations, because they cannot offer the career prospects and stability of larger organizations. However, in a study of health maintenance organizations, Wholey, Christianson, and Sanchez (1992) found that the liability of small size depended importantly on organizational form and was not necessarily a universal effect.

Carroll (1983) examined the liability of newness in a diverse sample of firms in fifty-two quite different industries and found support for the idea. Carroll and Delacroix (1982), studying Argentine and Irish newspapers, found that failure rates were related to age, and Freeman and Hannan's (1983) study of restaurants also observed age-dependent mortality. Freeman, Carroll, and Hannan (1983) explored the liability of newness using data on unions and semiconductor firms, an analysis continued in Hannan and Freeman (1989). The argument that many organizational routines and practices entail tacit knowledge and skill and that, until that knowledge is developed and those interdependencies effectively coordinated, organizations are at greater risk for failure implies that reorganizations or other substantial changes (such as a change in the leadership of the organization) should reintroduce at least some of the initial mortality risk, until the organization learns to operate under the new conditions. And, indeed, there is evidence that the succession of a publisher in newspapers (Carroll, 1984) and change in publication content and frequency in newspapers (Amburgey, Kelly, and Barnett, 1993) are associated with initially increased failure rates that then decline over time.

Both founding and mortality for a number of different organizational populations have been found to depend on density, or the number of organizations, and to do so in a curvilinear relationship. The interpretation is as follows. Both rates of organizational founding and mortality depend on two factors, legitimacy and competition. As the number of a particular form of organization in an environment increases, the legitimacy of that type or form increases, although at a decreasing rate (there are declining returns in legitimation to increasing numbers of organizations). By contrast, competition increases at ever higher rates as organizational density climbs and there are more and more demands on the carrying capacity of the niche (Hannan and Carroll, 1992). "Thus, growth in density from zero mainly legitimates an organizational form, but continued growth eventually generates enough competition to overwhelm the effect of legitimation. . . . As density rises from zero . . . founding rates rise initially and then fall, and mortality rates fall initially and then rise" (Hannan, Carroll, Dundon, and Torres, 1995, p. 510).

This curvilinear effect of density on organizational foundings has been demonstrated in studies of New York state life insurance companies (Budros, 1994), U.S. semiconductor firms (Hannan and Freeman, 1989), day care centers in Toronto (Baum and Oliver, 1992), Pennsylvania telephone companies (Barnett, 1990), automobile manufacturers in Europe (Hannan et al., 1995), and numerous other organizational populations including labor unions, Irish newspapers, U.S. breweries, and newspapers in Argentina (Hannan and Carroll, 1992; Baum and Powell, 1995). The effect on organizational mortality has been observed in an equally wide range of types of organizational populations (see Baum and Powell, 1995, pp. 534–535).

Although the empirical facts of density dependence and the liabilities of newness and smallness are no longer much in dispute, three issues remain. First, some argue that the age dependence of organizational mortality is a spurious result of unobserved heterogeneity. Assume, for instance, that some organizations at their founding have better-skilled management and that management skill is importantly related to survival. Organizations with less-effective management will fail early, which means that those organizations that survive have better management and are more likely to continue to survive. What looks like a liability of newness is really just a liability of poor management. Hannan and Freeman (1989) attempted to empirically distinguish their argument from this methodological problem and were able to demonstrate an age dependence effect nevertheless.

The second issue is the substantive meaning of the relationship of founding and mortality to organizational density, a concern because neither legitimation nor competition is often measured directly. Measuring legitimation by numbers of organizations has been particularly problematic to some (e.g., Zucker, 1989). Again, there are forceful replies (Hannan and Carroll, 1995), and efforts have been made to empirically demonstrate the validity of the theoretical ideas. A third, related problem arises because of the concern in much of the literature solely with demonstrating effects of density rather than fully understanding all the forces affecting organizational birth and death. This leads to models that may underspecify causes of birth (or failure) that vary with density and, as a consequence, lead to estimated density effects when there are, in fact, no such effects in better specified models. Wholey, Christianson, and Sanchez (1993) examined the founding of health maintenance organizations. They reported that:

> There are no density effects in the fully specified model, which is surprising given the consistent density effects reported by population ecologists. . . . We found nonmonotonic density effects that are consistent with ecological research in much simpler models. . . . This suggests that the nonmonotonic density effects in simpler models are a consequence of specification bias with density serving as a proxy for other processes affecting entry. Density effects disappear when we include comprehensive measures for these processes. (p. 178)

As Baum (1995, p. 178) has noted, density dependence ideas treat competition as a property of the population and consequently assume that each member of the population contributes equally to the competitive environment and experiences competition similarly. This seems unrealistic on its face, as there are organizations of different sizes that overlap in their market niches with competitors to varying degrees, and consequently the competitive effects should not necessarily be the same. This insight has led to refinements or modifications in the basic density dependence ideas. Baum and Mezias (1992) found that the failure rate of Manhattan hotels was greater the greater the intensity of competition from hotels of similar price, location, and size. Carroll and Wade (1991) found that an increase in density measured at the local geographic level had a greater effect on the failure rate. Baum and Singh (1994) developed the concept of overlap density and used it to study the failure rate of day care centers, measuring population overlap density in this instance in terms of the ages of children each day care center was licensed to serve.

Barnett and Amburgey (1990) argued that what might be important was not just population density but also population mass—the aggregate of the sizes of organizations in a population. They noted that larger organizations might generate more intense competition because such organizations enjoyed economies of scale and would deplete common resource pools to a greater extent. On the other hand, larger organizations may be less flexible and adaptive. They defined population mass as "population density with each organization weighted by its size" (p. 83). Their study of telephone companies in Pennsylvania found a mutualistic rather than a competitive mass effect, but the study measured mass "by the total number of subscribers of all existing companies in a given year" (p. 90). This measure of mass-dependent competition was not consistent with their own definition and could be argued to be a measure of total market size, not the size distribution of the competitors. Baum (1995, p. 181) has summarized the research on mass-dependent competition by noting that the empirical results were mixed. While density dependence ideas presume that each organization in a population competes with all other organizations, in models of size-localized competition, the basic argument is that the failure rate of organizations increases with the number of organizations of similar size in the population (p. 182). This prediction comes from the assumption that organizations of different sizes compete primarily with similarly sized organizations that have similar strategies and cost structures.

Closely related to size-localized competition is the idea of resource partitioning. In a study of newspapers, Carroll (1985) argued that competition among large, generalist organizations increased their failure rate but lowered the failure rate of small, specialist organizations that could serve small market niches neglected by the large, generalist firms. Carroll did observe that as the newspaper industry become increasingly concentrated, the failure rate of large, generalist newspapers increased while the failure rate of small, specialist newspapers (often published in foreign languages) actually fell. Similarly, Carroll and Swaminathan (1992) observed that as the level of concentration increased in the American brewing industry, the failure rate of microbreweries decreased. Baum (1995), studying the New York City hotel industry, found empirical support for each of these bases of competition and also noted that which form of competition predominated depended on period—there were temporal differences in the stages of competition. Thus, the empirical evidence suggests that competitive dynamics are better modeled using more refined measures of organizational similarity (size, price, geographical location, target population served, and so forth) rather than just aggregate population density.

What we have learned from the various ecological studies is that there is a liability in being new or young, a liability that recurs to some extent when there are reorganizations or important successions. There is also a liability to being small. We have learned that foundings are more likely and organizational mortality is diminished the fewer similar organizations there are and, conversely, that foundings are less likely and mortality is greater the more dense the population becomes. We have also learned in numerous studies that both foundings and mortality have a curvilinear relationship with population density because of the joint effects of legitimation and competition. The studies of particular industries have also examined more specific effects such as political and economic conditions that are relevant for understanding organizational birth and death in the particular population.

As a theory of performance, population ecology focuses attention on factors that may be substantively important but over which there is virtually no organizational control (e.g., age, size, and the density of competing organizations) except to the extent organizations can choose their competitive niche. But once that niche is chosen, given presumptions of inertia and the very real constraints that make entering and leaving market sectors difficult, a given organization's fate is largely in the hands of others and selection forces that are outside of its control. And even how to choose a niche is not clear from the empirical results. In the study most directly focused on performance (Barnett et al., 1994) and strategy, there was a paradoxical result: the very strategies that insulated organizations from competitive pressure and therefore enhanced their life chances also insulated organizations from the selection pressures that foster learning. The choice posed is

between enhanced survival and enhanced learning from competitive pressure—
surely a difficult decision that the research has thus far failed to address.

We know that there is a desire for a feeling of mastery and control on the
part of most people (Langer, 1983), so much so that individuals will act as if they
have control even in situations where they don't (e.g., by being willing to place a
larger wager on a game of chance such as throwing dice when they actually get
to throw the dice). One can only suspect that the control illusions and requirements of managers are at least as great if not greater than those of the subjects in
the experiments on the control illusion. Consequently, population ecology, for all
of its attractive elements and empirical support, is in its present versions reasonably far from a theory that permits knowledge to be translated into action. That
property limits not only its applicability but also its attractiveness in the multiparadigm organization theory marketplace in which it competes.

Human Resource Practices and Performance

As organizations have faced increasing competitive pressure, and as other sources
of competitive advantage such as product and process technology have become
somewhat less important because of the more rapid diffusion of technical information (Pfeffer, 1994), firms have tried to positively affect their performance
through their practices for managing their employees. There is a growing literature that documents the facts that (1) there are substantial differences in performance between the most and least effective firms or plants; (2) some significant
portion of that difference can be shown to be from differences in the management
of the employment relationship; (3) there is fairly consistent agreement on what
constitutes high-performance work practices; (4) there is conflicting evidence
about whether what constitutes "best practice" is or is not contingent on the firm's
strategy and whether or not the practices interact in producing their effects (i.e.,
it is important that they all be present at some level); and (5) there is evidence
that the diffusion of these so-called high-commitment work practices and their
persistence once they are implemented is not as great as one would expect given
their apparent effectiveness.

As to the first point, Womack, Jones, and Roos (1990, pp. 89, 90) documented differences of almost two to one between the most productive and least
productive automobile assembly plants operating in the same country and having
the same country of ownership, and differences in quality of more than three to
one among the comparable plants. For instance, the most efficient U.S.-owned
automobile assembly plant in North America took 18.6 person hours to assemble
a car, while the least efficient required 30.7 hours. The best U.S.-owned plant in
North America produced cars with on average 35.1 defects per 100 automobiles,
while the worst plant had a defect rate of 168.6 per 100. Ichniowski, Shaw, and
Prennushi (1993), in a study of integrated steel manufacturers, argued that the
most relevant dependent variable for that particular production setting was down-
time, the proportion of time the production line was shut down. They found a

600 percent difference between the most effective lines, which were shut down 2 percent of the time, and the least effective, which were down about 13 percent of the time.

There is also evidence that an important portion of the variation in economic performance is associated with differences in human resource practices. MacDuffie (1995), using data from the MIT study of the world automobile industry, observed a strong positive relationship between his measure of production organization and both quality and productivity. His production organization index included scales measuring the use of buffer inventories, work systems (including the use of work teams and suggestion systems), job rotation and decentralization, and human resource management policies (including contingent compensation, an emphasis on training, and limited differentiation in status). Previous but less comprehensive studies in the automobile industry had already demonstrated important effects of, for instance, participation in suggestion programs, involvement in quality of work life programs, and worker attitudes on both productivity and quality (Katz, Kochan, and Gobeille, 1983; Katz, Kochan, and Weber, 1985). The magnitude of some of the bivariate effects are astonishing. Katz, Kochan, and Weber (1985, p. 519) reported a bivariate correlation of 0.73 between participation in suggestion programs and product quality in their study of twenty-five General Motors' automobile assembly plants.

Kravetz (1988) examined the connection between human resource policies and financial performance for 150 of the 500 largest companies listed in *Forbes*. His measure of human resource progressiveness included the extensiveness of career development and training, participative management, flexible work schedules, and the degree of emphasis on people in the company culture. He found that the more progressive companies enjoyed 64 percent greater sales growth, 61 percent higher profit margins, four times the rate of increase in profits, and a larger increase in earnings per share than companies using less progressive human resource policies. Reviewing 131 field studies in North America between 1961 and 1991 that assessed the effects of changes in work systems, Macy and Izumi concluded that "there seems to be *large* overall performance improvements obtained from work innovation . . . and organizational development efforts" (1993, p. 265). A metaanalysis of forty-three studies of various forms of worker participation—participation in decision making, mandated co-determination, profit sharing, worker ownership (either through employee stock ownership or individual worker ownership of the firm's assets), and collective ownership—concluded that except for co-determination, all of the forms of worker participation were positively associated with productivity (Doucouliagos, 1995). Moreover, the effects of participation were larger in firms owned and controlled by workers compared to firms in which participation was granted by owners or managers to workers.

Ichniowski, Shaw, and Prennushi's (1993), study of thirty integrated steel production plants, using the percentage of time the line actually operated as the dependent variable, found that, controlling for technological factors, human resource systems had a significant effect on performance. Studying thirty steel minimills, Arthur (1994) observed a statistically and substantively significant relationship between how an organization managed its work force and measures of both productivity and turnover. He reported a statistically significant correlation between labor productivity and scrap rate, a result that is consistent with MacDuffie (1995) in indicating that quality and efficiency are positively related. Controlling for the plants' age, size, degree of unionization, and business strategy, using a high-commitment work system decreased the labor hours to produce a ton of steel and the scrap rate. Ichniowski (1986), in a study of nine unionized paper mills over the 1976–1982 period, observed a connection between employee relations practices and productivity, with the more grievances filed, the lower the productivity. Studies of the textile industry (Dunlop and Weil, 1995) and fifteen semiconductor wafer fabrication facilities (Brown, 1994) have also shown a relationship between how employees were managed and various industry-relevant measures of productivity.

One problem with many of these studies is that, because of their cross-sectional design, inferring causality is problematic. It is plausible that instead of financial performance resulting from high-commitment work practices, those organizations that are doing well are more willing and able to implement suggestion systems, allow participation, offer flexible work schedules, do more training, and other similar things. Note, however, that Macy and Izumi's (1993) review covered studies of change and found important effects. Ichniowski et al.'s (1993) study of steel mills reported that firms that changed their work systems to utilize more high-commitment practices increased their performance subsequently. And Huselid's (1995) study of 968 firms used a more rigorous statistical methodology and estimated sample selection bias to overcome this and other methodological problems. He observed a statistically significant impact of high-commitment work practices on turnover, sales per employee, profits per employee, and the market value of the firm. Again, these effects were substantively large. "A one-standard-deviation increase in High Performance Work Practices yields a $27,044 increase in sales and a $3,814 increase in profits. . . . The estimated per employee impact on firm market value [is] $18,614" (p. 662).

Welbourne and Andrews (1996) studied the five-year survival rate of 136 non-financial companies that began initial public offerings in 1988, using the firms' human resource policies as one predictor of survival. Since these policies were measured from the initial public offering document and the outcome variable, survival, occurred subsequently, causality is more unambiguously assessed. The study employed a sample of comparatively smaller firms than those used in other studies, extending the analysis to a different outcome (survival instead of productivity or quality) and to a different part of the size distribution. Welbourne and Andrews measured human resource policies by two indices: (1) a human resource value index composed of items such as the quality of employee relations (citing employees as a key strategic asset), having an executive with full-time human resources responsibility, and having an employee training program, and (2) a rewards index containing items assessing the extent to which the firm had stock plans, profit sharing, and other incentives for either management or all employees. For the whole sample the overall survival rate was 70 percent. Firms that were one standard deviation above the mean on the human resource value index had a 79 percent survival rate, while of firms one standard deviation below the mean, only 60 percent survived. The effect of rewards was even larger. The survival rates for firms one standard deviation above and one standard deviation below the mean were 87 percent and 45 percent, respectively. Welbourne and Andrews's results demonstrate yet again that human resource practices are both statistically significantly related to important performance outcomes and that these effects are substantively important.

Huselid's results indicated that there was little evidence for complementarity either among the various internal practices or between the internal practices and the firm's strategy. The data showed that the effects of the various high-performance practices were largely additive and noncontingent on a particular strategy. Ichniowski et al. (1993) did find evidence of complementarity among the various practices, and Arthur (1992) had found a relationship between strategy and the use of high-commitment or cost-reduction work practices in his study of steel minimills. Complementarity and the effectiveness of practices regardless of strategy may be contingent on the particular firms and their environment.

Although the various studies differ somewhat in what they include when they measure high-performance or high-commitment work practices, there is substantial overlap in the commonly accepted meanings of these terms. Figure 7-2 presents dimensions of work practices from a number of studies and indicates that there are a number of common themes across the studies. Specifically, high-performance work practices are characterized by higher levels of wages, employee skills, effort in selecting employees, and training and a set of practices associated with the devolution of power, including the use of quality circles or self-managed teams (Katzenbach and Smith, 1993; Mohrman, Cohen, and Mohrman, 1995; Seaman, 1995), fewer job classifications, more information sharing, and fewer supervisors. Having better-trained and more-carefully screened employees working a system that permits and, indeed, encourages them to use their skills results in higher levels of organizational performance.

The Diffusion of High-Performance Work Practices

Although there is little doubt that high-commitment work practices are diffusing (Osterman, 1994), there is also evidence that their adoption is neither extensive nor easily accomplished, particularly given their apparent substantial effects on organizational performance. For instance, Lawler et al. (1992) reported on the proportion of firms from the Fortune 1000 that had either not adopted a particular practice at all or used it with less than 20 percent of their employees. They found that, as of 1990, 90 percent of the firms made virtually no use of self-managing teams, 56 percent of the firms did not use profit sharing, 89 percent did not employ gain sharing, 79 percent did not use work-group or team-based incentives, 68 percent did not use job enrichment or job redesign, and 70 percent did not employ quality circles or problem-solving groups. Moreover, the "data indicate that the power sharing practices that had diffused most widely . . . are those that redistribute power and authority the least" (McCaffrey, Faerman, and Hart, 1995, p. 608). The Commission on the Skills of the American Workplace stated that " 'the vast majority' of U.S. employers aren't moving to 'high perfor-

Arthur (1994)
  decentralization
  participation
  general training
  skill level
  wage level
  bonus or incentives
  due process procedures
  span of control
  higher benefits
  social activities
  percent unionized

Womack, Jones, and Roos (1990)
  reduction of status differences
  contingent compensation
  high levels of training
  commitment to retain employees
  emphasis on quality
  elimination of buffers/inventories
  multiskilled workers
  emphasis on flexibility
  emphasis on commitment of workers

Huselid (1995)
  promotion from within
  information sharing
  training
  incentive compensation
  participation practices
  access to formal grievance procedure
  selectivity in recruiting
  surveys of employee attitudes
  formal job analysis
  merit-based performance appraisals

Ichniowski, Shaw, and Prennushi (1993)
  incentive pay
  selective recruiting and selection
  teamwork and cooperation
  employment security
  flexible job assignment
  knowledge and skill training
  communication of information
  quality of labor relations

Wood (1996)
  trainability as selection criterion
  commitment as selection criterion

career ladders and progression
teamworking
quality circles
long-term training budgets
workers responsible for own quality
job design to use workers' skills
regular briefings
flexible job descriptions
no compulsory redundancy
use of temporary staff to protect security of
  core work force
single-status terms and conditions of employment
formal assessment for production workers

Osterman (1994)
  self-directed work teams
  job rotation
  employee problem-solving groups
  total quality management

Lawler, Mohrman, and Ledford (1992)
  sharing of information
  amount and type of training
  performance-based rewards
  alternative reward systems (all-salaried pay,
    skill-based pay)
  power-sharing practices
  job enrichment or redesign
  self-managed work teams
  employment security
  suggestion system
  flextime
  employee stock ownership

Walton (1985)
  frequent use of teams
  job design combines doing and thinking
  flat organization structure
  minimum status differentials
  variable rewards; gain sharing or profit
    sharing
  pay for skill
  business data widely shared
  attempt to ensure employment stability
  employee participation on many issues
  mutuality in labor relations

Figure 7-2   Dimensions of High-Commitment/High-Performance Work Practices

mance' work organizations" (Karr, 1990, p. A4). Diffusion is equally slow in the United Kingdom. R. Locke reported that "no more than 2% of all establishments with more than 25 workers have quality circles or problem-solving groups. Team work and major alterations in job content are even more rare" (1995, p. 16).

In the textile industry, the existing bundle system of production, which is characterized by low wages, a high rate of occupational injury, and little career mobility, is favored by almost no one. Dunlop and Weil (1992) noted that many industry observers favored an alternative system of production called modular production, which could potentially solve problems of absenteeism, turnover, and labor shortages. Nonetheless, the diffusion of the modular production system and the abandonment of the bundle system has been slow:

> In 1985, 97% of all manufacturers used the bundle system, according to industry surveys. Although this figure decreased to 90% by 1988 and to 82% by 1992, given the economic pressures and the fact that industry publications were filled with articles advocating the new system, one might have expected more change. The components of the bundle system, such as individual (rather than group) piece rates and narrow (as opposed to broad) training also maintained their dominance in the industry. (Pfeffer, 1994, p. 83)

Moreover, there is evidence that even when adopted, high-commitment work practices such as quality of working life programs and quality circles have high mortality rates (Drago, 1988). Rankin (1986) estimated that about 40 percent of all employee involvement or quality of working life efforts failed within the first two to three years. Goodman's (1980) review of participation programs implemented during the 1970s indicated that after five years only one quarter of the quality of work life programs survived. A University of Michigan study (Cammann et al., 1984) of eight programs implemented between 1973 and 1978 discovered that by 1984, they all had been terminated.

A number of explanations for this diffusion failure have been offered. R. E. Cole (1989) has argued that the United States has very little social infrastructure to encourage the diffusion of these practices; in contrast, Japan has strong industry associations, and in Sweden the government has played an active role. He noted that Japanese and Swedish corporations were more oriented toward collective solutions to the various costs involved in starting small-group, participative activities and that they seemed to have a greater appreciation of the economizing benefits of collaboration than did comparable American managers. Levine and Tyson, asking, "if employee participation often has positive effects on productivity, why don't we see more of it?" (1990, p. 184), argued that the firm's environment, including capital market conditions and labor laws, create "market failures" in which efficient practices are not adopted because it is not sensible for a single firm to do so by itself. For instance, if only one or a few firms offer employment security, they face a potential problem of adverse selection, in which the least able and least hard-working employees will flock to those firms because of the disproportionate benefit of that security. Of course, if every firm offers the same policies, perhaps because of regulation, then there is no particular advantage or disadvantage to any single firm. Or, consider the problem of underinvestment in training. It may be irrational for a given firm to invest in training, particularly general training, when employees can leave and other organizations can capture the training benefits. But if every firm invested proportionately, there would not be the potential loss.

Belief systems may also be important in accounting for the relatively slow diffusion of management practices that appear to have high economic benefit. A. Kohn (1993) has implied that it is managerial ideology, and particularly a belief in external, often individually based incentives, that helps determine management practices. McCaffrey et al. noted that "participative systems reduce the chances of control of situations by managers . . . and increase the chances of stability; this will encourage the reassertion of controls" (1995, p. 604). They argued, "barriers to participative systems are embedded in social, economic, and political principles deeply valued in their own right. . . . The structures and attitudes impeding participative systems are usually valued more highly than the prospective gains from the systems" (p. 604). The idea that incentives take care of all problems, an idea derived from the economic model of behavior, would certainly not encourage an emphasis on team-based, more participative programs that emphasize intrinsic motivation and control.

McCaffrey et al. (1995) noted that participative methods made the most sense in precisely those situations in which they were least likely to be adopted— settings in which hierarchical and adversarial relations had substantially adversely affected performance through effects on commitment and the sharing of information. A review of the literature on cooperation in prisoner's dilemma games as well as the organization development literature on collaboration led these authors to propose four conditions in which collaborative, participative practices were likely to begin and survive: "(1) prior dispositions toward collaboration based on history, beliefs, and other residues of earlier actions; (2) social and political organization; . . . (3) the nature of incentives, issues, and values presently facing parties"; and "(4) leadership capacity and style" (p. 613).

Pil and MacDuffie (1996) have conducted one of the few studies that actually examined change in the use of performance-enhancing work practices over time, using data gathered in two rounds of surveys approximately five years apart from forty-three automobile assembly plants located around the world. They noted that the use of high-involvement work practices increased considerably during this period but that there was still substantial variation in the rate of increase of adoption of these practices. Their results showed, first of all, that performance problems did not predict the adoption of the practices. Contrary to their expectations, neither productivity nor quality in 1989 predicted the amount of change in the use of these practices over the ensuing period. Also counter to expectations, there was no evidence that the practices diffused more readily to plants that had either production workers or managers with less tenure—who, presumably, would have less commitment to the past and therefore resist change less. In fact, their results indicated that high-involvement work practices tended to diffuse more readily in plants with higher managerial tenure. They did find that changing the product produced by the plant—in this instance, model changeovers—facilitated the adoption of high-involvement work practices, but there was no effect of plant additions or expansion. They also found no effect for previous layoffs on change in the use of these ways of organizing work. They argued that the absence of an effect might reflect two counteracting forces—the tendency for layoffs to, on the one hand, create distrust and fear, which would make change difficult, but on the other hand to create the perception of the need for change and thereby unfreeze strongly held attitudes, thereby making change easier.

The Pil and MacDuffie study did not directly examine many of the factors that have been discussed as affecting the diffusion of high-performance work practices—for instance, managerial ideology, the environmental context, which obviously varies dramatically across the various nations in which their plants were located, or even the tendency for high-performance practices to diffuse more within a single corporation or geographic area compared to across organizational or geographic boundaries. The literature indicates that there are a number of potential explanations for why some firms adopt high-commitment work practices while others do not. What is clear is that this is an increasingly important area for research.

Conclusion

The four perspectives on organizational performance—the three reviewed in this chapter and the social model, with its emphasis on interorganizational linkages and structural position—do have some commonalities that have yet to be empirically realized. For instance, one could explore failure rates of organizations as affected by the density of competing firms using high-performance work practices, and the diffusion of such practices themselves could be modeled as an ecological process. Social relationships and network connections undoubtedly affect the pattern of diffusion of such practices. Just as Burt (1987) examined the diffusion of an antibiotic using concepts of structural equivalence to account for that process, so one could use similar methods and arguments to explore the diffusion of high-commitment work practices generally, or specific practices such as employee ownership or decentralization, in a network of organizations.

The models of performance also have some important differences, particularly in the extent to which they incorporate decision variables and therefore promote action. As already noted, typical ecological analyses incorporate few variables that are potentially subject to organizational or managerial discretion. Structural contingency theory suffers not from its disregard of normative implications but rather from its use of a set of concepts that are difficult to grasp and a theoretical structure that is better suited to multiple regression analysis than it is to being remembered and implemented. The network and employment system analyses of performance both offer some advantages of being theoretically grounded and empirically testable but also of being normatively focused and incorporating potential decision variables.

8

Organizations from a Critical
Theory Perspective

Much, although not all, of the literature on organizations seeks to address managerial problems—how to enhance organizational performance, how to exercise more effective control over behavior in the work place, how to create and manage organizational cultures, how to identify and develop leaders, and so forth. The dominant approach in this literature has been functionalist:

> The functionalist paradigm has provided the foundation for most modern theory and research on the subject of organizations. . . . The perspective . . . encourage[s] us to see the role of values as a separate variable in the research process. . . . Functionalist theory has typically viewed organization as a problematic phenomenon, and has seen the problem of organization as synonymous with the problem of 'efficiency' and, more recently, of 'effectiveness'. (Morgan, 1990, p. 15)

The language of efficiency and effectiveness, the presumption of voluntary exchanges and transactions (as with the economic model), and the invocation of environmental—competitive or regulatory—constraints and pressures are frequent in the organizations literature. Each of these linguistic and theoretical conventions has the effect of rendering many organizational outcomes as inevitable and produced without much intervention of human agency. Constraints, competition, and efficiency mean that what has occurred is either required for organizational survival or voluntarily preferred by those involved or both. The place of those harmed by the drive for efficiency, the fact that some are disadvantaged by organizational controls, and the possibility that social arrangements are and can be chosen is frequently absent from the discussion. Social scientists frequently make sense of what is—recall the retrospective accounts produced by economic models that demonstrate the efficiency of organizational arrangements—and make prescriptions based on social science theories to enhance managerial control. In this sense, many of those who do organization studies become "servants of power" (Baritz, 1960). This managerialist orientation, with its neglect of the contested organizational landscape, has provoked criticism:

> Most of the undesirable features of modern capitalistic society are not mentioned by organization theorists, presenting the appearance of value neutrality, but in actuality masking a politically conservative bias. This compromises the social function of the field to the point where organizational theory serves primarily the dominant interest of capital, rather than society at large. (Jermier, 1982, p. 204)

Perrow echoed many of the same themes:

> we are intellectual captives of the organizations we study, and thus are burdened with some unproductive assumptions. . . . We have failed to pay our dues to society by devoting . . . roughly a quarter of our efforts to applying our organisa-tional expertise to pressing public problems and in particular, those of the power-less. . . . I question the assumption that efficiency can be addressed by exam-ining survival, legitimacy, growth or profits, thus neglecting the multiple stakeholders within and without the organisation with quite different notions of . . . goal attainment. . . . We should question our evolutionary bias that sees big organisations as more complex, efficient, and selected by an indifferent envi-ronment, and instead see organisational birth, death and change as a process of decimation of forms and reduction of adaptability. (1992, p. 371)

In response to this prevailing managerialist and functionalist perspective, a number of variants of critical theory have arisen to challenge conventional depic-tions of organizations and to propose other theoretical lenses for understanding them. Critical theory or critical studies have emerged in law, the humanities, and the social sciences. One reasonable definition of critical theory (CT) is provided by Alvesson and Willmott: "A fundamental claim of the proponents of CT is that social science can and should contribute to the liberation of people from unnecessarily restrictive traditions, ideologies, assumptions, power relations, iden-tity formations, and so forth, that inhibit or distort opportunities for autonomy, clarification of genuine needs and wants, and thus greater and lasting satisfaction" (1992, p. 435).

There are a number of branches of critical theory, some of which operate largely in the realm of philosophical discourse and some that launch empirical challenges to existing organization theory orthodoxy. The focus here is on the more empirically grounded critical approaches. Organization theory is, after all, fundamentally a social science; although philosophy and moral reasoning are im-portant and interesting, critical theory has had and probably will have its most effect where it engages organization studies in a realm with testable empirical implications.

Much, although certainly not all, of critical organization theory derives from Marxist roots, and there have been a number of empirical studies in a Marxian tradition that challenged some of the received wisdom of organization theory. Consequently, we begin the review of critical theory in organizations with the Marxist critique and alternative conceptualization of organizations. We then move on to consider some other variants of critical theory applied to organizations, including feminist organization theory.

Marxist Versions of Organization Theory

The Marxist critique of organization theory was pursued most vigorously in the 1970s. In some sense this is not surprising, as the 1970s saw the end of the Vietnam War, a very politicizing event for American culture, Watergate and the resignation of President Nixon, and the economic stresses associated with oil shocks, inflation, and recession. It was a time of heightened political awareness and a questioning of the institutions of authority. Marxist theory provided a useful theoretical lens for that critique:

> the Marxist approach began essentially as a critique of the dominant rationalist views. . . . Marxists argue that organizational structures are not rational systems for performing work. . . . Rather, they are power systems designed to maximize control and profits. Work is divided . . . not to improve efficiency but to "deskill" workers, to displace discretion from workers to managers, and to create artificial divisions among the work force. . . . Hierarchy develops . . . as an instrument of control and a means of accumulating capital through the appropriation of surplus value. . . . Human relations . . . reforms are misguided because they do not challenge the fundamental exploitative nature of organizations; indeed they help to shore it up by assuming a congruence of goals. (Scott, 1992, p. 115)

There are two topic domains in which Marxist approaches pose the most direct challenge to traditional organization theory—in the structuring of work within enterprises and in the understanding of relations among enterprises and between enterprises and the state and the reasons for those relations. We consider each of these topics in turn.

A Critical View of the Employment Relation

Most approaches to understanding the structuring of the employment relation proceed from an efficiency rationale—governance arrangements that minimize both transaction and production costs prevail (Williamson, 1975). The presumed objective of control, whether achieved through the use of incentives or through socialization and inculturation, is enhanced organizational performance in a competitive marketplace. Although managerial motives may not be benign, managers are compelled by competitive pressures to manage the way they do. Contingency theories of organizations (e.g., Donaldson, 1985; Lawrence and Lorsch, 1967; Woodward, 1970) have an environmental or technological determinism to them, so in form they are quite parallel to economic reasoning—there are environmental exigencies of size, competition, or technology that virtually dictate what organizations and their managers must do in order to survive or prosper.

Marxist analysis challenges these arguments in two ways. First, it asserts that control, not efficiency, is the objective of organizing arrangements and that when there are trade-offs involved, efficiency concerns are frequently subservient to the achievement of control over the labor process. Marglin's (1974) analysis of the development of hierarchy during the industrial revolution, Stone's (1973) description of the development of job ladders in the steel industry in the late nineteenth century, and Clawson's (1980) review of the demise of the inside contracting and putting out system and their replacement by hierarchically structured employment relations all argue that changes in the structure of the employment relation emerged "as much from the desire to effect organizational control as from the need to apply continually advancing technology to production" (Goldman and Van Houten, 1977, p. 109). Edwards has argued that several factors enter the evaluation of profitability, including "the extent to which any technology provides managers with leverage in transforming purchased labor power into labor actually done" (1979, p. 112). Second, a critical or Marxist perspective argues that many of the prescribed (and often acknowledged as effective) mechanisms for achieving control of the work process are not benign and achieve their results at some substantial cost to the individuals working in organizations.

Empirically testing whether control is instituted to enhance efficiency or for other reasons is obviously difficult. One can observe outcomes or behavior much more unambiguously than motives. Four lines of evidence and argument may be relevant to the debate. First, there is evidence, already discussed, that there is less diffusion of high-commitment work practices, and particularly practices that involve fundamental changes in the power structure and in control of work, than one might expect given the effects of such practices on productivity and performance (e.g., Levine and Tyson, 1990; Pfeffer, 1994). Data from a General Accounting Office survey of the Fortune 1000 reported by Lawler et al. (1992) showed that self-managed teams and gain sharing (sharing financial benefits from increased performance accompanied customarily by some degree of control over the work process) were work-place changes that had diffused the least. By contrast, survey feedback and all salaried pay had diffused the most completely. Note that changing pay from an hourly to a salaried basis and collecting survey data and feeding it back involve less change in the control of work than going to self-managing teams. The data also indicate that the differences in diffusion cannot be explained by differences in perceived effectiveness of the changes. Similarly, the failure of decentralization to readily diffuse (Levine and Tyson, 1990) is consistent with a desire to maintain control.

Second, there is evidence that employers pursue control over the labor process and contest that control even when there are few or no apparent efficiency reasons for doing so. For instance, although Freeman and Medoff (1984) have documented the frequently positive and seldom harmful effects of unionization on productivity and profitability (see also Pfeffer, 1994, chap. 7), employers in the United States have resisted unionization vigorously (Kochan, Katz, and McKersie, 1986).

L. J. Griffin, Wallace, and Rubin (1986), studying employer resistance to unionization in the early 1900s, argued that such resistance was based importantly on a desire to achieve control over the labor process. They wrote, "Unionization is one of the most important market-driven mechanisms available to the working class in its struggles to achieve its interests. . . . Without labor organization and mobilization, the working class, especially in the U.S., due to its lack of a strong socialist party presence, would be structurally hindered in its collective action in market and state spheres" (p. 148). They noted that employers launched two major countermovements in the early 1900s to resist unionization—an open shop drive that began around 1903 and the "American Plan," a form of welfare capitalism that arose in the 1930s. In empirical estimates of the effects of employer resistance, organized in part by the National Association of Manufacturers, Griffin et al. found that "the NAM, its size and expenditures, significantly reduces *all* indicators of the strength and vitality of labor organization" (1986, p. 163, emphasis in original). Quoting industrialists, including Harry Frick, head of Andrew Carnegie's operations, Griffin et al. maintained that the fundamental issue was control: "Who, then, would control the factory? Management could control the labor process only if a 'transfer of skill'—from craft worker to manager—about production techniques occurred. This, in turn, was possible only if the power of the craft union . . . was broken" (1986, p. 150).

Third, there is evidence that, again at least in the United States, we are willing to spend vast sums of money on control over work. In medicine, for instance, Woolhandler and Himmelstein (1991) have estimated that almost a quarter of expenditures on health care in the United States are for administration and that this emphasis on supervision, administration, and monitoring accounts for about one-half of the difference in health care costs between the United States and Canada. These authors reported that in the late 1980s, there were more administrators in Blue Cross and Blue Shield in Massachusetts than there were in the entire Canadian health care system. Also, the United States for years has had the highest rate of prison incarceration in the world. Some would take this willingness to spend money on prisons as consistent with an emphasis on control. The previously discussed spread of electronic monitoring and surveillance, even in the presence of evidence demonstrating deleterious effects on customer service and motivation, is also consistent with this line of argument.

Fourth, Marxist analysis maintains that in the effort to effectuate control, jobs will be deskilled (Braverman, 1974; L. R. Goldberg, 1980). Unless skill is transferred from workers to managers or owners and jobs are comparatively easy to learn, workers will retain significant specialized knowledge that will limit their subordination. Braverman (1974) maintained that even if some jobs were gaining skill and autonomy—for example, engineers—other jobs were losing skills and autonomy, and thus he predicted an increasing polarization of jobs. The evidence on the deskilling of work, or even how to measure skill levels, is mixed (Spenner, 1983; Attewell, 1987). There is little convincing evidence that job skills have either gone down, as the Marxists predicted, or up, as those who see technological change and progress requiring more training and knowledge have maintained. Rather, some occupations and work places have experienced deskilling, while others have experienced skill upgrading (Adler and Borys, 1989). Bailey (1995, p. 33) has argued that there is a connection between the adoption of high-performance work practices and skill and education requirements. The partial diffusion of these practices means that skill and educational requirements have gone up where they have been adopted and have either stayed the same or gone done where more Taylorist forms of work organization persist. The mixed empirical results suggest that a more finely variegated theory of occupational change is required to understand this aspect of the evolution of work in America.

The inconsistent empirical results also highlight the problems in the definition and measurement of skill levels. Spenner has argued that there are at least two dimensions to skill: substantive complexity ("the level, scope, and integration of mental, manipulative, and interpersonal tasks in a job" [1990, p. 402]) and autonomy-control ("the discretion or leeway available in a job to control the content, manner, and speed with which tasks are done" [p. 403]). As he noted, "there is far more consistent evidence of deskilling with respect to the effect of technological change on levels of autonomy-control than on substantive complexity" (p. 404). Barley's (1988) review of this issue also highlights the important distinction between autonomy and skill. Thus, the practice of health maintenance organizations and insurance companies to require preauthorization for hospitalization and some expensive medical tests and procedures clearly limits physicians' autonomy, but it does not change the skill or knowledge required to do the work of a doctor.

Bailey noted that the "direct measurement of skill has proved to be extremely difficult" (1995, p. 28) and that even when such observations are made, the results measure the skills available and used rather than those that are optimal for doing the work. He noted that two indirect approaches to measuring skill levels were (1) measuring the relative earnings of workers with different levels of education and (2) measuring the growth of different occupations with presumably different skill requirements. The change in relative wages during the 1980s was consistent with the view that skill requirements were increasing, as the earnings difference between college graduates and high school graduates increased from 13 percent in 1979 to 38 percent by 1987 (p. 29). The analysis of the entire occupational distribution (as contrasted only with the ten fastest growing jobs) also suggests that "the new jobs that will be added over the next decade are disproportionately those that currently use more highly educated incumbents" (p. 30). Educational requirements may represent credentialism rather than actual learning required to do a task (Collins, 1979), so analyses relying on these indirect measures are inevitably somewhat problematic.

In his review of the literature on technical change, automation, and skill levels, Barley concluded: "current theories of technology and work are either too brutish or too brittle to capture the subtle but multiple ramifications of technical change. . . . Between the stark degradation heralded by the neo-marxists and the bright industrial utopia envisioned by the sociologists of automation, must lie a more nuanced depiction of events" (1988, p. 72).

Some of the earliest Marxist works on the labor process (e.g., Blauner, 1964) noted the alienating effects of achieving control over the labor process—which almost inevitably entails separating the planning of work from doing the work and a process of deskilling (Braverman, 1974). As competitive exigencies have required the involvement and commitment of employees' minds as well as their bodies, there has been a trend toward using high-commitment work practices

(Osterman, 1994). These practices often entail creating self-managing teams and increasing involvement and participation in the work place.

Yet these changes are not necessarily favorable in their effects on employees. As Barker (1993) demonstrated in an ethnographic study of an organization moving from hierarchical to team-based control, the new, value-based and peer-monitored control system was more powerful and complete in its effects than the hierarchical system it replaced. Adler's (1992) study of New United Motors provided ample evidence that the control of work under the new system was much more complete and efficient than under the old. The workers were possibly less alienated and more motivated, however, because now they were supervising each other. As M. Parker and Slaughter wrote in describing the NUMMI system and its reduction of absenteeism, "all the difficulties of one person's absence fall on those in daily contact with the absentee—the co-workers and immediate supervisor—producing enormous peer pressure against absenteeism" (1988, p. 43). Parker and Slaughter referred to the system as management by stress. The question is whether the team model is "creating an era of cooperation between workers and management that is rooted in coercion or consent" (Graham, 1995, p. 1).

Graham's (1995) participant observation study of a Subaru-Isuzu plant in the United States documented the tremendous pace of work and how that pace puts enormous pressure on employees, creating stress and even physical injury. Her study also documented how production exigencies frequently overrode formal company policies of egalitarianism and how, even in a nonunion environment, the work place demands provoked resistance. Garrahan and Stewart, interviewing a small number of workers from Nissan's plant in the United Kingdom, concluded that "the Nissan Way rests upon control through quality, exploitation via flexibility, and surveillance via teamworking" (1992, p. 139). A study of a small number of employees at the Mazda plant at Flat Rock, Michigan (Fucini and Fucini, 1990), also found dissatisfaction with the production system. A study predicting individual employees' attitudes toward lean production (Shadur, Rodwell, and Bamber, 1995) found that commitment to the company was the single best predictor, with attitudes toward the speed of the line being second in importance.

There is irony in the fact that the Taylorist system, with its emphasis on the analysis of work processes, has been perfected not by separating the planning of the work from its doing, as Taylor had proposed, but rather by having the workers participate in their own control and design their own work processes. Parker and Slaughter found that in the NUMMI system, every move a worker made was specified in greater detail than ever before. Because supervisors know the production process well from working on the line themselves, and because workers are involved in a process of continually improving (increasing the productivity) of their own jobs, there is a much more complete form of control achieved than in a more traditional hierarchy.

The Marxist analysis of the labor process soon came under criticism even from critical theorists (e.g., Burawoy, 1985; M. Reed, 1990). First, some argued that the representation of managers as all having the same interests and acting in a unified fashion was incorrect. Second, many writers noted that, whatever the interests and intent of managers and capitalists, workers were not as powerless as portrayed in many of the accounts. There was resistance to the imposition of managerial control, and indeed this resistance forms an important subtext in the detailed case analyses of the Japanese automobile plants (e.g., Adler, 1992; Graham, 1995). Third, there was a deterministic quality to the analysis that troubled some (e.g., Giddens, 1982) because of the limitations imposed on the study of conflict in the work place as a social process. Nevertheless, the so-called labor process theorists have been enormously influential in stimulating a discussion of work place control, not from the point of view of organizational efficiency or management but from the point of view of its determinants and its effects on workers.

The Concept of Class and Interorganizational Analysis

The concept of social class looms large in Marxist analysis, and a second way in which this line of thought has influenced organizational analysis is by operationalizing the construct of class and examining its empirical implications. One line of research has argued that class pertains to the relationship of individuals to the means of production, with capitalists owning the means of production and workers not having ownership. If class matters, then there should be economic returns to one's position in the capitalist ownership structure, controlling for such things as human capital endowments (e.g., education and experience), factors that obviously would also affect wages. There have been studies that do find an effect of "control" on wages, net of other factors. Wright and Perrone (1977), for example, found that the economic returns to education were less for workers than for employers or managers.

The concept of class raises the issue of class solidarity—are there connections among individuals that are defined by class lines that serve to structure interorganizational relationships and action? The relationship of class interests to the state is also an issue highlighted by Marxist theory. The concept of class challenges conventional organization theory by suggesting that organizational behavior such as political contributions and the composition of boards of directors reflect not some need to manage interorganizational dependence (Pfeffer and Salancik, 1978) but rather the pursuit of class interests that transcend organizational boundaries. There is evidence to suggest there are such class interests and they do have predictive power, but the interpretation of the evidence is sometimes challenged.

Palmer contrasted the two approaches to interorganizational analysis succinctly: "According to the interorganizational approach, organizations are entities that possess interests. . . . According to the intraclass approach, individuals within the capitalist class or business elite are actors who possess interests. Organizations are the agents of these actors" (1983, pp. 40–42).

Palmer (1983) argued that if interorganizational co-optive relations, maintained through directorship ties, were consequential for managing interorganizational dependence, such relations should be reconstituted when accidentally broken, for instance, by a death or retirement of the individual linking the two organizations. However, Koenig, Gogel, and Sonquist (1979) found that only 6 percent of single interlock ties were reconstituted, and Palmer (1983) concluded that only 15 percent of the ties could be construed as vehicles for interfirm coordination. Palmer concluded that rather than director interlocks linking organizations, organizations constituted arenas that linked the elite together. Palmer, Friedland, and Singh (1986) found that neither competitive constraint nor inter-industry transaction interdependence accounted for the reconstitution of broken ties, providing further evidence that director interlocks did not apparently serve interfirm coordination.

Another domain relevant to class solidarity is whether or not the business elite took coordinated political activity in spite of the apparent divergence of organizational interests around specific issues. For instance, Whitt (1979; 1980) studied five transportation issues determined by referenda in California during the period 1962–1974 and noted, "Even though there is good reason to expect that, for each issue, some companies would favor it and some would oppose it, the money in every case is virtually *all on one side or the other of the issue*" (1980, pp. 105–106). Whitt also observed a strong correlation between measures of firm size or stake in the issue and the amount contributed, which he took to indicate coordination of action. Dunn's (1980) study of the Weyerhaeuser family office provided an example of one possible coordinating mechanism and how it worked, while Domhoff (1974) has argued for the importance of social ties realized in clubs and other such settings for achieving intraclass coordination. There is evidence that corporate interlocks also help to structure business elite activity and that unity in perspective extends to political candidates as well as to the referenda studied by Whitt (e.g., Clawson and Neustadtl, 1989; Clawson, Neustadtl, and Bearden, 1986; Mizruchi and Koenig, 1986).

The final form of evidence mustered to show the importance of class has been demonstrating a structure to the ruling class (Domhoff, 1967; 1970; 1974). The argument is that there is an inner circle of elite business leaders that hold multiple directorships, articulate classwide business interests, and make decisions, for instance, on political contributions, with these general (as opposed to particular corporate interests) in mind. This structure is manifested in the frequency and centrality of both directorship ties and ties to other important organizations such as government, prestigious foundations and charities, and policy influencing bodies such as commissions and associations (Useem, 1979). Useem (1984) studied the inner circle in both the United States and the United Kingdom, examining board of director interlocks, philanthropic and political contributions, service on nonprofit boards, social origins, and membership on important government advisory committees. He wrote:

> Central members of the inner circle are both top officers of large firms and directors of several other large corporations operating in diverse environments. Though defined by their corporate positions, the members of the inner circle constitute a distinct, semi-autonomous network, one that transcends company, regional, sectoral, and other politically divisive fault lines within the corporate community. The inner circle is at the forefront of business outreach to government, nonprofit organizations, and the public. (p. 3)

The "inner circle" distinction is critical for this line of argument, because there is too much heterogeneity otherwise in business behavior to argue convincingly for the importance of class-based interests and action. But the inner circle argument makes logical sense. In any social structure, including individual organizations, those admitted to the highest levels of power and prestige are individuals who have been carefully filtered (J. C. March and March, 1977) and who exemplify and uphold the organization's central values and interests. There is no reason to believe that obtaining high-level positions in a structure that transcends organizational boundaries would not similarly depend on one's ability and willingness to advocate positions that serve the network as a whole.

Yet the idea of the unity of the ruling class is challenged by the plethora of hostile takeovers (Hirsch, 1986) as well as by the greater activism on the part of boards of directors in the 1990s to dismiss poorly performing CEOs—friends don't raid each other or fire each other. It is possible that both positions are partly correct. There may be an inner circle and an attempt to develop collective interests that transcend the parochial concerns of individual organizations (Useem, 1984, p. 5). At the same time, there are obviously pressures, including those from institutional investors (G. F. Davis and Thompson, 1994), that challenge this cozy relationship and threaten its stability. Which tendency—classwide coordination or the pursuit of individual organizational interests—dominates at any point in time is contingent on a number of environmental factors, and as Davis and Thompson (1994) noted, it is not just the ruling elite that can organize for collective action but their critics and investors as well.

Other Critical Theory

Marxist analysis emphasizes class, defined as the relationship to the means of production, as the fundamental distinction among people. Other critical theories, while similar in their opposition to the perceived hegemony and domination of the powerless, emphasize other bases of difference and oppression such as race and gender, for instance. Acker noted that feminist organization theory involved helping to "create the conditions for a fundamental reworking of organizational theories to account for the persistence of male advantage in male organizations" (1992, p. 248). There have been numerous studies documenting the persistent sex segregation of women and men into different occupations (Beller, 1982; Oppenheimer, 1968; Treiman and Hartmann, 1981), different organizational jobs and roles (Bielby and Baron, 1986), different hierarchical levels with differing authority (e.g., Wolf and Fligstein, 1979) with consequences for women's wages (Halaby, 1979), and studies have shown that, even controlling for hierarchical level, amount of experience, background credentials, and other factors, women almost invariably earn less than men (e.g., Ferber and Kordick, 1978; Fox, 1985; Madden, 1985). Acker distinguished these studies from feminist critical theory: "studies of women's economic and occupational inequality document the extent of the problems but give us no convincing explanations for their persistence or for the apparently endless reorganization of gender and permutations of male power. . . . The extensive literature on women and management documents difficulties and differences but provides no adequate theory of gendered power imbalance" (1992, pp. 248–249).

As an example, Pfeffer and Davis-Blake (1987) showed that salaries for both male and female college administrators decreased as the proportion of women in administrative positions in a given college or university increased and that in colleges and universities that paid less, the proportion of women administrators increased over time more than in settings in which pay was higher. The explanation was that women's work was socially devalued, and it had become taken for granted or institutionalized to pay less for "women's jobs." Calas and Smircich critiqued the study not for its findings but for its apparent silence about implications. They wrote: "they don't use institutional theory to question this situation—which defies the expected positive social consequences of an increased number of females in professional activities" (1992, p. 231).

Critical theory maintains that social science is never neutral, particularly with respect to issues of power, and that this needs to be more explicitly acknowledged in both theoretical development and empirical work. Thus, critical theorists argue that even texts that do not mention gender—or, perhaps, particularly works that do not seem to directly implicate gender—by this very omission contribute to the domination of women (e.g., Mumby and Putnam, 1992; Martin, 1994).

Feminist literature has criticized the separation of the public sphere of work and the private sphere of home and family life (Olsen, 1983; Martin, 1994). Although often portrayed as being gender neutral, some argued that "the reification of the public-private dichotomy gives organizations a justification for refusing to deal with the ways that home life and work life are inextricably intertwined" (Martin, 1994, p. 409). Because the division of home and child-rearing responsibilities are not gender neutral, there are differential effects of being married and having children on women's and men's careers (e.g., Pfeffer and Ross, 1982).

Writers have argued that the very language describing organizations has gender connotations. Acker noted that "the organization itself is often defined through metaphors of masculinity of a certain sort. Today, organizations are lean, mean, aggressive, goal oriented, efficient, and competitive but rarely empathetic, supportive, kind, and caring" (1992, p. 253). Similar arguments have been made about the literature on leadership (Calas, 1993); these arguments note that the language used to describe effective leadership behavior often has implicit connotations of maleness.

Critical theory also argues that there is implicit bias in what is chosen for study. The powerful are studied, the powerless—in terms of class, race, or gender—are frequently neglected. If men and women are differentially present in senior-level positions, for instance, studies of powerful managers will not have many women in the data. Sheriff and Campbell wrote, "Men have produced a body of organizational theory and research in which men are assumed to be the primary objects of study" (1992, p. 31).

The Role of Critical Theory in Organization Studies

Critical theory has a more explicit focus on social change than most social science. Nothing is to be taken for granted, and the goal of research is to help the powerless and excluded. Critical perspectives help organization theory progress by challenging conventional views—for instance, of organizational culture and commitment and the beneficent effects of high-commitment work practices. Critical theory literature can potentially help to ensure that important substantive arenas are not overlooked.

But there is a paradox. Even as critical theory adopts an explicitly political agenda, because of its acknowledged position of a comparative lack of power—excluded, for instance, from the power structure of most academic departments (Martin, 1994)—the more insistent and challenging it becomes, the less likely it is to have its intended effects. Eschewing a strategy of co-optation or even coexistence, some variants of critical theory demand different forms of theory and empirical analysis—qualitative, interpretive work as contrasted with quantitative analysis, as one instance. But one might question how direct challenges to the established order can succeed when they are launched from a position of less power, directly confront the established literature, and do so not on its own terms but on terms chosen and at times knowable only by those launching the critiques. In such a circumstance, it is all too easy for the dominant view to ignore theoretical and empirical challenges. Thus, the challenge for critical theory is to engage conventional analysis in ways that facilitate interaction rather than rejection. The very fact that "institutional conditions determine what kinds of knowledge are produced and what kinds of observation and interpretation come to be accepted as true" (Martin, 1994, p. 416) would seem to require taking those institutional conditions and social realities into account in determining both a theoretical and empirical strategy. In this regard, Marxist organization theory and its descendants possibly provide a fruitful model of what might be accomplished.

9

New Directions for Organization Theory

Three major themes recur in this overview of the field of organization studies and the concepts and controversies that characterize attempts to understand these ubiquitous social entities. First, there are subjects given comparatively short shrift by the field even though they are important in the environment and pose some interesting challenges for some strands of organization theory. Among such subjects are the changing natures of organization boundaries, the employment relation, and the size distribution of organizations, changes in managerial autonomy produced in part by changes in the capital markets, changing organizational demography as the work force composition changes and as organizations internationalize, and changes in the degree of wage inequality in organizations and, as a consequence, in the United States. There are also numerous subject domains in which important models of behavior make competing predictions and in which adherents of the various models tend to talk past each other, ignore competing points of view, and dismiss conflicting evidence, discussions about interdisciplinary cross-fertilization to the contrary.

Second, there is the issue of the very diversity of the field, its increasing differentiation, and the profusion of theories, concepts, and methods as the scope and boundaries of organization studies expand to incorporate ideas from whatever nearby disciplines seem to be useful at the time. And third, there is the idea that both of these facets of the field—what is ignored and the theoretical fragmentation—are consequences of the particular evolution and location of organization studies. In particular, because organization studies is located increasingly in business schools, particularly U.S. business schools, economics has come to play a larger role. In this interdisciplinary setting, fewer disciplinary anchors or forces guide or direct research, contributing to the theoretical diversity that has come to characterize the field. Also, by being housed in business schools, the managerial concerns focused often at the individual or at most the firm level of analysis loom large, and social policy and broader macrosocial issues such as wage inequality, size distributions, and the governance and control of organizations receive comparatively less attention. The particular research context favors an individualistic, careerist, and differentiated pattern:

> In North America the dominating agenda . . . is centered on individualistic competition over careers. . . . Specialization is promoted by the desire of each person to differentiate themselves from the mass. . . . The country with the largest number of professional researchers into organizations, the USA, would display the largest degree of competition and attempts at differentiation. . . . The overwhelming impression is of pluralistic diversity. (Donaldson, 1995, p. 6)

This last chapter builds on the review of the field accomplished in the preceding chapters by taking stock of the field's progress and offering some thoughts about useful future directions for research, paths to avoid, and ideas about the task of building organization theory. The last time I did this, I concluded that "the dominant perspective on action . . . has been the rational model of choice" and that "the vast majority of the research has focused on the individual level of analysis" (Pfeffer, 1982, p. 255). Because organizations are in fact "social entities characterized by demographic, relational, and physical (material?) structures" (Mirvis, 1981, p. 2), I argued that research on networks and social relations, organizational demography, and the physical design of organizations would be productive and useful. The ensuing years have seen at least two of those recommendations or predictions come to fruition. There has been extensive research on both organizational demography (e.g., Stewman, 1988; Mitman, 1992) and social networks (e.g., Burt, 1992). In both instances, there have been substantial advances in ideas, methods, and results.

By contrast, there has not been much attention given to physical design (e.g., Darley and Gilbert, 1985), and if anything there has been less research on this subject since the 1980s. And, as noted in chapter 7, the subject of organizational design has also diminished in the amount of research attention received. One of the things this final chapter does is to renew the call for research on the effects of the physical or built environment and to argue for a revitalization of research on other aspects of design. This is part of a recommendation for the field to become more phenomenon driven and to consider using issues of relevance as one way of navigating the thicket of ideas and concepts. This chapter also pursues another theme from the earlier review—a concern with the state of paradigm proliferation—although now the argument is more readily made that the costs of being unconcerned about the state of organization studies as a scientific activity are closer at hand.

How Is Organization Studies Doing?

If judged by the formation of new journals and the expansion of existing ones, the field of organization studies is doing well. *Organization Science, Journal of Management Inquiry,* and *Organization* are only three of several journals that have appeared since 1990. The *Academy of Management Journal* has recently expanded by 50 percent in publication frequency (from four to six issues per year) and has also expanded the size of each issue, and the *Academy of Management Review* is larger as well. The *Journal of Management* has enlarged its editorial board, scope, and ambitions. There is a vigorous and growing set of outlets for organizational research. Book publishing is also flourishing. More and more publishers have entered the field of business publishing, which includes publication of work on management and organizations, and the number of titles published has expanded virtually every year. Attendance at professional meetings is up substantially, as is the size and length of the program and membership in the Academy of Management.

If judged by the passion aroused by debates over whether or not dispositions are useful for understanding organizational behavior (House et al., 1996), whether a critical perspective on both organizations and organization theory is useful (Ferguson, 1984), whether the field should seek more paradigmatic unity (Van Maanen, 1995b), and whether the field is too functionalist (e.g., Martin, 1992b), intellectual activity in the field is vigorous. Indeed, the vigor and scope of organization studies make the task of providing an overview of the field daunting.

By some other indicators, however, a less sanguine view of the field emerges. Hambrick (1994) bemoaned organization studies' lack of influence on the world of practice and its corresponding lack of disciplinary power and attention. There is, for instance, a Council of Economic Advisors but no Council of Organizational (or Management) Advisors, even though both government and social policy could benefit from the insights and research of organization studies. Although economic statistics are gathered regularly by official agencies, statistics that would assist in studying organizations must still, for the most part, be gathered by individual scholars rather than by agencies with data gathering as their mission. The 1990s have witnessed efforts to sharply curtail federally funded research in the sciences generally, but it is the social sciences that are particularly hard hit as medical research, for instance, has been more successful in defending itself.

There is concern with the pace of the development of organizational knowledge and even if there is such progress in our understanding. Webster and Starbuck (1988) argued that knowledge was developing slowly, and they buttressed this claim by noting that the strength of relationships, as measured by the size of reported correlations on a variety of topics, was actually getting smaller rather than larger over time. Miner (1984) examined the connection between the usefulness, scientific validity, and frequency of mention by scholars for twenty-four organization theories. He found little correlation among the three measures. For example, more useful or more valid theories were no more likely to be frequently mentioned than less useful or valid ones. This disconnection between validity, applicability, and prominence is troubling for a field that aspires to be scientifically valid and useful for understanding and managing organizations. Barley and Kunda were concerned about the field's inability to get beyond an "Anglo-American vision of social order [that] rests on an opposition between mechanistic and organic solidarity, associated, respectively, with normative and rational ideologies of control" (1992, p. 386).

There are a number of things that might be done to help knowledge develop and to make the field more useful and usable by managers and policy makers. Some of these are suggested in what follows, but the discussion does not purport to be comprehensive. Addressing these issues requires the discussion and attention of all of those interested in organizations and their study.

Avoiding the Dangerous Liaison with Economics

As noted in the first chapter, there is evidence that organization studies is increasingly influenced by and preoccupied with an economic orientation or model of behavior. The study of organizations seems to be not so much bothered by physics envy (Van Maanen, 1995b) as it is by economics envy, which at the end of the day is potentially much more troublesome. After all, most of us don't really borrow physics theory too often to understand organizations (chaos theory notwithstanding), but the temptation to rely on rational economic models of choice and organizational behavior, regardless of their ability to develop novel insights or to produce empirically valid predictions, remains compelling. In their analysis of waves of managerial rhetoric, Barley and Kunda argued that the normative emphasis of the writing about organizational culture would be supplanted by a "resurgence of rationalism" (1992, p. 394). This prediction has turned out to be true and the trend was already well advanced at the time of their article.

Why should we care about this trend? Canella and Paetzold argued that we should not worry about the growing dominance of economic models in organization analysis: "Should members of another field wish to mount a hostile takeover of organizational science, we say 'let them come,' . . . recognizing that such a takeover requires the convincing of members of our field . . . that some particular perspective is the best one offered to date" (1994, p. 337).

But this argument is wrong on two counts. It is misleading in the first instance for its implications about the politics of knowledge. Those advocating an economic approach to organizational analysis (e.g., Barney and Ouchi, 1986; Hesterly, Liebeskind, and Zenger, 1990) have displayed a willingness—indeed, an eagerness—to take on topics traditionally left to psychologists, sociologists, and organizations scholars, topics, that is, such as organizational structure (Milgrom and Roberts, 1992) and the structuring and effects of rewards and incentives (Zenger, 1992). Many of those pushing an economic model are explicit in their view that this mode of analysis is intended to *replace*, rather than to *supplement*, other forms of organizational analysis. Thus, for instance, Jensen predicted "an impending revolution in organization theory" (1983, p. 324) based on emerging theoretical work in economics. Hirschleifer was even more direct: "The social sciences can be regarded as in a process of coalescing. As economics 'imperialistically' employs its tools of analysis over a wider range of social issues, it will *become* sociology and anthropology and political science. . . . As these other disciplines grow increasingly rigorous, they will not merely resemble but will *be* economics" (1977, pp. 3–4, emphasis in original).

Canella and Paetzold recognized that "science is not a magnificent march toward absolute truth, but a social struggle among the scholars of the profession to construct truth" (1994, p. 332). But the implication of this fact is that truth will not necessarily triumph since truth is itself socially determined. Or, the best perspective offered to date is determined not by some unambiguous empirical test but rather by which theory or perspective can muster the most social support for its definition of truth and organizational reality. Consequently, those factors that produce advantage in a social struggle will be important in determining which theoretical perspective triumphs, and unity in perspective and consensus are among the factors that provide the economic perspective with an edge in the contest among models and theories.

Being unconcerned about the proliferation of economic explanations of organizations is also wrong as a matter of science. Chapter 3 detailed just a portion of what is wrong with the economic model as a way of analyzing organizations. Ghoshal and Moran (1996) have made the argument that not only are economic models often theoretically and empirically misleading; they are also "bad for practice" and, by inference, a poor foundation on which to build public or management policy. "Organization economics . . . sees managers as untrustworthy and as requiring controls from superordinate levels in the organization" (Donaldson, 1995, p. 4), thereby contributing to a control-oriented set of management practices (e.g., the emphasis on hierarchy, incentives, and surveillance) that are both expensive and counterproductive. If this is true—and certainly more research and argument may be warranted—then there are important consequences for organizations themselves from the field of organization studies being seduced by economic logic and models. Recall that theories of behavior, to the extent they guide policies and practices, can become true through their very implementation (Frank, 1988; Pfeffer, 1994, chap. 4) because of the self-fulfilling, interconnected nature of behavior. Organizational scholars have an obligation to develop and test alternative models of behavior and not simply cede the field to economics.

Somewhat paradoxically, even as the various strands of organization theory may have become increasingly diverse and disconnected, the field as a whole has become more connected to adjacent social sciences that advocate the rational actor model of behavior. Even as debate about positivism has occurred within the field of organization studies, and even as critical perspectives have evolved, the field has come to be increasingly dominated by models and methods that would seem to epitomize what critical theory eschews. This is not to suggest that there aren't subcultures of organization theory that embrace the humanities, postmodernism, and critical theory or that there aren't those who seek to maintain a diversity of paradigms. But the current trend seems clear.

Avoiding Fads and Fashion by Pursuing a Strong Inference Research Strategy

One cause for the flirtation of the field with economic models is the absence of paradigmatic consensus over problems, theories, or research methods. This absence of a well-developed scientific paradigm makes experimenting with anything new or different more desirable. It also has the undesirable property of permitting taste, virtually unconstrained by scientific norms and standards, to run rampant. Two experienced organizations scholars with extensive experience as editors and reviewers made this point eloquently: "Even when a paper contains a well-articulated theory that fits the data, editors or reviewers may reject it or insist the theory be replaced simply because it clashes with their particular conceptual tastes" (Sutton and Staw, 1995, p. 372).

Organization studies, because of its lack of a strong anchor either in a discipline or in phenomena, is susceptible to being caught up by fads and fashion. Making this same observation, Zald wrote, "organizational studies follows the ratings, responding not only to academic fads but to the whims and foibles of academic hucksters and the problem definitions of corporate executives" (1993, p. 514). Eccles and Nohria noted that management theory was obsessed with newness, even though the "new" principles were essentially the same as the old ones: "Even a casual reading of the management literature over the past seventy-five years, both popular and academic, shows that every age 'discovers' these principles anew. . . . Even as the fundamental themes of management remain the same, the words used to express them constantly portray them as new" (1992, p. 5).

Following fads and fashion without some sense of a theoretical research agenda that can withstand the blandishments of novelty and uniqueness can cause problems for the development of the field of study, as Barley and Kunda noted: "to the degree that trends in organizational theory mirror trends in managerial discourse at large, our efforts may be neither cumulative nor pathbreaking. Instead, in the long run, the tenor of our theorizing may amount to little more than the turning of a small cog within a larger socioeconomic clock over which no one has control" (1992, p. 394).

Absent some consensus on the goals of the scientific enterprise, the temptation to be caught up in the new and to pursue "what's interesting" has a greater influence on the research process. The study of organizations would probably be well served to spend more time confronting data and phenomena and less time being fascinated by the new, the elegant, or the obscure for their own sake. Donaldson maintained that "the present degree of pluralism in US organization theory is excessive and harbours severe problems of incoherence, lack of cumulation, cynicism, faddism and despair that anything of lasting worth can be accomplished" (1995, p. 6). Commenting on the prevalence of the uniqueness value—"a prescription that uniqueness is good, and therefore organization scholars should attempt to make unique contributions to their discipline," Mone and McKinley wrote:

> M. S. Davis (1971) pointed out that the criterion for evaluating the importance of a social science theory is typically iconoclasm, rather than the theory's truth value. . . . Astley (1985) . . . argued that "the value attached to a theory, and the assessment of its contribution to scientific progress, is primarily determined . . . by its intellectual novelty." . . . Staw (1985) advocated a role for journals as generators of variety rather than selection-retention mechanisms. . . . Gioia and Pitre (1990) suggested that organizational science should strive to be original, and Martin (1992[b]) stated that we should "invent our own experiments, uncon-

strained by the usual ways of thinking and writing about empirical work." (1993, pp. 285; 286)

This value of uniqueness and innovation for its own sake, not for its truth value or for its ability to advance our understanding of organizations, is very much at variance with the use of a theory-building strategy employing the logic of strong inference. MacKenzie and House advocated a strong inference approach as a paradigm development strategy for organization studies. They described strong inference research as:

> based on the assumption that: (a) all theories, no matter how good at explaining a set of phenomena, are ultimately incorrect and consequently will undergo modification over time . . . and (b) the fate of the better theories is to become explanations that hold for some phenomena in some limited conditions. . . . A guiding principle of the strong inference research strategy is the Popperian position that pursuit of knowledge is more efficient when scientists deliberately set out to disprove theories, or seek rejections, than when they attempt to assemble proof for theories. (1978, p. 13)

They noted that "paradigm development research necessarily implies commitment to a program of research" (p. 21) and that this programmatic research approach "is counter to the 'success ethic' whereby researchers act as if they are 'piece workers' grinding out a quota of 'successes' per unit time, with bonuses given for above average productivity" (p. 21).

The uniqueness value has other adverse consequences for developing knowledge about organizations. It contradicts the idea of replication—even replicability—as well as the process for developing useful knowledge, because for knowledge to be useful it must be both replicable and replicated. The uniqueness value tends to favor complexity—simple ideas are less likely to be unique or to be "interesting." But, there is much to be said for parsimonious, simple theoretical ideas that can serve as a foundation for understanding organizations:

> If people are boundedly rational, constrained by rules and procedures, prone to act according to habit or custom, with unclear preferences, and subject to various forms of social influence, why do we think it necessary to develop such intricate models and such complex variables to describe them individually and in interaction? As others have noted, the phrase complex organizations may refer more to the organization theorists' portrayal of organizations than to the entities themselves (Weick, 1969, p. 1). . . . If we use relatively simpler processes and models, the world will appear to be simpler and more certain. . . . In our fascination with complexity, we overlook the potential for finding simpler models to describe the world. (Pfeffer, 1981a, p. 411)

Some argue that paradigm diversity stimulates innovation (Martin, 1992b; Morgan, 1990; Zald, 1993). The evidence on this point is far from clear. Zammuto and Connolly wrote that "the organizational sciences are severely fragmented" and that "this fragmentation presents a serious obstacle to scientific growth of the field" (1984, p. 30). They noted that "organization sciences incur costs in every area: teaching, administration, research, publication, advancement, and recognition" (p. 31). In a similar vein, Mone and McKinley maintained that "the rapid rate of innovation . . . is not necessarily strengthening our understanding or knowledge concerning organizations" (1993, p. 293). Commenting on the profusion of paradigms, Donaldson wrote:

> The academic institutional system in the USA which so fragmented organizational structural theory in the seventies and which has produced a plethora of conflicting paradigms may continue . . . generating distinctiveness through product differentiation. . . . The prospects may not be bright for an imminent reintegration of the currently competing paradigms. . . . Nevertheless, such a unified theory is needed . . . and it is the goal which all persons of good scientific conscience will wish to see achieved. (1995, p. 214)

If, as Donaldson has suggested, the prospects for developing a more unified theory are meager, and if the logic of strong inference or seeking some greater level of paradigm development are both unattractive (e.g., Van Maanen, 1995b), then another way of advancing knowledge is to anchor research concerns more in phenomena and in relevance.

The Advantage of Being Phenomenon Driven

The role of theory in the organization sciences is problematic. First of all, there are important disagreements about what theory is or should be. Van Maanen argued that "theory makes its way in intellectual communities (and beyond) as much by its style as by its theoretical claims, logic, sweep, empirical evidence, or methodological strictures" (1995a, p. 690). To some, rhetoric and theory are inseparable and almost indistinguishable (Van Maanen, 1995a; 1995b). There is even the question as to whether theory is useful. "Some prominent researchers have argued the case against theory. . . . The field first needs more descriptive narratives about organizational life" (Sutton and Staw, 1995, p. 378). Rich description, writing that is at times indistinguishable from literature or reporting, is necessary to build strong theory over time (Van Maanen, 1989). Others question whether the demands placed on scholars for both good theory and rigorous data are compatible or even feasible. Sutton and Staw (1995, p. 380–381) noted: "On the one hand, editors and reviewers plead for creative and interesting ideas. . . . On the other hand, authors are skewered for apparent mismatches between their theory and data. . . . Contradictory demands for both strong theory and precise measurement are often satisfied only by hypocritical writing."

On the other hand, some organization scholars argue for theory development and theory testing based on principles found in the natural as well as the social sciences. Sacks, one of the founders of conversation analysis, a branch of ethnomethodology, itself a qualitative branch of sociology, argued for the importance of methods that were replicable and that could be transferred to others: "When I started to do research . . . I figured that sociology could not be an actual science unless it was able to handle the details of actual events, handle them formally, and in the first instance, be informative about them in the direct ways in which primitive sciences tend to be informative, that is, that anyone else can go and see whether what was said is so" (1984, p. 26).

MacKenzie and House (1978) argued for the importance of not only developing theory but rejecting it when it did not fit the data, a method for cumulating knowledge and over time refining theories so that they were increasingly rigorous and applicable. Donaldson (1995) has argued not only for theory in general but for a specific theory, structural contingency theory, and has made the broader argument that cumulation and integration of insights and findings are important for the advance of organization studies.

Given these disagreements and the general absence of paradigmatic consensus, prospects for theory development may not be bright. Sutton and Staw wrote, "Lack of consensus on exactly what theory is may explain why it is so difficult to develop strong theory in the behavioral sciences" (1995, p. 372). In a similar vein, Weick noted "how hard it is in a low-paradigm field, in which people are novice theorists, to spot which of their efforts are theory and which are not" (1995, p. 387).

One way to navigate the morass of different theories, and one way to evaluate the theories that present themselves, is to ask the extent to which each theory or perspective is linked to a particular, important organizational phenomenon and affords insight into understanding that phenomenon. It is, in fact, possible to make the case that many of the prominent organization theories did, in fact, derive from a concern with specific, interesting phenomena. What happened, however, was that over time the theories became objects of discourse and development in and of themselves, often losing connection to their original foundations.

For instance, one important source of institutional theory was the observation that organizational goals and their associated technology were often only loosely coupled with actual organizational arrangements, including structures (J. W. Meyer and Scott, 1983). Another observation was the effect on the adoption of various practices of the mere frequency of adoption of similar practices in the environment rather than some technical or efficiency rationale for their use (e.g., Tolbert and Zucker, 1983). Much of the interest in social networks and the effects of the social environment on behavior came from the observation that organizational behavior was contagious, in a social network sense (e.g., G. F. Davis, 1991), and from the interest in the sources of the differences in individual career attainments and success (e.g., Granovetter, 1974). Resource dependence theory arose from observations of interorganizational influence (e.g., Pfeffer, 1972a). And the rationalizing model, with its concomitant effect on the analysis of organizational incentives and their consequences, derived in part from the observation that people often developed attitudes to be consistent with their behavior rather than the reverse (Aronson, 1972; Staw, 1980) and that it was the case that rewards often had perverse effects (A. Kohn, 1993).

Theoretical perspectives that have been less phenomenon driven have sometimes gotten themselves into trouble as a consequence. Economics, for example, often starts with a phenomenon—for example, the spread of the multidivisional structure, the prevalence of seniority-graded wage profiles—but doesn't investigate the cause of the phenomenon because it assumes the cause: efficiency. Rather, it models how an efficiency-based explanation, consistent with what is observed, can be derived. Because observations, in this mode of theorizing, can never be used to inform or develop the theory—rather, the theory is used to account for the observations—there cannot be any refutation or specifying of the scope conditions of the theory, and, as a consequence, there is also no development of the theory. Structural contingency theory (Donaldson, 1995) suffered from a different problem. Although it began with a phenomenon—differences in organizational structure and what might affect those differences and result from them—it fairly quickly moved to conceptualize the phenomenon using dimensions that were both far removed from practice and managerial conversation and also too complex and convoluted to be explained or recalled even to a scientific audience. In that sense, the theory departed from the original thing it began to explain— understanding organizational structures in the service of developing the science and practice of organizational design.

But design remains an important concern in organizations, and issues of design have much to recommend them as important ways of analyzing and understanding organizations. Pursuing a design perspective, broadly defined, would, therefore, be useful in advancing organizational analysis.

The Relevance of Design—Physical and Organizational

The effects of physical design on social behavior remain relatively unexplored in the organizations literature and in related social sciences. For instance, the topic of environmental psychology was only included in the *Handbook of Social Psychology* in its *third* edition (Darley and Gilbert, 1985). Organizations textbooks and courses typically ignore discussion of either the design of work environments or the effects of physical design on organizational behavior, even though it seems clear that "physical settings provide contexts for behavior" (Hatch, 1987, p. 387). One possible reason for the neglect of the topic is that it represents "a problem-centered rather than a theory-centered set of activities" (Darley and Gilbert, 1985, p. 949). As we have just seen, organization studies is often enamored with theory, or at least with the appearance of theory. Consideration of physical environments is consistent with the emphasis on phenomena that may be useful for developing understanding of organizations. As will be discussed shortly, these environments are themselves changing, which bears explanation, and have potent effects on behavior.

Since the mid-1990s, there has been some indication of a growing interest in the subject of design, both architectural design (F. Becker and Steele, 1995), product design (Sutton and Hargadon, 1996), and systems design. Becker and Steele have argued that considering organizational design and new work arrangements such as self-managed teams without considering the physical design implications is incomplete, because "as a work setting, an effective organization is best managed as a total integrated system that includes the physical facility, information technology, organizational policies and practices, and management style" (1995, p. xii). Moreover, there is a literature that documents a set of reliable findings with respect to design issues and design effects.

Darley and Gilbert noted: "an interior—an artificial construction that encapsulates or surrounds an occupant—influences behavior by virtue of its ambient qualities, its spatial and architectural arrangements, and its perceived purpose. . . . We may best gauge the influence of the built interior by examining the ways in which it impedes, constrains, alters, or facilitates purposive behavior" (1985, p. 969).

Springer summarized the findings of three major studies of the effects of the built environment on performance. The dimensions of the environment considered included acoustics (noise), visual (lighting and glare) and thermal (temperature and temperature variability) aspects, air quality, appearance, and spatial arrangement, including dimensions such as floor space, layout, the amount of personal storage, the work surface, and ease of circulation. He reported that "enhancements to white-collar workplaces have shown consistent performance improvements of between 10 to 15 percent" (1992, p. 46).

One aspect of physical space that has received some research attention is the effect of distance on interaction. "Empirical verification of the role played by propinquity in regulating interpersonal attraction seemed to bring to the fore the realization that one's friends are drawn from the population of persons one has met and that meeting requires the conjoint occupation of space" (Darley and Gilbert, 1985, p. 971). Festinger, Schachter, and Back (1950) studied a graduate student housing complex and noted how friendship patterns were correlated with visual access and with the likelihood of chance meetings. Furthermore, they observed that the number of friends a person had was affected by location in the housing complex and its influence on chance encounters. Hatch summarized a number of studies that observed "a relationship between distance and choice of interaction partners. . . . All of these researchers found an inverse relationship between the distance separating employees and the likelihood of communication occurring between them" (1987, p. 387). The effect of distance on interaction probably affects only certain forms of interaction, such as face-to-face. Conrath (1973), for example, noted that distance was inversely correlated with face-to-face interaction and telephone calls but not with written communication among employees.

The relationship between barriers, including physical barriers such as partitions and doors and social barriers such as having a secretary, and interaction is less clear. Some studies have found a negative relationship between settings with barriers and the amount of interaction (e.g., Gullahorn, 1952) and have reported that moving from a closed to an open office arrangement increased opportunities to interact and the apparent ease of communication (e.g., Brookes and Kaplan, 1972; Szilagyi and Holland, 1980). However, Oldham and Brass (1979) found that perceptions of supervisor feedback and friendship opportunities decreased after a move to an open office setting.

In one of the more comprehensive studies of the effects of physical space and other factors on interaction, Hatch, studying employees in two high technology organizations, found that:

> interactions among professional-technical workers . . . may be greater for workers who are given enclosed work spaces than for those lacking physical barriers.

> . . . Enclosure by partitions (or walls) and a door was found to be positively associated with the amount of time individuals reported working with others. Partition height was also positively related to reported amount of meeting time. . . . Enclosure supports interpersonal and group interaction. . . . Time reported to be spent building relationships was positively correlated with the use of a door. (1987, pp. 396–397)

Hatch's interpretation was that a certain amount of privacy and personal space was useful for building relationships and holding meetings and that an absence of privacy actually reduced interaction. Her study also found that task interdependence and task uncertainty were not related to self-reported interaction activity. The variables that were the primary focus of her study, the characteristics of physical space, accounted for a sizable portion of the variation in seven categories of self-reported work activity and in most instances explained more of the variance than either individual demographics, individual sociability scores, or the firm or type of job.

There is a second important way in which the physical environment affects organizational behavior. R. A. Baron has summarized the extensive literature on the influence of affect, "the mild, temporary shifts in current mood that virtually everyone experiences" (1993, p. 64), on a number of outcomes including negotiation, conflict, performance appraisals, task performance, and absenteeism and turnover. In a series of imaginative studies, Baron has demonstrated that "social factors, although of obvious importance, are clearly not the only source of positive and negative affect. Another set of factors that can produce shifts in current moods relates to aspects of the *physical environment*. Included here are such variables as ambient temperature, humidity, noise, crowding, air quality, lighting, and other features of the physical surroundings in which people work or interact" (p. 74). He reported effects of temperature on aggression, of pleasant scents on goal setting and self-confidence, and of lighting on a number of dimensions of work performance.

It is striking that organizations have undergone a number of transformations without the literature linking these changes very explicitly to considerations of the built environment. Two such changes come to mind. First, there is an increasing emphasis on working in teams and teamwork in organizations, particularly as the ranks of middle management have been decimated. A physical environment built to facilitate and encourage teamwork is one that looks different from one built to enhance managerial status or to promote individual, contemplative decision making. There are examples of redesigning built environments to promote a sense of team identification—for instance, when Volvo moved to a more team-based model of production in its Kalmar truck factory, it redesigned the layout to incorporate areas for each team that enhanced visual contact and promoted a sense of team identification. But, we have yet to fully understand what a team-based physical setting would encompass, and studies that relate the team orientation of the physical environment to the success of self-managed team interventions remain to be done.

Second, people now more frequently work off-site, in arrangements that entail telecommuting from home or that involve working at customer premises or on the road. Because physical space is expensive, some organizations have taken these new work arrangements as an opportunity to reduce their space require-ments and thereby cut occupancy costs. The idea is to provide individuals with space in a central office only when and as needed—an arrangement sometimes called "hoteling." Permanent storage with temporary work spaces reduces the need to provide offices that sit vacant while individuals are working off-site. Al-though this arrangement obviously saves space, it sends an interesting message about the importance of interacting with one's peers and colleagues and, indeed, about one's identification with the organization. Again, studies about the effects of this arrangement on organizational identification, commitment and turnover, career advancement (which often requires sponsorship and the building of net-works), and learning and idea sharing would be useful. As Darley and Gilbert noted, "layout serves not only to regulate communication but to communicate something of its own. . . . Interior layout serves as a signaling system that defines role, rights, and responsibilities" (1985, p. 972).

The neglect of physical design in the literature is related to the current ne-glect of organizational design. As one way of demonstrating this current neglect, consider the literature cited by one of the proponents of a design perspective. In his overview of the structural contingency literature, Donaldson (1995, p. 14) cited some sixty-one studies. Almost half of them were from the 1970s (thirty) and only two were from the 1990s. It is fair to state that the late 1960s and early 1970s were the heyday of academic interest in both structural contingency theory and organizational design. Although management consultants and practicing manag-ers remain interested in questions of design, the research literature has waned.

The problem is that both physical and organizational design share an "engi-neering" orientation to the field of organizations. Although the study of manage-ment has important historical roots in engineering, engineering is out, at least among many academics today. Even as consultants have come to play a larger role in producing books about organizations and organizational processes, and even as consulting firms and similar organizations are increasingly involved in doing studies and research about organizational issues, the response from re-searchers in academic settings seems to be profound ambivalence. Although many academics participate in these outside activities, within the academy there seems to be some dominant notion of theoretical purity. There seems to be an implicit belief that the way to retain both status and position is to be calculatively irrelevant. As a strategy of inquiry, it is not likely to work. As MacKenzie and House argued, "much is to be learned from applying the knowledge gained in the laboratory to outside settings. Application is not the sole justification for basic research, but it is certainly helpful in generating counter examples to a theory" (1978, p. 21). Their position, with which I concur, is that it is through "engi-neering" activities that one learns the extent to which a theory is useful and valid and hence acquires the empirical insight necessary to develop and revise theory.

Thus, there is a case to be made that organization studies would be well served to be both more phenomena driven and more concerned with the applica-bility of its ideas. In pursuing these goals, an emphasis on design seems war-ranted. The issue is not just that good theory is practical, to rephrase Lewin's old dictum. It is that in the welter of ideas that characterizes the field, the "engineering" application of those ideas provides one way of distinguishing those that help us understand organizations and those that don't.

Conclusion

Much progress has occurred in understanding the basic foundations of behavior, in developing and testing alternative models of behavior, in understanding social control, and in understanding the causes of organizational performance. But much remains to be accomplished. Empirical and theoretical work still often pays more attention to belief and ideology than to data, and connections among topics and tests of competing perspectives remain all too rare. Organization studies is trapped by its context and seems almost unconscious of this fact, limiting the likelihood of extending its research domain to be more explicitly comparative and historical and to address more directly social and organizational policy as well as description.

In reviewing the literature on organizational change, Barnett and Carroll (1995) noted that the field had developed in two separate, virtually isolated streams—one emphasizing the content of change or what actually changes in an organization, and the other focusing on the process of change or how change occurs. In reviewing that literature and its progress over the previous twenty years, the authors concluded that although process and content effects are different, there are important interactions between the two domains. They argued that "when researchers start recognizing and incorporating such notions into studies of the consequences of organizational change, it will be easier to sort out findings and to resolve apparently contradictory ones" (p. 233).

A similar comment applies to organization theory generally. The field could benefit from more connection between concerns of process and content. More comprehensive incorporation of issues—including the locus for causality of behavior, the models that explain behavior, fundamental understanding of social control processes, and the consequences of all of this for various outcomes including survival and performance—would help sort out findings and provide guidance for those seeking to understand organizations and for those who live in and manage them.

One particularly worthwhile domain in which process and content concerns converge is the translation of knowledge into action. There are many instances in which organizations know what to do (content) but have difficulty in actually implementing that knowledge (action). To understand how organizations fail to act on their knowledge, or, more prosaically, why well-informed individuals and organizations within them pursue ineffective activities and promote dysfunctional policies and practices, we will need to study not just "best practices" but "worst practices" as well. Population ecology has reminded the field of the importance of not selecting on the dependent variable and how much more can be learned by studying the full range of organizational performance and populations of organizations. The challenge for organization studies in the future is to find ways of understanding the connection between content and process, between knowledge and action, and between theory and practice. It seems that such a focus would provide some additional leverage for analyzing organizations. Most important, it is a way of thinking about analyzing organizations that could develop knowledge in organization science that would have both theoretical power and practical utility.

REFERENCES

Abegglen, J. C., and G. Stalk, Jr. (1985). *Kaisha: The Japanese corporation.* New York: Basic Books.

Abowd, J. M. (1990). Does performance-based managerial compensation affect corporate performance? *Industrial and Labor Relations Review, 43,* 52–73-S.

Abrahamson, E. (1996). Management fashion. *Academy of Management Review, 21,* 254–285.

Achen, C. H. (1986). *The statistical analysis of quasi-experiments.* Berkeley: University of California Press.

Acker, J. (1990). Hierarchies, jobs, bodies: A theory of gendered organizations. *Gender and Society, 4,* 139–158.

Acker, J. (1992). Gendering organizational theory. In A. J. Mills and P. Tancred (Eds.), *Gendering organizational analysis,* 248–260. Newbury Park, Calif.: Sage.

Adler, P. S. (1992). The learning bureaucracy: New United Motors Manufacturing, Inc. In B. M. Staw and L. L. Cummings (Eds.), *Research in organizational behavior: Vol. 15,* 111–194. Greenwich, Conn.: JAI Press.

Adler, P. S., and B. Borys (1989). Automation and skill: Three generations of research on the NC case. *Politics and Society, 17,* 378–383.

Aiello, J. R. (1993). Electronic performance monitoring. *Journal of Applied Social Psychology, 23,* 499–507.

Aiello, J. R., and A. Chomiak (1992). The effects of computer monitoring and distraction on task performance. Unpublished ms., Rutgers University.

Aiello, J. R., and C. M. Svec (1993). Computer monitoring and work performance: Extending the social facilitation framework to electronic presence. *Journal of Applied Social Psychology, 23,* 537–548.

Aldrich, H. E., and E. R. Auster (1986). Even dwarfs started small: Liabilities of age and size and their strategic implications. In B. M. Staw and L. L. Cummings (Eds.), *Research in organizational behavior: Vol. 8,* 165–198. Greenwich, Conn.: JAI Press.

Alexander, C. N., and G. W. Knight (1971). Situated identities and social psychological experimentation. *Sociometry, 34,* 65–82.

Alexander, J., B. Nuchols, J. Bloom, and S. Lee (1995). Organizational demography and turnover: An examination of multiform and nonlinear heterogeneity. *Human Relations, 48,* 1455–1480.

Alexander, V. D., and P. A. Thoits (1985). Token achievement: An examination of proportional representation and performance outcomes. *Social Forces, 64,* 332–340.

Allen, M. P. (1974). The structure of interorganizational elite co-optation: Interlocking corporate directorates. *American Sociological Review, 39,* 393–406.

Allen, R. W., D. L. Madison, L. W. Porter, P. A. Renwick, and B. T. Mayes (1979). Organizational politics: Tactics and characteristics of its actors. *California Management Review, 22,* 77–83.

Allen, S. A. (1978). Organizational choices and general management influence networks in divisionalized companies. *Academy of Management Journal, 21,* 341–365.

Allmendinger, J., and J. R. Hackman (1995). The more the better? A four-nation study of the inclusion of women in symphony orchestras. *Social Forces, 74,* 423–460.

Alvesson, M., and H. Willmott (1992). On the idea of emancipation in management and organization studies. *Academy of Management Review, 17,* 432–464.

Amabile, T. M. (1985). Motivation and creativity: Effects of motivational orientation on creative writers. *Journal of Personality and Social Psychology, 48,* 393–399.

Amabile, T. M., B. A. Hennessey, and B. S. Grossman (1986). Social influences on creativity: The effects of contracted-for reward. *Journal of Personality and Social Psychology, 50,* 14–23.

Amburgey, T. L., D. Kelly, and W. P. Barnett (1993). Resetting the clock: The dynamics of organizational failure. *Administrative Science Quarterly, 38,* 51–73.

American Management Association (1994). *1994 AMA survey on downsizing: Summary of key findings.* New York: American Management Association.

Amick, B. C., and M. J. Smith (1992). Stress, computer-based work monitoring and measurement systems: A conceptual overview. *Applied Ergonomics, 23,* 6–16.

Applebaum, E. (1987). Restructuring work: Temporary, part-time, and at-home employment. In H. I. Hartmann (Ed.), *Computer chips and paper clips: Technology and women's employment,* 268–310. Washington, D.C.: National Academy Press.

Archibald, W. P. (1974). Alternative explanations for self-fulfilling prophecy. *Psychological Bulletin, 81,* 74–84.

Argyris, C. (1972). *The applicability of organizational sociology.* London: Cambridge University Press.

Argyris, C. (1995). On actionable knowledge. Unpublished ms. Harvard University, Graduate School of Business Administration.

Arkes, H. R., and C. Blumer (1985). The psychology of sunk cost. *Organizational Behavior and Human Decision Processes, 35,* 124–140.

Armour, H. O., and D. J. Teece (1978). Organizational structure and economic performance: A test of the multidivisional hypothesis. *Bell Journal of Economics, 9,* 106–122.

Aronson, E. (1972). *The social animal.* San Francisco: W. H. Freeman.

Aronson, E., and J. Mills (1959). The effect of severity of initiation on liking for a group. *Journal of Abnormal and Social Psychology, 59,* 177–181.

Arrow, K. (1982). Risk perception in psychology and economics. *Economic Inquiry, 20,* 1–9.

Arthur, J. B. (1992). The link between business strategy and industrial relations systems in American steel minimills. *Industrial and Labor Relations Review, 45,* 488–506.

Arthur, J. B. (1994). Effects of human resource systems on manufacturing performance and turnover. *Academy of Management Journal, 37,* 670–687.

Arvey, R. D., T. J. Bouchard, Jr., N. L. Segal, and L. M. Abraham (1989). Job satisfaction: Environmental and genetic components. *Journal of Applied Psychology, 74*, 187–192.

Asch, B. J. (1990). Do incentives matter? The case of navy recruiters. *Industrial and Labor Relations Review, 43*, 89-S–106-S.

Ashforth, B. E., and A. M. Saks (1996). Socialization tactics: Longitudinal effects on newcomer adjustment. *Academy of Management Journal, 39*, 149–178.

Astley, W. G. (1985). Administrative science as socially constructed truth. *Administrative Science Quarterly, 30*, 497–513.

Atkinson, J. (1984). Manpower strategies for flexible organizations. *Personnel Management, 16*, 28–31.

Attewell, P. (1987). The deskilling controversy. *Work and Occupations, 14*, 323–346.

Austin, J. T., and K. A. Hanisch (1990). Occupational attainment as a function of abilities and interests: A longitudinal analysis using Project TALENT data. *Journal of Applied Psychology, 75*, 77–86.

Bacharach, S. M., and P. S. Tolbert (Eds.) (1992). *Research in the sociology of organizations: Vol. 10.* Greenwich, Conn.: JAI Press.

Baer, D., and S. Stolz (1978). A description of the Erhard Seminar Training (est) in terms of behavior analysis. *Behaviorism, 6*, 45–70.

Bailey, T. R. (1995). The integration of work and school. In W. N. Grubb (Ed.), *Education through occupations in American high school: Vol. 1, Approaches to integrating academic and vocational education*, 26–38. New York: Teachers College Press.

Baker, G. P., M. C. Jensen, and K. J. Murphy (1988). Compensation and incentives: Practice vs. theory. *Journal of Finance, 18*, 593–616.

Bantel, K. A., and S. E. Jackson (1989). Top management and innovations in banking: Does the composition of the top team make a difference? *Strategic Management Journal, 10*, 107–124.

Baritz, J. H. (1960). *Servants of power.* Middletown, Conn.: Wesleyan University Press.

Barker, E. (1984). *The making of a Moonie: Choice or brainwashing?* Oxford: Basil Blackwell.

Barker, J. R. (1993). Tightening the iron cage: Concertive control in self-managing teams. *Administrative Science Quarterly, 38*, 408–437.

Barley, S. R. (1988). Technology, power, and the social organization of work: Towards a pragmatic theory of skilling and deskilling. *Research in the sociology of organizations: Vol. 6*, 33–80. Greenwich, Conn.: JAI Press.

Barley, S. R. (1991). Contextualizing conflict: Notes on the anthropology of disputes and negotiations. In M. H. Bazerman, R. J. Lewicki, and B. H. Sheppard (Eds.), *Research on negotiation in organizations: Vol. 3*, 165–202. Greenwich, Conn.: JAI Press.

Barley, S. R., and G. Kunda (1992). Design and devotion: Surges of rational and normative ideologies of control in managerial discourse. *Administrative Science Quarterly, 37*, 363–399.

Barley, S. R., G. W. Meyer, and D. C. Gash (1988). Cultures of culture: Academics, practitioners, and the pragmatics of normative control. *Administrative Science Quarterly, 33*, 24–60.

Barnett, W. P. (1990). The organizational ecology of a technical system. *Administrative Science Quarterly, 35*, 31–60.

Barnett, W. P., and T. L. Amburgey (1990). Do larger organizations generate stronger competition? In J. V. Singh (Ed.), *Organizational evolution: New directions*, 78–102. Beverly Hills, Calif.: Sage.

Barnett, W. P., and G. R. Carroll (1987). Competition and mutualism among early telephone companies. *Administrative Science Quarterly, 32,* 400–421.

Barnett, W. P., and G. R. Carroll (1995). Modeling internal organizational change. *Annual Review of Sociology, 21,* 217–236.

Barnett, W. P., H. R. Greve, and D. Y. Park (1994). An evolutionary model of organizational performance. *Strategic Management Journal, 15,* 11–28.

Barney, J. B., and W. G. Ouchi (Eds.) (1986). *Organizational economics: Toward a new paradigm for understanding and studying organizations.* San Francisco: Jossey-Bass.

Baron, J. N. (1988). The employment relation as a social relation. *Journal of the Japanese and International Economies, 2,* 492–525.

Baron, J. N., F. R. Dobbin, and P. D. Jennings (1986). War and peace: The evolution of modern personnel administration in U.S. industry. *American Journal of Sociology, 92,* 350–383.

Baron, J. N., B. S. Mittman, and A. E. Newman (1991). Targets of opportunity: Organizational and environmental determinants of gender integration within the California civil service, 1979–1985. *American Journal of Sociology, 96,* 1362–1401.

Baron, J. N., and A. E. Newman (1990). For what it's worth: Organizational and occupational factors affecting the value of work done by women and non-whites. *American Sociological Review, 55,* 155–175.

Baron, J. N., and J. Pfeffer (1994). The social psychology of organizations and inequality. *Social Psychology Quarterly, 57,* 190–209.

Baron, R. A. (1993). Affect and organizational behavior: When and why feeling good (or bad) matters. In J. K. Murnighan (Ed.), *Social psychology in organizations: Advances in theory and research,* 63–88.

Barrick, M. R., and M. K. Mount (1991). The Big Five personality dimensions and job performance: A meta-analysis. *Personnel Psychology, 44,* 1–26.

Barrick, M. R., and M. K. Mount (1993). Autonomy as a moderator of the relationship between the big five personality dimensions and job performance. *Journal of Applied Psychology, 78,* 111–118.

Barry, B. (1978). *Sociologists, economists, and democracy.* Chicago: University of Chicago Press.

Bass, B. M. (1985). *Leadership and performance beyond expectations.* New York: Free Press.

Baum, J. A. C. (1995). The changing basis of competition in organizational populations: The Manhattan hotel industry, 1898–1990. *Social Forces, 74,* 177–205.

Baum, J. A. C., and S. J. Mezias (1992). Localized competition and organizational failure in the Manhattan hotel industry, 1898–1990. *Administrative Science Quarterly, 37,* 580–604.

Baum, J. A. C., and C. Oliver (1991). Institutional linkages and organizational mortality. *Administrative Science Quarterly, 36,* 187–218.

Baum, J. A. C., and C. Oliver (1992). Institutional embeddedness and the dynamics of organizational populations. *American Sociological Review, 57,* 540–559.

Baum, J. A. C., and W. W. Powell (1995). Cultivating an institutional ecology of organizations: Comment on Hannan, Carroll, Dundon, and Torres. *American Sociological Review, 60,* 529–538.

Baum, J. A. C., and J. V. Singh (1994). Organizational niches and the dynamics of organizational mortality. *American Journal of Sociology, 100,* 346–380.

Baumol, W. (1959). *Business behavior, value, and growth.* New York: Macmillan.

Bazerman, M. H., R. I. Beekun, and F. D. Schoorman (1982). Performance evaluation in a dynamic context: A laboratory study of the impact of prior commitment to the ratee. *Journal of Applied Psychology, 67,* 873–876.

Bazerman, M. H., and J. S. Carroll (1987). Negotiator cognition. In B. M. Staw and L. L. Cummings (Eds.), *Research in organizational behavior: Vol. 9*, 247–288. Greenwich, Conn.: JAI Press.

Bazerman, M. H., T. Magliozzi, and M. A. Neale (1985). The acquisition of an integrative response in a competitive market. *Organizational Behavior and Human Performance, 34*, 294–313.

Bazerman, M. H., and M. A. Neale (1982). Improving negotiator effectiveness under final offer arbitration: The role of selection and training. *Journal of Applied Psychology, 67*, 543–548.

Becker, B. E., and M. A. Huselid (1992). The incentive effects of tournament compensation systems. *Administrative Science Quarterly, 37*, 336–350.

Becker, F., and F. Steele (1995). *Workplace by design: Mapping the high-performance workscape*. San Francisco: Jossey-Bass.

Becker, G. S. (1962). Irrational behavior and economic theory. *Journal of Political Economy, 70*, 1–13.

Becker, G. S. (1964). *Human capital: A theoretical and empirical analysis with special reference to education*. New York: Columbia University Press.

Beer, M., B. Spector, P. Lawrence, D. Mills, and R. Walton (1984). *Managing human assets*. New York: Free Press.

Beller, A. H. (1982). Occupational segregation by sex: Determinants and changes. *Journal of Human Resources, 17*, 371–392.

Belous, R. S. (1989). *The contingent economy*. Washington, D.C.: National Planning Association.

Bem, D. J. (1972). Self-perception theory. In L. Berkowitz (Ed.), *Advances in experimental social psychology: Vol. 6*, 1–62. New York: Academic Press.

Bem, D. J., and A. Allen (1974). On predicting some of the people some of the time: The search for cross-situational consistencies in behavior. *Psychological Review, 81*, 506–520.

Bem, D. J., and D. C. Funder (1978). Predicting more of the people more of the time: Assessing the personality of situations. *Psychological Review, 85*, 485–501.

Berle, A., Jr., and G. C. Means (1932). *The modern corporation and private property*. New York: Macmillan.

Berscheid, E., and E. H. Walster (1969). *Interpersonal attraction*. Reading, Mass.: Addison-Wesley.

Besser, T. L. (1995). Rewards and organizational goal achievement: A case study of Toyota Motor Manufacturing in Kentucky. *Journal of Management Studies, 32*, 383–399.

Bielby, W. T., and J. N. Baron (1986). Men and women at work: Sex segregation and statistical discrimination. *American Journal of Sociology, 91*, 759–799.

Biggart, N. W. (1989). *Charismatic capitalism: Direct selling organizations in America*. Chicago: University of Chicago Press.

Blalock, H. (1967). *Toward a theory of minority group relations*. New York: John Wiley.

Blau, J. (1984). *Architects and firms*. Cambridge, Mass.: MIT Press.

Blau, P. M. (1955). *The dynamics of bureaucracy*. Chicago: University of Chicago Press.

Blau, P. M. (1970). A formal theory of differentiation in organizations. *American Sociological Review, 35*, 201–218.

Blau, P. M. (1973). *The organization of academic work*. New York: Wiley.

Blau, P. M. (1977). *Inequality and heterogeneity*. New York: Free Press.

Blau, P. M., and J. E. Schwartz (1984). *Crosscutting social circles: Testing a macrostructural theory of intergroup relations*. New York: Academic Press.

Blau, P. M., and W. R. Scott (1962). *Formal organizations*. San Francisco: Chandler.

Blaug, M. (1980). *The methodology of economics*. New York: Cambridge University Press.

Blauner, R. (1964). *Alienation and freedom: The factory worker and his industry*. Chicago: University of Chicago Press.

Bluen, S. D., J. Barling, and W. Burns (1990). Predicting sales performance, job satisfaction, and depression by using the Achievement Strivings and Impatience-Irritability dimensions of Type A behavior. *Journal of Applied Psychology, 75*, 212–216.

Boeker, W. (1989). The development and institutionalization of subunit power in organizations. *Administrative Science Quarterly, 34*, 388–410.

Boeker, W. (1992). Power and managerial dismissal: Scapegoating at the top. *Administrative Science Quarterly, 37*, 400–421.

Boland, L. A. (1979). A critique of Friedman's critics. *Journal of Economic Literature, 17*, 503–522.

Borjas, G. (1980). Wage determination in the federal government: The role of constituents and bureaucrats. *Journal of Political Economy, 88*, 1110–1147.

Borjas, G. (1982). The politics of employment discrimination in the federal bureaucracy. *Journal of Law and Economics, 25*, 271–299.

Borjas, G. (1983). The measurement of race and gender wage differentials: Evidence from the federal sector. *Industrial and Labor Relations Review, 37*, 79–91.

Bouchard, T. J., and M. McGue (1981). Familial studies of intelligence: A review. *Science, 212*, 1055–1059.

Bougon, M. G. (1983). Uncovering cognitive maps: The self-Q technique. In G. Morgan (Ed.), *Beyond method: Strategies for social research*. Beverly Hills, Calif.: Sage.

Bougon, M. G., K. E. Weick, and D. Binkhorst (1977). Cognition in organizations: An analysis of the Utrecht Jazz Orchestra. *Administrative Science Quarterly, 22*, 606–639.

Boulding, K. (1968). *The organizational revolution: A study of the ethics of economic organization*. Chicago: Quadrangle Books.

Bowman, E. H. (1963). Consistency and optimality in managerial decision-making. *Management Science, 9*, 310–321.

Boxman, E. A. W., P. M. De Graaf, and H. D. Flap (1991). The impact of social and human capital on the income attainment of Dutch managers. *Social Networks, 13*, 51–73.

Brass, D. J. (1985). Men's and women's networks: A study of interaction patterns and influence in an organization. *Academy of Management Journal, 28*, 327–343.

Brass, D. J., and M. E. Burkhardt (1993). Potential power and power use: An investigation of structure and behavior. *Academy of Management Journal, 36*, 441–470.

Braverman, H. (1974). *Labor and monopoly capital*. New York: Monthly Review Press.

Brehm, J. W. (1966). *A theory of psychological reactance*. New York: Academic Press.

Bresnen, M., and C. Fowler (1994). The organizational correlates and consequence of subcontracting: Evidence from a survey of South Wales. *Journal of Management Studies, 31*, 847–864.

Bridges, W. F., and W. J. Villemez (1994). *The employment relationship: Causes and consequences of modern personnel administration*. New York: Plenum.

Brief, A. P., A. H. Butcher, and L. Roberson (1995). Cookies, disposition, and job attitudes: The effects of positive mood-inducing events and negative affectivity on job satisfaction in a field experiment. *Organizational Behavior and Human Decision Processes, 62*, 55–62.

Brinkerhoff, R. O. (Ed.) (1989). *Evaluating training programs in business and industry*. San Francisco: Jossey-Bass.

Brockner, J., and J. Z. Rubin (1985). *Entrapment in escalating conflicts*. New York: Springer-Verlag.

Brockner, J., J. Z. Rubin, and E. Lang (1981). Face saving and entrapment. *Journal of Experimental Social Psychology, 17,* 68–79.

Brookes, M. J., and A. Kaplan (1972). The office environment: Space planning and affective behavior. *Human Factors, 14,* 373–391.

Brown, C. (Ed.) (1994). *The competitive semiconductor manufacturing human resources project: First interim report*. Berkeley: University of California, Berkeley, Institute of Industrial Relations.

Budros, A. (1994). Analyzing unexpected density dependence effects on organizational births in New York's life insurance industry. *Organization Science, 5,* 541–553.

Burawoy, M. (1979). *Manufacturing consent*. Chicago: University of Chicago Press.

Burawoy, M. (1985). *The politics of production*. New York: Verso.

Burns, L. R., and D. R. Wholey (1993). Adoption and abandonment of matrix management programs: Effects of organizational characteristics and interorganizational networks. *Academy of Management Journal, 36,* 106–138.

Burns, T., and G. M. Stalker (1961). *The management of innovation*. London: Tavistock.

Burrell, G., and G. Morgan (1979). *Sociological paradigms and organizational analysis*. London: Heinemann.

Burt, R. S. (1980). Autonomy in a social topology. *American Journal of Sociology, 85,* 892–925.

Burt, R. S. (1983). *Corporate profits and co-optation*. New York: Academic Press.

Burt, R. S. (1987). Social contagion and innovation: Cohesion versus structural equivalence. *American Journal of Sociology, 92,* 1287–1335.

Burt, R. S. (1992). *Structural holes: The social structure of competition*. Cambridge, Mass.: Harvard University Press.

Burt, R. S., K. P. Christman, and H. C. Kilburn, Jr. (1980). Testing a structural theory of corporate co-optation: Interorganizational directorate ties as a strategy for avoiding market constraints on profits. *American Sociological Review, 45,* 821–841.

Calas, M. (1993). Deconstructing charismatic leadership: Re-reading Weber from the darker side. *Leadership Quarterly, 4,* 305–328.

Calas, M., and L. Smircich (1992). Using the f-word: Feminist theories and the social consequences of organizational research. In A. J. Mills and P. Tancred (Eds.), *Gendering organizational analysis,* 222–234. Newbury Park, Calif.: Sage.

Calder, B. J. (1977). An attribution theory of leadership. In B. M. Staw and G. R. Salancik (Eds.), *New directions in organizational behavior,* 179–204. Chicago: St. Clair Press.

Caldwell, D. F., C. A. O'Reilly III, and J. H. Morris (1983). Responses to an organizational reward: A field test of the sufficiency of justification hypothesis. *Journal of Applied Psychology, 44,* 506–514.

Cammann, C., E. E. Lawler III, G. E. Ledford, and S. E. Seashore (1984). *Management-labor cooperation in quality of worklife experiments: Comparative analysis of eight cases*. Report to the U.S. Department of Labor. Ann Arbor: Survey Research Center, University of Michigan.

Campbell, J. P. (1990). An overview of the army selection and classification project (Project A). *Personnel Psychology, 43,* 231–239.

Canella, A. A., Jr., and R. L. Paetzold (1994). Pfeffer's barriers to the advance of organizational science: A rejoinder. *Academy of Management Review, 19,* 331–341.

Cappelli, P. (1995). Rethinking employment. *British Journal of Industrial Relations, 33,* 563–602.

Carlson, R. O. (1972). *School superintendents: Career and performance.* Columbia, Ohio: Merrill.

Carnevale, P., and A. Isen (1986). The influence of positive affect and visual access on the discovery of integrative solutions in bilateral negotiation. *Organizational Behavior and Human Decision Processes, 37,* 1–13.

Carroll, G. R. (1983). A stochastic model of organizational mortality: Review and reanalysis. *Social Science Research, 12,* 303–329.

Carroll, G. R. (1984). Dynamics of publisher succession in newspaper organizations. *Administrative Science Quarterly, 29,* 93–113.

Carroll, G. R. (1985). Concentration and specialization: Dynamics of niche width in populations of organizations. *American Journal of Sociology, 90,* 1262–1283.

Carroll, G. R., and J. Delacroix (1982). Organizational mortality in the newspaper industries of Argentina and Ireland: An ecological approach. *Administrative Science Quarterly, 27,* 169–198.

Carroll, G. R., and P. Huo (1986). Organizational task and institutional environments in ecological perspective: Findings from the local newspaper industry. *American Journal of Sociology, 91,* 838–873.

Carroll, G. R., and A. Swaminathan (1992). The organizational ecology of strategic groups in the American brewing industry from 1975 to 1990. *Industrial and Corporate Change, 1,* 65–97.

Carroll, G. R., and J. B. Wade (1991). Density dependence in the evolution of the American brewing industry across different levels of analysis. *Social Science Research, 20,* 271–302.

Carson, R. C. (1989). Personality. *Annual Review of Psychology, 40,* 227–248.

Castro, J. (1993). Disposable workers. *Time,* March 29, 1993, 43–47.

Chamberlain, K. (1988). On the structure of well-being. *Social Indicators Research, 20,* 581–604.

Chandler, A. (1962). *Strategy and structure: Chapters in the history of the American industrial enterprise.* Cambridge, Mass.: MIT Press.

Channon, D. F. (1973). *The strategy and structure of British enterprise.* London: Macmillan.

Chatman, J. A. (1989). Improving organizational research: A model of person-organization fit. *Academy of Management Review, 14,* 333–349.

Chatman, J. A. (1991). Managing people and organizations: Selection and socialization in public accounting firms. *Administrative Science Quarterly, 36,* 459–484.

Chatman, J. A., and S. G. Barsade (1995). Personality, organizational culture, and cooperation: Evidence from a business simulation. *Administrative Science Quarterly, 40,* 423–443.

Chatman, J. A., D. F. Caldwell, and C. A. O'Reilly (1995). Managerial personality and early career success: A profile comparison approach. Unpublished ms., University of California, Berkeley, Haas School of Business.

Chatman, J. A., and K. A. Jehn (1994). Assessing the relationship between industry characteristics and organizational culture: How different can you be? *Academy of Management Journal, 37,* 522–553.

Chertkoff, J. M., and M. Conley (1967). Opening offer and frequency of concession as a bargaining strategy. *Journal of Personality and Social Psychology, 7,* 181–185.

Child, J. (1972). Organization structure, environment, and performance: The role of strategic choice. *Sociology, 6,* 1–22.

Child, J. (1973). Predicting and understanding organization structure. *Administrative Science Quarterly, 18,* 168–185.

Child, J. (1975). Managerial and organizational factors associated with company performance, part 2: A contingency analysis. *Journal of Management Studies, 12*, 12–27.

Child, J., and R. Mansfield (1972). Technology, size, and organization structure. *Sociology, 6*, 369–393.

Christensen, K. (1995). *Contingent work arrangements in family-sensitive corporations.* Boston: Boston University, Center on Work and Family.

Cialdini, R. B. (1988). *Influence: Science and practice.* Glenview, Ill.: Scott, Foresman.

Cialdini, R. B., N. Eisenberg, B. L. Green, K. Rhoads, and R. Bator (1994). Undermining the undermining effect of reward on intrinsic interest: When unnecessary conditions are sufficient. Unpublished ms. Arizona State University, Department of Psychology.

Clawson, D. (1980). *Bureaucracy and the labor process: The transformation of U.S. industry, 1860–1920.* New York: Monthly Review Press.

Clawson, D., and A. Neustadtl (1989). Interlocks, PACs, and corporate conservatism. *American Journal of Sociology, 94*, 749–773.

Clawson, D., A. Neustadtl, and J. Bearden (1986). The logic of business unity: Corporate contributions in the 1980 election. *American Sociological Review, 51*, 797–811.

Clegg, S. R. (1990). *Modern organizations: Organization studies in the postmodern world.* London: Sage.

Coase, R. H. (1937). The nature of the firm. *Economica, 4*, 386–405.

Coase, R. H. (1978). Economics and contiguous disciplines. *Journal of Legal Studies, 7*, 201–211.

Coase, R. H. (1983). The new institutional economics. *Journal of Institutional and Theoretical Economics, 1*, 229–231.

Cohen, Y., and J. Pfeffer (1986). Organizational hiring standards. *Administrative Science Quarterly, 31*, 1–24.

Coker, D. A., M. A. Neale, and G. B. Northcraft (1987). Structural and individual influence on the process and outcome of negotiation. Unpublished ms. University of Arizona, College of Business.

Cole, R. E. (1979). *Work, mobility, and participation: A comparative study of American and Japanese industry.* Los Angeles: University of California Press.

Cole, R. E. (1989). *Strategies for learning.* Berkeley: University of California Press.

Cole, S. (1983). The hierarchy of the sciences? *American Journal of Sociology, 89*, 111–139.

Coleman, J. S. (1990). *Foundations of social theory.* Cambridge, Mass.: Harvard University Press.

Coleman, J. S., E. Katz, and H. Menzel (1966). *Medical innovation.* New York: Bobbs-Merrill.

Collins, J. C., and J. I. Porras (1994). *Built to last: Successful habits of visionary companies.* New York: HarperBusiness.

Collins, R. (1974). Where are educational requirements for employment highest? *Sociology of Education, 47*, 419–442.

Collins, R. (1979). *The credential society: An historical sociology of education and stratification.* New York: Academic Press.

Conrath, C. W. (1973). Communication patterns, organizational structure, and man: Some relationships. *Human Factors, 15*, 459–470.

Cook, K. S., R. M. Emerson, M. R. Gillmore, and T. Yamagishi (1983). The distribution of power in exchange networks: Theory and experimental results. *American Journal of Sociology, 89*, 275–305.

Costa, P. T., and R. R. McCrae (1988). Personality in adulthood: A six-year longitudinal study of self-reports and spouse ratings on the NEO Personality Inventory. *Journal of Personality and Social Psychology*, 54, 853–863.

Cowherd, D. M., and D. I. Levine (1992). Product quality and pay equity between lower-level employees and top management: An investigation of distributive justice theory. *Administrative Science Quarterly*, 37, 302–320.

Cropanzano, R., and K. James (1990). Some methodological considerations for the behavioral genetic analysis of work attitudes. *Journal of Applied Psychology*, 75, 433–439.

Cross, J. G. (1983). *A theory of adaptive economic behavior*. Cambridge: Cambridge University Press.

Crystal, G. S. (1991). *In search of excess: The overcompensation of American executives.* New York: Norton.

Cyert, R. M., W. R. Dill, and J. G. March (1958). The role of expectations in business decision making. *Administrative Science Quarterly*, 3, 307–340.

Cyert, R. M., and J. G. March (1963). *A behavioral theory of the firm*. Englewood Cliffs, N.J.: Prentice Hall.

Cyert, R. M., H. A. Simon, and D. B. Trow (1956). Observation of a business decision. *Journal of Business*, 29, 237–248.

Dahl, R. A. (1957). The concept of power. *Behavioral Science*, 2, 201–215.

Darley, J. M., and D. T. Gilbert (1985). Social psychological aspects of environmental psychology. In G. Lindzey and E. Aronson (Eds.), *Handbook of social psychology*, 3rd Ed., 949–991. New York: Random House.

D'Aveni, R. A. (1990). Top managerial prestige and organizational bankruptcy. *Organization Science*, 1, 121–142.

Davis, G. F. (1991). Agents without principles? The spread of the poison pill through the intercorporate network. *Administrative Science Quarterly*, 36, 583–613.

Davis, G. F., and T. A. Thompson (1994). A social movement perspective on corporate control. *Administrative Science Quarterly*, 39, 141–173.

Davis, M. S. (1971). That's interesting! Towards a phenomenology of sociology and a sociology of phenomenology. *Philosophy of the Social Sciences*, 1, 309–344.

Davis, S. (1984). *Managing corporate culture*. Cambridge, Mass.: Ballinger.

Davis-Blake, A., and J. Pfeffer (1989). Just a mirage: The search for dispositional effects in organizational research. *Academy of Management Review*, 14, 385–400.

Davis-Blake, A., and B. Uzzi (1993). Determinants of employment externalization: A study of temporary workers and independent contractors. *Administrative Science Quarterly*, 38, 195–223.

Deal, T., and A. Kennedy (1982). *Corporate cultures: The rites and rituals of corporate life.* Reading, Mass.: Addison-Wesley.

Deci, E. (1975). *Intrinsic motivation*. New York: Plenum.

Demb, A., and F. F. Neubauer (1992). *The corporate board: Confronting the paradoxes.* New York: Oxford University Press.

Dennison, D. (1990). *Corporate culture and organizational effectiveness*. New York: John Wiley.

Deutsch, M., and H. Gerard (1955). A study of normative and informational social influences on individual judgment. *Journal of Abnormal and Social Psychology*, 51, 629–636.

Diener, E. (1990). Challenges in measuring subjective well-being and ill-being. Working paper, University of Illinois, Urbana, Department of Psychology.

Digman, J. M. (1990). Personality structure: Emergence of the five-factor model. *Annual Review of Psychology*, 41, 417–440.

Dillon, R. L. (1987). The changing labor market: Contingent workers and the self-employed in California. *Special report to Senator Dan McCorquodale and Senator Bill Greene*. Sacramento, Calif.: Office of Senate Research.

DiMaggio, P. J. (1988). Interest and agency in institutional theory. In L. G. Zucker (Ed.), *Institutional patterns and organizations*, 3–21. Beverly Hills, Calif.: Sage.

DiMaggio, P. J., and W. W. Powell (1983). The iron cage revisited: Institutional isomorphism and collective rationality in organizational fields. *American Sociological Review*, 48, 147–160.

Domhoff, G. W. (1967). *Who rules America?* Englewood Cliffs, N.J.: Prentice Hall.

Domhoff, G. W. (1970). *The higher circles: The governing class in America*. New York: Random House.

Domhoff, G. W. (1974). *The Bohemian Grove and other retreats: A study in ruling class cohesiveness*. New York: Harper and Row.

Donaldson, L. (1985). *In defence of organization theory: A reply to the critics*. Cambridge: Cambridge University Press.

Donaldson, L. (1990). The ethereal hand: Organizational economics and management theory. *Academy of Management Review*, 15, 369–381.

Donaldson, L. (1995). *American anti-management theories of organization: A critique of paradigm proliferation*. Cambridge: Cambridge University Press.

Dooley, R. (1969). The interlocking directorate. *American Economic Review*, 39, 314–323.

Dosi, G. (1995). Hierarchies, markets, and power: Some foundational issues on the nature of contemporary economic organization. *Industrial and Corporate Change*, 4, 1–19.

Doucouliagos, C. (1995). Worker participation and productivity in labor-managed and participatory capitalist firms: A meta-analysis. *Industrial and Labor Relations Review*, 49, 58–77.

Dow, G. K. (1987). The function of authority in transaction cost economics. *Journal of Economic Behavior and Organization*, 8, 13–38.

Drago, R. (1988). Quality circle survival: An exploratory analysis. *Industrial Relations*, 27, 336–351.

Drago, R., and J. S. Heywood (1995). The choice of payment schemes: Australian establishment data. *Industrial Relations*, 34, 507–531.

Duncan, R. B. (1972). Characteristics of organizational environments and perceived environmental uncertainty. *Administrative Science Quarterly*, 17, 313–327.

Dunlop, J. T., and D. Weil (1992). Human resource innovations in the apparel industry: An industrial relations system perspective. Unpublished ms. Harvard University, Department of Economics.

Dunlop, J. T., and D. Weil (1995). Diffusion and performance of human resource innovations in the U.S. apparel industry. *Industrial Relations* (in press).

Dunn, M. G. (1980). The family office: Coordinating mechanism of the rule class. In G. W. Domhoff (Ed.), *Power structure research*, 17–45. Beverly Hills, Cal.: Sage.

Durkheim, E. (1949 trans.). *Division of labor in society*. Glencoe, Ill.: Free Press.

Ebers, M. (1995). The framing of organizational cultures. *Research in the sociology of organizations: Vol. 13*, 129–170. Greenwich, Conn.: JAI Press.

Eccles, R. G. (1985). *The transfer pricing problem: A theory for practice*. Lexington, Mass.: Lexington Books.

Eccles, R. G., and N. Nohria (1992). *Beyond the hype: Rediscovering the essence of management*. Boston: Harvard Business School Press.

Edelman, M. (1964). *The symbolic uses of politics*. Urbana, Ill.: University of Illinois Press.

Edwards, R. C. (1976). Worker traits and organizational incentives: What makes a "good" worker? *Journal of Human Resources*, 11, 51–68.

Edwards, R. C. (1979). *Contested terrain: The transformation of the workplace in the twenti-eth century.* New York: Basic Books.

Ehrenberg, R. G. (1990). Comment. In A. S. Blinder (Ed.), *Paying for productivity: A look at the evidence,* 88–94. Washington, D.C.: Brookings.

Ehrenberg, R. G., and M. L. Bognanno (1988). Do tournaments have incentive effects? NBER Research Working Paper No. 2638. Washington, D.C.: National Bureau of Economic Research.

Ehrenberg, R. G., and M. L. Bognanno (1990). The incentive effects of tournaments revisited: Evidence from the European PGA tour. *Industrial and Labor Relations Review, 43,* 74-S–88-S.

Eisenberger, R. (1992). Learned industriousness. *Psychological Review, 99,* 248–267.

Eisenhardt, K. (1989). Agency theory: An assessment and review. *Academy of Management Review, 14,* 57–74.

Ely, R. J. (1994). The effects of organizational demographics and social identity on rela-tionships among professional women. *Administrative Science Quarterly, 39,* 203–238.

Ely, R. J. (1995). The power in demography: Women's social constructions of gender iden-tity at work. *Academy of Management Journal, 38,* 589–634.

Emerson, R. M. (1962). Power-dependence relations. *American Sociological Review, 27,* 31–41.

Engelbrecht, A. S., and A. H. Fischer (1995). The managerial performance implications of a developmental assessment center process. *Human Relations, 48,* 387–404.

England, P., G. Farkas, B. S. Kilbourne, and T. Dou (1988). Explaining occupational sex segregation and wages: Findings from a model with fixed effects. *American Sociolog-ical Review, 66,* 147–168.

Enzle, M. E., and S. C. Anderson (1993). Surveillant intentions and intrinsic motivation. *Journal of Personality and Social Psychology, 64,* 257–266.

Etzioni, A. (1988). *The moral dimension: Toward a new economics.* New York: Free Press.

Evans, M. G., M. N. Kiggundu, and R. J. House (1979). A partial test and extension of the job characteristics model of motivation. *Organizational Behavior and Human Performance, 24,* 354–371.

Ferber, M. A., and B. Kordick (1978). Sex differentials in the earnings of Ph.D.s. *Industrial and Labor Relations Review, 35,* 550–564.

Ferguson, K. (1984). *The feminist case against bureaucracy.* Philadelphia: Temple Univer-sity Press.

Festinger, L. (1954). A theory of social comparison processes. *Human Relations, 7,* 117–140.

Festinger, L. (1957). *A theory of cognitive dissonance.* Stanford, Calif.: Stanford University Press.

Festinger, L., S. Schachter, and K. Back (1950). *Social pressures in informal groups.* New York: Harper.

Finkelstein, S. (1992). Power in top management teams: Dimension, measurement, and validation. *Academy of Management Journal, 35,* 505–538.

Finkelstein, S. (1996). Inter-industry merger patterns and resource dependence: A replica-tion and extension of Pfeffer (1972). Unpublished working paper, Dartmouth Col-lege, Tuck Graduate School of Business.

Finkelstein, S., and D. C. Hambrick (1990). Top-management-team tenure and organiza-tional outcomes: The moderating role of managerial discretion. *Administrative Sci-ence Quarterly, 35,* 484–503.

Finkelstein, S., and D. C. Hambrick (1996). *Strategic leadership: Top executives and their effects on organizations*. St. Paul, Minn.: West.

Fischhoff, B. (1982). Debiasing. In D. Kahneman and A. Tversky (Eds.), *Judgment under uncertainty: Heuristics and biases*. New York: Cambridge University Press.

Fligstein, N. (1985). The spread of the multidivisional form among large firms, 1919–1979. *American Sociological Review, 50*, 377–391.

Fligstein, N. (1987). The intraorganizational power struggle: The rise of finance presidents in large corporations, 1919–1979, *American Sociological Review, 52*, 44–58.

Fligstein, N. (1990). *The transformation of corporate control*. Cambridge, Mass.: Harvard University Press.

Fligstein, N. (1991). The structural transformation of American industry: An institutional account of the causes of diversification in the largest firms, 1919–1979. In W. W. Powell and P. J. DiMaggio (Eds.), *The new institutionalism in organizational analysis*, 311–336. Chicago: University of Chicago Press.

Fligstein, N., and P. Brantley (1992). Bank control, owner control, or organizational dynamics: Who controls the large modern corporation? *American Journal of Sociology, 98*, 280–307.

Fox, M. F. (1985). Location, sex-typing, and salary among academics. *Work and Occupations, 12*, 186–205.

Frank, R. H. (1984). Are workers paid their marginal products? *American Economic Review, 74*, 549–571.

Frank, R. H. (1988). *Passions within reason: The strategic role of the emotions*. New York: Norton.

Frank, R. H. (1990). A theory of moral sentiments. In J. J. Mansbridge (Ed.), *Beyond self-interest*, 71–96. Chicago: University of Chicago Press.

Frank, R. H., T. Gilovich, and D. T. Regan (1993). Does studying economics inhibit cooperation? *Journal of Economic Perspectives, 7*, 159–171.

Freeman, J., G. R. Carroll, and M. T. Hannan (1983). The liability of newness: Age dependence in organizational death rates. *American Sociological Review, 48*, 692–710.

Freeman, J., and M. T. Hannan (1983). Niche width and the dynamics of organizational populations. *American Journal of Sociology, 88*, 116–145.

Freeman, R. B., and J. L. Medoff (1984). *What do unions do?* New York: Basic.

French, J. R. P., Jr., and B. Raven (1968). The bases of social power. In D. Cartwright and A. Zander (Eds.), *Group dynamics, 3rd ed.*, 259–269. New York: Harper and Row.

Friedman, M. (1953). The methodology of positive economics. In M. Friedman, *Essays in positive economics*. Chicago: University of Chicago Press.

Fucini, J. J., and S. Fucini (1990). *Working for the Japanese*. New York: Collier Macmillan.

Funder, D. C., and C. R. Colvin (1991). Explorations in behavioral consistency: Properties of persons, situations, and behaviors. *Journal of Personality and Social Psychology, 60*, 773–794.

Gabor, A. (1990). *The man who discovered quality*. New York: Times Books.

Galanter, M. (1989). *Cults: Faith, healing, and coercion*. New York: Oxford University Press.

Galaskiewicz, J., and R. S. Burt (1991). Interorganization contagion in corporate philanthropy. *Administrative Science Quarterly, 36*, 88–105.

Galaskiewicz, J., and S. Wasserman (1989). Mimetic processes within an interorganizational field: An empirical test. *Administrative Science Quarterly, 34*, 454–479.

Galaskiewicz, J., and S. Wasserman, B. Rauschenbach, W. Bielefeld, and P. Mullaney

(1985). The influence of corporate power, social status, and market position on corporate interlocks in a regional network. *Social Forces, 64,* 403–431.

Galbraith, J. R. (1973). *Designing complex organizations.* Reading, Mass.: Addison-Wesley.

Gamson, W. A., and N. R. Scotch (1964). Scapegoating in baseball. *American Journal of Sociology, 70,* 69–76.

Gandz, J., and V. V. Murray (1980). The experience of workplace politics. *Academy of Management Journal, 23,* 237–251.

Gardner, J. W. (1990). *On leadership.* New York: Free Press.

Gargiulo, Martin (1993). Two-step leverage: Managing constraint in organizational politics. *Administrative Science Quarterly, 38,* 1–19.

Garrahan, P., and P. Stewart (1992). *The Nissan enigma: Flexibility at work in a local economy.* London: Mansell.

Garson, B. (1988). *The electronic sweatshop.* New York: Simon and Schuster.

Gavin, M. B., S. G. Green, and G. T. Fairhurst (1995). Managerial control strategies for poor performance over time and the impact on subordinate reactions. *Organizational Behavior and Human Decision Processes, 63,* 207–221.

Gaziel, H. H. (1994). Managerial studies and perceived job performance: An Israeli case study. *Public Personnel Management, 23,* 341–356.

George, J. M. (1989). Mood and absence. *Journal of Applied Psychology, 74,* 317–324.

George, J. M. (1991). State or trait: Effects of positive mood on prosocial behaviors at work. *Journal of Applied Psychology, 76,* 299–307.

George, J. M. (1992). The role of personality in organizational life: Issues and evidence. *Journal of Management, 18,* 185–213.

Georgenson, D. L. (1982). The problem of transfer calls for partnership. *Training and Development Journal, 36,* 75–78.

Gerhart, B. (1987). How important are dispositional factors as determinants of job satisfaction? Implications for job design and other personnel programs. *Journal of Applied Psychology, 72,* 366–373.

Gerlach, M. (1992). *Alliance capitalism: The social organization of Japanese business.* Berkeley: University of California Press.

Ghoshal, S., and P. Moran (1996). Bad for practice: A critique of the transaction cost theory. *Academy of Management Review, 21,* 13–47.

Giddens, A. (1982). Power, the dialectic of control, and class structuration. In A. Giddens and G. Mackenzie (Eds.), *Social class and the division of labour.* Cambridge: Cambridge University Press.

Gioia, D. A., and E. Pitre (1990). Multiparadigm perspectives on theory building. *Academy of Management Review, 15,* 584–602.

Gioia, D. A., and H. P. Sims, Jr. (1986). Introduction: Social cognition in organizations. In H. P. Sims, Jr., and D. A. Gioia (Eds.), *The thinking organization,* 1–19. San Francisco: Jossey-Bass.

Goldberg, L. R. (1990). An alternative "description of personality": The big-five factor structure. *Journal of Personality and Social Psychology, 59,* 1216–1229.

Goldberg, V. P. (1980). Bridges over contested terrain: Exploring the radical account of the employment relationship. *Journal of Economic Behavior and Organization, 1,* 249–274.

Goldman, P., and D. R. Van Houten (1977). Managerial strategies and the worker: A Marxist analysis of bureaucracy. *Sociological Quarterly, 18,* 108–125.

Goodman, P. S. (1980). Realities of improving the quality of work life. *Labor Law Journal, 31,* 487–494.

Gouldner, A. W. (1954). *Patterns of industrial bureaucracy.* Glencoe, Ill.: Free Press.

Graham, L. (1995). *On the line at Subaru-Isuzu.* Ithaca, N.Y.: Cornell University Press.

Granovetter, M. (1973). The strength of weak ties. *American Journal of Sociology, 78,* 1360–1380.

Granovetter, M. (1974). *Getting a job: A study of contacts and careers.* Cambridge, Mass.: Harvard University Press.

Granovetter, M. (1984). Small is bountiful: Labor markets and establishment size. *American Sociological Review, 49,* 323–334.

Granovetter, M. (1985). Economic action and social structure: The problem of embeddedness. *American Journal of Sociology, 91,* 481–510.

Granovetter, M. (1986). Labor mobility, internal markets, and job matching: A comparison of the sociological and economic approaches. *Research in Social Stratification and Mobility: Vol. 5,* 3–39. Greenwich, Conn.: JAI Press.

Granovetter, M. (1995). Coase revisited: Business groups in the modern economy. *Industrial and Corporate Change, 4,* 93–130.

Grant, R., and C. Higgins (1989). Monitoring service workers via computer: The effect on employees, productivity, and service. *National Productivity Review, 8,* 101–112.

Green, D. P., and I. Shapiro (1994). *Pathologies of rational choice theory: A critique of applications in political science.* New Haven, Conn.: Yale University Press.

Gresov, C., and C. Stephens (1993). The context of interunit influence attempts. *Administrative Science Quarterly, 38,* 252–276.

Greve, H. R. (1995). Jumping ship: The diffusion of strategy abandonment. *Administrative Science Quarterly, 40,* 444–473.

Greve, H. R. (1996). Patterns of competition: The diffusion of a market position in radio broadcasting. *Administrative Science Quarterly, 41,* 29–60.

Griffin, L. J., M. E. Wallace, and B. A. Rubin (1986). Capitalist resistance to the organization of labor before the New Deal: Why? How? Success? *American Sociological Review, 51,* 147–167.

Griffin, R. W. (1983). Objective and social sources of information in task redesign: A field experiment. *Administrative Science Quarterly, 28,* 184–200.

Guillen, M. F. (1994). *Models of management: Work, authority, and organization in a comparative perspective.* Chicago: University of Chicago Press.

Gullahorn, J. T. (1952). Distance and friendship as factors in the gross interaction matrix. *Sociometry, 15,* 123–134.

Gutek, B. A., A. G. Cohen, and A. M. Konrad (1990). Predicting social-sexual behavior at work: A contact hypothesis. *Academy of Management Journal, 33,* 560–577.

Gutek, B. A., and S. J. Winter (1992). Consistency of job satisfaction across situations: Fact or framing artifact? *Journal of Vocational Behavior, 41,* 61–78.

Hackman, J. D. (1985). Power and centrality in the allocation of resources in colleges and universities. *Administrative Science Quarterly, 30,* 61–77.

Hackman, J. R., and E. E. Lawler (1971). Employee reactions to job characteristics. *Journal of Applied Psychology, 55,* 259–286.

Hackman, J. R., and G. R. Oldham (1980). *Work redesign.* Reading, Mass.: Addison-Wesley.

Hage, J., and M. Aiken (1969). Routine technology, social structure, and organizational goals. *Administrative Science Quarterly, 14,* 366–376.

Halaby, C. N. (1979). Sexual inequality in the workplace: An employer specific analysis of pay differences. *Social Science Research, 8,* 79–104.

Hall, R. H., J. E. Haas, and N. J. Johnson (1967). Organizational size, complexity and formalization. *American Sociological Review, 32,* 903–912.

Hambrick, D. C. (1994). What if the academy actually mattered? *Academy of Management Review, 19,* 11–16.

Hambrick, D. C., and P. A. Mason (1984). Upper echelons: The organization as a reflection of its top managers. *Academy of Management Review, 9,* 195–206.

Hannan, M. T., and G. R. Carroll (1992). *Dynamics of organizational populations: Density, competition, and legitimation.* New York: Oxford University Press.

Hannan, M. T., and G. R. Carroll (1995). Theory building and cheap talk about legitimation: Reply to Baum and Powell. *American Sociological Review, 60,* 539–544.

Hannan, M. T., G. R. Carroll, E. A. Dundon, and J. C. Torres (1995). Organizational evolution in a multinational context: Entries of automobile manufacturers in Belgium, Britain, France, Germany, and Italy. *American Sociological Review, 60,* 509–528.

Hannan, M. T., and J. Freeman (1984). Structural inertia and organizational change. *American Sociological Review, 49,* 149–164.

Hannan, M. T., and J. Freeman (1989). *Organizational ecology.* Cambridge, Mass.: Harvard University Press.

Harder, J. W. (1992). Play for pay: Effects of inequity in a pay-for-performance context. *Administrative Science Quarterly, 37,* 321–335.

Harlan, A., and C. L. Weiss (1982). Sex differences in factors affecting managerial career advancement. In P. W. Wallace (Ed.), *Women in the workplace,* 59–96. Boston: Auburn House.

Hart, O., and B. Holmstrom (1987). The theory of contracts. In T. F. Bewley (Ed.), *Advances in economic theory—fifth world congress,* 71–155. New York: Cambridge University Press.

Hassard, J. (1990). An alternative to paradigm incommensurability in organization theory. In J. Hassard and D. Pym (Eds.), *The theory and philosophy of organizations: Critical issues and new perspectives,* 219–230. London: Routledge.

Hatch, M. J. (1987). Physical barriers, task characteristics, and interaction activity in research and development firms. *Administrative Science Quarterly, 32,* 387–399.

Haunschild, P. R. (1993). Interorganizational imitation: The impact of interlocks on corporate acquisition activity. *Administrative Science Quarterly, 38,* 564–592.

Haunschild, P. R. (1994). How much is that company worth? Interorganizational relationships, uncertainty, and acquisition premiums. *Administrative Science Quarterly, 39,* 391–411.

Haveman, H. A. (1993). Follow the leader: Mimetic isomorphism and entry into new markets. *Administrative Science Quarterly, 38,* 593–627.

Haveman, H. A. (1995). The demographic metabolism of organizations: Industry dynamics, turnover, and tenure distributions. *Administrative Science Quarterly, 40,* 586–618.

Heath, C. (1995). Escalation and de-escalation of commitment in response to sunk costs: The role of budgeting in mental accounting. *Organizational Behavior and Human Decision Processes, 62,* 38–54.

Heery, E., and J. Kelley (1988). Do female representatives make a difference? Women full-time officials and trade union work. *Work, Employment, and Society, 2,* 487–505.

Hernstein, R. J., and C. Murray (1994). *The bell curve: Intelligence and class structure in American life.* New York: Free Press.

Hesterly, W. S., J. Liebeskind, and T. R. Zenger (1990). Organizational economics: An impending revolution in organization theory? *Academy of Management Review, 15,* 402–420.

Hickson, D. J., C. R. Hinings, C. A. Lee, R. E. Schneck, and J. M. Pennings (1971). A strategic contingencies theory of intraorganizational power. *Administrative Science Quarterly, 16,* 216–229.

Hill, C. (1964). Discussion. *Past and Present, 29,* 63.

Hills, F. S., and T. J. Mahoney (1978). University budgets and organizational decision making. *Administrative Science Quarterly, 23,* 454–465.

Hinings, C. R., D. J. Hickson, J. M. Pennings, and R. E. Schneck (1974). Structural conditions of intraorganizational power. *Administrative Science Quarterly, 19,* 22–44.

Hirsch, P. S. (1986). From ambushes to golden parachutes: Corporate takeovers as an instance of cultural framing and institutional integration. *American Journal of Sociology, 91,* 800–837.

Hirsch, P. S., S. Michaels, and R. Friedman (1987). "Dirty hands" versus "clean models." *Theory and Society, 16,* 317–336.

Hirschleifer, J. (1977). Economics from a biological point of view. *Journal of Law and Economics, 20,* 1–52.

Hirschleifer, J. (1985). The expanding domain of economics. *American Economic Review, 75,* 53–68.

Hogan, R. (1986). *Manual for the Hogan Personality Inventory.* Minneapolis: National Computer Systems.

Holm, Petter (1995). The dynamics of institutionalization: Transformation processes in Norwegian fisheries. *Administrative Science Quarterly, 40,* 398–422.

Hornstein, H. A., E. Fisch, and M. Holmes (1968). Influence of a model's feelings about his behavior and his relevance as a comparison to other observers' helping behavior. *Journal of Personality and Social Psychology, 10,* 222–226.

Hornstein, H. A., H. N. Masor, and K. Sole (1971). Effects of sentiment and completion of a helping act on observer helping: A case for socially mediated Zeigarnik effect. *Journal of Personality and Social Psychology, 17,* 107–112.

Hough, L. M., N. K. Eaton, M. D. Dunnette, J. D. Kamp, and R. A. McCloy (1990). Criterion-related validities of personality constructs and the effect of response distortion on those validities. *Journal of Applied Psychology, 75,* 581–595.

House, R. J. (1977). A 1976 theory of charismatic leadership. In J. G. Hunt and L. Larson (Eds.), *Leadership: The cutting edge,* 189–204. Carbondale: Southern Illinois University Press.

House, R. J., and M. L. Baetz (1979). Leadership: Some empirical generalizations and new research directions. In *Research in organizational behavior: Vol. 1,* 341–423. Greenwich, Conn.: JAI Press.

House, R. J., A. Howard, and G. Walker (1991). The prediction of managerial success: A competitive test of the person-situation debate. In J. L. Wall and L. R. Jauch (Eds.), *Best Papers Proceedings, Academy of Management,* 215–219.

House, R. J., S. A. Shane, and D. M. Herold (1996). Rumors of the death of dispositional research are vastly exaggerated. *Academy of Management Review, 21,* 203–224.

House, R. J., W. D. Spangler, and J. Wyocke (1991). Personality and charisma in the U.S. presidency: A psychological theory of leader effectiveness. *Administrative Science Quarterly, 36,* 364–396.

Howard, A., and D. W. Bray (1988). *Managerial lives in transition: Advancing age and changing times.* New York: Guilford Press.

Howard, G. S., and P. R. Dailey (1979). Response-shift bias: A source of contamination of self-report measures. *Journal of Applied Psychology, 64,* 144–150.

Howe, W. J. (1986). The business services industry sets pace in employment growth. *Monthly Labor Review, 109* (April) 29–36.

Howell, J. M., and P. J. Frost (1989). A laboratory study of charismatic leadership. *Organizational Behavior and Human Decision Processes, 43*, 243–269.

Huber, J. (1990). Macro-micro links in gender stratification. *American Sociological Review, 55*, 1–10.

Hunter, J. E. (1986). Cognitive ability, cognitive aptitudes, job knowledge, and job performance. *Journal of Vocational Behavior, 29*, 340–362.

Huselid, M. A. (1995). The impact of human resource management practices on turnover, productivity, and corporate financial performance. *Academy of Management Journal, 38*, 635–672.

Ibarra, H. (1992). Homophily and differential returns: Sex differences in network structures and access in an advertising firm. *Administrative Science Quarterly, 37*, 422–447.

Ibarra, H. (1993a). Network centrality, power, and innovation involvement: Determinants of technical and administrative roles. *Academy of Management Journal, 36*, 471–501.

Ibarra, H. (1993b). Personal networks of women and minorities in management: A conceptual framework. *Academy of Management Review, 18*, 56–87.

Ibarra, H. (1995). Race, opportunity, and diversity of social circles in managerial networks. *Academy of Management Journal, 38*, 673–703.

Ibarra, H., and S. B. Andrews (1993). Power, social influence, and sense making: Effects of network centrality and proximity on employee perceptions. *Administrative Science Quarterly, 38*, 277–303.

Ichniowski, C. (1986). The effects of grievance activity on productivity. *Industrial and Labor Relations Review, 40*, 75–89.

Ichniowski, C., K. Shaw, and G. Prennushi (1993). The effects of human resource management practices on productivity. Working paper. Columbia University, Graduate School of Business Administration.

Irving, R. H., C. A. Higgins, and F. R. Safayeni (1986). Computerized performance monitoring systems: Use and abuse. *Communications of the ACM, 29*, 794–801.

Isen, A. M., and P. F. Levin (1972). Effects of feeling good on helping: Cookies and kindness. *Journal of Personality and Social Psychology, 21*, 384–388.

Izraeli, D. N. (1983). Sex effects or structural effects? An empirical test of Kanter's theory of proportions. *Social Forces, 62*, 153–165.

Jackson, P. B., P. A. Thoits, and H. F. Taylor (1995). Composition of the workplace and psychological well-being: The effects of tokenism on America's black elite. *Social Forces, 74*, 543–557.

Jackson, S. E., J. F. Brett, V. I. Sessa, D. M. Cooper, J. A. Julin, and K. Peyronnin (1991). Some differences make a difference: Individual dissimilarity and group heterogeneity as correlates of recruitment, promotions, and turnover. *Journal of Applied Psychology, 76*, 675–689.

Jacobs, J. A. (1992). Women's entry into management: Trends in earnings, authority, and values among salaried managers. *Administrative Science Quarterly, 37*, 282–301.

Jacoby, S. M. (1985). *Employing bureaucracy.* New York: Columbia University Press.

Jacoby, S. M. (1990). The new institutionalism: What can it learn from the old? *Industrial Relations, 29*, 316–359.

Jensen, M. C. (1983). Organization theory and methodology. *Accounting Review, 50*, 319–339.

Jensen, M. C., and W. H. Meckling (1976). Theory of the firm: Managerial behavior, agency costs, and ownership structure. *Journal of Financial Economics, 3*, 305–360.

Jensen, M. C., and K. J. Murphy (1987). Are executives' compensation contracts structured properly? Working paper no. 86-14, University of Rochester, Managerial Economics Research Center.

Jermier, J. (1982). Infusion of critical social theory into organizational analysis: Implications for studies of work adjustment. In D. Dunkerly and G. Salaman (Eds.), *The international yearbook of organization studies 1981*, 195–211. Boston: Routledge and Kegan Paul.

Johns, G. (1991). Substantive and methodological constraints on behavior and attitudes in organizational research. *Organizational Behavior and Human Decision Processes*, 49, 80–104.

Johnson, W. R. (1978). Racial wage discrimination and industrial structure. *Bell Journal of Economics*, 9, 70–81.

Jones, D. C., and T. Kato (1993). The scope, nature, and effects of employee stock ownership plans in Japan. *Industrial and Labor Relations Review*, 46, 352–367.

Judge, T. A. (1992). The dispositional perspective in human resources research. *Research in Personnel and Human Resources Management*, 10, 31–72.

Judge, T. A. (1993). Does affective disposition moderate the relationship between job satisfaction and voluntary turnover? *Journal of Applied Psychology*, 78, 395–401.

Judge, T. A., and C. L. Hulin (1993). Job satisfaction as a reflection of disposition: A multiple source causal analysis. *Organizational Behavior and Human Decision Processes*, 56, 388–421.

Kahn, L. M. (1993). Managerial quality, team success, and individual player performance in major league baseball. *Industrial and Labor Relations Review*, 46, 531–547.

Kahn, L. M., and P. D. Sherer (1988). Racial differences in professional basketball player's compensation. *Journal of Labor Economics*, 6, 40–61.

Kahn, L. M., and P. D. Sherer (1990). Contingent pay and managerial performance. *Industrial and Labor Relations Review*, 43, 107-S–120-S.

Kahneman, D., and A. Tversky (1979). Prospect theory: An analysis of decisions under risk. *Econometrica*, 47, 263–291.

Kalleberg, A. L., and M. E. Van Buren (1996). Is bigger better? Organization size and job rewards. *American Sociological Review*, 61, 47–66.

Kanter, R. M. (1977). *Men and women of the corporation*. New York: Basic.

Kanter, R. M. (1987). From status to contribution: Some organizational implications of the changing basis for pay. *Personnel*, 64, 12–37.

Kaplan, S. N. (1994). Top executive rewards and firm performance: A comparison of Japan and the United States. *Journal of Political Economy*, 102, 510–546.

Karr, A. R. (1990). Work skills panel urges major changes in school education, job organization. *Wall Street Journal*, June 19, 1990, A4.

Katz, D., and R. L. Kahn (1978). *The social psychology of organizations*, 2nd ed. New York: Wiley.

Katz, H. C., T. A. Kochan, and K. R. Gobeille (1983). Industrial relations performance, economic performance, and QWL programs: An interplant analysis. *Industrial and Labor Relations Review*, 37, 3–17.

Katz, H. C., T. A. Kochan, and M. R. Weber (1985). Assessing the effects of industrial relations systems and efforts to improve the quality of working life on organizational effectiveness. *Academy of Management Journal*, 28, 509–526.

Katz, R. (1982). The effects of group longevity on communication and performance. *Administrative Science Quarterly*, 27, 81–104.

Katzenbach, J. R., and D. K. Smith (1993). *The wisdom of teams*. New York: HarperCollins.

Kaufman, R. T. (1992). The effects of IMPROSHARE on productivity. *Industrial and Labor Relations Review, 45,* 311–322.

Kelley, H. H. (1971). *Attribution in social interaction.* Morristown, N.J.: General Learning Press.

Kenrick, D. T., and D. C. Funder (1988). Profiting from controversy: Lessons from the person-situation debate. *American Psychologist, 43,* 23–34.

Khandwalla, P. N. (1973). Effect of competition on the structure of top management control. *Academy of Management Journal, 16,* 285–295.

Khandwalla, P. N. (1974). Mass output orientation of operations technology and organizational structure. *Administrative Science Quarterly, 19,* 74–97.

Kidder, T. (1981). *Soul of a new machine.* Boston: Atlantic-Little, Brown.

Kiesler, C. A. (1971). *The psychology of commitment: Experiments linking behavior to belief.* New York: Academic Press.

Kilborn, P. T. (1991). Part-time hirings bring deep changes in U.S. workplaces. *New York Times,* June 17, 1991, A1.

Kipnis, D., and S. M. Schmidt (1988). Upward-influence styles: Relationship with performance evaluations, salary, and stress. *Administrative Science Quarterly, 33,* 528–542.

Kipnis, D., S. M. Schmidt, and I. Wilkinson (1980). Intraorganizational influence tactics: Explorations in getting one's way. *Journal of Applied Psychology, 65,* 440–452.

Kipnis, D., and R. Vanderveer (1971). Ingratiation and the use of power. *Journal of Personality and Social Psychology, 17,* 280–286.

Kirkpatrick, D. L. (1979). Techniques for evaluating training programs. *Training and Development Journal, 6,* 78–92.

Kochan, T. A., H. C. Katz, and R. B. McKersie (1986). *The transformation of American industrial relations.* New York: Basic Books.

Koenig, T., R. Gogel, and J. Sonquist (1979). Models of the significance of interlocking corporate directorates. *American Journal of Economics and Sociology, 38,* 173–185.

Kohn, A. (1993). *Punished by rewards.* Boston: Houghton Mifflin.

Kohn, M. L., and C. Schooler (1978). The reciprocal effects of the substantive complexity of work and intellectual flexibility: A longitudinal assessment. *American Journal of Sociology, 84,* 24–52.

Kohn, M. L., and C. Schooler (1982). Job conditions and personality: A longitudinal assessment of their reciprocal effects. *American Journal of Sociology, 87,* 1257–1286.

Konrad, A. M., and J. Pfeffer (1990). Do you get what you deserve? Factors affecting the relationship between productivity and pay. *Administrative Science Quarterly, 35,* 258–285.

Konrad, A. M., and J. Pfeffer (1991). Understanding the hiring of women and minorities: How gender and ethnic segregation is produced and reproduced in organizations. *Sociology of Education, 64,* 141–157.

Konrad, A. M., S. Winter, and B. A. Gutek (1992). Diversity in work group sex composition: Implications for majority and minority members. In P. Tolbert and S. B. Bacharach (Eds.), *Research in the sociology of organizations: Vol. 10,* 115–140. Greenwich, Conn.: JAI Press.

Kotter, J. P., and J. L. Heskett (1992). *Corporate culture and performance.* New York: Free Press.

Krackhardt, D. (1990). Assessing the political landscape: Structure, cognitions, and power in organizations. *Administrative Science Quarterly, 35,* 342–369.

Krackhardt, D., and L. W. Porter (1986). The snowball effect: Turnover embedded in communication networks. *Journal of Applied Psychology, 71,* 50–55.

Kramer, R. M., and D. M. Messick (Eds.) (1995). *Negotiation as a social process.* Thousand Oaks, Calif.: Sage.

Kramer, R. M., E. Newton, and P. L. Pommerenke (1993). Self-enhancement biases and negotiator judgment: Effects of self-esteem and mood. *Organizational Behavior and Human Decision Processes, 56,* 110–133.

Kramer, R. M., P. L. Pommerenke, and E. Newton (1993). The social context of negotiation: Effects of social identity and accountability on negotiator judgment and decision making. *Journal of Conflict Resolution, 37,* 633–656.

Kravetz, D. J. (1988). *The human resource revolution: Implementing progressive management practices for bottom-line success.* San Francisco: Jossey-Bass.

Kuhn, T. S. (1970). *The structure of scientific revolutions, 2nd ed.* Chicago: University of Chicago Press.

Kunda, G. (1992). *Engineering culture: Control and commitment in a high-tech corporation.* Philadelphia: Temple University Press.

Lachman, R. (1989). Power from what? A reexamination of its relationships with structural conditions. *Administrative Science Quarterly, 34,* 231–251.

Lambert, R. A., D. F. Larcker, and K. Weigelt (1993). The structure of organizational incentives. *Administrative Science Quarterly, 38,* 438–461.

Langer, E. J. (1983). *The psychology of control.* Beverly Hills, Calif.: Sage.

Larrick, R. P., and S. Blount (1995). Social context in tacit bargaining games. In R. M. Kramer and D. M. Messick (Eds.), *Negotiation as a social process,* 268–284. Thousand Oaks, Calif.: Sage.

Larrick, R. P., J. N. Morgan, and R. E. Nisbett (1990). Teaching the use of cost-benefit reasoning in everyday life. *Psychological Science, 1,* 362–370.

Larrick, R. P., R. E. Nisbett, and J. N. Morgan (1993). Who uses the cost-benefit rules of choice? Implications for the normative status of microeconomic theory. *Organizational Behavior and Human Decision Processes, 56,* 331–347.

Latane, B., and J. M. Darley (1970). *The unresponsive bystander: Why doesn't he help?* New York: Appleton-Century-Crofts.

Latis, S. J. (1976). *Method and appraisal in economics.* New York: Cambridge University Press.

Lawler, E. E., III (1981). *Pay and organizational development.* Reading, Mass.: Addison-Wesley.

Lawler, E. E., III, S. A. Mohrman, and G. E. Ledford, Jr. (1992). *Employee involvement and total quality management.* San Francisco: Jossey-Bass.

Lawrence, P., and J. Lorsch (1967). *Organization and environment.* Boston: Harvard University, Graduate School of Business Administration, Division of Research.

Lax, D. A., and J. K. Sebenius (1986). *The manager as negotiator.* New York: Free Press.

Lazear, E. P. (1979). Why is there mandatory retirement? *Journal of Political Economy, 87,* 1261–1264.

Lazear, E. P. (1981). Agency, earnings profiles, productivity, and hours restrictions. *American Economic Review, 71,* 606–620.

Lazear, E. P. (1989). Pay equality and industrial politics. *Journal of Political Economy, 97,* 561–580.

Lazear, E. P. (1995). *Personnel economics.* Cambridge, Mass.: MIT Press.

Lazear, E. P., and S. Rosen (1981). Rank-order tournaments as optimum labor contracts. *Journal of Political Economy, 89,* 841–864.

Lazersfeld, P. F., B. Berelson, and H. Gaudet (1944). *The people's choice.* New York: Columbia University Press.

Ledford, G. E., Jr., E. E. Lawler III, and S. A. Mohrman (1995). Reward innovation in *Fortune* 1000 companies. *Compensation and Benefits Review*, 27, 76–80.

Lee, C., S. J. Ashford, and P. Bobko (1990). Interactive effects of "type a" behavior and perceived control on worker performance, job satisfaction, and somatic complaints. *Academy of Management Journal*, 33, 870–881.

Lehman, D. R., R. O. Lempert, and R. E. Nisbett (1988). The effects of graduate training on reasoning: Formal discipline and thinking about everyday-life events. *American Psychologist*, 43, 431–442.

Leonard, J. S. (1990). Executive pay and firm performance. *Industrial and Labor Relations Review*, 43, 13-S–29-S.

Leontief, W. (1985). Interview: Why economics needs input-output analysis. *Challenge 28 (March-April)*, 27–35.

Lepper, M. R., and D. Greene (1975). Turning play into work: Effects of adult surveillance and extrinsic rewards on children's intrinsic motivation. *Journal of Personality and Social Psychology*, 28, 479–486.

Levin, I., and J. P. Stokes (1989). Dispositional approach to job satisfaction: Role of negative affectivity. *Journal of Applied Psychology*, 74, 752–758.

Levine, D. I. (1993). What do wages buy? *Administrative Science Quarterly*, 38, 462–483.

Levine, D. I., and L. D. Tyson (1990). Participation, productivity, and the firm's environment. In A. S. Blinder (Ed.), *Paying for productivity: A look at the evidence*, 183–237. Washington, D.C.: Brookings.

Lieberman, M. B., L. J. Lau, and M. D. Williams (1990). Firm-level productivity and management influence: A comparison of U.S. and Japanese automobile producers. *Management Science*, 36, 1193–1215.

Lieberson, S., and J. F. O'Connor (1972). Leadership and organizational performance: A study of large corporations. *American Sociological Review*, 37, 117–130.

Lin, N. (1982). Social resources and instrumental action. In P. V. Marsden and N. Lin (Eds.), *Social structure and network analysis*, 131–145. Beverly Hills, Calif.: Sage.

Lin, N., W. M. Ensel, and J. C. Vaughn (1981). Social resources and strength of ties. *American Sociological Review*, 46, 393–405.

Lincoln, J. R., M. L. Gerlach, and C. L. Ahmadjian (1996). *Keiretsu* networks and corporate performance in Japan. *American Sociological Review*, 61, 67–88.

Lingle, J. H., T. C. Brock, and R. B. Cialdini (1977). Surveillance instigates entrapment when violations are observed, when personal involvement is high, and when sanctions are severe. *Journal of Personality and Social Psychology*, 35, 419–429.

Lippitt, R. (1940). An experimental study of authoritarian and democratic group atmosphere. *University of Iowa Studies in Child Welfare*, 16, 43–195.

Locke, E. A., and J. F. Bryan (1966). The effects of goal-setting, rule-learning, and knowledge of score on performance. *American Journal of Psychology*, 79, 451–457.

Locke, E. A., E. Frederick, C. Lee, and P. Bobko (1984). Effect of self-efficacy, goals, and task strategies on task performance. *Journal of Applied Psychology*, 69, 241–251.

Locke, E. A., and G. P. Latham (1990). *A theory of goal-setting and task performance*. Englewood Cliffs, N.J.: Prentice Hall.

Locke, R. (1995). The transformation of industrial relations? In K. S. Wever and L. Turner (Eds.), *The comparative political economy of industrial relations*, 9–31. Madison, Wisc.: Industrial Relations Research Association.

Lodahl, J., and G. Gordon (1972). The structure of scientific fields and the functioning of university graduate departments. *American Sociological Review*, 37, 57–72.

Louis Harris and Associates (1991). *Laborforce 2000 survey.* New York: Louis Harris and Associates.

Lowin, A., and J. R. Craig (1968). The influence of level of performance on managerial style: An experimental object lesson in the ambiguity of correlational data. *Organizational Behavior and Human Performance,* 3, 440–458.

Luthans, F., and R. Kreitner (1975). *Organizational behavior modification.* Glenview, Ill.: Scott, Foresman.

Lykken, D. T., T. J. Bouchard, Jr., M. McGue, and A. Tellegen (1993). Heritability of interests: A twin study. *Journal of Applied Psychology,* 78, 649–661.

MacDuffie, J. P. (1995). Human resource bundles and manufacturing performance: Flexible production systems in the world auto industry. *Industrial and Labor Relations Review,* 48, 197–221.

MacKenzie, K. D., and R. House (1978). Paradigm development in the social sciences: A proposed research strategy. *Academy of Management Review,* 3, 7–23.

Macy, B. A., and H. Izumi (1993). Organizational change, design, and work innovation: A meta-analysis of 131 North American field studies—1961–1991. *Research in Organizational Change and Development:* Vol. 7, 235–313. Greenwich, Conn.: JAI Press.

Madden, J. F. (1985). The persistence of pay differentials: The economics of sex discrimination. In L. Larwood, A. H. Stromberg, and B. A. Gutek (Eds.), *Women and Work: An Annual Review:* Vol. 1, 76–114. Beverly Hills, Calif.: Sage.

Madison, D. L., R. W. Allen, L. W. Porter, P. A. Renwick, and B. T. Mayes (1980). Organizational politics: An exploration of managers' perceptions. *Human Relations,* 33, 79–100.

Main, B. G. M., C. A. O'Reilly III, and J. Wade (1995). The CEO, the board of directors, and executive compensation: Economic and psychological perspectives. *Industrial and Corporate Change,* 4, 293–332.

Manne, H. G. (1965). Mergers and the market for corporate control. *Journal of Political Economy,* 73, 110–120.

March, J. C., and J. G. March (1977). Almost random careers: The Wisconsin school superintendency, 1940–1972. *Administrative Science Quarterly,* 22, 377–409.

March, J. G. (1966). The power of power. In D. Easton (Ed.), *Varieties of political theory,* 39–70. Englewood Cliffs, N.J.: Prentice Hall.

March, J. G. (1978). Bounded rationality, ambiguity, and the engineering of choice. *Bell Journal of Economics,* 9, 587–608.

March, J. G., and J. P. Olsen (1984). The new institutionalism: Organizational factors in political life. *American Political Science Review,* 78, 734–749.

March, J. G., and J. P. Olsen (1989). *Rediscovering institutions: The organizational basis of politics.* New York: Free Press.

March, J. G., and H. A. Simon (1958). *Organizations.* New York: Wiley.

Marglin, S. A. (1974). What do bosses do? The origins and functions of hierarchy in capitalist production. *Review of Radical Political Economics,* 6, 60–112.

Markus, H., and R. B. Zajonc (1985). The cognitive perspective in social psychology. In G. Lindzey and E. Aronson (Eds.), *Handbook of social psychology,* 3rd ed.: Vol. 1, *Theory and method,* 137–230. New York: Random House.

Marris, R. (1967). *The economic theory of "managerial" capitalism.* London: Macmillan.

Marsden, D., and R. Richardson (1994). Performing for pay? The effects of "merit pay" on motivation in a public service. *British Journal of Industrial Relations,* 32, 219–242.

Martin, J. (1992a). *Cultures in organizations: Three perspectives*. New York: Oxford University Press.

Martin, J. (1992b). Escaping the inherent conservatism of empirical organizational research. In P. J. Frost and R. E. Stablein (Eds.), *Doing exemplary research*, 233–239. Newbury Park, Calif.: Sage.

Martin, J. (1994). The organization of exclusion: Institutionalization of sex inequality, gendered faculty jobs, and gendered knowledge in organizational theory and research. *Organization, 1*, 401–431.

Marwell, G. (1982). Altruism and the problem of collective action. In V. J. Derlega and J. Grzelak (Eds.), *Cooperation and helping behavior: Theories and research*, 207–226. New York: Academic Press.

Marx, K. (trans. 1967). *Capital*, Vol. 1. New York: New World Paperbacks.

McCaffrey, D. P., S. R. Faerman, and D. W. Hart (1995). The appeal and difficulties of participative systems. *Organization Science, 6*, 603–627.

McCain, B. R., C. A. O'Reilly, and J. Pfeffer (1983). The effects of departmental demography on turnover: The case of a university. *Academy of Management Journal, 26*, 626–641.

McGraw, K. O. (1978). The detrimental effects of reward on performance: A literature review and a prediction model. In M. R. Lepper and D. Greene (Eds.), *The hidden costs of rewards: New perspectives on the psychology of human motivation*. Hillsdale, N.J.: Erlbaum.

McGregor, D. (1960). *The human side of enterprise*. New York: McGraw-Hill.

Medoff, J. L., and K. G. Abraham (1980). Experience, performance, and earnings. *Quarterly Journal of Economics, 95*, 703–736.

Medoff, J. L., and K. G. Abraham (1981). Are those paid more really more productive? The case of experience. *Journal of Human Resources, 16*, 186–216.

Meindl, J. R., S. B. Ehrlich, and J. M. Dukerich (1985). The romance of leadership. *Administrative Science Quarterly, 30*, 78–102.

Mellor, S. (1995). Gender composition and gender representation in local unions: Relationships between women's participation in local office and women's participation in local activities. *Journal of Applied Psychology, 80*, 706–720.

Meyer, J. P., S. V. Paunonen, I. R. Gellatly, R. D. Goffin, and D. N. Jackson (1989). Organizational commitment and job performance: It's the nature of the commitment that counts. *Journal of Applied Psychology, 74*, 152–156.

Meyer, J. W., and B. Rowan (1977). Institutionalized organizations: Formal structure as myth and ceremony. *American Journal of Sociology, 83*, 340–363.

Meyer, J. W., and W. R. Scott (1983). *Organizational environments: Ritual and rationality*. Beverly Hills, Calif.: Sage.

Meyer, J. W., W. R. Scott, and T. E. Deal (1981). Institutional and technical sources of organizational structure: Explaining the structure of educational organizations. In H. D. Stein (Ed.), *Organization and the human services*, 151–178. Philadelphia: Temple University Press.

Meyer, M. W. (1972a). *Bureaucratic structure and authority*. New York: Harper and Row.

Meyer, M. W. (1972b). Size and structure of organizations: A causal analysis. *American Sociological Review, 37*, 434–440.

Meyer, M. W. (1975). Leadership and organizational structure. *American Journal of Sociology, 81*, 514–542.

Meyer, M. W., and L. G. Zucker (1989). *Permanently failing organizations*. Newbury Park, Calif.: Sage.

Milgrom, P., and J. Roberts (1988). An economic approach to influence activities in organizations. *American Journal of Sociology, 94,* S154–S179.

Milgrom, P., and J. Roberts (1992). *Economics, organization, and management.* Englewood Cliffs, N.J.: Prentice Hall.

Miller, Daniel J. (1995). CEO salary increases may be rational after all: Referents and contracts in CEO pay. *Academy of Management Journal, 38,* 1361–1385.

Miner, J. B. (1984). The validity and usefulness of theories in an emerging organizational science. *Academy of Management Review, 9,* 296–306.

Mintzberg, H. (1973). *The nature of managerial work.* New York: Harper and Row.

Mirvis, P. (1981). Personal correspondence: Review of *Organizations and organization theory.*

Mischel, W. (1977). The interaction of person and situation. In D. Magnusson and N. S. Endler (Eds.), *Personality at the crossroads: Current issues in interactional psychology,* 333–352. Hillsdale, N.J.: Erlbaum.

Mishel, L., and J. Bernstein (1995). *The state of working America, 1994–1995.* Washington, D.C.: Economic Policy Institute.

Mitchell, D. J. B., D. Lewin, and E. E. Lawler III (1990). Alternative pay systems, firm performance, and productivity. In A. S. Blinder (Ed.), *Paying for productivity: A look at the evidence,* 15–88. Washington, D.C.: Brookings.

Mitman, B. S. (1992). Theoretical and methodological issues in the study of organizational demography and demographic change. In S. B. Bacharach and P. S. Tolbert (Eds.), *Research in the sociology of organizations: Vol. 10,* 3–53. Greenwich, Conn.: JAI Press.

Miyazawa, S. (1986). Legal departments of Japanese corporations in the United States: A study on organizational adaptation to multiple environments. *Kobe University Law Review, 20,* 97–162.

Mizruchi, M. S. (1992). *The structure of corporate political action: Interfirm relationships and their consequences.* Cambridge, Mass.: Harvard University Press.

Mizruchi, M. S., and T. Koenig (1986). Economic sources of corporate political consensus: An examination of interindustry relations. *American Sociological Review, 51,* 482–491.

Mizruchi, M. S., and L. B. Stearns (1994). A longitudinal study of borrowing by large American corporations. *Administrative Science Quarterly, 39,* 118–140.

Mohr, L. (1971). Organizational technology and organizational structure. *Administrative Science Quarterly, 16,* 444–459.

Mohrman, S. A., S. G. Cohen, and A. M. Mohrman, Jr. (1995). *Designing team-based organizations: New forms for knowledge work.* San Francisco: Jossey-Bass.

Molotch, H. L., and D. Boden (1985). Talking social structure: Discourse, domination, and the Watergate hearings. *American Sociological Review, 50,* 273–288.

Mone, M. A., and W. McKinley (1993). The uniqueness value and its consequences for organization studies. *Journal of Management Inquiry, 2,* 284–296.

Montemayor, E. F. (1995). Review of Alfie Kohn, *Punished by Rewards: The Trouble with Gold Stars, Incentives Plans, A's, Praise, and Other Bribes. Personnel Psychology, 48,* 941–945.

Moore, W. L., and J. Pfeffer (1980). The relationship between departmental power and faculty careers on two campuses: The case for structural effect on faculty salaries. *Research in Higher Education, 13,* 291–306.

Morgan, G. (Ed.) (1983). *Beyond method.* Beverly Hills, Calif.: Sage.

Morgan, G. (1990). Paradigm diversity in organizational research. In J. Hassard and D.

Pym (Eds.), *The theory and philosophy of organizations: Critical issues and new perspectives*, 13–29. London: Routledge.

Morris, M. W., and K. Peng (1994). Culture and cause: American and Chinese attributions for social and physical events. *Journal of Personality and Social Psychology, 67,* 949–971.

Morris, S. (1973). Stalled professionalism: The recruitment of railway officials in the United States, 1885–1940. *Business History Review, 47,* 317–334.

Mowday, R. T., L. W. Porter, and R. M. Steers (1982). *Employee-organizational linkages: The psychology of commitment, absenteeism, and turnover.* New York: Academic Press.

Mowday, R. T., and D. G. Spencer (1981). The influence of task and personality characteristics on employee turnover and absenteeism. *Academy of Management Journal, 24,* 634–642.

Mowday, R. T., and R. I. Sutton (1993). Organizational behavior: Linking individuals and groups to organizational contexts. *Annual Review of Psychology, 44,* 195–229.

Mueller, F. (1995). Organizational governance and employee cooperation: Can we learn from economists? *Human Relations, 48,* 1217–1235.

Mumby, D. K. (1988). *Communication and power in organizations: Discourse, ideology, and domination.* Norwood, N.J.: Ablex.

Mumby, D. K., and L. L. Putnam (1992). The politics of emotion: A feminist reading of bounded rationality. *Academy of Management Review, 17,* 465–486.

Neale, M. A. (1984). The effect of negotiation and arbitration cost salience on bargainer behavior: The role of arbitrator and constituency in negotiator judgment. *Organizational Behavior and Human Performance, 34,* 97–111.

Neale, M. A., and M. H. Bazerman (1985). The effects of framing and negotiator overconfidence on bargainer behavior. *Academy of Management Journal, 28,* 34–49.

Neale, M. A., and M. H. Bazerman (1991). *Cognition and rationality in negotiation.* New York: Free Press.

Neale, M. A., and G. B. Northcraft (1986). Experts, amateurs, and refrigerators: Comparing expert and amateur decision making on a novel task. *Organizational Behavior and Human Decision Processes, 38,* 305–317.

Neale, M. A., and G. B. Northcraft (1990). Experience, expertise, and decision bias in negotiation: The role of strategic conceptualization. In B. H. Sheppard, M. H. Bazerman, and R. J. Lewicki (Eds.), *Research on negotiation in organizations: Vol. 2,* 55–75. Greenwich, Conn.: JAI Press.

Newton, T., and T. Keenan (1991). Further analyses of the dispositional argument in organizational behavior. *Journal of Applied Psychology, 76,* 781–787.

Nilakant, V., and H. Rao (1994). Agency theory and uncertainty in organizations: An evaluation. *Organization Studies, 15,* 649–672.

Nisbett, R. E., and L. Ross (1980). *Human inference: Strategies and shortcomings of social judgment.* Englewood Cliffs, N.J.: Prentice Hall.

Nkomo, S. M. (1992). The emperor has no clothes: Rewriting "race in organizations." *Academy of Management Review, 17,* 487–513.

Nord, W. (1969). Beyond the teaching machine: The neglected area of operant conditioning in the theory and practice of management. *Organizational Behavior and Human Performance, 14,* 371–397.

Northcraft, G. B., and M. A. Neale (1986). Opportunity costs and the framing of resource allocation decisions. *Organizational Behavior and Human Decision Processes, 37,* 348–356.

Northcraft, G. B., and M. A. Neale (1987). Experts, amateurs, and real estate: An anchoring-and-adjustment perspective on property pricing decisions. *Organizational Behavior and Human Decision Processes, 39,* 228–241.

Northcraft, G. B., and M. A. Neale (1994). *Organizational behavior: A management challenge.* Fort Worth, Tex.: Dryden Press.

Northcraft, G. B., M. A. Neale, and P. C. Earley (1994). Joint effects of assigned goals and training on negotiator performance. *Human Performance, 7,* 257–272.

Northcraft, G. B., and G. Wolf (1984). Dollars, sense, and sunk costs: A life-cycle model of resource allocation decisions. *Academy of Management Review, 9,* 225–234.

Ocasio, W. (1994). Political dynamics and the circulation of power: CEO succession in U.S. industrial corporations, 1960–1990. *Administrative Science Quarterly, 39,* 285–312.

Oldham, G. R., and D. J. Brass (1979). Employee reactions to an open-plan office: A naturally occurring quasi-experiment. *Administrative Science Quarterly, 28,* 267–284.

Olsen, F. (1983). The family and the market: A study of ideology and legal reform. *Harvard Law Review, 96,* 1497–1578.

Omi, M., and H. Winant (1986). *Racial formation in the United States: From the 1960s to the 1980s.* New York: Routledge and Kegan Paul.

Oppenheimer, V. K. (1968). The sex-labeling of jobs. *Industrial Relations, 7,* 219–234.

O'Reilly, C. A. (1977). Personality-job fit: Implications for individual attitudes and performance. *Organizational Behavior and Human Performance, 18,* 36–46.

O'Reilly, C. A. (1989). Corporations, culture, and commitment: Motivation and social control in organizations. *California Management Review, 31,* 9–25.

O'Reilly, C. A., and D. F. Caldwell (1979). Informational influence as a determinant of task characteristics and job satisfaction. *Journal of Applied Psychology, 64,* 157–165.

O'Reilly, C. A., and D. F. Caldwell (1980). Job choice: The impact of intrinsic and extrinsic factors on subsequent satisfaction and commitment. *Journal of Applied Psychology, 65,* 559–565.

O'Reilly, C. A., and D. F. Caldwell (1981). The commitment and job tenure of new employees: Some evidence of postdecisional justification. *Administrative Science Quarterly, 26,* 597–616.

O'Reilly, C. A., D. F. Caldwell, and W. P. Barnett (1989). Work group demography, social integration, and turnover. *Administrative Science Quarterly, 34,* 21–37.

O'Reilly, C. A., and J. A. Chatman (1986). Organizational commitment and psychological attachment: The effects of compliance, identification, and internalization on prosocial behavior. *Journal of Applied Psychology, 71,* 492–499.

O'Reilly, C. A., and J. A. Chatman (1994). Working smarter and harder: A longitudinal study of managerial success. *Administrative Science Quarterly, 39,* 603–627.

O'Reilly, C. A., and J. A. Chatman (1996). Culture as social control: Corporations, cults, and commitment. In B. M. Staw and L. L. Cummings (Eds.), *Research in Organizational Behavior: Vol. 18,* 157–200. Greenwich, Conn.: JAI Press.

O'Reilly, C. A., J. A. Chatman, and D. F. Caldwell (1991). People and organizational culture: A profile comparison approach to assessing person-organization fit. *Academy of Management Journal, 34,* 487–516.

O'Reilly, C. A., B. G. M. Main, and G. S. Crystal (1988). CEO compensation as tournament and social comparison: A tale of two theories. *Administrative Science Quarterly, 34,* 21–37.

O'Reilly, C. A., and K. H. Roberts (1975). Individual differences in personality, position in the organization, and job satisfaction. *Organizational Behavior and Human Performance, 14,* 144–150.

O'Reilly, C. A., R. C. Snyder, and J. N. Boothe (1993). Effects of executive team demography on organizational change. In G. P. Huber and W. H. Glick (Eds.), *Organizational change and redesign*, 147–175. New York: Oxford University Press.

O'Reilly, C. A., and B. A. Weitz (1980). Managing marginal employees: The use of warnings and dismissals. *Administrative Science Quarterly*, 25, 467–484.

Osterman, P. (1994). How common is workplace transformation and who adopts it? *Industrial and Labor Relations Review*, 47, 173–188.

Palmer, D. P. (1983). Broken ties: Interlocking directorates and intercorporate coordination. *Administrative Science Quarterly*, 28, 40–55.

Palmer, D. P., B. M. Barber, X. Zhou, and Y. Soysal (1995). The friendly and predatory acquisitions of large U.S. corporations in the 1960s: The other contested terrain. *American Sociological Review*, 60, 469–499.

Palmer, D. P., R. Friedland, and J. Singh (1986). The ties that bind: Organizational and class bases of stability in a corporate interlock network. *American Sociological Review*, 51, 781–796.

Palmer, D. P., P. D. Jennings, and X. Zhou (1993). Late adoption of the multidivisional form by large U.S. corporations: Institutional, political, and economics accounts. *Administrative Science Quarterly*, 38, 100–131.

Parker, M., and J. Slaughter (1988). Management by stress. *Technology Review*, 91, 38–44.

Parker, R. (1993). Can economists save economics? *American Prospect*, 13, 148–160.

Pascale, R. (1985). The paradox of "corporate culture": Reconciling ourselves to socialization. *California Management Review*, 27, 26–41.

Pascale, R. (1990). *Managing on the edge*. New York: Simon and Schuster.

Pearce, J. L., W. B. Stevenson, and J. L. Perry (1985). Managerial compensation based on organizational performance: A time series analysis of the effects of merit pay. *Academy of Management Journal*, 28, 261–278.

Pennings, J. (1975). The relevance of the structural-contingency model of organizational effectiveness. *Administrative Science Quarterly*, 30, 393–410.

Perrow, C. (1970a). Departmental power and perspectives in industrial firms. In M. N. Zald (Ed.), *Power in organizations*, 59–89. Nashville: Vanderbilt University Press.

Perrow, C. (1970b). *Organizational analysis: A sociological view*. Belmont, Calif.: Wadsworth.

Perrow, C. (1992). Organisational theorists in a society of organisations. *International Sociology*, 7, 371–379.

Pervin, L. A. (1985). Personality: Current controversies, issues, and directions. *Annual review of psychology*, 36, 83–114.

Pervin, L. A., and M. Lewis (1978). Overview of the internal-external issue. In L. A. Pervin and M. Lewis (Eds.), *Perspectives in interactional psychology*, 1–22. New York: Plenum.

Peters, T. J. (1978). Symbols, patterns, and settings: An optimistic case for getting things done. *Organizational Dynamics*, 7, 3–23.

Pettigrew, A. M. (1972). Information control as a power resource. *Sociology*, 6, 187–204.

Pettigrew, A. M. (1973). *Politics of organizational decision-making*. London: Tavistock.

Pettigrew, A. M. (1979). On studying organizational cultures. *Administrative Science Quarterly*, 24, 570–581.

Pfeffer, J. (1972a). Interorganizational influence and managerial attitudes. *Academy of Management Journal*, 15, 317–330.

Pfeffer, J. (1972b). Merger as a response to organizational interdependence. *Administrative Science Quarterly*, 17, 382–394.

Pfeffer, J. (1972c). Size and composition of corporate boards of directors: The organization and its environment. *Administrative Science Quarterly*, 17, 218–228.

Pfeffer, J. (1973). Size, composition, and function of hospital boards of directors: A study of organization-environment linkage. *Administrative Science Quarterly*, 18, 349–364.

Pfeffer, J. (1977). The ambiguity of leadership. *Academy of Management Review*, 2, 104–112.

Pfeffer, J. (1981a). Four laws of organizational research. In A. Van de Ven and W. Joyce (Eds.), *Perspectives on organization design and behavior*, 409–418. New York: Wiley.

Pfeffer, J. (1981b). Management as symbolic action: The creation and maintenance of organizational paradigms. In L. L. Cummings and B. M. Staw (eds.), *Research in Organizational Behavior: Vol. 3*, 1–52. Greenwich, Conn.: JAI Press.

Pfeffer, J. (1981c). *Power in organizations*. Marshfield, Mass.: Pitman.

Pfeffer, J. (1982). *Organizations and organization theory*. Marshfield, Mass.: Pitman.

Pfeffer, J. (1983). Organizational demography. In L. L. Cummings and B. M. Staw (Eds.), *Research in organizational behavior: Vol. 5*, 299–357. Greenwich, Conn.: JAI Press.

Pfeffer, J. (1985). Organizations and organization theory. In G. Lindzey and E. Aronson, *The handbook of social psychology, 3rd ed.*, 379–440. New York: McGraw-Hill.

Pfeffer, J. (1987). A resource dependence perspective on intercorporate relations. In M. S. Mizruchi and M. Schwartz (Eds.), *Intercorporate relations: The structural analysis of business*, 25–55. Cambridge: Cambridge University Press.

Pfeffer, J. (1991). Organization theory and structural perspectives on management. *Journal of Management*, 17, 789–803.

Pfeffer, J. (1992). *Managing with power: Politics and influence in organizations*. Boston: Harvard Business School Press.

Pfeffer, J. (1993). Barriers to the advance of organizational science: Paradigm development as a dependent variable. *Academy of Management Review*, 18, 599–620.

Pfeffer, J. (1994). *Competitive advantage through people: Unleashing the power of the work force*. Boston: Harvard Business School Press.

Pfeffer, J., and J. N. Baron (1988). Taking the workers back out: Recent trends in the structuring of employment. *Research in organizational behavior: Vol. 10*, 257–303. Greenwich, Conn.: JAI Press.

Pfeffer, J., and Y. Cohen (1984). Determinants of internal labor markets in organizations. *Administrative Science Quarterly*, 29, 550–572.

Pfeffer, J., and A. Davis-Blake (1986). Administrative succession and organizational performance: How administrator experience mediates the succession effect. *Academy of Management Journal*, 29, 72–83.

Pfeffer, J., and A. Davis-Blake (1987). The effect of the proportion of women on salaries: The case of college administrators. *Administrative Science Quarterly*, 32, 1–24.

Pfeffer, J., and A. Davis-Blake (1990). Determinants of salary dispersion in organizations. *Industrial Relations*, 29, 38–57.

Pfeffer, J., and A. Davis-Blake (1992). Salary dispersion, location in the salary distribution, and turnover among college administrators. *Industrial and Labor Relations Review*, 45, 753–763.

Pfeffer, J., and A. M. Konrad (1991). The effects of individual power on earnings. *Work and Occupations*, 18, 385–414.

Pfeffer, J., and N. Langton (1988). Wage inequality and the organization of work: The case of academic departments. *Administrative Science Quarterly*, 33, 588–606.

Pfeffer, J., and N. Langton (1993). The effect of wage dispersion on satisfaction, productivity, and working collaboratively: Evidence from college and university faculty. *Administrative Science Quarterly*, 38, 382–407.

Pfeffer, J., and J. Lawler (1980). Effects of job alternatives, extrinsic rewards, and behavioral commitment on attitude toward the organization: A field test of the insufficient justification paradigm. *Administrative Science Quarterly*, 25, 38–56.

Pfeffer, J., and H. Leblebici (1973). The effect of competition on some dimensions of organizational structure. *Social Forces, 52,* 268–279.

Pfeffer, J., A. Leong, and K. Strehl (1977). Paradigm, development, and particularism: Journal publication in three scientific disciplines. *Social Forces, 55,* 938–951.

Pfeffer, J., and W. L. Moore (1980a). Average tenure of academic department heads: The effects of paradigm, size, and departmental demography. *Administrative Science Quarterly, 25,* 387–406.

Pfeffer, J., and W. L. Moore (1980b). Power in university budgeting: A replication and extension. *Administrative Science Quarterly, 25,* 637–653.

Pfeffer, J., and P. Nowak (1976). Joint ventures and interorganizational interdependence. *Administrative Science Quarterly, 21,* 398–418.

Pfeffer, J., and C. A. O'Reilly (1987). Hospital demography and turnover among nurses. *Industrial Relations, 26,* 158–173.

Pfeffer, J., and J. Ross (1982). The effects of marriage and a working wife on occupational and wage attainment. *Administrative Science Quarterly, 27,* 66–80.

Pfeffer, J., and G. R. Salancik (1974). Organizational decision making as a political process: The case of a university budget. *Administrative Science Quarterly, 19,* 135–151.

Pfeffer, J., and G. R. Salancik (1977). Administrator effectiveness: The effects of advocacy and information on resource allocations. *Human Relations, 30,* 641–656.

Pfeffer, J., and G. R. Salancik (1978). *The external control of organizations: A resource dependence perspective.* New York: Harper and Row.

Pfeffer, J., G. R. Salancik, and H. Leblebici (1976). The effect of uncertainty on the use of social influence in organizational decision making. *Administrative Science Quarterly, 21,* 227–245.

Pil, F. K., and J. P. MacDuffie (1996). The adoption of high-involvement work practices. *Industrial Relations, 35,* 423–455.

Podolny, J. M. (1993). A status-based model of market competition. *American Journal of Sociology, 98,* 829–872.

Podolny, J. M. (1994). Market uncertainty and the social character of economic exchange. *Administrative Science Quarterly, 39,* 458–483.

Podolny, J. M., and J. N. Baron (1995, August). Resources and relationships: Social networks, mobility, and satisfaction in the work place. Paper presented at the Annual Meeting of the Academy of Management, Vancouver, Canada.

Pondy, L. R. (1978). Leadership is a language game. In M. W. McCall, Jr., and M. M. Lombardo (Eds.), *Leadership: Where else can we go?* 87–99. Durham, N.C.: Duke University Press.

Porac, J. F., and G. R. Salancik (1981). Generic overjustification: The interaction of extrinsic rewards. *Organizational Behavior and Human Performance, 27,* 197–212.

Presthus, R. (1978). *The organizational society, rev. ed.* New York: St. Martin's Press.

Pugh, D. S., D. J. Hickson, C. R. Hinings, and C. Turner (1968). Dimensions of organization structure. *Administrative Science Quarterly, 13,* 65–105.

Pugh, D. S., D. J. Hickson, C. R. Hinings, and C. Turner (1969). The context of organization structures. *Administrative Science Quarterly, 14,* 91–114.

Rafaeli, A., and R. I. Sutton (1991). Emotional contrast strategies as means of social influence: Lessons from criminal interrogators and bill collectors. *Academy of Management Journal, 34,* 749–775.

Rankin, T. (1986). Integrating QWL and collective bargaining. *Work-Life Review, 5,* 14–18.

Ree, M. J., and J. A. Earles (1991). Predicting training success: Not much more than g. *Personnel Psychology, 44,* 321–332.

Reed, M. (1990). The labour process perspective on management organization: A critique and reformulation. In J. Hassard and D. Pym (Eds.), *The theory and philosophy of organizations: Critical issues and new perspectives*, 63–82. London: Routledge.

Reed, T. L. (1978). Organizational change in the American Foreign Service, 1925–1965: The utility of cohort analysis. *American Sociological Review, 43*, 404–421.

Reichers, A., and B. Schneider (1990). Climate and culture: An evolution of constructs. In B. Schneider (Ed.), *Organizational climate and culture*, 5–39. San Francisco: Jossey-Bass.

Rosen, C. M., K. J. Klein, and K. M. Young (1986). *Employee ownership in America*. Lexington, Mass.: Lexington Books.

Rosen, S. (1986). Prizes and incentives in elimination tournaments. *American Economic Review, 76*, 701–715.

Ross, J., and B. M. Staw (1986). Expo 86: An escalation prototype. *Administrative Science Quarterly, 31*, 274–297.

Ross, J., and B. M. Staw (1993). Organizational escalation and exit: Lessons from the Shoreham nuclear power plant. *Academy of Management Journal, 36*, 701–732.

Ross, L. D. (1977). The intuitive psychologist and his shortcomings: Distortions in the attribution process. In L. Berkowitz (Ed.), *Advances in experimental social psychology: Vol. 10*, 173–220. New York: Random House.

Rumelt, R. P. (1974). *Strategy, structure, and economic performance*. Boston: Harvard University, Division of Research, Graduate School of Business Administration.

Russell, B. (1938). *Power: A new social analysis*. London: Allen and Unwin.

Sackett, P. R., C. L. Z. Dubois, and A. W. Noe (1991). Tokenism in performance evaluation: The effects of work group representation on male-female and white-black differences in performance ratings. *Journal of Applied Psychology, 76*, 263–267.

Sacks, H. (1984). Methodological remarks. In J. M. Atkinson and J. C. Heritage (Eds.), *Structures of social action: Studies in conversation analysis*, 21–27. Cambridge: Cambridge University Press.

Salancik, G. R. (1977). Commitment and the control of organizational behavior and belief. In B. M. Staw and G. R. Salancik (Eds.), *New directions in organizational behavior*, 1–21. Chicago: St. Clair Press.

Salancik, G. R., and J. Pfeffer (1974). The bases and use of power in organizational decision making: The case of a university. *Administrative Science Quarterly, 19*, 453–473.

Salancik, G. R., and J. Pfeffer (1977). Constraints on administrator discretion: The limited influence of mayors on city budgets. *Urban Affairs Quarterly, 12*, 475–498.

Salancik, G. R., and J. Pfeffer (1978a). A social information processing approach to job attitudes and task design. *Administrative Science Quarterly, 23*, 224–253.

Salancik, G. R., and J. Pfeffer (1978b). Uncertainty, secrecy, and the choice of similar others. *Social Psychology, 41*, 246–255.

Salancik, G. R., and J. Pfeffer (1980). Effects of ownership and performance on executive tenure in U.S. corporations. *Academy of Management Journal, 23*, 653–664.

Samuelson, P. A. (1963). Discussion: Problems of methodology. *American Economic Review Proceedings, 53*, 231–236.

Sanger, D. E. (1996). A U.S. agency, once powerful, is dead at 108. *New York Times*, January 1, 1996, pp. 1, 9.

Schein, E. (1985). *Organizational culture and leadership*. San Francisco: Jossey-Bass.

Schein, V. E. (1979). Examining an illusion: The role of deceptive behaviors in organizations. *Human Relations, 32*, 287–295.

Scherer, F. M. (1980). *Industrial market structure and economic performance*, 2nd ed. Chicago: Rand McNally.

Schneider, B. (1987). The people make the place. *Personnel Psychology, 40,* 437–453.

Schneider, B., H. W. Goldstein, and D. B. Smith (1995). The ASA framework: An update. *Personnel Psychology, 48,* 747–773.

Schoonhoven, C. B. (1981). Problems with contingency theory: Testing assumptions hidden within the language of contingency "theory." *Administrative Science Quarterly, 26,* 349–377.

Schoorman, F. D. (1988). Escalation bias in performance appraisals: An unintended consequence of supervisor participation in hiring decisions. *Journal of Applied Psychology, 73,* 58–62.

Schwartz, B. (1974). Waiting, exchange, and power: The distribution of time in social systems. *American Journal of Sociology, 79,* 841–870.

Scott, W. R. (1987). The adolescence of institutional theory. *Administrative Science Quarterly, 32,* 493–511.

Scott, W. R. (1992). *Organizations: Rational, natural, and open systems, 3rd ed.* Englewood Cliffs, N.J.: Prentice Hall.

Scott, W. R. (1995). *Institutions and organizations.* Thousand Oaks, Calif.: Sage.

Scully, G. W. (1974). Discrimination: The case of baseball. In R. G. Noll (Ed.), *Government and the sports business,* 221–273. Washington, D.C.: Brookings.

Seaman, R. (1995). How self-directed work teams support strategic alignment. *Compensation and Benefits Review, 27,* 23–32.

Sears, D. O., and C. L. Funk (1990). Self-interest in Americans' political opinions. In J. J. Mansbridge (Ed.), *Beyond self-interest,* 147–170. Chicago: University of Chicago Press.

Sears, D. O., R. R. Lau, T. R. Tyler, and H. M. Allen, Jr. (1980). Self-interest vs. symbolic politics in policy attitudes and presidential voting. *American Political Science Review, 74,* 670–684.

Seligman, D. L. (1992). *A question of intelligence: The IQ debate in America.* New York: Birch Lane Press.

Selznick, P. (1949). *TVA and the grass roots.* Berkeley: University of California Press.

Selznick, P. (1957). *Leadership in administration.* Evanston, Ill.: Row, Peterson.

Sen, A. K. (1977). Rational fools. *Philosophy and Public Affairs, 6,* 317–344.

Shadur, M. A., J. J. Rodwell, and G. J. Bamber (1995). Factors predicting employees' approval of lean production. *Human Relations, 48,* 1403–1425.

Shamir, B., R. J. House, and M. Arthur (1993). The motivational effects of charismatic leadership: A self-concept based theory. *Organization Science, 4,* 577–594.

Sheldon, M. E. (1971). Investments and involvements as mechanisms producing commitment in organizations. *Administrative Science Quarterly, 16,* 143–150.

Shell, R. L., and R. G. Allgeier (1992). A multi-level incentive model for service organizations. *Applied Ergonomics, 23,* 49–53.

Shenhav, Y. (1995). From chaos to systems: The engineering foundations of organization theory, 1879–1932. *Administrative Science Quarterly, 40,* 557–585.

Shenhav, Y., and Y. Haberfeld (1992). Paradigm uncertainty, gender composition, and earnings inequality in scientific disciplines: A longitudinal study, 1972–1982. In P. Tolbert and S. B. Bacharach (Eds.), *Research in the sociology of organizations: Vol. 10,* 141–172. Greenwich, Conn.: JAI Press.

Sheriff, P., and E. J. Campbell (1992). Room for women: A case study in the sociology of organizations. In A. J. Mills and P. Tancred (Eds.), *Gendering Organizational Analysis,* 31–45. Newbury Park, Calif.: Sage.

Shore, L. M., K. Barksdale, and T. H. Shore (1995). Managerial perceptions of employee commitment to the organization. *Academy of Management Journal, 38,* 1593–1615.

Shore, L. M., and S. J. Wayne (1993). Commitment and employee behavior: Comparison of affective commitment and continuance commitment with perceived organizational support. *Journal of Applied Psychology, 78,* 774–780.

Siehl, C., and J. Martin (1990). Organizational culture: A key to financial performance? In B. Schneider (Ed.), *Organizational climate and culture,* 241–281. San Francisco: Jossey-Bass.

Sigelman, L., H. Milward, and J. M. Shepard (1982). The salary differential between male and female administrators: Equal pay for equal work? *Academy of Management Journal, 25,* 664–671.

Sills, D. L. (1957). *The volunteers.* Glencoe, Ill.: Free Press.

Simon, H. A. (1947). *Administrative behavior.* New York: Macmillan.

Simon, H. A. (1963). Discussion: Problems of methodology. *American Economic Review Proceedings, 53,* 229–231.

Simon, H. A. (1964). On the concept of organizational goal. *Administrative Science Quarterly, 9,* 1–22.

Simon, H. A. (1978). Rationality as process and as product of thought. *American Economic Review, 68,* 1–16.

Simon, H. A. (1979). Rational decision making business organizations. *American Economic Review, 69,* 493–513.

Simon, H. A. (1985). Human nature in politics: The dialogue of psychology with political science. *American Political Science Review, 79,* 293–304.

Simon, H. A. (1991). Organizations and markets. *Journal of Economic Perspectives, 5,* 25–44.

Sims, H., A. Szilagyi, and R. Keller (1976). The measurement of job characteristics. *Academy of Management Journal, 19,* 195–212.

Singh, J. V., and C. J. Lumsden (1990). Theory and research in organizational ecology. *Annual Review of Sociology, 16,* 161–195.

Skinner, B. F. (1953). *Science and human behavior.* New York: Macmillan.

Smircich, L. (1983). Concepts of culture and organizational analysis. *Administrative Science Quarterly, 28,* 339–359.

Smith, K. G., K. A. Smith, J. D. Olian, H. P. Sims, Jr., D. P. O'Bannon, and J. A. Scully (1994). Top management team demography and process: The role of social integration and communication. *Administrative Science Quarterly, 39,* 412–438.

Smith, M. J., P. Carayon, K. J. Sanders, S. Y. Lim, and D. LeGrande (1992). Employee stress and health complaints in jobs with and without electronic performance monitoring. *Applied Ergonomics, 23,* 17–28.

Soref, M., and M. Zeitlin (1987). Finance capital and the internal structure of the capitalist class in the United States. In M. Mizruchi and M. Schwartz (Eds.), *Intercorporate relations: The structural analysis of business,* 56–84. Cambridge: Cambridge University Press.

South, S. J., C. M. Bonjean, W. T. Markham, and J. Corder (1982). Social structure and intergroup interaction: Men and women of the federal bureaucracy. *American Sociological Review, 47,* 587–599.

Spangler, E., M. A. Gordon, and R. M. Pipkin (1978). Token women: An empirical test of Kanter's hypothesis. *American Journal of Sociology, 84,* 160–170.

Spangler, W. D., and R. J. House (1991). Presidential effectiveness and the leadership motive profile. *Journal of Personality and Social Psychology, 60,* 439–455.

Spence, A. M. (1974). *Market signaling: Informational transfer in hiring and related processes.* Cambridge, Mass.: Harvard University Press.

Spenner, K. I. (1983). Deciphering Prometheus: Temporal change in the skill level of work. *American Sociological Review, 48,* 824–837.

Spenner, K. I. (1990). Skill: Meanings, methods, and measures. *Work and Occupations, 17,* 399–421.

Springer, T. J. (1992). Does ergonomics make good business sense? *Facilities Design and Management, II,* 46–49.

Starbuck, W. H. (1981). A trip to view the elephants and the rattlesnakes in the garden of Aston. In A. H. Van de Ven and W. F. Joyce (Eds.), *Perspectives on organization design and behavior,* 167–198. New York: Wiley.

Staw, B. M. (1974). Attitudinal and behavioral consequences of changing a major organizational reward: A natural field experiment. *Journal of Personality and Social Psychology, 29,* 742–751.

Staw, B. M. (1976). Knee deep in the Big Muddy: A study of escalating commitment to a chosen course of action. *Organizational Behavior and Human Performance, 16,* 27–44.

Staw, B. M. (1980). Rationality and justification in organizational life. In B. M. Staw and L. L. Cummings (Eds.), *Research in organizational behavior: Vol. 2,* 45–80. Greenwich, Conn.: JAI Press.

Staw, B. M. (1985). Repairs on the road to relevance and rigor: Some unexplored issues in publishing organizational research. In L. L. Cummings and P. J. Frost (Eds.), *Publishing in the organizational sciences,* 96–107. Homewood, Ill.: Irwin.

Staw, B. M., N. E. Bell, and J. A. Clausen (1986). The dispositional approach to job attitudes: A lifetime longitudinal test. *Administrative Science Quarterly, 31,* 56–77.

Staw, B. M., B. J. Calder, R. K. Hess, and L. E. Sandelands (1980). Intrinsic motivation and norms about payment. *Journal of Personality, 48,* 1–14.

Staw, B. M., and H. Hoang (1995). Sunk costs in the NBA: Why draft order affects playing time and survival in professional basketball. *Administrative Science Quarterly, 40,* 474–494.

Staw, B. M., and J. Ross (1980). Commitment in an experimenting society: An experiment on the attribution of leadership from administrative scenarios. *Journal of Applied Psychology, 65,* 249–260.

Staw, B. M., and J. Ross (1985). Stability in the midst of change: A dispositional approach to job attitudes. *Journal of Applied Psychology, 70,* 469–480.

Steers, R. M., and D. G. Spencer (1977). The role of achievement motivation in job design. *Journal of Applied Psychology, 62,* 472–479.

Steffy, B. D., and A. J. Grimes (1986). A critical theory of organization science. *Academy of Management Review, 11,* 322–336.

Stern, R. N., and S. R. Barley (1996). Organizations and social systems: Organization theory's neglected mandate. *Administrative Science Quarterly, 41,* 146–162.

Stewman, S. (1986). Demographic models of internal labor markets. *Administrative Science Quarterly, 31,* 212–247.

Stewman, S. (1988). Organizational demography. *Annual Review of Sociology, 14,* 173–202.

Stewman, S., and S. L. Konda (1983). Careers and organizational labor markets: Demographic models of organizational behavior. *American Journal of Sociology, 88,* 637–685.

Stillenger, C., M. Ebelbaum, D. Keltner, and L. Ross (1990). The "reactive devaluation" barrier to conflict resolution. Unpublished working paper, Stanford University, Department of Psychology.

Stinchcombe, A. L. (1965). Social structure and organizations. In J. G. March (Ed.), *Handbook of organizations*, 142–193. Chicago: Rand McNally.

Stinchcombe, A. L., M. S. McDill, and D. R. Walker (1968). Demography of organizations. *American Journal of Sociology*, 74, 221–229.

Stolzenberg, R. M. (1978). Bringing the boss back in: Employer size, employee schooling, and socioeconomic achievement. *American Sociological Review*, 43, 813–828.

Stone, K. (1973). The origins of job structures in the steel industry. *Radical America*, 7, 17–66.

Strickland, L. H. (1958). Surveillance and trust. *Journal of Personality*, 26, 200–215.

Sutton, J. R., F. Dobbin, J. W. Meyer, and W. R. Scott (1994). The legalization of the workplace. *American Journal of Sociology*, 99, 944–971.

Sutton, R. I. (1991). Maintaining norms about expressed emotions: The case of bill collectors. *Administrative Science Quarterly*, 36, 245–268.

Sutton, R. I., and B. M. Staw (1995). What theory is not. *Administrative Science Quarterly*, 40, 371–384.

Sutton, R. I., and A. Hargadon (1996). Brainstorming groups in context: Effectiveness in a product design firm. *Administrative Science Quarterly*, (in press).

Szafran, R. (1984). *Universities and women faculty*. New York: Praeger.

Szilagyi, A. D., and W. E. Holland (1980). Changes in social density: Relationships with functional interaction and perceptions of job characteristics, role stress, and work satisfaction. *Journal of Applied Psychology*, 65, 28–33.

Taylor, F. W. (1903). *Shop management*. New York: Harper.

Teece, D. J. (1981). Internal organization and economic performance: An empirical analysis of the profitability of principal firms. *Journal of Industrial Economics*, 30, 173–200.

Terborg, J. R., G. S. Howard, and S. E. Maxwell (1980). Evaluating planned organizational change: A method for assessing alpha, beta, and gamma change. *Academy of Management Review*, 5, 109–121.

Tetlock, P. E. (1985a). Accountability: The neglected social context of judgment and choice. In B. M. Staw and L. L. Cummings (Eds.), *Research in organizational behavior: Vol. 7*. Greenwich, Conn.: JAI Press.

Tetlock, P. E. (1985b). Accountability: A social check on the fundamental attribution error. *Social Psychology Quarterly*, 48, 227–236.

Tetlock, P. E. (1992). The impact of accountability on judgment and choice: Toward a social contingency model. In M. Zanna (Ed.), *Advances in experimental social psychology: Vol. 25*, 331–376. New York: Academic Press.

Tett, R. P., D. N. Jackson, and M. Rothstein (1991). Personality measures as predictors of job performance: A meta-analytic review. *Personnel Psychology*, 44, 703–740.

Thomas, J., and R. Griffen (1983). The social information processing model of task design: A review of the literature. *Academy of Management Review*, 8, 672–682.

Thompson, J. D. (1956). On building an administrative science, *Administrative Science Quarterly*, 1, 102–111.

Thompson, J. D. (1967). *Organizations in action*. New York: McGraw-Hill.

Thompson, J. D., and A. Tuden (1959). Strategies, structures, and processes of organizational decision. In J. D. Thompson, P. B. Hammond, R. W. Hawkes, B. H. Junker, and A. Tuden (Eds.), *Comparative studies in administration*, 195–216. Pittsburgh: University of Pittsburgh Press.

Tidball, M. E. (1980). Women's colleges and women achievers revisited. *Signs: Journal of Women in Culture and Society*, 5, 504–517.

Tolbert, P. S., and A. A. Oberfield (1991). Sources of organizational demography: Faculty sex ratios in colleges and universities. *Sociology of Education, 64*, 305–315.

Tolbert, P. S., and L. G. Zucker (1983). Institutional sources of change in the formal structure of organizations: The diffusion of civil service reform, 1880–1935. *Administrative Science Quarterly, 30*, 22–39.

Toren, N. (1990). Would more women make a difference? Academic women in Israel. In S. S. Lie and V. E. O'Leary (Eds.), *Storming the tower: Women in the academic world*, 74–85. London: Kogan Page.

Training (1992). Give 'em that old-time ambition. *Training*, February, 74.

Treiman, D. J., and H. I. Hartmann (1981). *Women, work, and wages: Equal pay for jobs of equal value*. Washington, D.C.: National Academy Press.

Tsui, A. S., and C. A. O'Reilly (1989). Beyond simple demographic effects: The importance of relational demography in superior-subordinate dyads. *Academy of Management Journal, 32*, 402–423.

Tsui, A. S., T. D. Egan, and C. A. O'Reilly. (1992). Being different: Relational demography and organizational attachment. *Administrative Science Quarterly, 37*, 549–579.

Tushman, M. L., W. Newman, and E. Romanelli (1986). Convergence and upheaval: Managing the unsteady pace of organizational evolution. *California Management Review. 29*, 1–20.

Tushman, M. L., and E. Romanelli (1983). Uncertainty, social location, and influence in decision making: A sociometric analysis. *Management Science, 29*, 12–23.

Tversky, A., and D. Kahneman (1974). Judgment under uncertainty: Heuristics and biases. *Science, 185*, 1124–1131.

Uchitelle, L. (1992). Clinton's economics point man. *New York Times*, November 21, 17.

Useem, M. (1979). The social organization of the American business elite and participation of corporate directors in the governance of American institutions. *American Sociological Review, 44*, 553–572.

Useem, M. (1984). *The inner circle*. New York: Oxford University Press.

Useem, M. (1996). *Investor capitalism: How money managers are changing the face of corporate America*. New York: Basic Books.

Van Maanen, J. (1989). Some notes on the importance of writing in organization studies. In *Harvard business school research colloquium*, 27–33. Boston: Harvard Business School.

Van Maanen, J. (1995a). Fear and loathing in organization studies. *Organization Science, 6*, 687–692.

Van Maanen, J. (1995b). Style as Theory. *Organization Science, 6*, 132–143.

Van Maanen, J., and E. H. Schein (1979). Toward a theory of organizational socialization. In B. M. Staw (Ed.), *Research in organizational behavior: Vol. 1*, 209–264. Greenwich, Conn.: JAI Press.

Vroom, V. H. (1976). Leadership. In M. D. Dunnette (Ed.), *Handbook of industrial and organizational psychology*, 1527–1551. Chicago: Rand McNally.

Wade, J., C. A. O'Reilly, and I. Chandratat (1990). Golden parachutes: CEOs and the exercise of social influence. *Administrative Science Quarterly, 35*, 587–603.

Wagner, J. A., III, and J. R. Hollenbeck (1992). *Management of Organizational Behavior*. Englewood Cliffs, N.J.: Prentice Hall.

Wagner, W. G., J. Pfeffer, and C. A. O'Reilly (1984). Organizational demography and turnover in top-management groups. *Administrative Science Quarterly, 29*, 74–92.

Walker, G. (1985). Network position and cognition in a computer software firm. *Administrative Science Quarterly, 30*, 103–130.

Walton, R. E. (1985). Toward a strategy for eliciting employee commitment based on policies of mutuality. In R. E. Walton and P. R. Lawrence (Eds.), *HRM trends and challenges*, 35–65. Boston: Harvard Business School Press.

Watson, D., L. A. Clark, and A. Tellegen (1988). Development and validation of brief measures of positive and negative affect: The PANAS Scales. *Journal of Personality and Social Psychology, 54*, 1063–1070.

Watson, D., and A. K. Slack (1993). General factors of affective temperament and their relation to job satisfaction over time. *Organizational Behavior and Human Decision Processes, 54*, 181–202.

Weber, M. (1946 trans.). *From Max Weber: Essays in sociology.* Edited by H. H. Gerth and C. W. Mills. New York: Oxford University Press.

Weber, M. (1947 trans.) *The theory of social and economic organization.* Edited by A. H. Henderson and T. Parsons. Glencoe, Ill.: Free Press.

Webster, J., and W. H. Starbuck (1988). Theory building in industrial and organizational psychology. In C. L. Cooper and I. Robertson (Eds.), *International review of industrial and organizational psychology*, 93–138. New York: Wiley.

Weick, K. E. (1964). The reduction of cognitive dissonance through task enhancement and effort expenditure. *Journal of Abnormal and Social Psychology, 68*, 533–539.

Weick, K. E. (1969). *The social psychology of organizing.* Reading, Mass.: Addison-Wesley.

Weick, K. E. (1979). Cognitive processes in organizations. In B. M. Staw (Ed.), *Research in organizational behavior: Vol. 1*, 41–74. Greenwich, Conn.: JAI Press.

Weick, K. E. (1993). Sensemaking in organizations: Small structures with large consequences. In J. K. Murnighan (Ed.), *Social psychology in organizations: Advances in theory and research*, 10–37. Englewood Cliffs, N.J.: Prentice Hall.

Weick, K. E. (1995). What theory is *not*, theorizing *is. Administrative Science Quarterly, 40*, 385–390.

Weick, K. E., and M. G. Bougon (1986). Organizations as cognitive maps: Charting ways to success and failure. In H. P. Sims, Jr., and G. A. Gioia (Eds.), *The thinking organization*, 102–135. San Francisco: Jossey-Bass.

Weiner, N., and T. A. Mahoney (1981). A model of corporate performance as a function of environmental, organizational, and leadership influences. *Academy of Management Journal, 24*, 453–470.

Weiss, H. M., and J. Adler (1984). Personality and organizational behavior. In B. M. Staw and L. L. Cummings (Eds.), *Research in organizational behavior: Vol. 6*, 1–50. Greenwich, Conn.: JAI Press.

Weiss, H. M., and J. Shaw (1979). Social influences on judgments about tasks. *Organizational Behavior and Human Performance, 24*, 126–140.

Weitz, J. (1952). A neglected concept in the study of job satisfaction. *Personnel Psychology, 5*, 201–205.

Weitzman, M. L., and D. L. Kruse (1990). Profit sharing and productivity. In A. S. Blinder (Ed.), *Paying for productivity: A look at the evidence.* Washington, D.C.: Brookings.

Welbourne, T. M., and D. M. Cable (1995). Group incentives and pay satisfaction: Understanding the relationship through an identity theory perspective. *Human Relations, 48*, 711–726.

Welbourne, T. M., and A. O. Andrews (1996). Predicting the performance of initial public offerings: Should human resource management be in the equation? *Academy of Management Journal, 39*, 891–919.

Westphal, J. D., and E. J. Zajac (1994). Substance and symbolism in CEO's long-term incentive plans. *Administrative Science Quarterly, 39*, 367–390.

Westphal, J. D., and E. J. Zajac (1995). Who shall govern? CEO/board power, demographic similarity, and new director selection. *Administrative Science Quarterly, 40,* 60–83.

Wharton, A. S. (1992). The social construction of gender and race in organizations: A social identity and group mobilization perspective. In P. Tolbert and S. B. Bacharach (Eds.), *Research in the sociology of organizations: Vol. 10,* 55–84. Greenwich, Conn.: JAI Press.

Wharton, A. S., and J. N. Baron (1987). So happy together? The impact of gender segregation on men at work. *American Sociological Review, 52,* 574–587.

White, S., and T. Mitchell (1979). Job enrichment versus social cues: A comparison and competitive test. *Journal of Applied Psychology, 64,* 1–9.

Whitt, J. A. (1979). Toward a class-dialectical model of power: An empirical assessment of three competing models of political power. *American Sociological Review, 44,* 81–100.

Whitt, J. A. (1980). Can capitalists organize themselves? In G. W. Domhoff (Ed.), *Power structure research,* 97–113. Beverly Hills, Calif.: Sage.

Wholey, D. R., J. B. Christianson, and S. M. Sanchez (1992). Organization size and failure among health maintenance organizations. *American Sociological Review, 57,* 829–842.

Wholey, D. R., J. B. Christianson, and S. M. Sanchez (1993). The effects of physician and corporate interests on the formation of health maintenance organizations. *American Journal of Sociology, 99,* 164–200.

Wiersema, M. F., and K. A. Bantel (1992). Top management team demography and corporate strategic change. *Academy of Management Journal, 35,* 91–121.

Wiersema, M. F., and A. Bird (1993). Organizational demography in Japanese firms: Group heterogeneity, individual dissimilarity, and top management team turnover. *Academy of Management Journal, 36,* 996–1025.

Williamson, O. E. (1964). *Corporate control and business behavior: Managerial objectives in a theory of the firm.* Englewood Cliffs, N.J.: Prentice Hall.

Williamson, O. E. (1975). *Markets and hierarchies: Analysis and antitrust implications.* New York: Free Press.

Williamson, O. E. (1985). *The economic institutions of capitalism.* New York: Free Press.

Williamson, O. E. (1991). Economic institutions: Spontaneous and intentional governance. *Journal of Law, Economics, and Organization, 7,* 159–187.

Williamson, O. E. (1993). Opportunism and its critics. *Managerial and Decision Economics, 14,* 97–107.

Williamson, O. E. (1995). Hierarchies, markets, and power in the economy: An economic perspective. *Industrial and Corporate Change, 4,* 21–49.

Williamson, O. E., and W. G. Ouchi (1981). The markets and hierarchies program of research: Origins, implications, prospects. In A. H. Van de Ven and W. F. Joyce (Eds.), *Perspectives on organizational design and behavior,* 347–370. New York: Wiley.

Wilson, T. D., and G. D. Lassiter (1982). Increasing intrinsic interest with superfluous external constraints. *Journal of Personality and Social Psychology, 42,* 811–819.

Winter, D. G. (1987). Leader appeal, leader performance, and the motive profiles of leaders and followers: A study of American presidents and elections. *Journal of Personality and Social Psychology, 52,* 196–202.

Wolf, W. C., and N. D. Fligstein (1979). Sex and authority in the workplace: The causes of sexual inequality. *American Sociological Review, 44,* 235–252.

Womack, J. P., D. T. Jones, and D. Roos (1990). *The machine that changed the world.* New York: Rawson Associates.

Wood, S. (1996). High commitment management and payment systems. *Journal of Management Studies, 33,* 53–77.

Woodward, J. (1965). *Industrial organization: Theory and practice.* London: Oxford University Press.

Woodward, J. (Ed.) (1970). *Industrial organization: Behaviour and control.* London: Oxford University Press.

Woolhandler, S., and D. U. Himmelstein (1991). The deteriorating administrative efficiency of the U.S. health care system. *New England Journal of Medicine, 324,* 1253–1258.

Wright, E. O., and L. Perrone (1977). Marxist class categories and income inequality. *American Sociological Review, 42,* 32–55.

Wrong, D. H. (1968). Some problems in defining social power. *American Journal of Sociology, 73,* 673–681.

Wyatt Company (1993). *Wyatt's 1993 survey of corporate restructuring-best practices in corporate restructuring.* New York: Wyatt Company.

Yoels, W. C. (1974). The structure of scientific fields and the allocation of editorships on scientific journals: Some observations on the politics of knowledge. *Sociological Quarterly, 15,* 264–276.

Zajonc, R. B. (1980). Cognition and social cognition: A historical perspective. In L. Festinger (Ed.), *Four decades of social psychology,* 180–204. New York: Oxford University Press.

Zald, M. N. (1993). Toward a reconceptualization of the foundations of the field. *Organization Science, 4,* 513–528.

Zammuto, R. F., and T. Connolly (1984). Coping with disciplinary fragmentation. *Organizational Behavior Teaching Review, 9,* 30–37.

Zeitlin, M. (1974). Corporate ownership and control: The large corporation and the capitalist class. *American Journal of Sociology, 79,* 1073–1119.

Zenger, T. R. (1992). Why do employers only reward extreme performance? Examining the relationship among performance, pay, and turnover. *Administrative Science Quarterly, 37,* 198–219.

Zenger, T. R., and B. S. Lawrence (1989). Organizational demography: The differential effects of age and tenure distributions on technical communication. *Academy of Management Journal, 32,* 353–376.

Zucker, L. G. (1983). Organizations as institutions. In S. B. Bacharach (Ed.), *Research in the sociology of organizations: Vol. 2,* 1–47. Greenwich, Conn.: JAI Press.

Zucker, L. G. (1989). Combining institutional theory and population ecology: No legitimacy, no history. *American Sociological Review, 54,* 542–545.

INDEX

absenteeism
  autonomy and, 38
  control and, 183
  effects on, 36
  heterogeneity and, 85
accountability, 152–53
achievement, 38
acquisitions, 88
additive interaction, defined, 37
adverse impact, 25–26
affect
  defined, 200
  design and, 200
  individual differences and, 28–29
  job satisfaction and, 32
  moods and, 33
  negotiation and, 153
  scales for, 31–32
  stability of, 31–32, 34
affective disposition, defined, 36. *See also*
    dispositions
African Americans. *See* minorities; race
age, 83
age dependence
  founding and mortality and, 165, 166
  heterogeneity and, 166
agency theory
  ambiguity and uncertainty and, 51
  contracts and, 46

defined, 45–46
  economic model and, 45–46
agents, defined, 46
agreeableness. *See* Big Five
alienation, 182–83
allocation. *See* resource allocation
ambiguity and uncertainty
  agency theory and, 51
  power and influence and, 143–45
  rewards and incentives and, 132
  transaction cost economics and, 51
anchoring-and-adjustment, defined, 152
applied psychology, defined, 11. *See also*
    psychology
ASA cycle, defined, 27
assertiveness, 147–48
asset specificity, 52
attendance at work. *See* absenteeism
attitudes. *See* job attitudes
  consistency of, 30
  twins and, 31
attraction-selection-attrition (ASA) cycle,
    defined, 27
attribution theory, defined, 79
authority
  defined, 138
  economic model and, 51
  efficiency and, 51
  power and influence and, 138, 146

industrial sociology and, 11–12
organization studies and, 6, 9–11, 13
standardization in, 9–10
entrapment activities, 69
entrepreneurship. *See* self-employment
environment. *See* design
equilibrium, economic model and, 45
Europe. *See also* France; Germany; Sweden; United Kingdom
business schools in, 13
organization studies in, 6
evolution, ecology and, 163–64
exchange, power and influence and, 147, 148
experience. *See* Big Five; tenure
expert power, defined, 141. *See also* power and influence
explicitness, 116
expressive orientation, defined, 37–38
external constraints
commitment and, 68
defined, 68
job satisfaction and, 68
leadership and, 127
externalization. *See also* internalization
defined, 19
design and, 200–201
economic model and, 51–52
gender and, 20
growth of, 18–20, 21–22
in Japan, 21
minorities and, 20
size distribution and, 21
social consequences of, 20
in United Kingdom, 20
in United States, 19–20
extraversion, defined, 34. *See also* Big Five

fads, fashion, and trends, 16, 193–96
family life, 187
feedback loops, 87
feminist organization theory, defined, 186. *See also* critical theory (CT); gender
field of vision, defined, 89
finance, 23
financial services, defined, 21
firing, 115–16. *See also* downsizing
force activation model, of power and influence, 138, 139

formality and formalization
of organizations, 9
size distribution and, 21
Fortune 500 companies, 21
founding and mortality
age dependence and, 165, 166
competition and, 166, 168
criticism of and support for, 163
density and, 166–67, 168
of high-commitment work system, 174
legitimacy and, 166, 168
framing, 151–52
France, earnings in, 23. *See also* Europe
free riding, defined, 75
fringe benefits, 21. *See also* rewards and incentives
full-time employees. *See* human resources
functionalist paradigm
defined, 17
management and, 177
fundamental attribution error
leadership and, 129–30
normative order and, 26–27

game theoretic approach, defined, 151
GCA. *See* intelligence
Gemeinschaft, defined, 103
gender
adverse impact on, 25–26
competition and, 94–95, 97
co-worker contact and, 94–95
demography and, 82–83, 85, 87–88, 93–94
earnings and, 88–89, 96, 106, 186–87
externalization and, 20
Griggs v. Duke Power and, 25–26
heterogeneity and, 85
job satisfaction and, 95
management and, 97
mobility and, 94–95
networks and, 96–97
power and influence and, 148
public-private dichotomy and, 187
role models and, 97
same-gender co-workers and, 96, 97
selection criteria and, 25–26
self-employment and, 20
status and, 96–97
structure and, 82

motivation
　growth need strength and, 37
　negotiation and, 153
　rewards and incentives and, 111
multidivisional structures, 159–60

natural selection
　criticism of, 43
　defined, 43
　performance and, 156
　rationality and, 44
　timing and, 44–45
negative affect. *See* affect
negotiation
　affect and, 153
　anchoring-and-adjustment and, 152
　constituent accountability and, 152–53
　decision making and, 151–52, 153–54
　education and, 154
　experience and, 154
　framing and, 151–52
　interpersonal processes and, 5–6
　motivation and, 153
　power and influence and, 150–55
　social identity and, 153
　social model and, 153
　tenure and, 154
　ubiquity of, 150
net benefit rule, defined, 46–47
networks. *See also* social model
　concepts of, 60–62
　constraint and, 61
　earnings and, 97
　effects of, 58–60
　gender and, 96–97
　in Japan, 60
　legitimacy and, 58
　measurement of, 64
　mergers and, 59
　minorities and, 96–98
　performance and, 58–60
　resource dependence theory and, 62
　resource flow and, 58
　social model and, 56–58, 60
　status and, 61–62
　strong versus weak ties and, 60
　structural holes in, 97
　structure and, 82
　Structure (computer program) and, 60
　of suppliers, 21

neutral interlocks, defined, 64. *See also* networks
new economics of personnel, defined, 106–7
"new employment contract," 18
newness, liability in, 165–66, 168
nonwhites. *See* minorities; race
normative control. *See also* control
　growth of, 103
　social psychology and, 102
normative order. *See also* culture
　behavior and, 26–27
　causality and, 26–27
　fundamental attribution error and, 26–27
　influences on, 76
　institutionalization and, 76
　personal values and 39
　selection and, 101

Occam's Razor, defined, 43
OCP, 121–22
off-site employment. *See* externalization
operant conditioning
　behavior and, 25
　defined, 105
　rewards and incentives and, 105
opportunism
　defined, 45, 46, 47
　economic model and, 45–46
　self-interest compared to, 45
　transaction cost economics and, 46, 47
opportunities, defined, 82
organizational behavior, 32–33
organizational culture. *See* culture
Organizational Culture Profile (OCP), 121–22. *See also* culture
organizational demography. *See* demography
organizational ecology. *See* ecology
organizational mortality. *See* founding and mortality
organizational performance. *See* performance
organizational psychology, 11. *See also* psychology
organizational selection, 36
organizational sociology, 12. *See also* sociology
organizational structure. *See* structure

turnover (*continued*)
  person-situation fit and, 39
  social integration and, 84–85
  social model and, 56
  tenure and, 83–85
  top management teams and, 90
twins
  heredity versus environment and, 31
  job attitudes of, 31
  job interests and, 31
  studies of, 31, 36

U-form hypothesis, defined, 159
uncertainty. *See* ambiguity and uncertainty
underwritings, defined, 62
unionization. *See also* politics
  earnings and, 106, 108
  internalization and, 52, 53
  size distribution and, 21
  variable pay and, 108
United Kingdom. *See also* Europe
  CEOs in, 23
  earnings in, 23
  externalization in, 20
  high-commitment work system in, 174
  variable pay in, 105
United States
  behavior in, 26–27
  business schools in, 13
  CEOs in, 23
  control in, 22
  earnings in, 23
  externalization in, 19–20
  high-commitment work system in, 172–74
  organization studies and, 13
  rewards and incentives in, 23, 104–5
  size distribution and, 21

takeovers in, 22
top management teams in, 85
variable pay in, 104–5
unrealistic models, 43–44
upper-echelons theory of management
  characteristics of, 89
  heterogeneity and, 92
  top management teams and, 91–92

validation, 25–26
values. *See* normative order
variable pay. *See also* earnings
  criticism of, 113–14
  defined, 104
  growth of, 104–5
  implementation of, 110
  performance and, 113
  politics and, 109
  unionization and, 108
  in United Kingdom, 105
  in United States, 104–5
variation, 161
verbal ability, 33. *See also* intelligence
vision, field of, 89
volition, 116

wages. *See* earnings
waiting and delay, 147
weak interlocks, defined, 64. *See also* networks
weak ties, 61
Weber, Max, 12
whites. *See* race
women. *See* gender
"women's work," classification and devaluation of, 96, 187. *See also* gender
worker participation, defined, 170
work processes, 183